JAMES F. SCOTT
Saint Louis University

FILM
THE MEDIUM
AND THE MAKER

Holt Rinehart and Winston, Inc.
NEW YORK CHICAGO SAN FRANCISCO ATLANTA DALLAS
MONTREAL TORONTO LONDON SYDNEY

For my children, Adrienne and Jamie

Copyright © 1975 by Holt, Rinehart and Winston, Inc.
All rights reserved
Library of Congress Cataloging in Publication Data
Scott, James F
    Film, the medium and the maker.
    Bibliography: p.
    1. Moving-pictures—Aesthetics. I. Title.
PN1995.S418   791.43'01   74-26611
ISBN 0-03-079445-5
Printed in the United States of America
 678   090   98765432

PREFACE

In the following pages I have attempted a description of film aesthetics that balances the claims of art and technology. If there is justification for adding to the already considerable literature in this field, it lies in a belief that the integration of mechanical and imaginative factors is something most film criticism has not yet achieved.

The book is oriented to seeing films rather than making them. But it assumes that seeing films properly requires us occasionally to give up our theatre seats to look through the viewfinder of a camera or venture among the gadgets of the cutting room and the sound studio. I have tugged the reader in this direction not to fill his head with nuts and bolts but to give some hint of the creative options the available technology offers the prospective filmmaker. My only consciously cultivated bias (beyond the mechanical one) is the assumption that most filmmaking involves more people than the film director and that his subordinates should have more credit than they normally get for the work they do.

Since the approach is not strictly that of the historical survey, I have built the chapters around comparatively few examples rather than exhaustively catalogued all films potentially relevant to the discussion. This leads to regrettable but seemingly unavoidable omissions. I have decided, for instance, to use *A Nous, la Liberté* to represent the early sound film. But I do not mean to suggest that musical comedy under René Clair's direction was necessarily better than musicals directed by Ernst Lubitsch or Rouben Mamoulian—*Monte Carlo* or *Love Me Tonight,* for example. The last thing film criticism needs at the moment, is a preemptive list of superimportant "masterpieces" that could be imposed upon unsuspecting undergraduates. I would like to see teachers select films for study according to their own tastes, using this text less to ascertain what films to look at than to show students how to look at films in general.

54782

For those who might want to follow rather closely the format I have chosen, each chapter provides information on the availability of films singled out for discussion. The filmography at the end of the book is more general, though the emphasis is upon pictures with some specific pedagogical relevance. The reader should nevertheless acquaint himself with the *Index to 16mm Educational Films,* I–III (National Information Center for Educational Media: University of Southern California, Los Angeles, 1973) and with both the *1970 Catalog: Educational Motion Pictures* (Audio Visual Center: University of Indiana, Bloomington, 1970) and its *Cumulative Supplement,* 1974. The catalogs of the various 16mm distributors of fiction and nonfiction films are also indispensable aids to film study and can be procured from the firms cited under Film Distributors Code on page 329. From these it should be possible for a teacher to put together a series of films that could be approached through my methodology without being bound to my choice of examples and illustrations.

Neither the footnotes nor the bibliography do full justice to those who have assisted me in shaping this work. In particular I would like to thank Richard M. Barsam of Richmond College (CUNY) for his close reading of the whole manuscript in its formative and again in its final stages; the contribution of Jack C. Ellis, University of Texas at Austin, and Harlan Mendenhall, Southern Illinois University at Carbondale, were equally valuable. I also appreciate the help of Eileen Rossi, whose expertise in the analysis of film acting sharpened my understanding of this special professional discipline. I would like to thank the Audio-Visual department of Ruhr University, Bochum, West Germany, for the facilities they unstintingly put at my disposal during my 1972–1973 residence on that campus. These resources made possible the close image-by-image analysis of certain films that otherwise could not have been so thoroughly examined. I want to mention the contribution of my wife Carolyn, to whom I owe more of my ideas than could ever be acknowledged in conventional citations. There is no substitute for the immediate on-the-spot interaction which takes place when two people have just shared the experience of seeing a motion picture. Any mistakes of fact or judgment in the book, however, are my own.

JAMES F. SCOTT

Saint Louis University

CONTENTS

1
AN APPROACH TO FILM

"Auteur" Criticism and its Limitations   2

Preeminence of the director in current critical theory. Analysis of Peter Wollen, *Signs and Meaning in the Cinema*. "Auteur" approach to Howard Hawks and John Ford. Approach of Andrew Sarris. Some omissions and unanswered questions. Disturbing exclusion of film technology. Effect of evolving technology upon film history.

Filmmaking as a Cooperative Art   9

Importance of interaction in creative filmmaking. Relationship of director to cameraman. Case of Ingmar Bergman and Sven Nykvist. Comparable involvement of the director with the scenarist and the actors. Role of the film editor. Collaboration of Arthur Penn and Aram Avakian. Further complexities of interaction: Marlon Brando's enlargement of *The Godfather*.

2
COMPOSITION   21

Composing with the Camera   24

The Moving Image   24

Invention of cinematography. Enthrallment with physical motion. Early strategies for simulating motion: "Irising" and "undercranking." Applications in *The Joyless Street, The Wild Child, The Rink, City Lights, Tom Jones, A Clockwork Orange*. Development of slow-motion photography. Applications in *Bonnie and Clyde, Ski the Outer Limits*.

The Moving Camera   32

Camera movements and their significance. The pan: *The Lower Depths*. Tracking: *Viridiana*. Booming: *Ugetsu*. Tilting: *The World of Apa, The Loneliness of the Long Distance Runner*. Conjunction of camera and subject movement: *The Gospel According to St. Matthew, Umberto D.* Significance of stasis: *The Seven Samurai.*

Composing with Lenses   37

Basic Lens Variables: Focal Length and Aperture   38

Definition of focal length. Its relationship to framing. Normal, wide-angle, and telephoto lenses. Definition of aperture. Concept of lens "speed." Use of f/stops. Relationship of lens variables to composition: their effect upon perspective and depth of field.

Wide-Angle, Deep-Field Composition   43

Pioneering work of Soviet cinematography with wide-angle lenses. Sergei Eisenstein's analysis of wide-angle effects. Eisenstein and Edouard Tisse: *Strike* and *Potemkin.* Vogue of wide-angle composition in the U.S.A. Concomitant interest in reduced apertures and expanded depth of field. Contribution of Gregg Toland. Collaboration of Toland and Orson Welles: *Citizen Kane.* Persistence of this approach: *Odds against Tomorrow.*

Soft-Textured and Long-Lens Composition   52

Preference for open apertures. Concomitant softness of texture. Strategies of open-aperture composition. Spatial arrangement: *The Iron Horse.* Following focus: *The Last Command.* Motivated softness: *The Bank Dick.* The turn to longer lenses. Characteristics of telephotos. Softness and selective focus: *Elvira Madigan* and *Adalen 31.* Compression of space and retardation of motion: *Battle of Algiers, The Graduate, The Confession.*

New Lenses, New Optical Systems   61

Cinerama, Todd-A-O, and Cinemascope   61

New wide-field systems. Image qualities and production costs. Emergence of CinemaScope: Leon Shamroy's photography in *The Robe.* Other approaches to the scope system: Max Ophuls and Christian Matras in *Lola Montes;* Federico Fellini and Otello Martelli in *La Dolce Vita.*

Zoom Lenses and Special-Effects Lenses   66

Introduction of the zoom lens to cinematography. New optical effects: "Crash" effects: *Who's Afraid of Virginia Woolf?* Perspective disturbance: *Medium Cool.* Probing and distancing: *Psycho* and *The Beast Must Die.* Subjective effects: *Adrift.* Fish-eye lenses: *Seconds.*

3
LIGHTING   73

Lighting in the Era of Orthochrome   77

The Daylight School of American Cinematography   79

Tendency toward naturalism in American photography of the 1910s. Extension of this orientation to cinema. Billy Bitzer and D. W.

Griffith, *Birth of a Nation*. William Daniels and Erich von Stroheim, *Greed*.

The Arc Lights of Germany   83

Hostility to naturalism in German art and drama. Impact of Robert Wiene's *Dr. Caligari*. Expressionistic lighting effects in *Nesferatu*. Collaboration of F. W. Murnau with Fritz Wagner.

Lighting with Panchromatic Film   86

The Studio Look   88

Panchrome in the studios. Introduction of tungsten lamps. Migration of German cameramen to Hollywood. Concept of "formula" lighting. Theory and practice of cameraman John Alton. Collaboration of Lee Garmes and Josef von Sternberg: *Shanghai Express*.

Persistence of Motif Lighting and Emergence of the Available-Light School   94

Motif lighting of Robert Krasker for Carol Reed in *Odd Man Out*. Haskell Wexler and Mike Nichols, *Who's Afraid of Virginia Woolf?* Raoul Coutard and available-light cinematography. Coutard and Jean-Luc Godard. Coutard and François Truffaut: *Shoot the Piano Player*. Flexibility of panchrome stock.

Lighting with Color Film   103

From Technicolor to Tripack   104

Evolution of color cinematography. The role of the Kalmuses. Bert Glennon and Natalie Kalmus: *Drums along the Mohawk*. More ambitious expressiveness of *Black Narcissus*. Introduction of Eastmancolor. Work of Teinosuke Kinugasa and Kohei Sagiyama in *Gate of Hell*. Further innovations of *Black Orpheus*.

Contemporary Innovations in Color   112

The available-light approach to color photography. Robert Surtees' "prefogging" in *The Graduate*. Expressionistic color filtration in *2001: A Space Odyssey*. Subjectivist uses of color: *Red Desert*. Various special color effects: *King Murray, Butch Cassidy, Alluros*.

**4
SOUND**   119

Basic Technology   120

The concept of a sound score. Integration and orchestration of noise. Systems of sound recording, Disc sound. Optical sound. Magnetic sound. Sound mixing.

The Sounds of Silence   124

Role of the organ in silent cinema. Efforts to re-create live sound. Stan Kann's organ concerts for *The Hunchback of Notre Dame* and *Phantom of the Opera.* Implicit sound notation in silent film: *Greed, October, Strike.* René Clair and *Two Timid People.*

The Age of Optical Sound   129

The Musical Dimension   131

The musical idiom as an extension of silent-film technique. Interest of various composers in the sound film. Vogue of musical comedy. Collaboration of Georges Auric and René Clair: *A Nous, la Liberté.* The symphonic film. Collaboration of Eisenstein and Sergei Prokofiev: *Alexander Nevsky.*

The Voice-Music-Effects Mix   140

Unimaginative use of voice in the early sound film. Some exceptions: the Marx brothers, Chaplin. Orson Welles and the impact of radio. Sound without image: Welles' "panic broadcast." Sound mix of *Citizen Kane.* Extensions of technique: *The Lady from Shanghai, The Stranger.*

The Advent of Magnetic Sound   145

The Wild-Sound Movement   147

Economy and portability of magnetic tape. Market for authentic documentary in the television industry. New documentary teams: Richard Leacock and D. A. Pennebaker. Automatic sound synchronization: *Primary* and *Don't Look Back.* Frederick Wiseman: *High School.*

Word and Image: Experiments in Counterpoint   154

Other applications of magnetic recording. Ficticious sound: *Divorce Italian Style.* Ironic and allusive sounds: *Contempt.* Sound and the moving camera: *Targets.* Sound as voice-over commentary: *Diary of a Mad Housewife.*

Tricky Mixes, New Noises: Distorted and Electronic Sound 159

The mix and the moving camera; mixing in voice collage Possibility of creatively reshaping everyday sound. The effect of off-speed recording: *Throne of Blood.* Filtered sound: *The Long Day's Dying.* Electronic noise: *One Day in the Life of Ivan Denisovitch.* A new dimension in sound: *The Conversation.*

5
STORY AND SCRIPT   167

Rhetorical Structures   170

The Argumentative Approach to Script   170

Jean Renoir and the problem-oriented scenario. The "October Group." Renoir and Jacques Prévert: *The Crime of Monsieur Lange.* Prévert's capacity for consolidation. His poetic and allegorical tendency. Renoir and Charles Spaak: *Grand Illusion.* Primacy of the spoken word and the complete scene. Persistent interest in argument and social analysis.

Symbolic and Associative Structures 179

Alternative conceptions of structure. Ingmar Bergman as scenarist. His symbolic and subjectivist orientation. Symbolic language in *The Seventh Seal*. Associative structure in *Wild Strawberries*.

Picaresque Structures 184

Action Genres: Scripts for Spies and Cowboys 184

Collaboration of Dudley Nichols and John Ford. Nichols' conception of script. His scripting of *The Informer*. Primacy of the visual. Ford, Nichols, and *Stagecoach*. Relatedness of language to the action structure.

The Neorealist Scenario 189

Redefinition of structure in neorealism. Role of Cesare Zavattini. His collaboration with Vittorio De Sica. Harmony of speech and movement in *The Bicycle Thief*.

The Anti-Story 195

The Rejection of "Plot" 195

Michelangelo Antonioni as disciple of Zavattini. Deliberate violation of expectations as to structure. *L'Avventura* as inversion of motifs in the "adventure story." Rejection of the climactic. Substitution of alternative values.

Reconceptions of Speech and Action 202

Jean-Luc Godard as scenarist. Renewal of interest in the verbal. Dependence upon improvisation. The Brechtian use of dialogue in *La Chinoise*. Interest in extended monologue. Verbal dimension of *Weekend*.

6
ACTING AND STAGING 209

The Actor as Icon 210

Special nature of film acting. Effects of framing upon performance. Interaction of the actor with decor and ensemble. Bergman's treatment of the actor: *The Passion of Anna*. Alternative approach to framing in Antonioni. Antonioni and Monica Vitti. Variation in the iconography of the film frame: Glenn Ford and Sidney Poitier in *Blackboard Jungle*.

Foundations of Film Acting: Gestural Style 217

The Style of Physical Comedy 217

The art of Charles Chaplin. Centrality of body gesture: *The Idle Class, The Immigrant*. Ingenuity with costume: *The Gold Rush,*

Shoulder Arms. Increasing importance of decor: *City Lights.* Involvement of both decor and ensemble: *Modern Times.* Alternative orientation of Buster Keaton. Keaton's more elaborate gymnastic skills. Capacity to extend and modify a routine: *College, The General.*

        Biomechanics and Constructivism   226
Theories of Vsevolod Meyerhold. Interest in Chaplin. Promotion of the acting ensemble above the individual performer. Innovations in stagecraft and design. Meyerhold's influence upon Eisenstein. *Potemkin* and *Strike.* Eisenstein's demands upon the actor. Testimony of Nicolai Cherkasov. Cherkasov's performance in *Alexander Nevsky* and *Ivan the Terrible.*

        Expressionism and its Derivatives   232
The school of Max Reinhardt. His sensitivity to lighting, costume, decor. His disciples in the cinema: Paul Wegener, F. W. Murnau, Fritz Lang. Expressionist impact upon Josef von Sternberg. Sternberg's work with Emil Jannings and Marlene Dietrich. Reinhardtesque performance and choreography in *The Blue Angel.*

    Styles in Transition   239
    The Hollywood Studio Style   240
Functional and pragmatic tendencies of Hollywood studio style. Testimony of Henry Fonda. Personalization of stereotypic roles: Humphrey Bogart. Possibility of greater theatricalism: George Cukor's handling of Greta Garbo in *Camille.* Alfred Hitchcock's emphasis upon minimal performance: Joseph Cotten in *Shadow of a Doubt.* Changes wrought in the 1950s. Contrast of acting styles in *The Tin Star.*

        The Impact of Stanislavsky   247
New sources of theatrical talent. Elia Kazan and Lee Strasberg at the New York Actors Studio. Their indebtedness to Konstantin Stanislavsky. Their emphasis upon the interiorization of a role. Kazan, Marlon Brando, and *On the Waterfront.* Rod Steiger as Actors Studio performer. His role in *The Pawnbroker.* His personal testimony.

        Improvisation, Formalism, and Continuing Experiment   254
Other conceptions of "naturalism": Stanislavsky and V. I. Pudovkin. Handling the nonprofessional actor: *Deserter.* Pudovkin and Italian neorealism: Roberto Rossellini and *Paisan.* Fellini and François Périer in *The Nights of Cabiria.* Continuing interest in formalistic approaches to acting: Peter Brook, Ken Russell, and Glenda Jackson. *Marat/Sade* and *Women in Love.*

7
EDITING AND ASSEMBLY   261
    Basic Principles of Editing   262
Editing as a source of motion and metaphor. Cuts and dissolves. Superimposition: *Psycho, The Birds.* Editing in conjunction with

composition, lighting, color: *Easy Rider, Last Year at Marienbad, War and Peace.* Editing with respect to sound: *Topkapi.* Putting together a sequence: *High Noon.* Editing in its historical context.

Montage in the Silent Film   267

The Continuity Principle   268

Lev Kuleshov as analyst of the editing process. Results of his experiments. Pudovkin as disciple of Kuleshov. Conception of montage in *Mother.* Matching of motion. Contrasts of size. Interaction of objects. Complex intellectual montage.

The Collision Principle   272

Eisenstein's differences with Pudovkin. Emphasis upon maximum conflict: *Old and New.* Use of superimposition: *Strike.* The moving figure and the moving object: *October, Strike,* and *Potemkin.*

Montage in the Sound Film   278

Studio Specialization and its Consequences   278

Shifts of directorial emphasis. Introduction of the "montage sequence." Formulaic versus imaginative montage. Contribution of Slavko Vorkapitch: *Viva Villa* and *The Good Earth.* Use of the symbolic dissolve in Sternberg and John Huston. The special case of *Fantasia.*

Editing within the Genres: The Thriller   281

Susceptibility of the thriller to dynamic cutting. The example of *M.* Hitchcock's interest in editing. Collaboration with Alma Reville. Pace and rhythm in *North by Northwest.* Continuity of movement: *Foreign Correspondent.* Dissolves and superimpositions: *Shadow of a Doubt, The Wrong Man.* Treatment of sound: *Notorious.* Mood and suspense: *Psycho.*

Editing Beyond the Genres   291

Relationship of editing to the conventions of the genre film. New approaches to cutting by Fellini: *I Vitelloni.* Subjective and disjunctive editing in the French "New Wave." Collaboration of Henri Colpi and Alain Resnais. From *Guernica* to *Hiroshima, Mon Amour.* Interweaving of past and present; interrelated montage of sight and sound. Influence of Resnais-Colpi upon Truffaut and Godard.

The Short Film   297

The Compilation Film   298

Nature of the compilation film. Compilation as documentary and propaganda: Frank Capra. New turn in the compilation film: *Night and Fog.* Short compilation film in America: Charles Braverman. Braverman's editorial innovations: *American Time Capsule, The World of '68, The Sixties.* The compilation film as parody: Bruce Connor and *A Movie.* As jazz improvisation: *Cosmic Ray.*

The Lyrical Film   303

Transcendence of narrative form. Lyricism of the straight cut:

Hilary Harris, *Nine Variations on a Dance Theme*. Lyricism with more sophisticated opticals: Francis Thompson, *N.Y., N.Y.* Ed Emshwiller, *Totem;* Norman McLaren, *Pas de Deux.*

8
CONCLUSION

309

Integration of functions in filmmaking. Levels of collaborative achievement. Mechanical integration: "Mission Impossible." Failure of integration: *The Misfits*. Technical and thematic integration: *The Searchers*. Some suggestions for the reorientation of film criticism.

Suggested Further Reading   319

Suggested Further Viewing   324

Film Distributors Code   329

Index   333

I
AN APPROACH TO FILM

Film is our liveliest, but not our likeliest, art. It defies our expectations of what art should be. It is mechanical in its mode and collectivist in its inspiration, which seems sometimes to make it an art without an artist.

Few deny that there is aesthetic achievement in filmmaking. But which member of the production team is the achiever? Is it the head cameraman who set up the visuals or the editor who sorted them after they were shot? Is it the actor who intoned the lines or the scenarist who gave him lines to intone? Or is the artistry perhaps a more basically mechanical matter, something connected with the choice of lenses, the success of color correction, the fidelity of the sound mix, in other words, something owed to the combined skill of an ensemble of technicians? Actually, filmcraft includes all these specialties and others as well. A good film is the work of many hands, most of them devoted to adjusting the controls of expensive precision instruments. Exceptional among the arts, filmmaking is always a cooperative venture and, more than that, it always involves a silent partnership between man and machine.

"AUTEUR"
CRITICISM
AND ITS LIMITATIONS

Preeminence of the director in current critical theory.
Analysis of Peter Wollen, Signs and Meaning in the Cinema.
"Auteur" approach to Howard Hawks and John Ford. Ap-
proach of Andrew Sarris. Some omissions and unanswered
questions. Disturbing exclusion of film technology. Effect
of evolving technology upon film history.

Although an occasional reviewer may still attribute the success of a picture to anyone from the producer to the popcorn girl, current criticism tends to associate film art with the imagination and energy of the director, whose spirit presides over the entire operation. Lewis Jacobs reflects these assumptions in his *An Introduction to the Art of the Movies,* where he describes cinema as "the director's art." [1] Working from this premise, he represents film criticism as a salute to great directors, men of genius who, "in their efforts to become more expressive, discovered the special characteristics of the medium, extended the limits of technique and propelled the movies into deeper and more original forms of composition." This view of the director originated in France during the late 1940s and is usually known as the "auteur" theory. It assumes, quite simply, that the director is the "author" of the picture, or as Alexandre Astruc said in 1948, that the auteur-director is a man with his own "camera-stylo," a man who uses the camera as his personal fountain pen.[2] According to this theory, later elaborated by critics associated with *Cahiers du Cinéma,* the director is a stylist and thinker with a unique signature, recognizable in every film that he makes. Whatever its limitations, the auteur theory is the most interesting reference point in contemporary film criticism.

Undoubtedly, the auteur approach has a great deal to recommend it. It relieves us of the impression (too often held over from the theatre) that the director is just a kind of shop foreman who keeps track

---

[1] (New York: The Noonday Press, 1960), p. 3.

[2] "The Birth of a New Avant-garde: *La Camera-stylo,*" *The New Wave,* ed. Peter Graham (Garden City, N.Y.: Doubleday & Company, Inc., 1968), pp. 17–22. Reprinted from the series *Cinema One* by permission of Martin Secker & Warburg Limited.

THE DIRECTOR AS AUTEUR: Current critical theory makes the director responsible for the filmic conception that will be executed by various members of the production team. Here director Akira Kurosawa demonstrates the kind of sword thrust he wishes actor Toshiro Mifune to use in a scene from *The Seven Samurai*. Photographs reproduced through the courtesy of Yoichi Matsue, producer of the film.

of the equipment and manages the manpower. It calls our attention to the unity of particular pictures and invites us to see continuity in the work of directors who take charge of their films. It gives credence to the verbal shorthand by which we speak of "an Ingmar Bergman film," "another work by Michelangelo Antonioni," or "John Ford's America." Above all, though, it asks us to take the cinema seriously, to put it on the same footing with literature and painting, to stop thinking of it as a circus, a burlesque show, or a way to keep children off the streets at night. The clearest contribution of the auteur critics has been to improve the pedigree of motion-picture art.

So far, the most impressive exposition of the auteur theory has been provided by Peter Wollen in *Signs and Meaning in the Cinema.*[3] Among other things, the book illustrates the auteur conception of the director by analyzing in great detail the films of John Ford and Howard Hawks, showing how each has shaped his raw material according to his personal vision of America and of the world. In searching for "a core of repeated motifs" characteristic of each director, Wollen concludes that the two men entertain radically different views of man and society which dictate the elaboration of their respective themes. For Hawks, man is isolated, insignificant, capable only of momentary satisfaction through "the camaraderie of the exclusive, self-sufficient, all-male group." Ford, on the other hand, "finds transcendent values in the historic vocation of America as a nation, to bring civilization to a savage land, the garden to the wilderness." Hence, though both directors may work in the same genres (the western, the war film) and occasionally use the same stars (John Wayne, for example), their films diverge absolutely, articulating mutually incompatible ideals of heroism, justice, and moral achievement. Moreover, these rival visions of life determine the situations and dramatic conventions typical of the two directors. Hawks' forbidding stoicism pushes his heroes toward adventure and defiance epitomized in gang wars (*Scarface*, 1932), big-game hunts (*Hatari*, 1962), or military exploits (*Air Force*, 1942). But Ford's patriotic conservatism, while allowing for explosive action, leads finally toward marriage (*My Darling Clementine*, 1946), law (*The Man Who Shot Liberty Valance*, 1962), and the extension of civilized restraint (*Stagecoach*, 1939; *Wagonmaster*, 1950; etc.). According to Wollen, the object of film criticism should be this act of "decipherment, decryptment," by which we learn to pick out the central concerns of a director, just as he identifies, quite perceptively, the persistent interests of Hawks and Ford.

So brief a summary can hardly do justice to the wealth of insight in

---

[3] (Bloomington: Indiana University Press, 1969). This and the following citations of Wollen are from his chapter entitled "The Auteur Theory," pp. 74–115.

Wollen's analysis, which surely reflects favorably upon the assumptions of auteur criticism. But for all its brilliance, the discussion of Ford and Hawks seems curiously abstract and incomplete. What do their films look like? Is the camera mobile or anchored in one place? Are the scenes long and continuous or are they broken up into fragments? Is the sound track noisy or quiet? Does the look and sound change from picture to picture or are certain preferences constant through the careers of the two directors? These questions are never raised, since Wollen does not think them pertinent. "A great many features of films," he says, "have to be dismissed as indecipherable because of 'noise' from the producer, the cameraman, or even the actors." While these other aspects of a film may "sway us or please us or intrigue us," they are, according to this version of auteur theory, "simply . . . inaccessible to criticism." Perhaps, however, the auteur school has gone slightly astray in dismissing so much of the film experience as mere "noise."

Consider, for instance, the films of Ford and Hawks. It is undoubtedly true, as Wollen maintains, that Ford's pictures are wrought out of antinomies: "garden versus wilderness, ploughshare versus sabre, settler versus nomad, European versus Indian, civilized versus savage, book versus gun, married versus unmarried, East versus West." Yet what first strikes me about this director is not his moral categories so much as his unfailing pictorial sense. Thinking of Ford's films, I remember water glistening in the sun as it flies from the wheels of a stagecoach; I remember the shadows of Indians that portentously announce their later appearance; I remember the rugged buttes of Monument Valley, which speak eloquently of the stamina and courage of anyone who might make his home amid such unpromising surroundings. And as I recall these images I remind myself that Ford had at his disposal several of the best cameramen Hollywood ever turned out, including Bert Glennon, Joseph August, and Gregg Toland. Hawks, on the other hand, I remember better from the play of voices, the witty exchanges of Bogart and Bacall in *To Have and Have Not* (1944), or the comic malapropisms of Paul Muni in *Scarface*. These films were scripted, respectively, by William Faulkner and Ben Hecht, two scenarists who fully understood the ways of words. Somehow, I doubt that these facts are irrelevant — that Ford's cameramen and Hawks' writers can be dismissed as noisemakers who may, if not carefully controlled, distract attention from the director.

Andrew Sarris, an American proponent of auteur criticism, deals wittily, but not quite satisfactorily, with these problematic points. While admitting that "an expert production crew could probably cover up for a chimpanzee in the director's chair," he insists that, when "the quasichimpanzee" directs, the auteur function shifts elsewhere among the filmmaking team.[4] Hence "if Joe Pevney directed Garbo, Cherkasov, Olivier, Belmondo, and Harriet Andersson in *The Cherry Orchard,* the resulting spectacle might not be completely devoid of merit with so many subsidiary *auteurs* to cover up for Joe." Yet why this must be a "cover-up" is not immediately evident. Nor is the issue clarified by Sarris' further extension of the debate: "Marlon Brando has shown that a film can be made without a director. Indeed, *One-Eyed Jacks* is more interesting than many films with directors. . . . One can talk about photography, editing, acting, but not direction. The film even has personality, but like *The Longest Day* and *Mutiny on the Bounty* it is a cipher directorially." This may be. Yet why should we be so embarrassed about discussing the photography, editing, acting, and "personality" of *One-Eyed Jacks*? Furthermore, why should we apologize for thinking of Brando himself as a creative force?

These strictures against auteur criticism are in no way intended to minimize the role of the director. He is clearly the most important person on the set, since his influence touches every phase of production. But he uses his power, it seems to me, more as a skillful diplomat than as a military dictator. He has a certain technology at his disposal, about which he usually needs advice; he may shoot from a prefabricated script, and his stars may be inclined to drift toward parts they have played before; his editor, though not a publicly prominent figure, may have definite ideas about how the film should be cut. He must accommodate to his machinery and interact with his staff. Far from denying the director's creativity, however, these considerations merely change the nature of the creative act. It is not privatistic, but cooperative; not exclusively spiritual, but mediated through the performance of a machine. The film director reveals his talent through his ability to elicit and judge the talent of others; his inspiration is embodied in his capacity to inspire his associates, calling into play their mechanical or professional expertise. This means, in effect, that the figure I shall hereafter call the "filmmaker" is really a kind of composite person, a team more than an individual, though a team coordinated by the wide-ranging skills of the director.

Perhaps the most serious limitation of auteur criticism is its neglect of film technology. The auteur critics are more likely to think of a film as something that happens in the mind of a great artist than as something that happens in the chemical response of silver-halide granules. They know, of course, that motion pictures are made of celluloid and shot with cameras, just as other aestheticians know that paintings are made with paint, that architecture assumes an acquaintance with en-

---

[4] This and the following citations of Sarris are from "Notes on the Auteur Theory in 1962," *Film Culture Reader,* ed. P. Adams Sidney (New York: Praeger and Co., 1970), pp. 121–135. © 1970 by permission of Praeger Publishers, Inc.

gineering, and that a sculptor is not likely to be indifferent toward either his marble or his chisels. But they follow the lead of other schools of aesthetics in emphasizing the artist's transcendence of his physical medium. Hence they continually betray a bias on behalf of moral abstractions, which seems foreign to the intense concreteness and material immediacy of the cinema.

For film is a decidedly mechanical art, much more than painting, or music, or literature. The pen does not make the poem, nor the brush the portrait, nor the violin the concerto, though in the latter two instances the instrument distinctly contributes to artistic execution. But in a greatly more exacting sense the tools of the filmmaker prompt and shape his creative achievement. In the cinema, we perceive motion only because the camera runs at a speed that deludes the eye; we see objects, not as they would appear if we were standing in front of them, but according to the perspective rendered by a particular lens; we experience bright and dark, not so much because of their true light values as because of the sensitivity of the film stock and the intervention of a mechanical diaphragm. Voice and noise have not always been part of the cinema, nor has continuous, full-spectrum color. These emerged as imaginative resources only after a slow and laborious technical evolution. Nor does this process ever promise to come to completion. In today's cinema, just as in yesterday's, a new mode generally depends upon a new machine — perhaps a new camera (such as those that make possible extreme slow motion), or a new stock to feed into it (such as ultra light-sensitive color film), or a new lens to fasten onto it (such as a zoom lens or a long telephoto). Even such minor mechanical contrivances as cranes, dollies, and portable power systems affect the pace and rhythm of a shot. The matter of which causes what, whether the imagination creates the technology or the technology the imagination, is simply a question of the chicken and the egg. They are too deeply entwined to ever be separated.

Let one example stand for the many that are available. Recently rock singer Frank Zappa attached his name to a film called *200 Motels* (1971). Zappa is not an auteur, and the film has little to recommend it from the standpoint of content. There are a few good gags in the picture, along with a scene or two in which television game shows and talk shows are wittily parodied. But it is loose, directionless, lacking in consistent thematic interest. What sustains attention, however, is a dazzling display of technical virtuosity, made possible by the importation of electronic imagery into cinema.

200 Motels is a photographic reproduction of a video tape. This is what gives its colors a shimmering iridescent quality quite unlike anything seen on the screen before. It is also what accounts for the ghostly double exposures, the tendency of images to linger like strange vapor trails in the midst of a new scene. At the same time, the video technology allows for a bewildering array of "special effects" which, though possible in a purely photographic system, would be prohibitively expensive and time-consuming. Hence at one moment The Mothers of Invention are shown with orange faces and green hands; then their hands turn blue while their faces assume normal flesh tones; then, only an instant later, the blues shift to the faces, and normal coloration returns to the hands. This random distortion has no carefully controlled meaning, though it is entirely in keeping with the trancelike, surrealist mood of the film. Meaningful or not, however, these devices of video are certain to affect the future of cinema. The effects we observe in *200 Motels* can be induced almost as easily as we can twirl the color dials of the living-room television set. And this is bound to have implications for motion pictures of the next decade. We will soon have to reckon with a new generation of directors anxious to explore more thoroughly the visual potential of this technological breakthrough.

So important is the visual surface of a motion picture that it can virtually override the film's explicit "meaning." Thus it is fairly simple to think of films which are really cameramen's pictures, even though they have been meticulously supervised by an auteur-director. An ideal example is Frederic Rossif's *To Die in Madrid,* a documentary of the early 1960s which memorializes the agony of the Spanish Civil War. A comparatively low-budget production which uses archive footage and features nonactors, it would seem exactly suited to the aspirations of an auteur. All he need do is step in and take charge of the heterogeneous mass of visual material collected from film archives in France, Spain, and Germany. Rossif has done precisely this. He sorted the footage, coached several narrators, inserted appropriate descriptions to reconstruct the political world of the 1930s, and developed a pro-Republican sound track to engraft his personal interpretation of events upon the scenes we see. He also did his own editing, adding further to his control of the picture. Thus we typically see Franco's Fascists in conjunction with walls, towers, and solid masses, while the Republicans are often associated with trees, fields, and open space. In context, Rossif makes these emblems of their respective personalities. Severe and imperious, Franco's armies stand for tradition, discipline, and strict authority; careless and casual, the Loyalists represent what is natural, spontaneous, and open to new experience. Thus arranged, *To Die in Madrid* certainly bears the personal signature of its director.

Yet the real beauty of the film lies not so much in these imposed controls as in its photographic texture. The recovered footage represents the combined skill of more than a hundred anonymous cameramen whose motives and ambitions are lost to us. Whatever their intentions — to do an onerous job, to report adversely upon Franco, to be on hand at this dress rehearsal for World War II — they left posterity the basic substance of a great work of art, statistical probability always placing some few of them in the right place at the right time. Look at the shots of the Nazi raid of Guernica. No one chose the bleak twilight setting; the hour of the attack was set by the German command, apparently anxious to strike as the shops closed and the streets filled. But the cameramen adapted admirably to difficult circumstances. The blanched images, resulting from hasty efforts to secure enough light, are exactly right for the scene. The suggestion of coldness in this sunless light, the vague brightness — how perfectly congruent this is with the panic-stricken faces and dizzied movements of those caught in the open as the bombs begin to fall. With such material at his disposal, the director's job was half finished the moment he began. Rossif's film had been in the vaults for twenty years; he just had to find it.

FILMMAKING AS A COOPERATIVE ART

Importance of interaction in creative filmmaking. Relationship of director to cameraman. Case of Ingmar Bergman and Sven Nykvist. Comparable involvement of the director with the scenarist and the actors. Role of the film editor. Collaboration of Arthur Penn and Aram Avakian. Further complexities of interaction: Marlon Brando's enlargement of The Godfather.

Given these inherent limitations of auteur criticism, what I would offer in its place is an approach that assumes a kind of collective creativity, in which various members of the production team participate through interaction. Surely, at the very least, this would be true of the head cameraman, because he is the direct link between the director and the technology that must be adapted and controlled. But the scenarist and the actor are also important, for they have indispensable professional skills that not every director can incorporate into his own personality. The same holds true of the editor, though he gets less space than the star in the credits. Naturally these parties also interact with each other, not just with the director himself.

Over the years various professional cameramen have made a significant contribution to the development of cinematic style. Fritz Wagner and Karl Freund gave films of the twenties and thirties a new look with the acute angling and off-center composition of their shots. Ernest Haller, Lee Garmes, and James Wong Howe pioneered in the use of low-key, high-contrast lighting for American gangster films, conferring quality upon third-rate melodramas by visual means alone. During the late thirties and early forties Gregg Toland revolutionized both studio and location photography through his unprecedented experiments with lenses and lighting in films made for John Ford, Orson Welles, and William Wyler. Right at the moment, the enthusiasm of Raoul Coutard and Henry Decae for available-light photography and handheld camera work has made these effects dominant in almost all films of the French "New Wave" directors, these two men having shot the majority of films attributed to Jacques Demy, François Truffaut, and Jean-Luc Godard. Coutard and Decae have helped make the new wave of the 1960s a unified surge instead of just a succession of individual ripples. The frontiers crossed by cameramen of this caliber are at least as important as the ground covered by almost any of the directors for whom they have worked.

Ideally, of course, the head cameraman thinks along with the director, matching suggestion with suggestion, merging image with idea. Before a single frame is exposed, the cameraman is on hand to assist the director in defining the "photographic idea" of a picture, i.e. to help the director clarify his feelings about composition, lighting, color, and whatever else is relevant to the visuals. It is not uncommon to find the director and his head cameraman surveying the set together, making notes and exchanging questions, each man equipped with a range finder to check out composition and a light meter to measure the angle and intensity of the light.

So sensitive is the relationship here that many directors have worked almost exclusively with one head cameraman, or at least shown a distinct preference for two or three above all others. Early in the 1900s, Billy Bitzer shot all the major films of pioneer director D. W. Griffith, making his imagination felt in classic scenes from *Birth of a Nation* (1914) and *Intolerance* (1916). During the formative phase of Soviet cinema, Edouard Tisse did all the photography for the films of Sergei Eisenstein, traveling halfway around the world with him to shoot *Que Viva Mexico*. On the contemporary scene, director Alain Resnais has generally consigned his visuals to Sacha Vierny, while Luchino Visconti

DIRECTOR AND CAMERAMAN: While filmmaking in some sense proceeds from the private inspiration of the director, this vision is mediated through the technical skill of his cameraman, a fact that makes their relationship a very sensitive one. Here Ingmar Bergman (seated left) and Sven Nykvist (at camera) work together during the shooting of *Persona* (1966). Photograph courtesy of Svensk Filmindustri.

typically collaborates with Giuseppe Rotunno. Sometimes a director associates himself with a particular cameraman all the while he is working in a particular style. Federico Fellini, for example, used cameraman Otello Martelli for nearly all the films he did in the idiom of neorealism, but when this director took a new road in *8½* (1963) it was in the company of another photographer, Gianni di Venanzo.

The career of Ingmar Bergman further underscores this last point. Through most of the 1950s he used Gunnar Fischer as his head cameraman; then with *The Virgin Spring* (1960) he shifted this responsibility to Sven Nykvist. The change presaged an entirely new look in Bergman's films, attributable, it would certainly seem, to the differing photographic tastes of the two cameramen. While Fischer liked to work in the studio, with lots of glancing lights, spot effects, and complex shadows, Nykvist prefers to shoot outdoors, in simple setups, with as few lights as possible. This shows up markedly in the difference between the Fischer-conceived visuals of *The Magician* (1958) or *Wild Strawberries* (1957) and the films of Bergman's trilogy (*Through a Glass Darkly,* 1961; *Winter Light,* 1962; and *The Silence,* 1963) which bear the impress of Nykvist. In these latter films, though they are by no means identical in their photographic style, we always see what Nykvist calls "the simplicity that does not disturb." [5]

It is probably safe to conjecture that Nykvist's style became appealing to Bergman because the cameraman at this stage of his career was moving along the same path as the director. Bergman had worked briefly with Nykvist (who shot the interiors for *The Naked Night,* 1953) in the early 1950s, but the partnership at that time proved inconsequential. By the later 1950s, however, Nykvist's feelings about photography were changing radically and he was reaching out toward a new style. Writing about this transformation of taste, Nykvist remarked in 1962: "As I look back now in retrospect on all the tricky experiences I have had in filming forty features, I am sometimes appalled. I am reminded of effectively lighted spots and a swarm of double shadows on the set walls. I see needless backlighting on a beautiful woman's hair; and big, exaggerated foregrounds — made only to create a great dramatic perspective in the picture. In short, what I see is overworked pictures." Bergman was rethinking his own approach to filmmaking at exactly the same time, so he and Nykvist were able to collaborate very fruitfully. "Ingmar Bergman and I promised each other when we started with *The Virgin Spring,*" says Nykvist, "there would be no beauty effects." Since then, "the goal has always been the same: to keep it simple." Hence the multiple close-ups, the spare decor, the minimal camera movement, which we know as hallmarks of the films Bergman has made during the last decade.

Bergman begins with a general photographic conception which he passes along to Nykvist for particularization. Of *The Silence,* for example, Nykvist recalls: "When Bergman handed me the script, he explained the dream effect he wanted: 'There must not be any of the old hackneyed dream effects, such as visions in soft focus or dissolves. The film itself must have the character of a dream.' "

This led Nykvist to screen several test rolls with Bergman and then choose an exceptionally light-sensitive film stock, Eastman Double-X, as the emulsion to use in shooting the picture. The effect Bergman sought also led the cameraman to have the stock processed in such a way as to emphasize its high-contrast characteristics, very noticeable in the finished product. This is one way the director and his cameraman

[5] This and the following citations of Nykvist are from his interview with the editors of *American Cinematographer* (October 1962), pp. 613 ff.

interact. Sometimes the photographic idea evolves while Nykvist and Bergman are on location together, as in the case of *Through a Glass Darkly*: "We traveled daily," says Nykvist, "between the camps and the location in the early, cloudy-grey light and we noticed how many fine impressive graphic values were to be seen, and that whenever the sun broke through the overcast momentarily, how it instantly killed the many delicate shades of light, arresting the graphic play between highlights and subtle shadows." The shared experience of the two men led on this occasion to a decision to shoot *Through a Glass Darkly* largely under the weather conditions Nykvist describes. The scenes are bright, but rarely hot with sharp sunlight, except at the close of the picture where the more intense light fulfills a significant dramatic purpose. When even so magisterial a director as Bergman depends to this extent upon the photographic advice of Nykvist, the crucial role of the head cameraman seems clearly established.

Filmmaking of course is much more than photography, and for this reason other types of craftsmanship or discipline are demanded. There is a script to be designed, actors to articulate it, and an editor to shape the footage the cameraman has shot. Some directors try to play all these roles themselves, while others are inclined to delegate more authority to their subordinates. Bergman, being a man of the theatre, almost always writes his own scripts and enters intensely into rehearsals with his actors. We can see the strength of his attraction to these phases of production in the close relationship he has formed with performers like Liv Ullmann, Ingrid Thulin, Bibi Andersson, Gunnar Björnstrand, and Max von Sydow. Jean Cocteau also scripted his own films but never worked quite so closely with a repertory company of actors. Some American directors, like Josef von Sternberg and Elia Kazan, also have strong ties to the theatre but were not nearly so interested in writing their own scripts as in setting the stage and directing the performers. Von Sternberg's professional intimacy with Marlene Dietrich is legendary, while Kazan in the 1950s dealt almost as single-mindedly with various graduates of the New York Actors Studio. This phase of production seems considerably less important to directors like Fellini and Antonioni, both of whom concentrate more energetically upon the editing process.

Whatever the approach of the director, however, there is usually a place for creative inspiration of other members of the production team. Jean Renoir and Marcel Carné, for example, are certainly auteur-directors, indeed two of the finest talents ever to emerge in the French cinema, yet each man had cause to be grateful for the sensitive scripts prepared by Jacques Prévert. More recently, British playwright Harold Pinter's scenarios for Joseph Losey have given this director a critical acclaim he never before enjoyed. The psychological complexity of

Losey films such as *The Servant* (1963), *Accident* (1967), and *The Go-Between* (1971) owe at least as much to Pinter's resonant dialogue and calculated pauses as to the director's baroque imagery. Besides, when Losey doesn't have a Pinter script at his disposal he seems to have trouble maintaining those nuances of mood which are the mark of his mature style. Pinterless, *Boom* (1968) was pretty much of a bust. The same holds true for the contribution of the actor. Obviously the Marx brothers are chiefly responsible for the comic zest of the films they played in, even though they never sat in the director's chair. By the same token, Chaplin was doing his own thing long before he dissociated himself from Sennett, and the same holds true for Buster Keaton, Jerry Lewis, and Jacques Tati.

Sometimes an actor makes a still more significant mark. Unlike the director, he has a way of becoming a kind of culture hero, and his public image occasionally does filmmaking a decided service. Humphrey Bogart imediately comes to mind. Having established himself as the sympathetic tough guy, he assumes pretty much the same stance whether he is directed by John Huston, Howard Hawks, or Michael Curtiz. Furthermore, his resistance to substantial deflection from this role more than once was a clear asset to the director who took charge of him. Is it coincidental that Huston made many of his best films while working with Bogart? I hardly think so. I would say, rather, that the public image of Bogart interlocked and counterbalanced the personal imagination of this director. Bogart's tough-mindedness, his sense of irony, often seems to have protected Huston from the bucolic sentimentality to which he is prone. This is one reason why *Key Largo* (1948), *Beat the Devil* (1954), and *The Treasure of Sierra Madre* (1948) are better pictures than superambitious catastrophes such as *Moby Dick* (1956) and *The Bible* (1966). Bogart saved Huston by bending the director's imagination toward a more astringent definition of heroism, a service which probably could never have been rendered by Gregory Peck. But the influence is reciprocal. If Bogart provided Huston with a credible hero, Huston conferred pace and form upon what in Bogart pictures may become just a digressive display of crusty fortitude. Mutual assistance is the key to relations between the director and his stars.

The editor's effort, while equally important, is harder to spell out. There is, though, the Hollywood adage "We'll save it in the cutting room," which testifies to the importance of this phase of production. One reason the editor remains obscure is that most directors here take

DIRECTOR AND ACTOR: Naturally the relationship between the director and the principal performers in the picture is one that demands constant interaction and collaboration. Here Ingmar Bergman (back to camera) rehearses Max von Sydow as assistant notes details on script. From the collection of Cinemabilia, New York.

a rather active role. The obvious examples are Eisenstein and V. I. Pudovkin, the Soviet directors who founded what is usually called "montage." But contemporary directors like Resnais, Godard, and Alfred Hitchcock have also shown much interest in what happens at the moviola. At the same time, however, editing is not a one-man job. Resnais has had a lot of help from Henri Colpi and Chris Marker, two talented editors who have now begun to acquire directors' reputations. And Godard, though himself a genius with shears and splicers, has always collaborated closely with Agnes Guillemot. Similarly, Anthony Gibbs, Karel Reisz, and Kevin Brownlow have brought editing in the British cinema up to its present standards of sophistication. The compliment that Agnes Varda paid to the man who cut her first feature film might well apply to many anonymous contributions from the cutting room: "By scrupulously editing my film," she admitted, "he allowed me to clarify my own thoughts." [6]

Aram Avakian, editor of Arthur Penn's *The Miracle Worker* (1962) and *Mickey One* (1964), emphasizes the relative independence of the editor as he speaks reminiscently of his own work on these films: "Any director in his right mind will leave his editor alone until the first cut is finished. The notion that the director works continuously with the editor in cutting the film is a myth. It only happens that way when the director is also a cutter. Usually, the director is there to screen the material after it has been cut in some form and when he's needed, that is, when something isn't going right. Some directors will come into the screening room for three or four days to make sure the editor shares a basic understanding and then leaves [sic] the editor alone to edit the picture." [7] Naturally this doesn't mean the director gives up his supervisory role: "When the director feels his intention in a specific sequence is not being served, or well enough, he will come into the cutting room and go over the footage with the editor cut by cut. But there are whole large portions of a film where the director will just say 'Go.' "

Avakian's practical experience with Penn tends to support his general claims about director-editor relations. Penn came to the cinema in the late 1950s fresh from a string of successes as a Broadway theatre director. Anxious to advertise his feeling for the cinematic, he immediately began experimenting with a bold editorial style, energetically but a bit clumsily carried out in *The Left-Handed Gun* (1957). When Avakian took over as Penn's editor for *The Miracle Worker*, however, he tried

---

[6] This compliment paid to Alain Resnais is cited in Roy Armes, *The Cinema of Alain Resnais* (New York: A. S. Barnes and Co., Inc., 1968), p. 31. Reprinted by permission of the Tantivy Press and A. S. Barnes and Co., Inc.

[7] This and the following citations of Avakian are from his "On the Editor," in *Movie People*, ed. Fred Baker (New York: Douglas Book Corporation, 1972), pp. 123–145.

to push the director toward a more conservative approach to the cutting: "It seemed to me," he says, "that jump cutting was out of keeping with the classical character of *The Miracle Worker* [a film biography of Helen Keller] and the period in which it was set [turn-of-the-century America]." But these considerations of genre and period did not impress the director as much as they did Avakian, and a dispute over the proper editorial strategy ensued. "We had a big discussion . . . about how the famous fight scene between Anne [Anne Bancroft, as Helen's tutor] and Patty [Patty Duke, as Helen] ought to be cut. Arthur wanted me to do it with a lot of jump cuts, and at first I resisted, but he finally pushed me into it."

The ultimate consequence, however, was not a clear-cut victory for either party. Both were enriched. Penn, says Avakian, had called for "energy, energy, jump-cut it," and the editor responded dutifully. Yet, Avakian continues, "when I had edited about three minutes of the scene that way, I decided I'd better show it to him to see how he felt about it. We went into the screening room. Arthur took a seat in the front, and I deliberately sat in the back so I could watch his reaction. I watched his head over the back of his chair. Two minutes into the scene, he had slipped completely out of sight. I could just about hear him muttering to himself — 'He's out of his mind.' I asked him what he thought and he said aloud, 'Well, you might have overdone it a little. Too much energy in this thing.' "

On the strength of this reaction, Avakian went back to the cutting room and did another version of the scene, smoother than the one he had just shown to Penn but not so tame as the one the editor himself had first envisioned. Furthermore, in the process of recutting the sequence, Avakian came to see the logic of Penn's impulses. The editorial disturbances conformed well to the film's theme. "I feel now," concludes Avakian, "that Arthur was right in the first place. Jump-cut, jump-cut, a deaf-dumb-blind kid getting hit, repeatedly, from out of that black corner." In other words, the cutting of this scene became a learning experience for both men. Avakian taught Penn something about practical technique, while Penn showed his editor that exceptional thematic concerns may call for a heterodox spirit in the cutting room. The much more complex but still scrupulously well-motivated cutting style of *Mickey One* owes much to what the two men learned from each other. Here again, though on a more abstract and expressionistic plane, disjunctive editing expresses the psychic pressure upon the central character.

To my mind the principle of cooperative creativity is very nicely illustrated by a scene from *The Godfather* (1972), largely conceived and executed by the leading actor, Marlon Brando. The scene is the death of old Don Corleone, long the iron-willed master of an East Coast

Mafia clan but now in failing health and gradually ceding power to his son Michael. The film was authoritatively directed by Francis Coppola and effectively scripted by Mario Puzo, author of the novel on which the film is based. Neither director nor scenarist, however, made much provision for the death scene of Corleone, though the internal logic of the picture demanded some amplitude of treatment. Hence Brando, trained in the deeply felt psychological realism of the Actors Studio, was invited to invent some stage business to flesh out an otherwise skimpy scene. What resulted, happily, was a whole new dimension of meaning.

The problem of the scene, I would suggest, was in some sense a mechanical one, the fact that what was in the novel didn't lend itself very well to photography. In the book Puzo describes the Don's death in metaphors of heat and light:

> Quite suddenly it felt as if the sun had come down very close to his head. The air filled with dancing golden specks. Michael's oldest boy came running through the garden toward where the Don knelt and the boy was enveloped by a yellow shield of blinding light. . . . Death hid behind that flaming yellow shield ready to pounce on him and the Don with a wave of his hand warned the boy away from his presence.[8]

The language here is highly visual and at first glance seems to ask for a photographic approach. But how exactly would you shoot it? Though it is easy enough to create blinding yellow flashes with a stroke of the pen, such strokes of the camera tend to fall too heavily upon the visual surface of a picture. The color could be deliberately distorted with a light-yellow filter. Or the heat could be simulated with a partial over-exposure that would bleach out the green leaves of the Don's garden. Or the lens shade could be left off the camera, allowing stray light to get into the lens and create little bubbles of sun flare. We have seen all these things before, however, and they have become optical clichés. Wisely, the director opted for a solution involving the actor rather than the cameraman.

Since the Don is alone, though, except for Michael's very young son, the scene cannot be built up verbally, through conversation. It calls for mime, body gesture, subtle yet significant action. With this in mind Brando began working with the child, his only available partner. Soon he had shoved a piece of fruit in his mouth, making a kind of monster mask to get the boy in a game they would enact in front of the camera. This proved exactly the right approach, not just because it elicited highly authentic reactions of fright from the child but also because

8 (Greenwich, Conn.: Fawcett Publications, Inc., 1969), p. 409. © 1969. By permission of G. P. Putnam's Sons.

Brando had accidentally hit upon a kind of symbol for the personality of the Don himself.

As it is finally played in *The Godfather,* the scene between Brando and the child becomes one of the most expressive elements in the film. We find the Don in his quiet garden, where Puzo had placed him in the novel, dutifully taking care of his vegetables, just as he has spent his late life in the comfortable privacy of his estate, looking after the interest of his family and his property. The garden image itself is thus rather significant, a metaphor suggesting the Don's protective paternalism. Immediately before the scene he has conferred for the last time with his son Michael, reluctant heir to the Corleone crime empire. He frets over Michael almost as if he were a child, then in a more reflective mood, apologizes for the life he is escorting his son into. Both these motifs are made more meaningful, certainly more visible, in Corleone's death scene. Here the son has been replaced by the grandson, yet the relationship, the laying of hands on the next generation, remains consistent. Corleone first takes a spray gun (a stage prop added in the picture) and teaches the child how to eliminate predatory insects, indirectly introducing the theme of killing, which is one of the chief occupations of the clan. Then, playfully, he turns himself into a monster to casually amuse the grandson. But the monster mask, which inadvertently disturbs the child, is also a piece of self-revelation, analogous to the slightly guilt-ridden confession Corleone has made to Michael in the previous scene. Having revealed himself morally to the child at the same time he has introduced him to a death-dealing weapon, old Corleone collapses and dies, secure in the belief that the next generation has been suitably oriented to the business of the family. In its inception, the scene was merely intended to give the actor something to do before he died, but as articulated by Brando it brought to summation the major themes of the film.

The chapters that follow propose to explore the inner dynamics of film art, giving appropriate attention to technology, craftsmanship, and directorial supervision. The great directors receive their kudos — Fellini for his visual imagination, Welles for his expertise with sound, Bergman for his scripts and his unfailing skill with actors, Eisenstein for his encyclopedic grasp of the whole production process — but I have also tried to give a voice to other members of the filmmaking team. This sometimes means looking at composition and lighting from the standpoint of the cameraman or thinking about sound from the perspective of a musician or the man who runs the mixer. It doesn't mean getting too deeply into gears and gadgets, only enough to see what technical factors impinge upon the aesthetic experience. Since scripting, staging, and editing are an equally integral part of film art, I have also attempted to include the people who adapt novels, put on greasepaint, or sit at the moviola, occasionally letting them explain their own discipline in their own words. By allowing for the complexity of their relations to the director, we shall ultimately, I believe, have more insight into what it means to be an auteur.

List of Films Discussed *

GODFATHER, THE   177 min.   FNC
MIRACLE WORKER, THE   107 min.   UAS
THROUGH A GLASS DARKLY   91 min.   JAN
TO DIE IN MADRID   90 min.   AUD-BRA
200 MOTELS   not presently available

* See pp. 329–331 for key to film distributors code.

2
COMPOSITION

Films begin in the viewfinder of a camera. Its rectangular shape prescribes the borders of an imagined world. This is not the real world, for it lacks the "all aroundness" we experience every time we roll our eyes or turn our heads. It is also a flat world, where dense, three-dimensional objects have been reduced to shadows and crushed into a single surface. It is a special kind of world, continuously created by the movements of the camera and rigorously governed by the optics of its lenses. This is the world that the filmmaker presides over. He is a man of vision who has learned to see with a mechanical eye.

Like painting, photographic composition involves the balance, tension, and interplay of lines and masses. Like theater, it also requires an understanding of stage properties essential to a scene. But motion pictures give us neither the abstract geometry of a Delacroix canvas nor the concrete tactility of an Ibsen set. The camera fashions a unique version of a physical scene — in images that seem solid or fluid, soft or sharp, spacious or constricted, depending upon where the machine is mounted and what lens is called into play. In the hands of an able craftsman, the optical system does more than merely record: it selects, features, and evaluates the material upon which it reports. Camera and lens do not just locate objects in space and time; each act of placement is also an exercise in composition.

At the most elementary level, composition entails handling the camera — placing it with respect to its subject; moving it at a calculated pace when it pans, tilts, or tracks; adjusting the running speed of its crank or motor, so that the action it records seems either dizzily swift or elegiacally slow. Each of these factors affects the look, but more importantly, the tone and feel of the filmic world.

Consider at the outset so matter-of-fact a thing as the camera's orientation to its subject. The filmmaker's first creative opportunity is to select his view, to choose a tiny fraction of the visual world before him as structurally and texturally suited to his imaginative interests. This is what is at stake when he frames a shot. He can weight down the picture space with rocks and rooted trees and squatty buildings, or lighten it with leaves and clouds and spires. He can feature clean, straight, uninterrupted lines, or complicate his pictorial rectangle with all sorts of bric-a-brac to mask, cut, and subdivide it. He can coax us to the center of action with arching boughs that point inward, or force us to keep our distance with forbidding fences that rise up in the foreground. He can soothe us with restful horizontal arrangements, unsettle us with slashing diagonals, or dazzle us with eye-catching radials. When he studies a character, he has further options. He can shoot the heroine from a full-in-the-face viewpoint or catch her from an oblique angle. He can let the camera stare down at her, haughtily, almost contemptuously, or from a low mount he can frame her against a quiet cloud-dappled sky. If he should choose to be more daring, he might even tip the camera to right or left, so that it is no longer aligned with the flow of gravity or the predictably level horizon line. From this setup the visual field loses its customary stability. Skyscrapers lean at impossible slants, vertical cliffs become strange overhangs, bridges and viaducts point uphill. Such changes of camera position necessarily effect changes of tone.

We get much greater complexity the moment the camera begins to move. It glides upward to measure the height of a tower, pans gently to follow the *entrechats* of a dancer, swishes wildly to catch the confusion of combat, or dollies in gradually to separate a face from the crowd. Often these movements have no special import, and, like good prose, they simply achieve variety without calling attention to themselves. But motion also has mimic potential; it is always a source of metaphor. If the camera is prowling around the set, the scene carries overtones of restlessness, whatever the actors might be doing or saying. When camera movements are startling and bold, the tempo of the action seems to quicken accordingly. If movement is rough and jerky, as when the cameraman packs the rig around on his shoulders, the impression this usually leaves is one of disorder and disturbance, or at least casualness and extreme informality. For better or worse, movement tends to carry meaning.

Besides the camera, another mechanical element that profoundly affects composition is the lens system. Lenses determine the texture of the image and the scale of objects within the frame. Does the actor in the foreground tower over his antagonist toward the rear of the set? This has more to do with the lens on the camera than with the relative sizes of the two men. Lenses alter our impressions of distance, drawing faraway objects up to the camera or pushing near ones farther away. They also influence both camera movement and subject movement in more ways than most people notice. Some lenses do strange things to perspective when the camera is tilted; others blur and fuzz the image when it is panned. Some lenses enhance the illusion of forward progress; others suppress such movement, seeming to freeze the subject in space. Used expressively, lenses translate amassed detail into symbolic decor, establish and adjust pictorial emphasis, convert random movement into poetic gesture. They dramatize whatever they depict.

From this it follows that the filmmaker must be constantly attentive to optics. Will a 100mm lens magnify a church spire to a point that it dominates the vertical axis of a scene? Will the face of the leading lady stay in sharp enough focus to show the anger in her eyes as she lurches toward the camera? Such questions, meaningless to painting or stagecraft, are the virtual core of cinematic composition. "How does this scene look?" is a misformed question. "How will *this lens in conjunction with this camera setup* make it look?" is the correct reformulation. Once this point is grasped, we can appreciate how filmmakers choose among alternative ways of seeing. Although these may seem natural, even inevitable, in a certain dramatic context, they are often as distinct from human vision as the colors of a Rembrandt landscape are distinct from the hues of the physical world. This is what makes the much vaunted "realism" of photography relative rather than absolute and what admits the filmmaker to the realm of the artist. In deciding where to put the camera, what lens to put on it, and how to maneuver each in keeping with the natural movement of his subject, the filmmaker enters a sphere where taste and judgment take priority over automatic reportage.

COMPOSING WITH THE CAMERA

n motion pictures, mastering composition means mastering movement. At the most basic level, this simply involves capturing the energy of a moving subject—a single actor raising his fist in defiance, a team of infantry sweeping over a ridge, or perhaps something inanimate yet pictorially exciting, like a raging fire or turbulent surf. But composition also entails creating, accentuating, or altering movement; this might be done by masking the frame, changing the running speed of the camera, or simply moving the tripod. Above all, the filmmaker must interpret the significance of motion, finding the way in which movement conveys the feel of a dramatic situation and unlocks the hidden meaning of a scene. Historically, composing with the camera has meant the search for an increasingly more flexible technology and for the imagination to use it with sensitivity and discretion.

THE MOVING IMAGE

Invention of cinematography. Enthrallment with physical motion. Early strategies for simulating motion: "Irising" and "undercranking." Applications in The Joyless Street, The Wild Child, The Rink, City Lights, Tom Jones, A Clockwork Orange. *Development of slow-motion photography. Applications in* Bonnie and Clyde, Ski the Outer Limits.

Before it became possible to think of film as an art form, it was necessary to develop a camera specifically designed to record motion. It had to have all the accouterments of its early ancestors, but also required radically new mechanical drives. These were necessary to force film through the camera at a rate of at least 10 frames per second, the threshold beyond which the eye is deceived into interpreting a succession of individual frames as a single dynamic event. Eadweard Muybridge didn't have such a camera in the 1870s when he made his first efforts to record the unposed movement of trotting horses. Instead, he simulated motion with multiple cameras triggered in rapid succession, each catching a further phase of the animals' strides. Though this contrivance satisfied the fundamental condition of cinematography, it was hopelessly awkward, noteworthy as aspiration rather than achievement. The "photographic gun" Jules Marey perfected in the 1880s was a major improvement, since it was one machine and not a dozen. But the Marey camera would run only in short bursts, to do photography of minimally short duration.

Full-fledged cinematography waited upon several refinements of the next decade, notably the sprocket wheel, the so-called Latham loop, and the synchronized shutter. The first of these devices made it possible to advance film through the camera at uniform speeds; the second reduced the stress which builds up as film is unwound from a large spool; the third, perhaps the most important innovation, eliminated blur and distortion resulting from unwanted movement of the film at the instant of exposure. Together these inventions put into the hands of filmmakers a camera which could be cranked at speeds adequate to smoothly record motion and geared to allow stable, sharply focused exposures of relatively long filmstrips. Knowing the labor that went into early experiments with the motion-picture camera should help us appreciate the simple photographic ambitions of these pioneering days. Louis Lumière's turn-of-the-century picture *Arrival of Train at Station* (1895), is not a work of soaring imagination. But the flight of the Wright brothers was similarly unspectacular. Like the event at Kitty Hawk, Lumière's film marks the opening of an era.

The further history of motion-picture cameras represents increasing sophistication of an achieved design. Throughout the next seventy-five years we can discern a continuing effort to build lighter, more durable, and more adaptable cameras, suited to every kind of compositional demand. As early as the 1910s there was an effort to get the camera on wheels, or to get it up in the air, as in the shots from the giant tower built for *Intolerance* (1916). The 1920s and 1930s brought still more elaborate rigs for trucking and lifting the camera, like the gigantic but mobile cranes and booms from which Busby Berkeley's musicals were invariably shot. Perhaps of greater significance, however, has been the steady pressure to miniaturize the camera, to make it more portable and in all ways more suited to unstaged location photography. Though the noise-muffling devices of the early sound era and the large-gauge cameras of the 1950s temporarily worked at cross-purposes with this effort to reduce camera size, two world wars and five decades of news photography have exerted overwhelming counterpressure. The same progress is evidenced in the synchronous drives which move film through the camera. The hand-cranked machines of the first cinematographers gave way within two decades to motorized equipment. Although the first effect of this transition was to freeze the camera at a fixed running speed, the long-term result was to provide a much greater range of speeds than hand-cranks could ever make possible. Of course, technology is not an escalator that automatically raises art to new heights. We do not necessarily have aesthetic progress every-time a character dies in slow motion or a camera whirls around the set in a helicopter. The imagination must humanize the available tech-nology, relieving it of easy clichés and accommodating it to serious dramatic purposes.

From its inception the cinema has been enthralled by the simple fact of motion. Lumière memorialized the moving train, forcing his audi-ence to duck away from the screen as it roared into the forespace of the frame. American director Edwin Porter added galloping horses and blazing six-guns in *The Great Train Robbery* (1903), giving the western the mobile props it would lean on for all the forseeable future. Mean-while Lumière's great contemporary Georges Méliès filled his studio with tumbling clowns and high-stepping dancing girls, creating forma-tions and routines that would live on in countless comedies and musi-cals. Movement soon became an integral feature of plot, as is demon-strated in chase scenes from *Intolerance* and *Birth of a Nation* to *Z* (France, 1969) and *The French Connection* (U.S.A., 1971). Even the emotional clichés of cinema typically involve the moving image: hope is a bright sun bursting through fragments of cloud; forgiveness is the lines of a stern face softening into a smile; impending disaster is leaves swept from the trees by rising winds. Though mere mobility does not insure artistic distinction, it is a fairly predictable constant of cinematic composition.

From the standpoint of modern cinema, the easiest way to enhance movement is to move the camera in conjunction with the subject. But early filmmakers, lacking sophisticated dollies and an efficient system of through-the-lens focusing, pioneered in treatments of the moving image appropriate to the technology of their day. This gave us such strategies as "irising" and "undercranking," two hallmarks of the silent era which became part of the permanent visual vocabulary of motion pictures. Irising simulates motion by masking portions of the picture space, thus changing the shape and size of the frame; undercranking exaggerates motion by slowing down the running speed of the camera, wildly ac-

THE IRIS SHOT. One of the filmmaker's options is to alter the shape of the frame, perhaps (as in this shot from *Birth of a Nation*) narrowing the picture space to a tiny oval, to con-centrate the viewers' attention on one particular element. Irising was accomplished in the early days of cinema by manipulating an external diaphragm attached to the camera and was thus part of the cameraman's art. Photograph from The Museum of Modern Art/Film Stills Archive.

celerating the apparent movement of cops, custards, or crashing cars.

The iris is an external diaphragm which is mounted in front of the lens to form a kind of extended barrel. Because of its circular shape, the iris as it is closed down transforms the film frame from a rectangle to an oval, either large or small, depending upon the cameraman's adjustments. Its chief purpose is to achieve selectivity, centering attention upon a few details encompassed within the standard rectangle. But it also contributes to the illusion of movement, as if the camera were suddenly to advance upon the principal subject of the shot, or draw back to encompass an entire scene.

The use of the iris for centering and selecting is well illustrated in one of the best German films of the silent era, *The Joyless Street* (1925). Directed by G. W. Pabst, the picture is poignant meditation upon the fate of depression-ridden Austria. One unifying motif of the film is musical, conveyed visually on the silent screen by extensive shots of bands and performers, always ready to strike up a melody. Their insistent strumming, which floats through all the cafés of polite society, is a desperate effort to maintain the facade of "gay Vienna" while breadlines gather in the street. The film moves toward the explosion of these pretenses, and this drift is completed in a narrowly oval iris that comes in the next to last scene. The elegant café now stands empty, the musicians have forsaken their instruments, and the camera roves over them in silence. Then the iris is closed down upon the drum and cymbal, the most conspicuous emblems of the tinny arrogance which can no longer maintain itself against the squalid realities beyond café walls. The shot requires no verbal commentary; the camera itself has spoken.

We don't see much of the iris anymore, since its functions have been assimilated into other types of camera movement. Instead of irising in to pick out one subject among several, the cameraman of the 1930s or 1940s would dolly the camera forward, while his counterpart of today would resort to a zoom lens. When the practice of irising is now revived, as it has been, occasionally, by the contemporary generation of French filmmakers, it ordinarily is done with a special process camera called an "optical printer" and is not introduced in the original exposure. No matter, though, for the effect is the same, and often very persuasive, as when director François Truffaut calls it into play in *The Wild Child* (1970). Truffaut of course is aware that he is dealing in archaism, but he is willing to risk looking slightly manneristic in order to evoke the period atmosphere of premodern France. Here the iris might be thought of as part of the camera's costume. Purists may find the analogy Truffaut draws between "primitive" cinematography and the primitivism of his hero a little far-fetched, but this doesn't keep the effect from being visually persuasive. The film is episodic, and most scenes begin or end with an iris that marks a stage in the acculturation of the young savage. Having opened the picture by irising in upon the unkempt, animal-like face of the fierce boy perched in a tree, Truffaut's cameraman closes *The Wild Child* by irising in upon the now washed, combed, and thoroughly civilized face of the same boy ascending a household stairway. The two shots measure all that has been gained (and a few things that have been lost) in the hero's progress from brute to man.

Besides changing the shape of the film rectangle, cameramen of the silent era also enhanced movement by altering the running speed of the camera. This makes the action seem either exceptionally slow or breathtakingly fast. In technical terms, it simply involves mismatching the speed of camera and projector. The projectors of this period were cranked at somewhere between 16 and 24 frames per second; hence on-screen action looked normal if the camera recording the action were running at approximately the same speed. Running the camera faster than 24 frames per second (say, at 30, 36, or 48) produces the effect of slow motion, since the projector then runs less fast than the camera. Running the camera at less than 16 frames per second, however (say, at 12, 10, or 8), produces the effect of acceleration, since the projector then runs faster than the camera. Known colloquially as "undercranking," this latter effect — by far the easier to produce with a hand-powered camera — became one of the staples of silent comedy.

Mack Sennett had learned in the early teens that the speed-up effects of undercranking were the ideal way to add vigor to creaking vaudeville stunts, and the cameramen at Keystone were instructed to apply this technique to all chases, brawls, and hairbreadth escapes. Though the approach gained many cheap laughs for second-rate comics, it also passed into the mature art of Buster Keaton and Charlie Chaplin. Although Chaplin's mimetic skill and Keaton's acrobatic agility are probably unequaled anywhere in the history of cinema, neither performer was reluctant to let the camera support and embellish his comic antics. Chaplin's skating, dancing, and boxing routines almost always involve an undercranked camera, as is clear from the gyrating near-catastrophes of *The Rink* (1916) or the fantastic fisticuffs of *City Lights* (1931). Endlessly imitated, both well and badly, comic undercranking (the term is now purely metaphoric, since all cinecameras have mechanical drives) can still be seen in such noteworthy modern films as *Tom Jones* (Britain, 1963) and *A Clockwork Orange* (Britain, 1971).

Although undercranking is usually associated with comedy, it would be a mistake to imagine it restricted to scenes of raucous laughter. The German expressionists sometimes undercranked the camera in fantasy sequences, as in the phantom chariot ride in *Nosferatu* (1922) that carries the hero to the castle of Count Dracula. More typically, undercranking is gathered into the service of "realism," as is the case in many action sequences from the early 1900s onward. In the famous battle on Lake Chudskoye in *Alexander Nevsky* (U.S.S.R., 1938) the clash of contending armies is shot at a systematically reduced camera speed, so that by the end of the sequence the victorious Russians are driving their foe from the field with absolutely phenomenal speed and power. Similar strategies are standard practice in today's studios, where scenes of intense action, whether they involve soaring jets, screeching police cars, or barroom fisticuffs, are shot at 18, rather than the standard 24, frames per second. This slight reduction of camera speed assures that the tempo of the action will be quickened, yet the eye will not take it to be abnormal or unnatural, just vigorous and convincing.

In spite of these facts, modern cinema has gleaned some of its most noteworthy effects by altering motion in the opposite direction, using high-speed motor-driven cameras to "overcrank" scenes that seem to encourage slow-motion treatment. Although imitated badly in many ultraviolent films of the late 1960s, the slow-motion death of Bonnie and Clyde is authentically effective, paradoxically distancing us from the event by stylizing it so intricately and at the same time forcing us to endure each detail of it for an inordinately extended interval. After we have allowed ourselves to be caught up in the lilt of banjo music and undercranked chase scenes, this device brings home the stark painfulness of death by violence in a peculiarly persuasive way. But it is perhaps not the fiction film that has used slow motion most effectively. The cameras of the 1960s, some of which have the capacity to shoot at as much as 400 frames per second (sixteen times as fast as conventional running speed), make it possible for the cinema to analyze motion never before accessible to exploration — the fierce wingbeats of an attacking eagle, the split-second timing of a karate kada, the graceful tumbling of a skier in flight. Extreme slow motion is what makes possible the exhilarating lyricism of *Ski the Outer Limits* (U.S.A. 1968), much of which was shot at 400 frames per second. Here actions almost too fast for the eye are stalled and lengthened, so that the lightning-quick acrobatics of the ski slope become floating arabesques in a fantastic aerial ballet.

SLOW-MOTION PHOTOGRAPHY. Modern high-speed cameras make it possible to stall and delay movement, so that abrupt and precipitous action comes to seem dreamlike and poetic. Here, with the camera running at 400 frames per second, the skiers appear to float in space as they display their gymnastic skills. From *Ski the Outer Limits;* courtesy Pyramid Films, distributors.

THE MOVING CAMERA

Camera movements and their significance. The panning:
The Lower Depths. *Tracking:* Viridiana. *Booming:* Ugetzu.
Tilting. The World of Apu, The Loneliness of the Long
Distance Runner. *Conjunction of camera and subject
movement:* The Gospel According to St. Matthew, Umberto
D. *Significance of stasis:* The Seven Samurai.

These specialized gestures notwithstanding, the most familiar forms of cinematic movement involve physical motion of the camera — tilting, panning, tracking, booming, or swiveling in some even more complex way. The camera has been relatively mobile since about nineteen fifteen, more so since the twenties, when Karl Freund let it roam freely around the set of *The Last Laugh* (Germany, 1924). Since World War II it has been able to climb skyscrapers, crawl under tables, almost turn handsprings in order to follow the action or catch the mood of a scene. What is at stake in all these situations, of course, is not the mechanical agility of the camera but the imaginative dynamism of the filmmaker. The movements that succeed the best are neither the simplest nor the most complex, but those that mime the thematic configurations of the scene.

Sometimes a single camera movement gives meaning and motive to an entire picture, as is the case in the elaborate 360-degree pan that opens Akira Kurosawa's version of *The Lower Depths* (Japan, 1957). Manipulated by Kazuo Yamasaki, the camera slowly spins to show us a prohibitively enclosed world, looking up to tall cliffs that offer no escape for the entrapped inhabitants of this sunken pit of the world. The take begins with the camera fixed upon a small temple, seen from afar and from a very low angle as an emblem of decency and propriety; then the camera slowly revolves on its tripod, maintaining an invariantly high horizon line in the frame as it completes its circular arc before returning to the environs of the temple, where two acolytes now stand while pouring trash and garbage into the pit. The shot concludes with a slight dip as the camera is momentarily drawn into the downward drift of the refuse. We are thus told in one sweeping movement where the action of this film will take place and what the respectable world thinks of the protagonists to whom we are about to be introduced.

While the camera movement that opens *The Lower Depths* is exceptionally intricate, the one that concludes *Viridiana* (Spain, 1961) is effortlessly simple. Merely a smooth, slow tracking shot, it is powerfully expressive, encapsulating director Luis Buñuel's meditation upon the fate of contemporary Spain. As Buñuel sees it, this is a nation bereft of its traditional Catholicism, yet reoriented only to the pragmatic, Amer-

THE ART OF FRAMING: In *Ugetsu,* as in any well-composed film, the placement and movement of the camera reflects the mood of the scene. Photograph courtesy of Janus Films.

icanized secularism of the NATO era. His heroine runs the gamut of loyalties from life-denying religiosity, through sentimental socialism, to the complete cynicism which holds her enthralled at the end of the picture. By this time she has accepted the amorous embrace of her cousin, which helps initiate her to sex, card games, and fourth-rate jazz. The last take of the film seems to be Buñuel's comment upon the pilgrimage of Viridiana. It begins as a relative close-up of the heroine embracing her lover in his brightly lit, musically resonant quarters; then the camera slowly backs through the door into chambers that savor of old Spain. Without making a judgment, the final images juxtapose two worlds — one artificially gay with glare and noise, the other full of lustrously tasteful furniture, but empty of humanity and permanently dark. The tracking camera stalls and holds without pointing in any new directions, just as the dramatic progression of this film leaves us with no solution to the problems posed.

Camera movements may also express the subjective consciousness of the protagonist, as does the boom shot at the end of *Ugetsu,* another fine Japanese film of the 1950s.

Unlike *Viridiana, Ugetsu* attests to man's ability to learn from his mistakes, and the learning process of the hero is represented in a graceful lift of the camera at the close of the film. The plot features a man who repeatedly victimizes himself and others through his refusal to see the worth of common things. Eventually relieved of this moral blindness, he rises up from consultation with Buddhist monks to begin life anew. At this point the camera also booms up from the low mount maintained through the entire picture, now for the first time offering an overview of a sunny landscape peopled by tillers of the soil. Their work appears beautiful, dignified by the communal rhythm the high angle of the camera allows us to see. As we look down from this new vantage point we participate in the growth of the film's protagonist. The camera movement has graphically expressed the expansion of his moral sympathies.

Obviously the camera moves at other times than in the first or last minute of a picture, always with a full range of expressive possibilities. There is an unforgettable moment in *The World of Apu* (India, 1959) where an unexpected tilt of the camera coincides with a climactic turn of mind. Frustrated and disappointed at his inability to live up to youthful ideals, Apu considers suicide, comes to no decisive conclusion, yet drifts listlessly to the railroad track where he may throw himself under the wheels of an oncoming train. We see Apu and the train in a series of conventional crosscuts, but the camera suddenly pulls away from these subjects to gaze absentmindedly at an empty sky. Though it is hard to summarize the significance of this abrupt gesture, we seem forced to experience the inner void which has brought him to this pitch of desperation. Perhaps too, we sense a faint foreshadowing of Apu's psychic recovery. The image suggests blankness, but also openness, the mind's release from foul memories. Hence we are not surprised to find in the next cut that he has physically avoided the train; the tilt of the camera seems to say he has already mentally avoided its thundering wheels.

A more complicated tilt plus pan gets us into the psychic life of the hero in *The Loneliness of the Long Distance Runner* (Britain, 1962). Temporarily beyond the confines of an unappealing English reformatory, delinquent hero Tom Courtenay momentarily fancies himself free of oppressive adult restriction. As he indulges this fantasy, the camera articulates it with exquisite fidelity, rolling back to a full vertical tilt, then twirling lazily on the tripod to take in the full expanse of leaves, sun, and sky. The graceful spiral which adds image to image in random succession is the perfect pictorial equivalent of Courtenay's adolescent daydream.

What happens when both camera and subject move? Lots of things — but for the moment let one example stand for a whole range of possibilities. In *The Gospel According to St. Matthew* (Italy, 1964) we are presented with a dynamic Christ who talks while he travels and who is often photographed while moving away from the camera. Generally speaking, retreat and withdrawal imply weakness, the banishment of a character to the background of a scene. In this case, however, the fact that the camera follows the moving figure — even physically pursues him — converts weakness to strength. We don't see Pasolini's Nazarine as a cowering or timorous man but as someone who has more important things to do than pose for pictures. (No doubt he would like to avoid having his face printed on a Vatican holy card.) The camera assumes the position of Christ's disciples, always struggling to keep up with this mission-ridden man, always straining to catch the look of heroic commitment on his face when he glances back to shout instructions at his slightly bewildered followers. The hand-held camera, bouncing and bobbing to snatch glimpses of the master, strengthens our sense of Christ's command over those who accompany him down the dusty roads of Galilee.

If camera mobility means this much to composition, quite naturally the camera's quiet moments can also be memorably evocative. There are surely times when it should simply stand still to let the action, or inaction, unfold. One such moment occurs at the opening of *Umberto D* (1952), a vintage product of Italian neorealism. As the film begins, a group of pensioners are in the midst of a march to dramatize grievances against officialdom, and the file of participants is headed toward the camera. They march in step and with apparent determination. From behind them, however, a public bus slowly presses into their midst, cuts their ranks, and soon drives them helter-skelter through the foreground in search of safety. Each movement here holds meaning. The fanlike scattering of the demonstrators visually exemplifies the disintegration of their efforts to organize against the government, while the clumsy faltering of individual marchers attests to the age and infirmity of the group. On the other hand, the bus moves with a completely different rhythm — linear, methodical, relentlessly efficient as the "public-service" industry it represents. Neither malicious nor merciful, it simply respects its schedules, pushing aside the puny humanity that has momentarily cluttered the public streets but which has now been chased to the outer edges of the picture space. Any move of the camera into this complex web of interacting subjects would clearly be intrusive and irrelevant.

The camera is similarly immobile at the conclusion of *The Seven Samurai* (Japan, 1954), in a gesture of elegiac tranquillity that perfectly complements the fierce action of earlier scenes. For three hours of screen time intense physical combat has been shot from every conceivable range and angle. Yet in its last moments the film grows very quiet, with only the minimal movement essential to underscore a very important point. The seven samurai were hired to protect a small village from bandit raids; they have succeeded, though the persistent battles have disastrously depleted their ranks. Four are dead, buried under immense mounds in the background of the scene. One has left their ranks to court a local village girl. The two who survive are standing with their backs to the camera, staring at the graves of their comrades, whose swords stick up impressively out of the burial mounds, drawing the eye beyond the immediate foreground and into the depths of the picture space. The camera is steady, unmoving, throughout what seems a very long take. The living protagonists are also completely static, almost as if they were sculptured figures belonging to the burial monuments. All

CAMERA RANGE AND ANGLE. The camera's orientation to the subject obviously has an important bearing on how the subject looks. A high-hung camera shooting down from a steep angle tends to dwarf or "crush" the subject by concealing its height (top). A low-mounted camera (bottom) tends to produce an opposite effect, exaggerating the impression of height (note the elongated neck of the bird) as in bottom photograph. The change of camera position also affects the relationship of the subject to the background and visual environment. Note that at top and center the bird seems blocked or encumbered by the overhanging vegetation; below, it seems to be breaking free of entanglements. Photographs by Carolyn D. Scott.

that moves is the sand which the wind blows off the tops of the distant mounds. This utterly unobtrusive movement is more expressive than anything that might be done with the camera; the drifting sand testifies to the erosion of a whole way of life, the passing into oblivion of a heroic species.

COMPOSING WITH LENSES

Rarely in cinematic composition is the performance of the camera apart and distinct from that of the lens. The camera may pan, track, or bounce on someone's shoulders, but it is the lens that etches an image upon celluloid. As cameras have evolved over the years, becoming lighter and more maneuverable while acquiring motor drives and other accessories, lenses too have developed, undergoing many changes of design and gaining startling new capacities. These have a remarkable bearing upon film art, largely determining the visual style that marks a particular epoch. For this reason it is wise to look closely at how lenses render what they record.

The mechanical basics of lenses can be stated quite simply. All depend upon the optical principle of refraction, i.e., the slowing and consequent bending of light which occurs when its rays pass from a less dense medium (air) to one more dense (glass). This bending accounts for the special properties of different lenses. The curve of all camera lenses is convex, which means that light is brought to approximately a single focal point behind the lens, thereby forming an image upon the film stock and gathering enough illumination to properly expose it. The lens thus compresses in two dimensions a phenomenal world that exists in three, and this fact necessitates all the calculation and compromise which make up the history of photo optics.

BASIC LENS VARIABLES: FOCAL LENGTH AND APERTURE

Definition of focal length. Its relationship to framing. Normal, wide-angle, and telephoto lenses. Definition of aperture. Concept of lens "speed." Use of f/stops. Relationship of lens variables to composition: their effect upon perspective and depth of field.

Two technical characteristics of lenses bear in a particular way upon composition; these are *focal length* and *aperture*. Focal length determines the "covering power" of the lens, that is, how broad an area is included in the framing; aperture, on the other hand, determines the so-called speed of the lens, that is, how sensitive it is to light. Each of these technical variables has an important, though perhaps not immediately obvious, effect upon composition. Focal length, for example, affects the proportion and scale of objects in a particular shot; it establishes the optical perspective in which we see the scene in front of the camera. Aperture determines the basic exposure; it dictates whether we shall see a scene as brightly lit or light-deprived. It also

FOCAL LENGTH AND COVERING POWER. The area covered in a particular shot depends crucially upon the focal length of the lens. Here the range of the camera remains constant while four different lenses are used to compose the scene: 28mm "wide-angle" lens (*below*), 50mm "normal" lens (*opposite page, top*), 105mm "portrait" lens (*center*), and 210mm "telephoto" lens (*bottom*). Short-focal-length lenses give what are conventionally termed "establishing shots" in which the whole set is visible, while lenses of long focal length (especially the 210mm) provide the isolation and selectivity of close-ups. Short lenses used at very close range will also create close-ups, of course, while long lenses at exceptionally great distance from the subject can place it in a visual context, as does an establishing shot (for example, in the center still, where the subject is flanked by candle and glass). Photographs by Carolyn D. Scott.

controls the texture of the image, contributing substantially to our impression of its softness or sharpness.

Described in the simplest possible language, focal length refers to the physical length of the lens barrel, i.e., the distance between the lens glass and the film stock upon which it focuses light. Lenses of different structure vary widely as to focal length. Some bring light to focus very gradually, passing it down a relatively long lens barrel: these are called long-focal-length lenses, or just long lenses. Others bring light to focus very quickly, at a point almost immediately behind the lens glass: these are called short-focal-length lenses, or short lenses. For purposes of 35mm motion-picture photography, any lens more than 2½ inches long is called a long lens. Any lens less than 1½ inches long is called a short lens. Lenses between 1½ and 2½ inches long (i.e., any lens about 2 inches long) are referred to as lenses of "normal" focal length, meaning that they are neither exceptionally short nor exceptionally long. The only complicating factor is that lens lengths are usually quoted in millimeters rather than inches. Hence the phrase "short lens" usually means a lens of 20 to 35mm; a "normal lens" means a lens of 40 to 60mm; and long lens means one of 75 to 135mm, and sometimes means a lens of still greater focal length.

The critical point about lens length is that it determines how much the camera sees. Long lenses always have a narrow "angle of view," meaning that they take in comparatively little of the world in front of them. Point a long lens (say, one of 135mm focal length) across the street and it will swallow up the intervening space, showing nothing more than the front porch of your neighbor's house. Short lenses, on the other hand, have what is called a wide viewing angle, meaning that they cover a much greater area. Take off the 135mm lens and replace it with one of 35mm; then look across the street again. Now the field will include the porch, the house, the terrace and sidewalk, as well as the boulevard in front of the house and perhaps some of the opposite sidewalk on which the tripod is mounted. Quite a difference. These variations of covering power make possible much of the creativity achieved in composing with lenses.

Differences of focal length suggest certain obvious ways in which lenses may be used. Short lenses are ideal for "establishing shots," which show us the whole theater of action. Normal lenses work very well for various kinds of "medium-range" shots, intended to show three or four people standing close together. Long lenses are standard for "close-ups," since those in the 85 to 135mm family tend to cover just the head and shoulders of the actor when they are used at their proper range. The habit of using lenses in this fashion gives us several other names under which they are known. Short lenses, because they take in a whole scene, are known as "wide-angle" lenses; long lenses, which restrict the framing to an actor's face, are usually called "portrait" lenses. Lenses of extremely long focal length are typically referred to as "telephoto" lenses; they circumscribe the viewing angle so severely that they seem to magnify distant subjects, much like a telescope.

The other crucial mechanical element in composition is lens aperture; this refers to the size of the opening through which light is admitted to the film. We might think of the lens aperture as a window that lets light flow down an otherwise dark corridor (the lens barrel) into a room beyond (the camera). Obviously, if the window is large, in relation to the length of the corridor, the room at the opposite end will be relatively well illuminated. Conversely, if the window is small in relation to the corridor, the room is sure to be quite dark. Lenses with large apertures (like big windows) gather in lots of light, making it easy to achieve a proper exposure, even on a dark day, or in twilight, or while shooting in somebody's basement. Lenses with such apertures are said to be "fast," i.e., highly sensitive to light. Lenses with smaller apertures gather less light, and hence must be used where there is more ample illumination, say, in sunshine, bright shade, or with the support of studio lamps. Such lenses are said to be "slow," meaning that they are relatively insensitive to light. There is quite an important relationship, especially significant in historical terms, between the "speed" of a lens and its focal length: fast lenses are usually lenses of near normal focal length; extremely long lenses (keep in mind a very long corridor from the analogy above) tend to be slow.

Lens apertures are ordinarily described in what is called "f/stops" or "f/numbers." These measure, in a rather complicated way, the diameter of the lens opening. According to this system, small f/numbers designate large lens openings, while larger numbers indicate reduced lens apertures. The standard progression of f/stops is as follows: f/1.4; f/2; f/2.8; f/4; f/5.6; f/8; f/11; f/16; f/22. On this scale, the light sensitivity of the lens is cut in half as we proceed from one interval to the next. The fastest lenses on today's market have apertures of f/1.4 or f/2; slow lenses, by contemporary standards, have apertures of f/4, f/5.6, or in the case of very long lenses, perhaps f/8. This means, notice, that a fast f/2 lens is four times more light-sensitive than a rather slow f/4 glass, while a very fast f/1.4 is eight times more light-sensitive than a quite slow f/5.6 lens. Thus the difference between fast and slow lenses is terribly important to a cameraman who is working in less than ample light.

When light is abundant, however, the lens need not be used at its maximum aperture. An adjustable diaphragm allows the cameraman to shut out light coming through the lens, just as a shade lets us screen out some of the light that comes in a window. In other words a lens with a maximum aperture (also called a "relative aperture") of f/2 might be used at f/2.8, f/4, or any other stop down to f/22. The process of setting a lens at less than full aperture is called "stopping down" the lens. By stopping down, the cameraman can shoot in very bright light that would otherwise result in overexposure. But adjusting the aperture in this way does more to the image than change the basic exposure. Hence, like choosing a lens of a particular focal length, choosing a particular aperture has aesthetic as well as practical significance.

What bearing then do lens length and aperture have upon the art of composition? Focal length affects composition because it determines perspective, the relative size of each object in the frame, as well as the impression we have of the distance between them. Short lenses (more commonly called wide-angle lenses) are said to create "strong" perspective, meaning that the objects in the immediate foreground seem very large in comparison to those in the background. And since the scale of objects affects our perception of distance, short-lens composition also enhances our sense of space, making objects seem rather far removed from one another. On the other hand, long lenses (usually called portrait lenses if they are moderately long, and telephotos if they are very long) are said to create "weak" perspective, meaning that the scale of objects does not taper off pronouncedly from foreground to background. By the same token, space seems compressed, objects crowded one upon the other. Anyone familiar with television commercials should be able to recognize both short-lens and long-lens perspective: short lenses are used to make the front seat (or the trunk) of a compact car seem spacious and roomy; long lenses are used in airline ads, where the sun seems close enough to touch from the jet silhouetted against it. Lenses of normal focal length (say, 40 to 60mm) seem not to alter scale or space in a remarkable way, since they render perspective in approximately the same manner as the human eye. Many scenes are shot with lenses of normal focal length, since they are fast, present no problems in tilting or panning (as other lenses sometimes do), and rarely call attention to themselves. Other scenes may be shot with moderately short (say, 35mm) or moderately long (say, 85mm) lenses, which — while influencing perspective — do not produce effects ordinarily discernible to the average moviegoer. Some filmmakers, however, have always been interested in exploring the view of the world made possible by lenses of exceptional focal length.

Lens aperture affects composition because it largely determines what is called "depth of field." This term, which is easier to illustrate than to define, refers to the relative softness or sharpness of the image from foreground to background. Look, for example, at a photograph of three people, one standing rather near the camera, one somewhat further removed, and the third a still greater distance away. Are all three faces in sharp focus? If so, the picture is said to have good depth of field, i.e., retains sharp focus into the depths of space. More likely, however, one or even two of the faces will be slightly out of focus, in which case the picture is said to have poor field depth, or less pejoratively, shallow field depth. As the aperture of a lens is opened up to its maximum, the field depth of the image is progressively reduced. Conversely, as a lens is stopped down (particularly if it is stopped down to as much as f/11 or f/16) the depth of field is progressively improved. Through the control of aperture a good cameraman controls the texture of the image, softening or sharpening it as the atmosphere of a particular film or a specific scene might dictate. It is also the case, moreover, that short lenses tend to have better field depth than long ones, at least when used at fairly close range. Thus we find in cinematography a fairly consistent affiliation between wide-angle and deep-field composition. Those who like short lenses also like stopped-down apertures. Similarly, since long lenses tend to lack field depth, the "telephoto syndrome" goes hand in hand with softness of texture.

WIDE-ANGLE, DEEP-FIELD COMPOSITION

Pioneering work of Soviet cinematography with wide-angle lenses. Sergei Eisenstein's analysis of wide-angle effects. Eisenstein and Edouard Tisse. Strike *and* Potemkin. Vogue *of wide-angle composition in the U.S.A. Concomitant interest in reduced apertures and expanded depth of field. Contribution of Gregg Toland. Collaboration of Toland and Orson Welles:* Citizen Kane. *Persistence of this approach:* Odds against Tomorrow.

Directors, theorists, and cameramen of the Soviet Union were among the first to get intensely interested in the creative use of lens lengths. Generally, they experimented with wide-angle composition, since in the 1920s telephoto lenses were usually too slow for cinematography. The Russians' efforts to handle short lenses in a pictorially revolutionary way are epitomized in the writings of Sergei Eisenstein, which grew out of his continuous collaboration with cameraman Edouard Tisse. We can see Eisenstein's sensitivity to optics in one of the assignments he gave his students while teaching at the State Institute of Cinematography in Moscow. As reported by one of his pupils in *Lessons with Eisenstein,* this shooting exercise in connection with *Crime and Punishment* makes clear how everything from the look of the set to the manner of the actor flows from the choice of lenses.[1]

[1] See Vladimir Nizhny, *Lessons with Eisenstein,* tr. Ivor Montague and Jay Leyda (London: George Allen & Unwin, Ltd., 1962). The exercise is described in "Mise-en-Shot " pp. 93–139.

Suppose, Eisenstein says, you were shooting the scene from this novel where Raskolnikov kills the old woman whom he imagines to be the instrument of universal oppression. Suppose, too, you had decided to compose with a 28mm lens. Where would you put it and how would you place the performers so as to get the benefit of its unique optical characteristics?

To respond intelligently, we must place a prior question. What is unique about the way a short lens sees a scene? First of all, it achieves its superior covering power by giving a very expansive view of the immediate foreground. And while elongating the foreground, it reduces the scale of objects well removed from the camera. This is why short lenses serve so efficiently as scenic lenses: they can sweep in the skyline of a whole city or pull down into the frame the jagged cliffs of a steep canyon. But we can see that Eisenstein's selection of a 28mm lens for work at close quarters is itself unusual. It forces him to take account in his composition of those exaggerations and distortions which are an inherent feature of short-lens foregrounds.

Where will Eisenstein put the camera? It should be mounted high, he says, so that the actor will approach it closely as he penetrates the stage space, and is left free to move underneath it, leaving the frame without making an orthodox lateral exit. This means, though, that we must expect swift changes of proportion as Raskolnikov and the old woman gyrate around one another very near to the camera. The strategy Eisenstein envisions is first to augment the stature of Raskolnikov's victim by bringing her up to the lens, then use perspective to emphasize the murderer as he begins his aggressive moves.

FOCAL LENGTH AND SPATIAL PERSPECTIVE. Lenses of different focal length used at ranges that allow them to cover the same field give startling changes of perspective, i.e., the scale of objects and their relationship to one another. The progression here is from a 28mm lens (*top*) to a 50mm lens situated approximately twice as far away (*center*) to a 105mm lens situated twice as far from the subject as the 50mm and four times as far away as the 28mm (*bottom*).

Note the predictable "wide-angle" effects in top shot: the enlarged head of the figure on the bowl in the foreground, the impression of spaciousness in the dish of the bowl itself, the apparent elongation of the grid behind the bowl, the suggestion of great distance between the two candles as measured by the respective size of the candles themselves. The impression of spaciousness is greatly curtailed (50mm lens *center*), even though the field covered is almost exactly the same: the grid now seems tightly wedged between bowl and backdrop and the candles no longer look so far apart. This "compression" effect is most noticeable, however, with the 105mm lens (*bottom*), where the grid has disappeared altogether (as has the free space on either side of it), the bowl now seems to lie sideways across the picture space instead of at the fairly pronounced angle seen at top, and the space between the two candles has been almost completely swallowed up. Photographs by Carolyn D. Scott.

When the scene opens, the old moneylender physically dominates because she is so near the camera; Raskolnikov seems a restless dwarf at the rear of the set. But the distortion expresses Raskolnikov's paranoid tendency to confer power upon his insignificant antagonist. Eisenstein pauses at this point to remind his students that from this position on stage Raskolnikov must make broad gestures with his hands and cape to call attention to his presence. With the 28mm lens, a slight facial movement would go unnoticed. Answering this necessity, Raskolnikov advertises himself with a great flourish of his garments as he extracts the hatchet from its hiding place. By this time he is advancing into the forespace, growing greater and more menacing with each stride toward the camera. To escape, the moneylender stumbles still nearer the camera. Her torso vanishes, leaving only her head at the lower left of the frame in a gigantic, grotesque close-up. Then the last, meticulously planned detail. Raskolnikov attacks, holding the hatchet at arm's length over his head, bringing it nearer the camera than any other object in the scene. The swinging hatchet and the vulnerable skull: this form of visual synecdoche gives content to the climax. The recessional movement is equally well planned. Struck dead, the old woman topples backward out of a distorted, short-lens close-up into a shrunken heap on the floor. She seemed to Raskolnikov's twisted mind a potent adversary; now, from its high-angle mount the camera sees her objectively as the puny victim of senseless rage. Raskolnikov similarly loses stature as he hurries away from the camera and gropes for the door. By refusing to use the short lens in a conventionally "right" situation, Eisenstein offers a convincing interpretation of Dostoevsky achieved in exclusively optical terms.

Eisenstein acquired this expertise with short lenses in his films of the 1920s, where, in consultation with Tisse, he constantly experimented with proportion and perspective. Tisse came to the cinema with a background in painting that sensitized him to composition and added to that a short career as a newsreel photographer where he apparently made much use of wide-angle lenses. He immediately brought this experience into play in his work for Eisenstein, shooting the crowd scenes from *Strike* (1924) with short lenses at long range and high angle, photographically diminishing the strikers, just as they are humanly diminished and morally humiliated by czarist autocracy. And of course the famous crowd choreography of *Potemkin* (1925) — the file of marchers past the fallen Vakulinchuk, the frenzy of the Odessa steps — depends upon short-lens composition. But Tisse also uses the 28mm glass in less conventional ways. It endlessly elongates a vacant corridor in *Strike*, emphasizing the emptiness of the business world when denied the cooperation of the proletariat. In *Potemkin* he uses the short lens in a comparably ambitious way, playing off the exaggerated scale of foreground objects against the reduced stature of men in the background.

This approach is just right for the drama on the quarterdeck where mutinous sailors find themselves threatened by the military authority of the ship's officers. Tisse composes much of this sequence from a point right behind the heavy guns of the *Potemkin,* which when shot with a wide-angle lens loom massively while the sailors beyond them seem scarcely larger than ants. Seen in this perspective the guns carry the symbolic freight Eisenstein has attached to them: they perfectly exemplify the might of czardom tyrannically dominating the men who swab the decks and choke on spoiled meat.

After this decade of experiment in the Soviet Union, American cinematographers of the late 1930s developed an interest in wide-angle composition, adding a further emphasis upon stopped-down apertures and increased depth of field. While the wide-angle look was certainly not new to the American cinema, the insistence upon absolutely sharp images, clearly etched through a succession of receding planes, was a decisive innovation and absolutely dependent upon the use of reduced lens apertures. In 1930, most Hollywood films were shot at f/4 or f/5.6, to spare the studio the cost of raising light levels on the set. By 1940, Gregg Toland was beginning his experiments with f/8 and f/11 apertures, availing himself to a new technology that made such undertakings practicable. This new machinery included several elements. After 1935, lens makers began to coat the surfaces and barrels of their glasses, in order to control flare and curb light loss. This period is also distinguished by experiments with new high-refraction/low-diffusion glass. These advances in construction made lenses appreciably faster, while improving resolution and facilitating the removal of optical faults. This, together with the introduction of lighting units of more intensity, renewed the prestige of short lenses and shifted the interest of Hollywood cameramen toward stopped-down apertures. The movement is virtually personified in Toland, one of the most inventive cinematographers in American film history.

Toland is the comparatively rare example of a highly talented cameraman who had no aspirations to become a director but who influenced the development of cinema far more than many would-be "auteurs." As head cameraman for John Ford, William Wyler, and Orson Welles, he had abundant opportunity to experiment with short lenses at stopped-down apertures, leaving the stamp of his visual style upon such films as *The Grapes of Wrath* (1940), *The Westerner* (1940), and *Citizen Kane* (1941).

Toland may have first adopted the 24mm lens to relieve the filmed plays he shot for Ford and Wyler of their theatrical look. At least this could be said of *The Long Voyage Home* (1940) and *The Little Foxes* (1941). But the design is more complicated in the last reel of *The Grapes of Wrath,* where Toland employs a very short lens to dramatize the import of Tom Joad's departure from family and friends. Silhou-

RELATIVE APERTURE AND DEPTH OF FIELD. By "stopping down" or "opening up" the lens aperture, the cameraman can either deepen or make shallower the field of sharp focus recorded by the camera. Stopped-down apertures enhance field depth while relatively open lens apertures cause it to diminish. Shot at the stopped-down aperture of f/16, the design on the small vase in the foreground (top) is in sharp focus, as are the centerpiece and even the vase at the back of the set. The carvings on the wooden bowl to the left are also photographically legible throughout the recesses of space. Shot with the same lens and at the same distance from the subjects, but at the relatively open lens setting of f/2, the depth of field is much shallower and the general impression is of "softness" (bottom). The centerpiece remains sharp, since it is located in the focal plane, but the design on the vase in the foreground is seriously blurred and the sharpness of outline of the vase at the back has begun to be lost. Photographs by James F. Scott.

etted against a bright horizon, Joad's stature is radically diminished, in keeping with the film's emphasis upon the limitedness of individual effort. At the same time, though, the impression of spaciousness implicit in the wide-angle view of a well-lit horizon subtly suggests that Tom's future remains open to his further effort. In this sequence, the stopped-down aperture does not figure importantly, but it certainly does in the picture that brought Toland international renown, *Citizen Kane*. For in the brash twenty-five-year-old Orson Welles, he found a director whose daring in dramatics matched the cameraman's enthusiasm for optical innovation. Given a free hand with the composition, Toland accomplished his masterpiece of short-lens, deep-field photography.

In an interview granted shortly after completion of the film, Toland admirably summarizes its novelty. "We pre-planned our angles and composition," he says, "so that action which would ordinarily be shown in direct cuts would be shown in a single, longer scene . . . often one in which important action might take place simultaneously at widely separated points in *extreme foreground* or *background* [my italics]." [2] To obtain these effects he used a short 24mm lens and supplemented the natural deep-field properties of its optical system with continuously stopped-down photography, itself made possible by the high light intensity of new studio lamps developed for technicolor. The picture was a landmark in several respects. But these mere technical achievements would have meant little were it not for the way the photography complements the dramatic values of *Citizen Kane*.

The film is a study of megalomania, the power craze of a love-deprived child, Charles Foster Kane, who develops a newspaper syndicate, enters politics, courts scandal, and eventually builds for himself a huge pleasure palace to attract the attention he failed to receive as a lonely adolescent. Given this theme the use of deep-field photography is ideal to convey the extensive ambience of the protagonist. Throughout the picture we never cease to sense the presence of Kane; his spirit dominates the set as completely as his personal power touches every one of his acquaintances. This impression the film gives of power exercised from afar no doubt owes much to the forceful acting of Welles in the title role. But this actor remains continually present only because of the remarkable spatial tolerance of Toland's lens. In one scene, for instance, Kane shrieks defiance at his gubernatorial opponent as the latter descends a flight of stairs, walking away from the speaker and into the camera. According to the usual logic of composition, the scene should belong to Kane's enemy, since it is he who advances into the forespace, looming larger and larger as he steps toward the camera. Still Kane holds his own, on the strength of his voice, of course, and as

[2] "Realism for *Citizen Kane*," *American Cinematographer* (February 1941), pp. 54–55.

SHORT LENS, DEEP FIELD COMPOSITION: Intensely sharp focus through all the receding planes of the picture space is the hallmark of Gregg Toland's photography for *Citizen Kane*. Note too the exaggerated size of objects in the foreground, an unfailing mark of short-lens composition. © 1941—RKO Radio Pictures, a division of RKO General, Inc. Photograph from The Museum of Modern Art/Film Stills Archive.

a result of the low mount of the camera, yet most importantly because his facial features remain sharp enough that we can read stern conviction in the glint of his eyes and the set of his jaw. Typical of the whole picture, the photography here is functional, not just a display of virtuosity. Texture articulates theme, and the medium confirms the message.

Toland also creatively uses perspective in conjunction with the stopped-down aperture, depending on the 24mm lens to open up space and enhance foregrounds quite remarkably. Again, the composition is functional, emphasizing Kane's alienation from the world around him. In one scene, for example, Kane's wife Susan lounges in the forespace of the frame, clumsily assembling a puzzle, while across the room her husband stands imperiously beside an ornamental fireplace, his face kept sharp by Toland's remarkable field depth. Though Kane feigns an interest in Susan, we immediately perceive their estrangement. The lens shows their psychic separation by opening up a cavernous distance between them: the room they share is as wide as a football field. The lens also magnifies Susan's puzzle in the foreground, further reinforcing our sense of her retreat into a private world which she herself has fabricated and which excludes the influence of her husband.

A further consequence of short-lens, stopped-down composition is that it almost always contributes to the dynamism of the image. The great depth of field provided by a stopped-down aperture permits the actor to move boldly in space, unworried that his face might slip out of focus, just as the fact of field depth accords equal freedom to the camera. It can roll laterally on a dolly, rise abruptly on a crane, or dart among the players while strapped to the chest of the cameraman without necessitating intricate follow-focus procedures or unwittingly fuzzing up the image. At the same time, the way the short lens renders perspective (especially anything so short as the 24mm glass Toland used for *Kane*) causes all forms of movement to seem more pronounced. Since strong perspective makes distant objects seem further away from the camera than is actually the case, anything approaching the camera always appears to leap forward with a tremendous rush, just as objects moving away from the camera quickly recede into the depths of space. Toland himself was well aware of such phenomena and once remarked that "in many ways the most potent and provoking phase of composition is accentuation through movement."[3] Certainly the enhanced mobility of both the camera and the performers is much in evidence in *Citizen Kane*, where it contributes handsomely to the mood of psychic turbulence and distress.

[3] "Composition of the Moving Image," *The Movies as Medium*, ed. Lewis Jacobs (New York: Farrar, Straus & Giroux, Inc., 1970), p. 71. But Toland's discussion of this question should be read in its entirety, pp. 67–75.

Largely on the strength of Toland's example, short-lens perspectives and narrow-aperture sharpness set style in both Europe and America for the next two decades. We find them still in vogue in one of the better American gangster films of the late 1950s, *Odds against Tomorrow*, which neatly encapsulates all the features of this approach to composition.

Directed by Robert Wise, who handled the editing for *Citizen Kane*, *Odds against Tomorrow* was shot with nothing longer than a 30mm lens, and cameraman Joseph Brun used much shorter 18mm and even 14mm lenses for panoramic composition. Brun says he chose the shortest of these lenses "not merely for its great depth of field and extremely wide angle, but for its presence and participation and its wonderful rendition of architectural perspective." [4] This puts the case very well. The picture interprets the fate of urban society (always present to the eye in the sweep of the New York skyline) through the behavior of three underworld characters driven to crime by society's malfunctions — an embittered police officer, a psychopathic ex-marine, and a disaffiliate black musician. Together they plan and execute a bank robbery, by which they intend to settle their quarrel with respectable society, but which aborts and destroys them when they prove unable to control the fear and hostility they bear toward one another. The film is rich in crisp images, forceful perspectives, and abrupt movements to and from the camera. Faces are constantly caught in fierce grimaces with every line sharply etched; chins jut out at severe angles. The fist that reaches into the forespace to threaten one of the protagonists looks gigantic, and the ladder up which another tries to escape seems 500 feet tall. Motion too is exaggerated. Speeding automobiles lurch into sudden prominence, while desperate men flee down preternaturally long alleys with astonishing speed. This treatment of visual detail is ideally suited to convey the tension and violence that pervades the film.

SOFT-TEXTURED
AND LONG-LENS COMPOSITION

Preference for open apertures. Concomitant softness of texture. Strategies of open-aperture composition. Spatial arrangement: The Iron Horse. *Following focus:* The Last Command. *Motivated softness:* The Bank Dick. *The turn to longer lenses. Characteristics of telephotos. Softness and selective focus:* Elvira Madigan *and* Adalen 31. *Compression of space and retardation of motion:* Battle of Algiers, The Graduate, The Confession.

[4] "Filming Formula for *Odds against Tomorrow*," *American Cinematographer* (August 1959), p. 478.

While Soviet cinematographers of the 1920s explored the potential of wide-angle lenses, their American counterparts took a greater interest in softening textures through the use of relatively open apertures. This inclination went hand in hand with a tendency to choose lenses of normal or slightly longer than normal focal length, since their restricted covering power was less likely to advertise the absence of sharpness in the overall picture space. This particular approach to composition reached its apex at the beginning of the studio era, when open apertures effectively disguised the artificiality of mock-up sets or backdrops and helped glamorize various Hollywood starlets. After an interval of two decades, however, the soft look was revived in the 1960s, as long telephoto lenses first became practicable in cinematography. The 1960s, of course, do not merely repeat the 1930s, since exceptionally long lenses bring into the cinema not only softness of texture but their own special perspective characteristics.

Savoring the quiet luster of an f/4 close-up, American cinematographers of the late 1920s brought the soft look to faces, sets, and even outdoor locations. Used tastelessly, this compositional strategy might give us a bare-shouldered, round-faced heroine weeping deliciously into a vaseline-smeared portrait lens which effaces every blemish from her body. But open-aperture composition need not be sentimental or sticky. It could just as easily seem natural, expressive, and lyrical. In any event, it was an almost necessary accommodation to problems of image sharpness that became critical during this era.

Open apertures appreciably reduce field depth, especially with lenses of 50 to 100mm, or longer, which always have more limited spatial tolerance. These apertures thus challenge the cameraman either to find ways to disguise softness or ways to make it seem appropriate.

Such questions came to the forefront in the late twenties largely because of a special problem in the manufacture of lenses. The lenses of the teens and earlier were not well corrected for what is called "chromatic aberration," that is, the failure of light of different colors (hence different wave lengths) to come to focus in the same plane. In the teens and early twenties, this failure of rectification was inconsequential, since the film stocks of that day registered only daylight or arc light, both of which are predominantly blue, and hence of relatively uniform wave lengths. In the middle 1920s, the introduction of new film stocks, sensitive to red as well as blue and green, necessitated more careful correction for chromatic aberration than lens manufacturers immediately achieved. To some extent, then, the open-aperture approach, which uses softness strategically, was an effort to make a virtue of necessity. The stocks were not fast enough to let the filmmaker overcome softness by using extremely narrow apertures; so what was sought instead was the pleasing graduation of textures that f/4 makes possible.

By restricting compositional possibilities, open apertures encourage great care in placing the camera. As always, it is the foreground of the image that causes the most trouble, thus promoting a photographic idiom which features faces averted from the camera toward a focal center somewhat removed in space. Setups from innumerable films might be summoned for illustration, where characters assemble in diagonal, or wedge, or radial formation in order to give weight and body to the foreground yet not soften the lines of the human face. These arrangements are anticipated even in films not otherwise notable for their soft look. In a classic scene from Ford's *The Iron Horse* (1924), for example, the foreground is anchored by close-ups of railway work-

SELECTIVE FOLLOW-FOCUS COMPOSITION: While the dramatic situation may sometimes call for image sharpness throughout the visual field, the filmmaker can also achieve telling effects through selective focus. Here in *The Last Command*, the plane of sharp focus does not extend beyond the sight line of the protagonist, a fact which greatly enhances our sense of his importance. Photograph from the private collection of Herman G. Weinberg.

ers standing along the tracks, while the compositional weight of this material is balanced by the massive, still sharply focused presence of an arriving locomotive in the background. The focal center of the shot is midway between the train and the railway workers, featuring two men in the middle distance whose faces are turned toward the camera. The shooting in this sequence takes full advantage of the forespace, yet the turning of faces from the camera makes the softening of the image perfectly tolerable, even attractive, as it seems to confer a dignified anonymity upon this mass of men. Effacement of foreground detail through silhouette lighting is another device to offset the problem of field depth.

When composing with open apertures, another way to get around the problem is to supply motive for the softening of the background images. This was done in countless "follow-focus" sequences of the period (and after), where the cameraman picked up his subject in the middle distance and then accommodated the focal field to his movement. There's a particularly nice example of "motivated" softness in Bert Glennon's photography for Josef von Sternberg's *The Last Command* (U.S.A., 1928). A story within a story, the film unfolds in flashback, detailing the fall from power of a Russian general who finds his place of exile in postwar Hollywood. On one occasion Duke Sergeus Alexander (Emil Jannings) imagines himself reviewing the troops, and the lens is used to heighten the power of his presence. His face, as we would expect, is kept absolutely sharp as he strides grandly into the camera, but more than that, his sight line, meeting and moving beyond the glance of successive soldiers, seems to determine the sharpness of the other faces. As Sergeus passes each of the underlings, the soldier's face begins to soften and soon fade into an anonymous blur. The general's nod makes and unmakes the men of the ranks, a fact gracefully underscored in the texture of the image.

Inasmuch as such careful composition is often impractical, other filmmakers found other solutions. One approach, especially attractive in adventure or comedy films, makes background softness enhance our sense of movement, or evoke feelings of confusion and disorientation. Aren't moving objects always blurred? Fine. Have the cameraman focus the lens upon the entrenched gunner in the foreground, paying little attention to the attacking airplanes that swoop down upon the scene from the recesses of space. These will have the sharpness of full definition only for a moment as they pass directly overhead, but this lack of clarity will strengthen the sense we have of the chaos of combat. Or, if the subject is comic, mount the camera on the automobile which carries the protagonists through the streets of the city and let the blurred faces of passersby vouch for the dizzying pace at which the car travels and the general bewilderment its misdoings provoke. This strategy is in force as late as 1941 for the madcap climax of *The Bank Dick*. W. C. Fields, unwilling chauffeur to a fugitive bank robber, bangs and bounces through the tidy streets of Lumpoc, past dozens of mystified townsfolk whose fuzzy facial attitudes plastically exhibit their discomfort in the presence of these strange goings-on.

In 1941 this softness of backgrounds might already have seemed anachronistic, since Toland's work in America and Jean Bachelet's composition for Jean Renoir in France had already begun to tug the cinema in an entirely different direction. But the wide-angle preferences of the 1940s and 1950s were also a temporary phenomenon, eventually giving way to a kind of "telephoto syndrome" that developed in the early 1960s. Naturally, lenses of 75 to 100mm had almost always been used in close-ups, even though a Toland or a Brun might sometimes elect to shoot even faces with a 30mm or 35mm lens. From the mid 1950s onward, however, manufacturers began to push lenses of 135mm, 150mm, and 200mm, which had once been thought of mostly as tools for the professional wildlife photographer. Optical research related to World War II had made such glasses appreciably more light-sensitive, fast enough for convenient use in commercial cinema, though they were often still slower than shorter lenses and had to be used at more open apertures. Furthermore, as the longer lenses became popular, some fllmmakers began to experiment with portrait-length lenses (say, 85mm) for panoramic instead of close-up takes. If a "wide-angle" lens could be used for close-ups simply by poking it right in the face of the performer, why couldn't a "portrait" lens be used to shoot a whole battlefield? All that need be done was to set the camera far enough away to give the longer lens the same covering power that a wide-angle lens would have when placed much nearer the subject. As soon as filmmakers began to think along these lines, another revolution in the treatment of texture and perspective was at hand.

Long lenses, especially those of telephoto length, have optical characteristics exactly opposite to the properties of wide-angle lenses. In addition to reducing depth of field, they also compress space, giving a flatter (and not always flattering) impression of faces as well as merging one plane with another as they relate foreground to background. A 300mm shot of a row of telephone poles, for example, makes each appear a near neighbor of the others, while a 30mm fix of the same scene opens great gaps between each pole. For exactly that reason, telephotos curtail the illusion of movement toward the camera, making such advances seem unnaturally slow. Obviously, the degree to which any of these effects is noticeable depends upon the length of the lens in use. Telephotos start at something like 150mm (which gives 3x magnification) and back all the way up to 500mm or even 1000mm, which give 10x and 20x magnification, respectively.

Telephotos are ideal for a certain kind of screen-filling facial close-up, since their magnifying power extracts the full expressive potential of small gestures. It is lenses of this family that emphasize the wry smiles of Marcello Mastroianni, the pouty lips of Jeanne Moreau, or the soulful eyes of Max von Sydow. Inasmuch as these micro-gestures are central to the revelation of personal psychology, the recent improvement of long lenses has sophisticated the language of the cinema. When director Akira Kurosawa chose to have *The Seven Samurai* shot predominantly with long lenses, the effects he says he sought were those of "solidarity and intimacy."[5] Generally speaking, these effects are inherent to the long lens.

We should not conclude, however, that long lenses affect composition only through their superior dramatization of fine points in an actor's performance. Their field properties and their implications for perspective are equally important to film language. They reintroduce soft foregrounds and unfocused depths, as in open-aperture composition of the early thirties, but with certain differences. They rarely glamorize like the portrait lens at f/4, since they render very crisp images at the plane of principal focus, even though the field of sharp focus is thin as a knife edge. This fact also promotes what is known as "zone focusing," where the plane of principal focus is changed in the midst of a shot. What was sharp becomes soft, and vice versa, thus altering the emphasis and orientation of a scene. The field properties of long lenses are shown to advantage in two pictures which Jorgen Persson shot for Bo Widerberg in the late 1960s, *Elvira Madigan* and *Adalen 31*.

In *Elvira* (1967), one of the most technically accomplished films to come out of Sweden in this decade, the long-lens treatment of textures interlocks perfectly with the thematic concerns. The film recounts the doomed romance of two lovers who escape social convention and professional commitment for one brief summer of hedonistic ecstasy before a suicide pact cuts short their lives. A little trite in its plot and too obvious in its foreshadowing of disaster to be truly suspenseful, *Elvira Madigan* succeeds as a motion picture chiefly because of the way the gauzy, soft-focused imagery evokes the evanescent, shimmering beauty of sun-drenched Swedish landscapes. Sexten and Elvira are typically caught in sharp focus, but the world they inhabit has no depth. As the two protagonists venture down a forest path, consumed in affection for each other, the ferns and leaves in the foreground have neither shape nor form, deprived of the definite bounding lines that sharp-focus shooting would give them. Lacking substance, they become mere flecks of varicolored light. The sinister dimension of the

---

[5] Quoted in Joseph L. Anderson and Donald Richie, *The Japanese Film: Art and Industry* (Rutland, Vt.: Charles E. Tuttle Co., Inc., 1959), p. 273; by permission of Charles E. Tuttle Co. Inc.

film is equally present in the imagery. The first time Sexten and Elvira make love the tree in the left foreground remains out of focus, an ill-defined shadow casting its suggestive darkness across the bright scene of consummated love. "We must reclaim our knowledge of the grass," Sexten once tells his brother, in a speech that sums up the meaning of the film; "we must appreciate the significance of small things." This speech verbally summarizes the argument of *Elvira Madigan*. But what gives it dramatic vitality is the photographic concentration upon a single plane of focus: like Sexten, the camera attends to one thing at a time. The lens reports upon reality yet represents it according to the consciousness of the hero.

Adalen 31 (Sweden, 1969) is a very different kind of picture, featuring laborers instead of lovers, strikes and riots instead of hand-swinging strolls through the woods. But Jorgen Persson again makes ample use of long lenses, sometimes zone-focusing the lens to withhold a detail and then force it upon us in a startlingly dramatic way. We are again in the glistening sun of a Swedish summer, though the charm of the landscape in no way conceals the malaise of the rural community it envelops. People go hungry among blooming flowers and grow rageful amidst parklike greenery. Persson's photography takes full account of this ironic contrast between scene and situation on the occasion when angry workers decide on a march to Lund to express their grievances. They are met by the army in a surprise move that frustrates their demonstration and takes several lives. In a nicely planned sequence, the soldiers emerge out of a picture-postcard setting through an adjustment of the focus knob. The lens is first focused on the foreground where the marchers, in a picnic atmosphere of bands and banners, are making their way along the road to Lund. The background is soft, though not completely unfocused (since we have a stopped-down lens at fairly long range), and we have the impression we see pretty clearly a roadside vista of shrubs, rocks, and flowers. But we haven't seen as clearly as we thought. The focus now is shifted to the background, revealing fixed bayonets amid the shrubs and soldiers crouched in the grass. The garden is garrisoned. The handling of focus allows us to appreciate this fact at about the same time it becomes evident to the demonstrators.

Lenses of telephoto capacity also affect perspective in ways valuable to the filmmaker. Their narrow angularity together with their tendency to compress one plane into another accounts for their ability to close up the space between objects. This will turn a long string of ships into a task force or a loose assemblage of stray soldiers into a tight formation. The impact of telephoto treatment of crowd scenes is amply evident in *Battle of Algiers* (Italy, 1966), a quasi-documentary picture chronicling the rebellion of Moslem nationalists against French colonial authority. Riot scenes shot with long lenses carry in their basic com-

LONG LENS, SHALLOW-FIELD COMPOSITION. The telephoto lens normally gives photographic sharpness only in a single plane in front of the camera, reducing all else in the picture space to a riddle of blurred shapes and forms. The effect, however, can be both aesthetically pleasing and psychologically convincing, as in Jorgen Persson's photography for *Elvira Madigan*. Courtesy Europa-Film, Stockholm.

position the atmosphere of pressure, the sense of continuous jostling and pushing. Because the lenses pull background buildings more prominently into the frame, the streets and squares of the city seem clogged beyond their capacity with every crowd that gathers. And the compacting of planes in these same scenes further congests row upon row of unsettled, restive masses of men. The violence which erupts thus seems the inevitable outcome of a culture under unbearable stress.

Inasmuch as long lenses compress space, they also retard apparent movement toward the camera: the distant subject already seems near, so doesn't soon seem nearer. The stalling which results from a telephoto fix admirably fulfills its comic purpose at the conclusion of *The Graduate* (U.S.A., 1967) when Dustin Hoffman makes his long race to the church to save the girl he loves from the fraternity fink who is about to marry her. In a scene which both imitates and parodies the thousand Hollywood rescues it resembles, the hero goes through a whole cycle of comic frustrations before his car runs out of gas and he finds himself forced to do the last lap of the chase on foot. It's at this point that the camera is equipped with the gigantic 500mm telephoto, and its immense compression turns Hoffman's frenzied rush into an exercise of running in place. True to the tradition, he finally gets the girl, but not before the lens itself has intervened as the last barrier in the obstacle course he must run. Given the mode of comedy, this photographic extravagance is allowable. In fact, it is a delight.

In *The Confession* (France, 1970), far different tonally from either *Battle of Algiers* or *The Graduate*, Raoul Coutard uses a telephoto to both compress space and delay forward progress. The scene is near the beginning of the picture, when Yves Montand, playing the harassed Czech official Artur London, is being shadowed by Stalinist agents. After several failing efforts to learn why he is under suspicion, he resigns himself to the humiliation of constant surveillance and simply tries to stay as far away as possible from his eventual captors. But we sense the element of futility in Coutard's optical treatment of the action. London's car weaves through the streets of Prague, always trailed by government spies. The long-lens shots compact the distance between the two automobiles, so that London's vehicle continually seems about to be overtaken. Through this shooting strategy the hero's psychic oppression is vividly dramatized. When he finally makes a fitful attempt to elude his pursuers, the lens still stands in the way. The car accelerates, but doesn't seem to move forward. The stalked political prey has been immobilized in space. This freezing effect is further underscored in the conversion of the camera to slow-motion speed for the climactic moments of London's capture. Once used largely for bird-watching, long lenses now constitute one of the most valuable visual resources of cameramen and directors.

NEW LENSES, NEW OPTICAL SYSTEMS

After 1950, mostly in response to competition from television, the film industry began to invest in new optical formats that would give pictures a wider and deeper look. The same years brought several new types of lenses, some to service the various "wide-screen" systems, others to extend the capability of standard formats, and a few for trick photography and special effects. The most important of these innovations are the scope lens, the zoom lens, and a peculiar-looking distortion lens known as the fisheye.

During the ferment of the early 1950s, some producers sought to widen the arc on the screen through multiple camera systems or with cameras built to accept oversized film stocks. This gave us, respectively, Cinerama and Todd-A-O. Naturally these formats required nonstandard lenses. But in the long run the most important of the new wide-screen processes was one called CinemaScope, which employed a funnel-shaped lens of highly exceptional design. The scope lens had covering power which approached that of Cinerama and Todd-A-O, yet could be adapted to a standard-gauge camera handling 35mm film stock. Because of their efficiency and economy, scope lenses are now incorporated at some stage of production into nearly all wide-screen systems, even those that make use of 55mm and 65mm film stocks.

CINERAMA, TODD-A-O, AND CINEMASCOPE

New wide-field systems. Image qualities and production costs. Emergence of CinemaScope: Leon Shamroy's photography in The Robe. *Other approaches to the scope system: Max Ophuls and Christian Matras in* Lola Montes; *Federico Fellini and Otello Martelli in* La Dolce Vita.

The earliest of the wide-field systems to attract popular attention was the Cinerama process, which employed three 27mm lenses whose fields adjoined and slightly overlapped one another to form a remarkably broad photographic arc. Developed by Fred Waller from a World War II device to train air-gunnery students, Cinerama achieved an "all-aroundness" and consequent stereoscopic illusion which was the wonder of 1952. When the novelty wore off, however, the system was too limited to survive. The frame lines marking the three images were imperfectly concealed by the combs designed for that purpose, and the expense of processing and projection finally proved prohibitive. Cinerama's contribution was to whet the popular appetite for the more practicable wide-field systems that soon replaced it.

Todd-A-O, which first stretched across American screens with *Oklahoma!* (1955), was vastly more sophisticated than Cinerama. Using the most advanced lenses designed by American Optical (the "A-O" of the trade name), this system offered the covering power of Cinerama without the difficulty of synchronizing three cameras to form a single image. The large-gauge film (70mm) improved the clarity of the image, while its 12.5mm super-wide-angle lens provided the same all-aroundness that was the reputed glory of Cinerama. Todd-A-O was a fine optical system, now preserved with some modifications in Super Panavision and Camera 65. But the camera equipment was bulky, the lenses presented some difficulties in panning, and the image it created (especially with the 12.5mm lens) was susceptible to serious curvilinear distortion. Above all, there was the question of expense. Roughly speaking, films that use 70mm stock cost twice as much to make as films shot in 35mm. And if you count the costs of shipping, handling, and storing, they mount up in the same way. For these several reasons, Todd-A-O and its successors have lost ground to CinemaScope during the last two decades.

CinemaScope was inaugurated with *The Robe* (U.S.A., 1953) and has proved highly satisfactory as a wide-field photographic system. Europeanized under several rubrics, exported to Japan as TohoScope, and known to later American cinema in the mutant forms of Panavision 35, SuperScope, and VidoScope, this format has clearly established its durability. The system utilizes a single lens of "anamorphic capacity," that is, one which registers an exceptionally wide horizontal field, but then records this registration upon a conventional 35mm negative by compressing or squeezing the image. After this distortion is rectified by an anamorphic component in the projector, the image again looks normal, while re-creating the very wide arc of the original shot. In their breadth of coverage, scope lenses somewhat resemble conventional wide-angle lenses, but the two should never be confused. Although scope lenses have the same visual sweep of wide-angle lenses in the horizontal dimension, they render scale and perspective quite differently. This fact holds considerable significance for film composition.

On first seeing the wide arc of CinemaScope one enthusiast cried, "It's like taking off blinders, people will see things they've never seen before." Not everyone was so enthusiastic, however: asked about the wide-screen scope format French filmmaker Jean Cocteau sniffed, "The next time I write a poem I'll get a big sheet of paper." The most considered reaction came from Leon Shamroy, who handled the photography for *The Robe*: "CinemaScope is most effective if the characters, not the camera, do the moving. If the camera is moved too much it wastes the ability of the lens to see more than ever before." [6] This was only a half-truth, but one that fully expressed the habits of scope composition in the 1950s. In film after film, the camera looked on quiescently while "casts of thousands" were expected to provide the necessary amount of pictorial dynamism. Such an approach also encouraged the accumulation of bric-a-brac, useful for filling waste space on the screen and also for creating obstacles that milling crowds or marching camels would be forced to wind around in gracefully pictorial arabesques. What this represented, in effect, was an attempt to apply Tolandesque techniques of wide-angle, narrow aperture photography to the scope format. But filmmakers soon emerged who would use the new system in more imaginative ways.

The scope format is used effectively in *Lola Montes* (France, 1955), although without radical departure from Shamroy's precedent in the handling of anamorphic lenses. Cinematographer Christian Matras shies away from long lenses, but the interior decor and the elaborate bric-a-brac picked up in the wide-angle composition is highly relevant to the film. The heroine is a very independent and self-emancipated creature decidedly out of place amid the formalities and proprieties of nineteenth-century Europe. As the camera threads its way around Ophuls' highly ornamented set, always composing Lola amid arches, curtains, tracery, and interior furnishings, we get a powerful sense of the way the culture impairs her movement, confines her to permissible roles, and threatens to crush her adventurous spirit. Matras' very special-looking "non-close-ups," i.e., one-shots with an enormous amount of waste space in them, are also functional. When Lola is finally forced to become a circus performer, we see her perched alone on a high trapeze, her face spotlighted against the vast emptiness of open space behind her head. A conventional, closely cropped image here would have ruined the effect. In these final moments of her life, she is absolutely estranged from the world she sprang from, exalted but utterly alone. The compositional strategy beautifully underscores this heroic isolation.

A film which extended the options of wide-field composition in a still more startling way was Federico Fellini's *La Dolce Vita* (1959),

[6] "Filming the Big Dimension," *American Cinematographer* (May 1953), p. 232.

which proved that the scope format entailed no necessary loss of intimacy or mobility. At the same time, Otello Martelli's photography continued to take advantage of the anamorphic lens' capacity to deal with architectural backdrops and the random business of the modern city.

The architectural setting of *La Dolce Vita* is made relevant from the opening shot, where we see a long line of broken aqueducts stretched out along the horizon. These emphasize pictorially how modern Rome has lost contact with the living water that nourished her ancient culture. The cityscapes and interior decor have similar relevance and always advance the film's thematic thrust. The bacchic dance of Anita Ekberg means more because it is enacted in the pagan baths of Caracalla. We better appreciate the media-conscious modernism of Marcello because we so often meet him along the Via Veneto, plying his trade among its bright lights, double-parked cars, and reveling tourists. Even the interiors of villas or palaces, lonely yet full of echoes, profit from lenses that emphasize their expansiveness as well as articulate the details of their decor. The scope lens, because of the way it renders perspective, is unrivaled for this purpose.

To understand how the scope lens treats scale and perspective, and how this bears upon *La Dolce Vita*, it is simply necessary to remember what happens when the horizontal field is squeezed onto conventional film stock in order to achieve wider coverage. Suppose, for example, that the squeeze ratio is approximately 2:1, which was the case with CinemaScope in the 1950s. This means that a 50mm lens (i.e., a lens of normal focal length), when equipped with a scope adapter, acquires the covering power of a 25mm lens. Similarly, a 100mm lens, when outfitted for scope, has the covering power of a 50mm lens. In either case, however, the scope lens retains the perspective characteristics of its true focal length, i.e., those of a 50mm lens in the first case and those of a 100mm lens in the second. For this reason, scope lenses never have the telltale "wide-angle look" of greatly enlarged foregrounds and sharply diminished backgrounds. This is why the aqueducts from the opening sequence of *La Dolce Vita* remain visually prominent, sizable enough to call attention to themselves. The same holds true for other objects that make up the background decor. Bottles are noticeable on distant nightclub tables, vases remain conspicuous on faraway shelves. The scope lens of normal focal length achieves wide-angle coverage without reducing small objects to flyspecks in the recesses of space.

In *La Dolce Vita*, Fellini did nothing really revolutionary when he used the scope lens for wide-angle composition. Other directors had achieved remarkable vistas with 40mm or 50mm scope lenses, even though they filled this impressive picture space with meaningless bric-a-brac or hordes of merely ornamental people. But in this film Fellini also investigated how scope lenses of long focal length could be employed in unconventional ways. Cameraman Martelli stood by him through these days of restless experiment, apparently often looking askance at some of the things Fellini tried to do. In a recent comment on *La Dolce Vita*, Martelli says of his director: "He wanted to use perspective according to his fantasy, often completely in contradiction to the principles governing the use of certain lenses." [7] Instead of principles, Martelli might have said habits, since his further comments show how tastebound were the supposed ultimates involved. In some scenes, continues the cameraman, "Federico wanted to use only long-range lenses: 75 millimeters, 100, even 150. These are supposed to be used for close-ups, for portraits; however, he wanted to use them while the camera was in motion. What mattered to him was really to focus upon the character, and he was hardly concerned at all about the effect this might have upon the depth of field." Such boldness shattered the frozen immobility of the CinemaScope image. "It gave a certain style to the film," concludes Martelli, ". . . a concentration within the frame, a distortion of the characters and the setting."

At the discretion of the director, Martelli shot several scenes quite differently than they would have been handled in a conventional approach to scope. There is, for instance, a scene in *La Dolce Vita* where several children pretend to have witnessed a miracle, an apparition of the Blessed Virgin. A huge crowd gathers, soon followed by pressmen, photographers, and television cameramen with their regalia of searchlights and microphones. Eventually the crowd gets rained on, the children become hysterical, and a near riot erupts. Had the scene been shot at MGM it almost certainly would have been done with a scope lens of relatively short focal length, so that its wide-angle coverage could take in the whole multitude at a single, steady glance, making it unnecessary to pan or tilt the camera and at the same time preserving sharp focus over the whole area. Perhaps there would be a few static close-ups shot with a longer lens, for the sake of what Hollywood calls "intimacy" or "involvement." But Fellini reverses photographic conventions by ordering virtually all of the scene shot with long lenses. This means we rarely see the whole arena of the action and that much of what we do see is seriously out of focus. Notice, too, that the soft focusing is greatly more conspicuous in the scope system, since even the long lenses cover a comparatively wide field (the 100mm lens, for example, takes in about the same field as a 50mm lens of standard

---

[7] This and the following citations of Martelli are from the interview with him reprinted in *Federico Fellini: An Investigation into His Films and Philosophy* by Gilbert Salachas, translated by Rosalie Siegel. © 1963 by Editions Seghers, Paris. Used by permission of Crown Publishers, Inc., New York.

design). Because the scene is shot this way we are allowed to perceive the surging crowd only as isolated bodies darting in and out of the frame, or in and out of focus. They jostle their immediate neighbors, their wet umbrellas momentarily catch the light, then they lurch away into fuzz and shadow.

Though the scene violates every formula that then prevailed for the use of scope, it effectively captures the chaos into which the dramatic action at this point dissolves. With *La Dolce Vita* the scope lens fully established itself as an artistic resource.

ZOOM LENSES AND SPECIAL-EFFECTS LENSES

Introduction of the zoom lens to cinematography. New optical effects. "Crash" effects: Who's Afraid of Virginia Woolf? *Perspective disturbance:* Medium Cool. *Probing and distancing:* Psycho *and* The Beast Must Die. *Subjective effects:* Adrift. *Fisheye lenses:* Seconds.

While the scope lens was finding its aesthetic bearings, the optical industries were perfecting "zoom" lenses, so-called because of their variable focal length. These change the framing and proportioning of the image without changing the position of the camera, just as if one removed a short lens from the camera and replaced it with a long one. Zoom lenses found an immediate and welcome place in cinematography since they could compensate for the relative immobility of big 70mm cameras, or cameras burdened with anamorphic adapters. Naturally, however, zoom lenses could be used just as effectively outside the wide-screen formats. By the early 1960s they were standard equipment for most American, European, and Japanese filmmakers.

In the last decade, composing with lenses has been greatly facilitated by the extensive use of zooms. These can provide anything from about a 25mm wide-angle viewpoint to a 250mm telephoto fix, depending upon the focal length for which they are set in a particular shot. Since focal length depends not only upon lens curvature and the refractive power of the glass but also upon the arrangement of lens components, it is possible to alter the position of these components by means of a mechanical lever and thus radically change the coverage of the lens. Such flexibility was first achieved at the expense of high resolution, and the varifocal lenses of the early fifties were decidedly inferior as to image sharpness. There was also a problem of steadiness in the experimental days, arising from failure to completely coordinate movements of the zoom lever to the changes of focal length these movements effected. But the situation was quickly remedied. The resolving power of the Angenieux and Panavision zooms of the sixties is as high as most lenses of absolute focal length, and this refinement of varifocal lenses now gives the filmmaker one lens with an infinite number of fixed focal lengths.

The refinement of zoom lenses has introduced to the cinema a phenomenon known as "optical traveling." When the lens is zoomed toward its telephoto setting, the field of the image is reduced and, in a certain sense, the camera appears to advance upon its subject. Of course optical traveling is quite different from real camera movement, since it is accompanied by those changes of spatial tolerance and perspective we described in connection with long and short lenses. As the cameraman closes in upon a face, the background goes soft, pictures on the wall becoming blurs of color or shadow, lamps in the corner becoming vague halos of shimmering light. Used with discretion, the zoom allows movements toward or away from the subject faster than any that could be made with a tracking camera; it also makes possible more complex maneuvers, especially when the take involves movements up and down. Though subject to abuse (some cameramen can't resist using the zoom lever as a slide trombone), the zoom has added to the language of cinema visual flourishes unknown before its arrival.

One of these might be called the "crash" effect, where the camera seems to leap forward in space — toward a gun carelessly discarded by a fleeing robber, a book on the table that suddenly acquires special importance, or a face caught in a moment of crisis. This last possibility is seen to advantage in Who's Afraid of Virginia Woolf? (U.S.A., 1966), a picture saved from excessive theatricality mostly through judicious manipulation of lenses. The first game of the evening to which Burton and Taylor (as George and Martha) treat their unsuspecting houseguests is a family fight, evidently much rehearsed, though always informally. To the astonishment of the naive couple who have dropped in for a nightcap, the old marrieds run the gamut of insult and vituperation before George gets a gun and pretends to shoot his wife. As this transpires, the camera registers the shock on the faces of all concerned with a series of unexpected, darting zooms, which isolates each expression and discriminates among several reactions. The shooting is as abrupt and brutal as the manner of George himself. The zoom lens violates the privacy of each participant in the scene, as if hurrying him into a response he is reluctant to make. It shatters the etiquette of the parlor more forcefully than the taunts the husband hurls at his wife.

The zoom has another effect uniquely its own, in evidence anytime it is used in conjunction with camera movement. Zooming while panning, for example, creates the disturbing sense of moving in two directions at the same time. Though discouraged in professional manuals, such gestures decidedly have their place. Again Haskell Wexler's photography comes to mind, this time the very ambitious camera work of *Medium Cool* (U.S.A., 1969). He is shooting a love scene, which is saturated with the sadomasochistic qualities of the protagonist's personality; hence the deliberate effort to make the tryst of the lovers seem as emotionally destructive as possible. He chooses a hand-held camera, which unsteadies the scene from its outset, but the larger disturbances are enacted by repeated changes of the lens setting. As we move from telephoto to wide-angle fixes, and back again, and back again, the lovemaking couple lurches wildly in space, jerked toward the camera, pushed away from it, then brought close again. They seem as little in control of their own bodies as the hapless lovers of Dante's *Inferno* who are pitched about by the winds of lust. Then the camera begins to pan and tilt while continuing a succession of zooms: the floor falls away under our feet, the walls give way at the corners, the furnishings of the room change shape before our eyes. What Wexler accomplishes is total visual disorientation, the exact optical equivalent to the psychic inquietude of the lovers themselves.

Just as zooms can burst in upon something hitherto unnoticed, they can also simulate the effect of hovering, as if undecided how closely a scene should be studied, or from what vantage point. Zooming makes it possible to inch forward in a kind of quizzical probing, then stall, change directions, and begin anew. The zoom lens may survey a street, glide toward the moving traffic at the first intersection, then swing toward the pedestrians on the left-hand sidewalk, and come in tight to catch a face in the crowd. Or it may do what it does at the opening of *Psycho* (1960), one of Alfred Hitchcock's more ingenious thrillers, in which the prolonged zoom of the first sequence seems as whimsical as the director himself. The original orientation gives us a long shot of an American city, after which the camera zooms slowly into the scene, pausing courteously to let the caption "Phoenix, Arizona" appear briefly on the screen. Following this nod to the audience, the lens continues its swoop until it hesitantly comes to rest on one particular hotel window. Naturally, this is the window behind which Janet Leigh is quarreling with her lover, thus precipitating all the tragic misadventures to come. In this instance the lens has become an extension of Hitchcock's own personality — witty, intensely self-conscious, and unfailingly able to find skeletons in the closet, even if the closet is the size of Phoenix.

While in *Psycho* the zoom pulls us into the picture, *The Beast Must Die* (France, 1969) shows us the reverse of this gesture, the film concluding with a long, slow retreat from the subject. Directed by Claude Chabrol in the Hitchcock vein, the film is highly melodramatic, featuring manslaughter, deliberate murder, and finally the suicide of the narrator-protagonist. The last shot, expertly negotiated by Jean Rabier, is a kind of distancing device, an effort to restore artistic repose. While we listen to the protagonist make his confession, the camera is fixed on the sailboat he has taken out into the quiet harbor; the zoom lens is in the telephoto position, so that we seem fairly close to the ship. As the monologue progresses, the camera is gradually swung away from the boat while the lens executes a slow zoom toward its wide-angle setting. Although zooming and panning together does not ordinarily produce a smooth effect, here the two movements are so closely integrated as never to disturb the eye. The camera eventually executes a full-circle pan, coming to rest with the sailboat again centered in the frame. But the visual orientation is completely different, since the lens is now operating from its extreme wide-angle position. By the time the protagonist has informed us of his decision to drown himself, we have come to feel infinitely removed from him, no longer fitfully caught up in his affairs. The director asks us to judge the suicide dispassionately, with the same detachment implicit in the vast space between us and the tiny craft almost lost in the empty expanse of sea.

The same sense of finality, but without restfulness, is conveyed in the succession of zoom shots at the close of *Adrift* (Czechoslovakia, 1970). This carefully crafted fantasy from Czechoslovakia deals with the disintegration of a marriage and with the guilt feelings of a husband who has ceased to love his wife. As the film builds to its tragic conclusion director Jan Kadar concentrates upon the irrevocable rupture within the family, and Vladimir Novotny's photography forcefully supports the dramatic line. Feeling intensely upset but bent upon returning to his wife, the distraught husband begins running toward their home. But a series of reverse zooms overrides his personal movements. He continues to struggle forward, but repeated thrusts of the lens from telephoto to wide-angle settings seem to push the house away from him, wrest it from his grasp. The lens says unmistakably, "You can't go home again," even though the distraught husband seems unwilling to admit the futility of his frantic physical effort.

In this scene from *Adrift*, the zoom lens performs a kind of magic, overthrowing what is literally possible for the sake of what is psychically plausible. This often happens in the cinema, where lens optics may be used to represent subjective reality, not the world as it is but the world as it appears to someone under stress, drugs, or alcohol. While lenses ordinarily make things look real, though a trifle exaggerated, they can just as easily produce bizarre, gothic, or surrealistic effects. Nonspherical lenses introduce grotesque distortions, causing figures to bulge and swell when they enter one area of the frame, then shrink and shrivel as they move to another. Lenses with prismatic components distort in another way, usually somewhat more attractively, fracturing a single image, so that it is multiplied and reduplicated throughout the frame. One of the most striking distortion lenses, however, is the fisheye, which is simply an inordinately short (6 to 10mm), extreme wide-angle lens. Fisheye composition is always recognized by its fantistically exaggerated foregrounds and its pronounced curvilinear distortion. While the use of such special-effects lenses is ordinarily confined to lyrical and experimental films, we occasionally find fisheye perspectives in a commercial fiction film, as in *Seconds* (U.S.A., 1966).

Directed by John Frankenheimer and shot by James Wong Howe, *Seconds* is a nightmare science-fiction thriller about the rejuvenation of corpses. It features a cadre of ghoulish doctors who prey upon man's eternal wish to be reborn, to gain a new identity. The hero of *Seconds* eventually becomes the doctors' victim, realizing only at the last moment what fate is in store for him. His comprehension of this fate is something that deserves singular treatment, which it receives in Howe's ambitious fisheye composition.

In the climactic scene, the central note of the hero's awareness is that there is no escape. Hence it is fully appropriate that the hands of the medical assistants who strap him down should be monstrous, utterly nonhuman. Nor should it bother us that their arms, similarly close to the camera and wildly exaggerated as to size, are themselves as large as all the rest of their bodies. What we see here is not the real world, but the subjective insight of a beaten man, overwhelmed by irresistible, diabolic strength. The other distortions of the visual field give further support to the subjectivizing effects of the sequence. The rectangular doorjamb bends in a weird curve, the heads of characters in the background shrink to midget proportions, all to the purpose of amplifying the general mood of terror. Fortunately, Frankenheimer had the discretion to use these effects sparingly so that they do not lose their leverage.

Even Frankenheimer's discrete use of a distortion lens, however, poses problems as to composition. Cameraman Howe apparently felt the pressure of these when he complained: "On *Seconds* I didn't want that . . . bug-eye lens. I wanted that journey to the operating theatre to be done in a simple style." [8] Whether or not his nervousness was well founded, Howe's suspicion of distortion photography underlines a very important point. Moments of visual eccentricity are hard to match up with photographic normalcy. Perhaps this explains why so few directors are willing to risk the special effects which are made possible by the lenses of extreme wide-angle capacity now in circulation.

[8] Charles Higham, ed., *Hollywood Cameraman: Sources of Light* (London: Thames and Hudson, 1970), p. 75. The interview with Howe might well be read in its entirety, pp. 75–97. Reprinted by the joint permission of Indiana University Press, publishers in the United States, and Martin Secker & Warburg Limited, publishers in London of the *Cinema One* series.

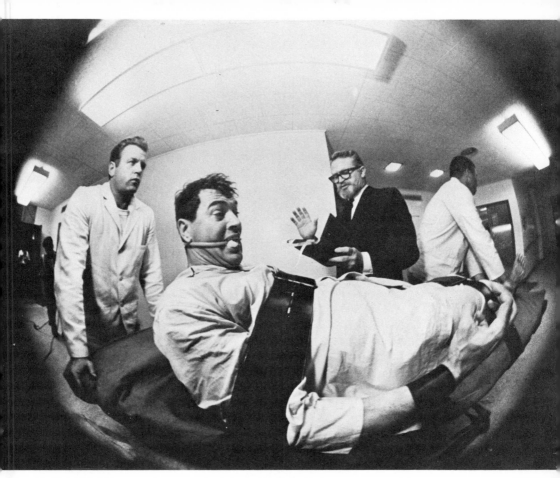

IMAGE DISTORTION AS METAPHOR: Lenses record reality in a manner that may differ radically from the perspective provided by the human eye. Hence the possibility of grotesque, expressionistic distortion, such as provided by the "fish-eye" composition in this climactic scene from *Seconds*. Note how the enlargement of belts and straps in the foreground contributes to the impression of inescapable doom. By permission of Paramount Pictures, Inc. Photograph, British Film Institute, London.

The handling of cameras and lenses is a classic case of artistic accommodation to a machine. The filmmaker composes with his inner eye but calls upon the engineer to objectify the image his mind entertains. Working within a limited technology, the imagination itself is constrained. Lumière at the turn of the century was delighted with the snapshot realism he had achieved in *Arrival of Train at Station*. Later imaginations conceived more grandly as technology answered their needs. Though every opportunity to innovate is an opportunity to err, few creative spirits have put aside the chance to experiment, and this has given the cinema its forward thrust over the last half-century. And the process continues. The laboratories are already at work on optical systems that will challenge directors of the eighties and nineties.

List of Films Discussed

ADALEN 31   not presently available
ADRIFT   not presently available
BANK DICK, THE   73 min.   UNI, TWY, SWA
BATTLE OF ALGIERS   123 min.   AUD-BRA, ADF
BEAST MUST DIE, THE   not presently available
BONNIE AND CLYDE   111 min.   WAR, TWY
CITIZEN KANE   119 min.   AUD-BRA, FNC, JAN
CITY LIGHTS   87 min.   RBC
CLOCKWORK ORANGE, A   125 min.   WAR
CONFESSION, THE   not presently available
DOLCE VITA, LA   180 min.   AUD-BRA
ELVIRA MADIGAN   90 min.   COL
GOSPEL ACCORDING TO ST. MATTHEW, THE   136 min.   AUD-
   BRA
GRADUATE, THE   105 min.   AVCO
IRON HORSE, THE   165 min.   FNC, MMA
JOYLESS STREET, THE   90 min.   MMA
LAST COMMAND, THE   95 min.   MMA
LOLA MONTES   110 min.   AUD-BRA
LONELINESS OF THE LONG DISTANCE RUNNER, THE   103 min.
   WRS, TWY
LOWER DEPTHS, THE   127 min.   AUD-BRA
MEDIUM COOL   110 min.   FNC
ODDS AGAINST TOMORROW   95 min.   UAS
POTEMKIN   67 min.   AUD-BRA, MMA, TWY
PSYCHO   109 min.   CCC, UNI
RINK, THE   20 min.   SWA
ROBE, THE   135 min.   FNC
SECONDS   106 min.   FNC
SEVEN SAMURAI, THE   141 min.   AUD-BRA
SKI THE OUTER LIMITS   25 min.   PYR
TOM JONES   127 min.   UAS
UGETSU   96 min.   JAN
UMBERTO D   89 min.   JAN
VIRIDIANA   90 min.   AUD-BRA
WHO'S AFRAID OF VIRGINIA WOOLF?   129 min.   WAR
WILD CHILD, THE   85 min.   UAS
WORLD OF APU, THE   103 min.   AUD-BRA

3
LIGHTING

The right light is as basic to cinema as the right lens. As we have seen, it affects the performance of lenses, improving their resolution when it is ample and impairing their efficiency when it is scarce. But light does much more than provide adequate exposure. It rounds objects to three dimensions and relates each to the others as a pictorial unit. It gives emphasis to specific detail and tone to a total scene. It is the film-maker's chief source of mood and metaphor. To the creative camera-man or director, as much as to Vermeer or Velázquez, light is the radi-ant energy which vivifies the surface of geometric space.

Light interprets the world it illumines. It is inseparable from the dra-matic values we connect with particular films. The harsh sunlight which sears the dust of Death Valley is what gives point to the desperation we feel at the end of *Greed* (U.S.A., 1923). But sunlight can glow as well as glare, imparting a warmer dramatic atmosphere less likely to imply frayed nerves, unrelieved tensions, or devastated hopes. There is abun-dant sunshine in *The Two of Us* (France, 1966), but it is softened by shadow and tempered by foliage, becoming the visible sign of an in-ward love that joins two generations. When clouds cool and diffuse the daylight, then we are likely to get the unflattering naturalism of Rossel-lini or De Sica, in whose films a persistent drabness seems to reduce the stature of the characters, disqualifying them for conventionally

LIGHT AND MOOD. The impression we gain of objects is strongly affected by the way they are illuminated. With conventionally balanced lighting, accomplished in this case by two spot floods with vinyl diffusers mounted on either side of the subject (*top*), the image is detailed, well-modeled, and three-dimensional. With the silhouette lighting of two undiffused spot floods mounted behind and below (*center*), the image loses its modeling and three-dimensionality; new elements attain prominence (note the stronger impression of the grid and the suggestion of ripples in the backdrop). Other effects are achieved through the still more exceptional and more severely unbalanced light accents of one undiffused spot flood mounted in front of and below the subject (*bottom*). Here the overexposure of one area of the picture gives the subject a ghostly, iridescent appearance totally different from that at top. Photographs by Carolyn D. Scott.

heroic roles. Remember Ricci and Bruno from *The Bicycle Thief* (Italy, 1948), almost swallowed up by the rain-soaked, uniform grayness of street and sky?

Artificial light offers a further array of tones and accents. Brilliant highlights from glass and silverware make the sets of a Lubitsch comedy sparkle like the overpolished wit of his heroes and heroines. But the intense, antiseptic brightness of white hospital walls heightens the pain of lost fertility in *The Pumpkin Eater* (Britain, 1964) and of lost love in *This Sporting Life* (Britain, 1963). Or there may be something in the quality, more than the intensity, of the light source that gives it a particular flavor. In the last moment of Antonioni's *The Eclipse* (Italy, 1962), the camera is fixed upon a fluorescent streetlamp, whose ice-blue coldness perfectly matches the uncompassionate insight his would-be lovers have attained about themselves and each other. This light is worlds removed from the candle-flame intimacy of romantic films like *Camille* (U.S.A., 1937), or *Queen Christina* (U.S.A., 1933). And none of these lights has much in common with the dim, high-contrast illumination which sets the mood for air raids, gang wars, and grave robbing. No wonder photographer-director Josef von Sternberg says "the drama of light when used effectively creates a flowing image that remains when the image itself has vanished."

When the filmmaker works in color, lighting effects become still more crucial. Slight underexposures make things look much darker than in black and white, while colors quickly bleach out if the light gets even a little too intense. The glare of dust in the parching sun might hardly register in tones of gray, but the drained-out blues it etches on color stock are the most memorable aspect of the picnic scene in *Bonnie and Clyde* (U.S.A., 1967). Semiopaque glasses or plastics, and even facial makeup, all take light more impressively in color, as we know from *Blow-up* (Britain, 1966) and *Satyricon* (Italy, 1969). Lit with the right accents, color also enables the filmmaker to feature an otherwise negligible detail. Would anyone notice the subliminal intercuts in *Marnie* (U.S.A., 1964) except for the fact that they are done in bright red?

Just as framing depends upon the lens and the camera, lighting depends upon the film stock. How bright is the scene? Which shadows will seem obtrusive? How strong is the contrast between light and dark areas of the exposure? These questions involve chemical characteristics of the emulsion and cannot be trusted to the commonsense judgments of the eye. Whether a stock records in color or black and white, two of its characteristics are of overriding importance — its speed, or light sensitivity, and its spectral response. In the case of color stock, it is also necessary to take account of what is called color temperature.

"Light sensitivity" is a measure of the speed with which the stock's light-responsive emulsion absorbs incoming illumination. Film-stock emulsions consist of silver-halide granules which are irreversibly altered by contact with light. The chemical changes in these granules are what constitutes an exposure. When these granules are relatively large (as in a so-called rough-grain film), the stock will be highly sensitive to light and can be adequately exposed at a relatively low level of illumination. Such film stocks are called "fast." When the silver granules are small, however (as in so-called fine-grain film), the stock will be much less responsive to light and require much higher levels of illumination for correct exposure. Such stocks are called "slow." The speed (fast or slow) of a film stock is ordinarily measured as ASA (American Standards Association) numbers or DIN (Deutsche Industrie Norm) numbers. In both systems, the faster stocks are represented by the higher numbers. For example, one of today's fast stocks might have an ASA rating of 400, while a slow stock would have a rating of 40. Slow and fast are relative terms, of course, and almost all stocks of the 1970s would be faster than almost any stock of the 1920s. For through the years there has been a continuing search for film stocks of increasingly higher speed that remain relatively fine grained (since fine-grained stocks always produce sharper images).

"Spectral response" is a further characteristic of all film stocks, denoting their sensitivity to various wave lengths of the color spectrum, from the short wave lengths of the blue family down to the long wave lengths of red. Spectral response is as important to black-and-white stocks as it is to color-sensitized emulsions, even though black-and-white stock reacts to the visible spectrum only in tones of gray. The black-and-white stocks used in cinematography until the late 1920s, the "orthochrome" emulsions, were primarily responsive to the blue spectrum, much less sensitive to green and yellow light, and almost completely insensitive to red. The stocks in use since the late 1920s, however, the "panchromatic" emulsions, are sensitive to all colors of the spectrum, though these also respond somewhat more strongly to blue. Because of this variation of spectral response, orthochrome stock registers hue and color very differently from panchrome. Furthermore, these two types of stock must be matched to appropriate light sources: orthochrome could only be used in the predominantly blue light of day, or with carbon arc lamps, whose color characteristic is also blue; panchrome, on the other hand, matches a much wider variety of light sources, even the decidedly reddish hue of tungsten filament bulbs.

"Color temperature," a near relative of spectral response, offers a more exact way of calibrating the color quality of light, achieving the precision necessary to color cinematography. It measures the color of light in terms of the heat of the light source. As anyone who has ever handled a gasoline stove should remember, relatively cool fires have a reddish appearance while very hot fires burn blue. For purposes of photography, these temperature changes are measured in Kelvin degrees. The lower temperatures (2000–3500°K) denote the red family while the higher temperatures (5000–10,000°K) designate the blues. A candle flame, for instance, has a color temperature of about 2000°K, a household bulb about 2800°K, a modern photoflood either 3200 or 3400°K, and the old carbon arc lamps about 5000°K. Daylight, on the other hand (emitted from the hottest imaginable light source), has a color temperature upwards of 5000°K. Unlike black and white, color emulsions must be balanced to light of a particular color temperature, either the high temperature of arc and daylight or the lower temperature of tungsten sources. This is not for the sake of correct exposure, as with orthochrome and panchrome, but to prevent distortion of color. Daylight color stocks turn orange when exposed to tungsten illumination, while "studio" stocks contaminate toward blue when exposed to daylight.

Historically and aesthetically, motion-picture lighting divides into three distinct categories, corresponding to the use of orthochrome, panchrome, and finally color emulsions. The first major break in the continuous maturation of lighting styles occurs in the late 1920s, as new panchromatic stocks come into general use, replacing the hitherto universal orthochromes. Increasingly more fine-grained and more light-sensitive, panchrome still holds an important place in cinematography as the standard black-and-white emulsion. Since 1950, however, its primacy in the film industry has been steadily eroded by more extensive use of color. The aesthetics of lighting is the history of accommodations made to these basic stocks.

LIGHTING IN THE ERA OF ORTHOCHROME

The "age of orthochrome" (that terrible mouthful of words seems unavoidable) extends back to 1873, when H. W. Vogel first added to silver-bromide film stock the dyes that extend its color receptivity beyond the blue spectrum into the green and the yellow. Thus orthochromatic stock was already available when the eccentric Mr. Muybridge first captured the motion of trotting horses and when Jules Marey built his ingenious "photographic gun," forerunner of the motion-picture camera. Orthochrome was the stock that all the great early cinematographers first learned to use, though many — Edouard Tisse, Karl Freund, and William Daniels, for example — lived on into the era of panchromatic emulsions. Since it obviously conditioned their tastes and expectations, we might do well to consider its chief characteristics. Kevin Brownlow in *The Parade's Gone By* calls orthochrome a "crisp" stock,[1] which is a good term, though perhaps in need of further clarification, since nonphotographers may associate crispness more with this morning's bacon than with yesterday's celluloid. If orthochrome gives crisp images, how is this crispness achieved? And how do we know it when we see it?

The best way to describe orthochrome, I think, is to call it a shape-sensitive film rather than a shade-sensitive film. In strong, bright sunshine it tends toward pictorial uniformity, with few glossy highlights or gauzy shadows; but when light is scarce or seriously unbalanced, it registers deep, sharp shadows, creating stark outlines and bold silhouettes. The reason for these special characteristics is the stock's almost complete insensitivity to orange and red. Everything in the red family of color photographs on orthochrome as black — not just deep shades of crimson, but also pink, vermilion, and red-related colors like peach, or magenta, or russet. Even green does not register strongly, which means that the world of trees and foliage readily becomes a set of black shapes against a bright sky. Orthochrome's blindness to red also has a further consequence. Not only does it fail to record the middle-gray scale when exposed to daylight, but also with orthochrome it is difficult to open up shadows using artificial fill light. Small incandescent bulbs of 250 to 500 watts, which make ideal light supplements for panchrome, have practically no effect upon orthochrome stock. It is sensitive only to the giant blue carbon arcs, which produce streaming, searchlight effects, very difficult to delicately scatter or diffuse. This is why studio lighting around 1910 and the 1920s so often consists of burning highlights amid seas of darkness.

There are situations, however, where the limitations of orthochrome become positive advantages. It is simply a question of working with, not against, the material bias of the medium. It might be roughly compared to designing with stained glass — the limitations aren't noticeable unless the artist tries to turn his glasswork into an oil painting. One supremely valuable quality of orthochrome is that it discourages the sentimental pretty-pretty lighting setups that became a trademark of both Hollywood and Paris during the 1930s. It invites either a harshly naturalistic approach to lighting, which relishes unhighlighted, slightly grainy prints, or a nightmarish, high-contrast expressionism, deliberately artificial but powerfully symbolic. One style prevails in the out-of-doors atmosphere of American cinema during the late teens and early twenties;

[1] (New York: Alfred A. Knopf, Inc., 1968), p. 213.

the other triumphs in the arc-lit world of Germany right after World War I. Each school seems to have taken the course that climate and culture ordained, leaving behind in its masterworks a record of these divergent artistic interests.

THE DAYLIGHT SCHOOL
OF AMERICAN CINEMAPHOTOGRAPHY

Tendency toward naturalism in American photography around 1910. Extension of this orientation to cinema. Billy Bitzer and D. W. Griffith, Birth of a Nation. William Daniels and Erich von Stroheim, Greed.

American cinema in the years from 1910 to 1925 had a pronounced affection for daylight. Filmmakers rushed to the West Coast at this time not just to avoid debts and taxes but also to seek out the sun. Whether exaggerated or not, the 350 days of sunshine forecast by the Los Angeles chamber of commerce had great appeal. Even the major studios of this period respected sunshine far more fully than their counterparts of the 1930s, running up their warning flags when clouds loomed upon the horizon, and setting their great mirrors to redirect sunrays when these streamed through the large glass roofs. And if the grand film-growing greenhouses of Hollywood relished daylight, so too did the influential journals devoted to artistic photography. It was during the late teens that Alfred Stieglitz, long a tastemaker in aesthetic circles, turned his prestigious magazine *Camera Work* into a forum to celebrate a new photographic naturalism. He extolled the "brutally direct" exposures of Paul Strand at the expense of more romantic schools of American photography which still aped the painterly artifice of French impressionism. This bias toward realism, manifest at several levels of seriousness in American culture, is what prompted Billy Bitzer to study the Civil War photos of William Brady before undertaking to shoot *Birth of a Nation*. It also pushed William Daniels into close association with Erich von Stroheim, as they prowled Polk Street together, seeking out authentic locations for *Greed*.

Bitzer's work for Griffith betrays the same ambivalence toward naturalism that marks the director himself, but his outdoor photography typically profits from the crispness of orthochrome. Bitzer was justly proud of the lovely cameo portraits he did of Lillian Gish under controlled studio conditions, and never regretted the time he spent rigging lamps, planning shadows, or softening facial features with reflectors and diffusers of every kind. He also achieved other studio effects that are most remarkable, considering the capacities of orthochrome stock. There is an unforgettable moment in *Broken Blossoms* (1919) when

ORTHOCHROME IN DAYLIGHT. The high-contrast characteristics of orthochrome stock here bleach out the possible gradations of gray (note the virtual disappearance of the horizon line into the sand, the strong shadows cast by the crouching figures) to create an atmosphere of extreme harshness in the last moments of *Greed*. Photograph, The Museum of Modern Art/Film Stills Archive.

Bitzer's lighting changes the whole character of Griffith's self-effacing Oriental hero. Prior to the scene, this character has epitomized innocence and vulnerability; now suddenly, as he bends over the heroine, we see a sinister element in his personality, created by the slightly underexposed photography and the thin net grid the cameraman has placed between lens and subject. This unexpected coarsening and darkening of his features is a tremendous tour de force. Brilliant as such lighting techniques are, however, they do not represent the most prescient of Bitzer's photographic instincts. They prove he could fancy up orthochrome, making it yield subtle webs of shadow we ordinarily expect only with panchromatic stock. But such delicacy is achieved at cross-purposes with the orthochromatic medium. This is why Bitzer's reconstruction of Civil War scenes in *Birth of a Nation* is more effective, though less striven for.

In these, utilizing the strengths of orthochrome, he constantly composes in hard, clean lines. As the Union army advances with rifles ablaze, the bright smoke from exploding powder vividly frames the troops that Bitzer has wisely chosen to photograph from the rear. Or again, as Sherman undertakes his march to the sea, Bitzer raises his camera to a high angle which nearly eliminates the horizon line, forcing us to concentrate on the powerful diagonals etched into the landscape. From this perspective, the road traveled by the troops looks like a jagged gash through the dark foliage — almost a symbol of the wound inflicted upon the Confederacy by Northern penetration of Georgia's heartland.

Bitzer's rugged portraiture of the natural world was not lost upon Erich von Stroheim, an actor and assistant to Griffith in *Birth of a Nation* who was about to begin his own career as a director. When he did so, with *Blind Husbands* (1919), he immediately struck up a professional friendship with William Daniels, another cinematographer of strong naturalistic proclivities. These two men worked closely together on the ambitious outdoor photography of *Foolish Wives* (1921) and then achieved permanent fame two years later when Stroheim dramatized Frank Norris' sprawling novel *McTeague*. This, of course, is what became *Greed*, a film that is a landmark in the aesthetics of lighting and shows orthochrome to the best possible advantage. The visuals alternate between glare and gloom, but always with complete appropriateness to the dramatic situation.

Of the major cameramen to come out of Hollywood, Daniels is probably one of the most accommodating. He assists a director without trying to replace or override him. In a recent interview he is quoted as saying, "I think the photographer should be an *inventor of detail,* adding to the imagination of a director with his own scientific skills." [2] This may be too modest an estimate of Daniels' contribution to *Greed,* but it correctly notes his willingness to let Stroheim take the lead in planning the picture. He thought Stroheim a bit of a prima donna, but he admired the outdoor locations the director had chosen for *Foolish Wives* and never regretted the difficulties they had in shooting *Greed* under even more rigorously lifelike conditions. Like Bitzer's best composition in *Birth of a Nation,* Daniels' photography in *Greed* extracts the full potential of orthochrome to render distinct lines and sharp contrasts.

Predictably, the street scenes are very well done. As McTeague courts Trina on the boulevards of San Francisco, the sunshine brightens the heroine's sentimental glances and brings out the appointments of her wardrobe. The crisp imagery makes her seem all the more starchily prim, as Daniels' head-to-heels framing shows us the flowers in her bonnet, the lace on her sleeves and collar, the striped parasol trailing at her side. But the indoor photography is equally eloquent, in spite of

[2] Higham, *Hollywood Camerman,* pp. 57–58. The interview in its entirety runs pp. 57–74. Reprinted by the joint permission of Indiana University Press, publishers in the United States, and Martin Secker & Warburg Limited, publishers in London of the *Cinema One* series.

the much more precarious lighting arrangements. The decision to use real interiors, as in all scenes of McTeague's flat, was almost unheard of in the early twenties, yet Stroheim's hunger for authenticity could be appeased only by real walls and real ceilings. This allowed, the director admits, "very few lamps" and required "making full use of the daylight which penetrated through the windows." Though "this was not always to the camera-man's liking," he continues, ". . . we got some very good photographic results."[3] Indeed they did. They got sharp crosslights which render faces very unhandsomely and leave grimy shadows in various corners of the rooms. Yet this is just the right accent to catch the sordidness of McTeague's world.

There are two scenes from *Greed* that everyone singles out for praise — McTeague's overwrought bourgeois wedding and his grisly last hours in the Death Valley desert. They are not only central dramatic nodes of the picture but also triumphs of photographic imagination.

In the first, the atmosphere is festive and the shadows have temporarily flown. To insure indoor exposures that were equivalent to daylight, Daniels supported the available illumination with powerful arcs, concealing their smokiness with a wedding-day decor which includes pipes, cigars, and candles. The high light level is what makes possible that magnificent shot through the window where we look past the romantic glee of the bridal party, past the prim white curtains, outside to the street, where a funeral procession is marching solemnly to a different drummer. In this shot we are asked to measure the private emotions of the lovers against the total environment of American life that eventually destroys them. And the effect is entirely the result of Daniels' lighting. Its intensity assures the in-depth sharpness of the image, while its balance distributes emphasis equally over the two widely separated planes of action. But most importantly, its imprint upon orthochrome is what accounts for the selective high contrast between the dense black of the mourners and the gay whites of the bridal party.

The scene in Death Valley requires pictorial ingenuity of another kind, yet it too is composed in lines and masses, without subtle gradations of shade. Draftsmanlike, rather than painterly, it achieves a simplicity unknown in Norris' prose, which is severely realistic in theme but ornate and involuted in style. In this last sequence of *Greed* there are few props, no sets, and no fill lights — just an endless expanse of sand and sky. Studied from a distance, McTeague and Marcus are swarthy specks dwarfed by distant mountains; up close, their dust-caked clothes seem to make them part of the earth they stand on. The blanched dryness of the entire area gives special point to the metaphors of draining and dying central to the dramatic action. Water

---

[3] Quoted in Joel Finer, *Stroheim* (Berkeley: University of California Press, 1968), p. 26.

spilled from a punctured canteen momentarily changes the look of the sand, but the wetness almost instantly vanishes, leaving the landscape as parched as before. The mule is shot, twitches convulsively for a terrible moment, then becomes a lifeless heap. So also with McTeague's ambitions, ironically evaluated by the stark photography. His compulsive ambition, first imagined under similarly harsh surroundings, has now come full circle, driving him back to the animal world he sought to escape through manners, marriage, and middle-class acquisitions. By brute strength and fierce will he has conquered the world, but his kingdom includes only an empty canteen, a dead mule, and a corpse handcuffed to his side. Stroheim originally planned that the symbols of McTeague's social success should be gold tinted, to contrast with the bleached-out emptiness of his demise. Even without these special embellishments, however, the scorching sunlight of the last shot pronounces resonantly upon the futility of human ambition.

THE ARC LIGHTS OF GERMANY

Hostility to naturalism in German art and drama. Impact of Robert Wiene's Dr. Caligari. *Expressionistic lighting effects in* Nosferatu. *Collaboration of F. W. Murnau with Fritz Wagner.*

While Bitzer, Daniels, and documentarists like Robert Flaherty were investigating the possibilities of natural light, German cameramen of the same period, as well as the directors who set them to their tasks, were developing their skills under much different inspiration. In central Europe, and especially in Germany, the expressionist school was strong in all the arts, particularly painting and theater. From the first decade of the century, painters like Emil Nolde and Erich Heckel had been in explicit revolt against the dappled outdoorsiness of French impressionism, and their tendency toward abstraction soon began to set style in photography, persuading representative figures like László Moholy-Nagy to preach against "the narrow rendering of nature." [4] The theater also acceded to these priorities, following the lead of Reinhard Sorge, who introduced the German stage to deliberately deformed sets and self-consciously artificial lighting arrangements. Inevitably, the impress of this movement was felt in the cinema, to which directors like Robert Wiene and F. W. Murnau turned after careers in painting, and to which other filmmakers like Paul Wegener brought extensive theatrical experience. When economic exigencies of the Wei-

[4] Quoted in Siegfried Kracauer, *Theory of Film* (Oxford: Oxford University Press, 1965), p. 10.

mar period called for a film product distinct from that of Hollywood, these men gave their pictures a visual surface totally different from the look of *Greed*.

The lighting of American films of this era ordinarily involves the selective use of dark detail against a relatively well-illumined background. In Germany, we see the exact reverse: brilliant streaks or pools of light surrounded and almost swallowed up by darkness. Both sunlight and searchlight, however, are fully compatible with the characteristics of orthochrome. In fact, the high-contrast tendencies of this stock are in many ways ideally suited to the theoretical tenets of expressionist art. Reacting against the delicate light balances which unify the impressionist canvas, artists of the German school sought to disrupt and fragment pictorial space with intense highlights and opaque masses, rejecting rounded forms in favor of slashing lines. But what they did with color and oil is very close to what almost necessarily results when orthochrome is exposed to the hot, highly directional beams of studio arc lamps, if these go unsupported by strong daylight or the efficient use of reflectors. As early as 1916 director Paul Wegener had called for a cinema of "nothing but moving surfaces," which would "transcend the lines and volumes of the natural." [5] Once cameramen and technicians had mastered the silhouette and spotlight composition of the stage, they were fully prepared to invest this vision of reality with physical form. Their handling of light thus gave filmmakers unparalleled opportunity to probe the secrets of the soul.

The Cabinet of Dr. Caligari (1919), which initiates German expressionist cinema, is photographically undistinguished and owes more to art direction and set design than to the camera work. It is this film, however, that established the visual conventions of the genre and forged a solid link between cinema and the plastic arts. Hermann Warm and Walter Röhrig, who built and painted the sets, were both former members of "Der Sturm," a clique of expressionist painters very influential around 1910. They sought to control the visuals of the picture by extraphotographic means, angling the architecture into structurally impossible shapes and strewing painted shadows over floors, walls, and rooftops. Their work robbed the photography of challenge, though these daring falsifications of light values remain an ocular tour de force. It remained the task of more talented cameramen like Fritz Wagner to give the expressionist attitude toward light and form a truly photographic articulation.

Murnau's *Nosferatu* (1922), a version of Bram Stoker's *Dracula*, is a triumph of expressionist lighting, ably executed by Fritz Wagner. It improves upon *Caligari* in several ways, most obviously in substituting

[5] Quoted in Lotte H. Eisner, *The Haunted Screen* (Berkeley: University of California Press, 1969), p. 33.

real shadows for daubs of black paint, but also by playing off outdoor landscapes, rendered naturally, against the eerie, haunted interiors that symbolize the dark recesses of man's unconscious mind. Unlike in *Caligari*, there is a world of sunshine and sanity against which to measure the cavernous diabolism of the vampire's lair. Dramatically, the film isn't completely successful. Dracula carries around more coffins than one vampire can gracefully manage, and the rats, though momentarily chilling, are a little cliché. Not all the cinematography works either. When Wagner undercranks the camera to achieve accelerated motion (suggesting the magical swiftness of Dracula and his servant), modern audiences usually laugh. But Wagner's lighting of the indoor sets is always expert, and his manipulation of mobile shadows is symbolically persuasive.

Wagner's shadows are superbly appropriate to carry the themes that come together at the climax of the film. As Dracula invades Nina's home to claim her as another victim, Murnau converts pat images of horror into impressive dramatic configurations. During these moments we never see Dracula physically, only his shadow which steals up the stairwell and approaches the bedroom door. These silhouette shots give the vampire a special status. He is not a man, merely the husk of a

ORTHOCHROME WITH ARC LIGHT: The high contrast effects of orthochrome were also put to good use in evoking the shadow-haunted world of German expressionism, here exemplified in *Nosferatu*. Photograph courtesy of Janus Films.

human form, empty of everything but darkness and existing only to suck life out of others. Perhaps the form itself is ambiguous, or so it seems as we are forced to stare at the intrusive image. The hands are claws, the nose is the beak of a scavenger. These predatory suggestions are relevant, as are those associated with his posture — hunched, bent forward, as if frozen in a stance of permanent aggression, and made doubly grotesque by contrast to the severe verticals the advancing shadow eclipses. Dracula's entrance to Nina's bedroom gives a final touch of sadistic eroticism to these already powerful graphics. Insubstantial fingers, preternaturally elongated by their distance from the light source, now crawl across the heroine's white gown, finding and clutching her breasts in their spastic grasp. At this point Dracula follows his shadow into the picture, as if suddenly enfleshed by the sensate contact he compulsively seeks out. Whether we read this scene politically, as an intuition of the dark threat to Weimar democracy, or psychoanalytically, as an expression of Murnau's homosexual insecurity, it perfectly illustrates Wagner's photographic mastery of light and shade. Orthochrome was often used well, but rarely better than in *Nosferatu*.

LIGHTING WITH PANCHROMATIC FILM

While Fritz Wagner and his German colleagues were garnering kudos for their expressionistic use of orthochrome, a new technology was gradually making obsolete its bleached whites, dense blacks, and persistent graininess. During the late 1920s panchromatic film stock won a place on the commercial market, bringing in its wake a substantially different approach to lighting. High-wattage tungsten lamps now began to replace the cumbersome, smoky carbon arcs which had been the staple of studio lighting for twenty years. And since the tungsten units were more mobile and easier to handle than arc lights, panchrome stock soon gave both European and American cinema the smooth, carefully modeled "studio look" characteristic of the 1930s and 1940s. Of course the new stock did not really force directors and cameramen into the studio; such force as there was came from the introduction of sound recording, and its demand for a superquiet environment. But whatever complex factors created the studio fetish, panchrome emulsions tempted filmmakers to stay indoors where they could take advantage of their opportunity to completely control the lighting. Only after the intervention of World War II did panchrome acquire its present reputation as a superb stock for use in unstructured, uncontrolled available-light photography.

The first panchromatic emulsions were introduced around 1910 by the French technician Léon Gaumont, but it was Eastman Kodak of Rochester that first made it a commercial item in 1923. Ironically, it was first developed not for studio photography but as an outdoor film useful in the treatment of cloudscapes — always difficult to film in orthochrome. Skylight is spectrally blue, whereas clouds tend to reflect equally all bands of the spectrum. This means that to the human eye they are generally brighter than the tone of the sky. But these differences did not record on blue-sensitive orthochromatic stock, blind to the spectral characteristics distinguishing skylight from cloud-reflected light. Panchromatic film, however, registered clouds very well, so well that they soon came down from the sky and claimed a place in the studio.

Hollywood cameraman Charles Rosher had experimented with panchrome as early as 1919, but it was Robert Flaherty's *Moana* (1926) that really alerted filmmakers to the full possibilities of the new stock. Flaherty had planned to shoot his film in orthochrome, as he had his earlier *Nanook of the North* (1920), where the blue-sensitive stock had proved quite adequate to treat the high-contrast blacks and whites of the frozen Hudson Bay area. But *Moana* was shot in the color-rich South Sea islands, whose multiple, glancing, mingling lights were beyond the susceptibilities of orthochrome. The dappled Samoan land and seascape dissolved in fuzzy imprecision as Flaherty made his first efforts to film it. Then one of his cameras malfunctioned, which prompted him to experiment with another that was loaded with panchrome. According to his wife, the results were astonishing. "When the rushes were screened," she says, ". . . the figures jumped right out of the screen. They had roundness and modelling and looked alive . . . and retained their full beauty of texture. The setting immediately acquired a new significance." [6] Having awakened to the precision with which pan stock records the scale of gray, Flaherty did most of the further filming in early morning or late afternoon, when long shadows and yellow-red sunlight would add to the graceful chiaroscuro of *Moana*. Quietly, almost by accident, this maker of documentaries had made a revolution in the film industry.

[6] Quoted in Arthur Calder-Marshall, *The Innocent Eye: The Life of Robert J. O'Flaherty* (New York: Harcourt Brace and Company, Inc., 1963), p. 109.

THE STUDIO LOOK

Panchrome in the studios. Introduction of tungsten lamps. Migration of German cameramen to Hollywood. Concept of "formula" lighting. Theory and practice of cameraman John Alton. Collaboration of Lee Garmes and Josef von Sternberg: Shanghai Express.

But if the varicolored luxuriance of Samoa more fully yielded its beauties to a panchromatic emulsion, then why couldn't the new stock uncover similar shades amid the manufactured *mise en scène* of Pathé, Metro, or Paramount? And it could. All that was needed was a cadre of art directors to gild the studio lilies and a set of lights to match the various hues of the tropical sun. These latter were not long coming. Mole-Richardson company of Hollywood, founded in 1927, set out specifically to build more versatile lighting units utilizing both arc and tungsten illumination, and these were soon being marketed all over the world. Competitors added further to the available supply of lamps, which now varied not just in size and weight but in matters crucial to photography, like temperature, wattage, reflectance, and penetration. By 1928, when Kodak's new negative was christened "M. P. Negative Panchromatic Type I," the lighting industry had begun to put at the cameraman's disposal a full array of studio lamps. He could still use arcs for basic illumination, as was done in the age of orthochrome, or if he wanted warmer tones there now were incandescent lamps of comparable intensity.

Furthermore, there was a welter of smaller lights, not just a back light to illumine the rear wall of the set and a kicker light to help model the face of the star, but also an eye light, a clothes light, and a hair light to further enchance tones and textures. Often there were even "baby spots" to throw highlights on drapes, furniture, and silverware. It was during this period that flashgun kisses (which lit up the faces of hero and heroine in their first embrace) took their place beside dry-ice fogs and wind-machine thundershowers as standard studio paraphernalia. And of course with new lights came new shadows — cast by "scrims," "cookies," "gobos," or any one of fifty other gadgets which might cast the shape of a lamp or a tree branch across an otherwise bare studio wall. No wonder the cameraman now came to be known as the "director of photography," a title more in keeping with his new managerial responsibilities.

Naturally filmmakers didn't exactly seal themselves into studios around 1930, and the lots that adjoined these gigantic facilities remained open to the light of day. But as control lighting became ensconced in the profession, the studio method substantially affected outdoor photography, particularly through the impetus it gave to the use of filters. Filters, of course, were of little value so long as the stock was orthochromatic, but with the coming of panchrome emulsions it became possible to alter the natural gray scale in pictorially exciting ways. Red filters, for example, will darken a bright sky, since they admit only red light to the lens while skylight is predominantly blue. Yellow filters also darken skies, though less pronouncedly, while green filters are ideal for highlighting (i.e., brightening) the leaves of trees. The expatriate cameraman and technician Eugen Schüfftan, fresh from his work in the studios of Germany, set style for French films of the 1930s with the excellent filtration photography he did for Marcel Carné. Schüfftan's perpetually glowering skies are a visual equivalent of the destructive fate that broods over *Port of Shadows* (1938), and they are equally congruent with the dramatic tone in *Rules of the Game* (1939), which Jean Bachelet shot for Renoir. In this latter film, Bachelet uses increasingly dense sky filtration to foreshadow impending catastrophe, even though the dialogue remains at the level of brittle comedy. More ambitious filtration effects are also possible, such as using a dense red filter while underexposing the stock by as much as two f/stops. This technique rather convincingly disguises day as night, especially if artificial light sources, such as glowing streetlamps or automobile headlights, are part of the composition. While without substantial aesthetic significance, this approach to lighting further advertises the priority of artifice in the studio method.

This syndrome dominated filmmaking at least until the middle 1940s, and in most of the world, much beyond this date. The fierce spotlights and flickering torches of expressionism were much modified in transit from orthochrome to pan stock and from Germany to Hollywood or Paris, but the principle of absolute light control was powerfully reinforced by these changes in technology and production. One consequence of this (not always a happy one) was the emergence of what we might call "formula" lighting. In this scheme, every genre is assigned a "key" on the scale of bright to dark and then lit in accordance with its dramatic tone. Comedy is gay, hence brightly lit, or "high key," in keeping with its upbeat outlook and shimmering costumes. Moods either more sinister or more sublime ask for low-key treatment, usually accorded to mysteries, melodramas, and martyrologies. It was these that taxed studio hands to the utmost in manipulating flashlight, firelight, candlelight, or light through stained-glass windows. Such effects came from lights that never were on land or sea, but their persuasive simulation of the real kept every scene alive with looming, suggestive shadows.

The pressure of studio precedent is nicely illustrated in the memoirs of Hollywood cinematographer John Alton, whose *Painting with Light* (1949) is an excellent retrospective testimonial to the ambitions of the

1930s and 1940s. With infinite patience and without the slightest trace of irony, Alton goes through the whole glossary of stock lighting effects, from "Mystery Lighting" to "The Hollywood Close-Up." For the most part the book simply takes for granted that these formulas are ideal for the moods and modes in question, yet he has amateur anthropology at his fingertips to put down anyone who might dispute the point. "*Mystery in lighting,*" he assures us, "is not a Hollywood invention; it is as old as man himself. There is an age-old saying that all evil happens at night; that while sunlight is beneficial to mankind, the cold clear rays of the moon are supposed to produce its opposite effect." [7] And if moonlight is mysterious, lightning is even more conducive to terror: "Because of its sudden, and to primitive man, mysterious appearance, and the death and destruction it brought in its wake, [lightning] has certain unhappy associations in the mind of man." From this account it would seem that studio lighting formulas have the blessing of Cassirer, Malinowski, and Claude Lévi-Strauss, even though Alfred Hitchcock might protest this convention with the daylight atrocities that mark his thrillers.

Occasionally Alton notes the existence of another approach to lighting, reminding us that "people are getting tired of the chocolate coated photography of yesterday." But the concessions to naturalism are limited, amounting only to the admission that the "light of some *real* fires, such as that of a forest fire, is strong enough to register on our present day sensitive film [my italics]." In other words, one way to photograph a forest fire would be to go out and actually take a picture of a forest fire. But this grudging nod to the world beyond the studio simply attests to the spell which its lamps cast during the thirties and forties.

Fortunately for the art of motion pictures, the cameramen who set style for the studios were better technicians than philosophers, and their achievements are often of singularly high quality. One of the best was Hollywood's Lee Garmes, whose work with Sternberg in the thirties fully assimilated studio practice while retaining fine personal touches with low-key illumination. Although Sternberg was fascinated by the look of German expressionism, Garmes became famous, and added to the director's fame, by imitating the balanced low-lit scenes of Dutch baroque painting. He knows the values of panchrome and his shadows are carefully graduated, not nearly so sharp and steep as those in the haunted houses of *Caligari* and *Nosferatu*.

"Ever since I began," says Garmes in a retrospective interview, "Rembrandt has been my favorite artist. . . . And of course I've followed him in my fondness for low key. If you look at his paintings, you'll see an

[7] (New York: The Macmillan Company, 1949), p. 44. Further citations of Alton are on pp. 44–56. Copyright 1949 by Macmillan Publishing Co., Inc.

awful lot of blacks. No strong highlights. You'll see faces and you'll see hands and portions of clothing he specifically wants you to notice, but he'll leave other details to your imagination." [8] With minor modifications, this could pass for a description of Garmes' own shooting style. When he utilizes daylight for exteriors, it is again with the performance of Rembrandt in mind: "I've always used his technique of north light — of having the main source of light on a set always coming from the north. He used to have a big window in his studio ceiling or at the end of the room that always caught that particular light." Naturally this facilitates low-key photography. Since it absolutely avoids harsh, high-contrast sunrays, north light provides balanced illumination, dim yet not dark, and free of sharp shadows, perpetually ready for whatever modifications the cinematographer wishes to make.

Garmes first connected himself with Sternberg after the Vienna-born director had done ten films in America, then junketed briefly to Germany where he made The Blue Angel in 1930. Sternberg returned to the U.S.A. the next year, bringing back Marlene Dietrich and a love of Teutonic shadows that stayed with him through Morocco (1930), Dishonored (1931), An American Tragedy (1931), and Shanghai Express (1932), all films made with Garmes handling the photography. Although there is some dispute about who was primarily responsible for the effects, Sternberg and Garmes together evolved a vocabulary of low-key setups whose sophistication helps account for the long-term prestige of studio photography.

Concerning his own contribution, Garmes says, "I had already established the Rembrandt style by Morocco," but his photography for Shanghai Express is generally thought superior, a critical judgment which to me seems correct. By this time he had had ample opportunity to experiment in lighting the face of Dietrich, giving it the sultry, vampish look that cast her as the dark lady of the silver screen. "Dietrich took the north light very well," recalls Garmes, "although for some shots I changed the style, making one side of the face bright and the other side dark. . . ." Out of all this comes the veiled, gauze-enclosed, shadow-shrouded figure whose journey from Peking to Shanghai is the best remembered railway trip in the history of motion pictures. Nor is it Dietrich alone upon whom Garmes lavishes his skill. The train, the travelers, and the troops who threaten them are all evoked with authority.

Shanghai Express opens in streaming arc-light sunshine (arc lamps, unlike the natural sun, have an uncanny ability to always pick out the star), but Dietrich's veil already checkers her face with a dark web

[8] This and the following citations of Garmes are from "North Light and Light Bulb: Conversations with Cameramen," Sight and Sound (Autumn 1967), pp. 193–196. Reprinted by permission of Sight and Sound.

as she prepares to board the train. Soon she is behind glass, and the shooting is into shadow, the heroine's black dress and hat absorbing whatever light penetrates the train's interior. After departure, Garmes frequently catches Dietrich in corridors, which are dim but momentarily lit up by glancing lights from unseen sources. He also seats her in corners, where she can be isolated in light-deprived close-ups, or envelops her in cigarette smoke when she gathers with a crowd. She is often placed behind drawn blinds that silhouette her impressively, deep gray against a somewhat more silvery foreground. As we would expect, special lighting graces her climactic scenes. While she worries over the fate of her lover, her fingers and hands are spotlighted with a single, high-intensity flood lamp, which emphasizes the contorted gestures that mix nervous desperation with fitful prayer. When she surrenders to the diabolic Commander Chang, the wooden slats of a half-closed door throw shadowy bars across her face and shoulders.

Like many pilgrimages before it, *Shanghai Express* is a journey into the dark places of the soul, and Garmes' shots characteristically sensitize us to the moral underworld we are entering. There is brightness at the moment of departure, but daylight soon fades as we are caught up in the drama of civil war. The visuals are decidedly low-key in the scene where government troops stop the train to search for a rebel officer, the set illumined by only one apparent light source, which throws long shadows and outlines an ominous-looking bayonet in the foreground. The tonalities here prefigure the still more sinister events of the rebel raid, which is shot in still deeper darkness, the raiders visible as shadows against steam when they slip over the tops of railway cars. This blackness is not only charged with ill-defined menace, but reflects the uncertainty and skepticism which is the core of the picture. While clumsily verbalized in the script, the theme of discovery through crisis comes through fully in the photography. The underlit scenes, teasing in their partial perspectives, deny us penetration of the physical landscape, just as the characters are denied insight into themselves and their fellow passengers. However hackneyed certain lighting formulas might become, we have no reason to resent their application to films like *Shanghai Express*.

THE STUDIO LOOK: Panchromatic film stocks revolutionized film lighting, bringing about smooth, carefully controlled chiaroscuro. In contrast to the stark blacks and whites of orthochrome, the new stocks allowed perfect graduation of the tones of grey. It also encouraged the use of filters, scrims, and gauzes, as evidenced in Josef von Sternberg's work with lighting cameraman Lee Garmes in *Shanghai Express*. From the private collection of Herman G. Weinberg.

PERSISTENCE OF MOTIF LIGHTING
AND EMERGENCE OF
THE AVAILABLE-LIGHT SCHOOL

Motif lighting of Robert Krasker for Carol Reed in Odd
Man Out. *Haskell Wexler and Mike Nichols,* Who's Afraid
of Virginia Woolf? *Raoul Coutard and available-light cinematography. Coutard and Jean-Luc Godard. Coutard and
François Truffaut:* Shoot the Piano Player. *Flexibility of
panchrome stock.*

The studio system, with its expert visual formulas, had persistent appeal. And why not? It let the filmmaker set each lamp at
exactly the right angle, study the light balances implicit in every movement, even evaluate the contour and density of shadows cast on the
rear wall. Any form of decoration or symbol, from the shadow of
blowing leaves to the shape of a chandelier, was immediately at hand.
There need be no mistakes. But the eyes inevitably tired of these prefabricated harmonies, yearning, it seems, for an unexpected flash or a
bare wall, unadorned by baroque shadows. Hence rigid lighting
schemes began to lose their appeal sometime in the late 1940s, leading directors and photographers to renew their interest in real-life
locations. This generated two contemporary schools of lighting, one
which we might call the "motif" approach, and another, more restricted and demanding, which is usually known as "available-light"
photography. One continues to respect the principle of close control
in lighting; the other holds dogmatically to the belief that "light is
where you find it."

New technology played some part in reducing the sway of the studio. In the late 1930s, Agfa introduced its new "Supreme" stock and
Kodak began to market "Plus-X"; both were sensitive, fine-grain emulsions that reduced the need for support light by more than 30 percent.
The next decade saw changes in recording that eliminated the problems of the sound camera. But most of all, cameramen had their conception of lighting changed by the authentic, on-the-spot reportage
of World War II. This is what gave us *Open City* (Italy, 1945), *Shoeshine*
(Italy, 1946), and the worldwide changes in the look of films that followed in their wake.

Yet if studio lighting sometimes hardened into cramping formulas,
it also made a permanent contribution to cinematography. This is preserved in motif lighting of the fifties, sixties, and seventies, which seeks
to maintain some control of the "light key," while varying it according
to dramatic need or the demands of location shooting. It may be neither
high-key nor low-key, but multikey, fluctuating in response to complex
changes of moral atmosphere that distinguish a particular picture.

Sir Carol Reed's *Odd Man Out* (1946) is a simple, but significant example of this approach. Shot by Robert Krasker on location in Belfast and London, it is lit in strict conformity to dramatic occasion yet works out all lighting arrangements with convincing naturalness. The last day in the life of the Irish revolutionary Johnny McQueen is recorded in changing lights of morning to night, as sunshine gives way to cloud, fog, snow, and finally darkness. Moreover, as daylight fades, different kinds of artificial light convey the ambiguous import of his last hours.

Though depicting a bank robbery, *Odd Man Out* begins on a hopeful note, establishing the basic decency of the thieves, who steal not for personal gain, but to finance guerrilla insurgency against government power. At this point they expect to avoid loss of life and make a clean escape, hopes that seem well-founded in the open sun-illumined world of the first scene. By the time this sequence is over, however, Johnny McQueen has killed a guard, received wounds in an exchange of shots, and fallen from the getaway car as it speeds off. The sky now darkens and never clears as we follow Johnny through a series of failing efforts to tend his injuries and rejoin his companions.

As his strength ebbs and his hopes decline, Johnny is studied against increasingly more dismal skyscape, fog and snow bringing early twilight which challenges the ingenuity of Krasker's photography. It is after dark, though, that the camera gets its most expressive effects, picking up the eerie glow of wet cobblestones and calling attention to the weblike shadows thrown by outdoor fire escapes. The light-dark antithesis also supports the dramatic contrast between outside and indoors, central to the theme of exile and exclusion. But these contrasts go beyond the obvious stereotypes. Darkness isolates yet also protects; light restores community yet raises the risk of exposure. In the pub where Johnny attempts to find refuge, the positive connotations of brightness are deceptive; he is betrayed by apparent friends. In the home of strangers, however, he finds sympathy, and the low-lit sets, in spite of their superficially negative valence, seem to augur a willingness to cooperate in Johnny's concealment. Back on the streets again, Johnny's face is illumined for the last time by light from the indoor world; the lamp is extinguished, and he is cut off from the civilities of home and family. He is now like a wounded animal, tracked and destroyed by anonymous hunters.

In the tragic finale, Krasker's lighting again plays the supreme role. Johnny is seen clearly, though in low light, as he leans upon his girl friend Kathleen, who has finally caught up with him; both are backed against a wire fence, which reflects enough light to make itself emphatically present as symbolic decor. The police pursuing this couple are present only as a loose network of flashlights which gradually encircles the fugitives. The lights draw closer, though the broken arc they

MOTIF LIGHTING. The progression of light tones in a film often corresponds to the evolution of the dramatic line, as is the case with Robert Krasker's photography for *Odd Man Out:*

The sun shines brightly at the beginning of the picture as we look out over the roofs and chimneys of Belfast. At this point the revolutionary cadre, here firming up last-minute details, entertains bright hopes for the success of the mission about to begin. *(Above, left.)*

Sunlight is still abundant in the scene of the bank robbery undertaken to net funds for the organization, but here the protagonists flee into ominous shadows down the street where their getaway car waits. *(Above, right.)*

Soon rain, fog, and early darkness obliterate the sense of optimism that once prevailed, reducing the protagonists to anonymous silhouettes, lost and confused amid a labyrinth of murky streets. *(Opposite page, left.)*

Rain changes to snow in the tragic finale, in which Johnny and Kathleen are encircled and shot by police. *(Right.)* Note how the light-reflectancy of the snow gives a cold brightness unaccompanied by real illumination, while headlights from police cars and flashlights carried by the individual officers serve to conceal rather than reveal identities. Just as the political issues of the film are never fully clarified, so also do the light accents of the picture promote confusion and disorientation. Courtesy Janus Films.

create in the darkness does not seem compositionally powerful. Their advance is relentless, yet reluctant, lacking anything which might be construed as heroic authority. Entrapped, Johnny shoots at the wavering ring of lights. In return, there are flashes of fire, and he falls. Kathleen picks up the gun and starts shooting. More bursts of fire from the darkness. She falls, and the drama is over. But the opacity of the scene is unrelieved. Some have disturbed the social order, for reasons that remain obscure, and society has cut them down. Is this justice or mere mechanical expediency? This matter remains as inscrutable as the details of the shrouded scene.

A more recent, and somewhat more unusual example of motif lighting is found in *Who's Afraid of Virginia Woolf?* Shot both in the studio and on the campus of Smith College, this adaptation of Edward Albee's play illustrates the careful discrimination of tones that contemporary

film stock and lighting equipment make possible. Fortunately, director Mike Nichols had in head cameraman Haskell Wexler one of the very best young talents in Hollywood. Though quite familiar with the casual lighting schemes of documentary, whose tendencies he had incorporated into the shooting of Elia Kazan's *America, America* (1963), Wexler chose in *Who's Afraid of Virginia Woolf?* to utilize all the lighting resources available. He did, however, put them to use in a boldly imaginative way. The light progressively interprets the dramatic movement, gradually changing from sharp to soft as, in the course of their endlessly vituperative exchanges, George and Martha become a little more tolerant of one another, a little more relaxed toward their situation.

In evolving his lighting scheme for the set, Wexler consciously departed from the original staging, which he evidently didn't care for. "The stage version of the play upset me greatly," he admits, "because it seemed unrelenting and inhuman right up to the very end." [9] But he liked the way Burton and Taylor construed the lead roles, apparently following Nichols' directorial effort to suggest "there is some human compassion, some spark of warmth between these people that goes beyond the horrible game they play." This approach to the script prompted Wexler to fashion a photographic surface that would support it. "I felt," he concludes, "that a gradual softening of the light would help establish the idea that they had reached the beginning of the end of this mad game they were playing." Every device in or out of the studio — filters, diffusers, overexposure, crosslighting, etc. — is drawn into the control of light Wexler required to visually articulate this reading of the dramatic line.

The opening sequence of the picture is visually gripping. We see George and Martha strolling across the grounds of an Ivy League

[9] This and the following citations of Wexler are from the interview with him in *American Cinematographer* (August 1966), pp. 530 ff.

campus, the scene decorated by scattered leaves and lit in a conventionally picturesque glow. The only false note is the shambling walk of the couple, which could signify romantic languor, but hints more nastily at drink and fatigue. In spite of this preparation, there is an element of shock in the first verbals, where we find George and Martha at each other's throats almost from the moment they first cross the threshold of home. This startling release of pent-up fury is enhanced by the lighting, which is charged with glare from the first second the switch is thrown. It almost pains the eyes. To get this effect, Wexler deliberately shot the opening indoor scene at one f/stop overexposed; in other words, with the aperture open enough to admit twice the light for normal exposure. He uses no filters or diffusers to scatter the hard, penetrating, highly directional illumination of strong flood lamps; the light is contrived to sting us, just as Martha tongue-lashes her husband. It seems most harsh amid the bright-white surfaces of the kitchen, giving point to the wife's oft-repeated "What a dump!" But there is no relief from Wexler's fierce illumination even when we join the guests in the living room.

Intensity is just one of the devices Wexler uses to invest the picture with harsh tones. The placement of lights is also important. He wants to make Elizabeth Taylor look as unglamorous as possible, to turn her, he says, into a "sloppy, fading voluptuary, her disheveled hair streaked with grey, her eyes bearing the ravages of too much alcohol and too little sleep." Part of this assignment belongs to the make-up department, of course, but Wexler's extensive crosslighting, and lighting from unflattering angles, contributes to the flabbiness of the leading lady, while exaggerating the shadows under her eyes. He also takes advantage of the color temperature of the lights to a degree unusual for black-and-white photography. In the most violent scene of the film, set in a sleazy nightspot where George is worsted in a scuffle with his academic colleague, the lighting is keyed by the blue-violet tones of fluorescent light from the jukebox. Like the crosslights, it treats the face badly, registering on black-and-white stock as bright but cruelly cold. It is fitting that such light should surround the protagonists at the moment of their most complete humiliation.

At the conclusion of *Virginia Woolf*, there is at least some hint of relief. We have lived through a sadomasochistic nightmare, but as dawn breaks a few of the specters that haunt the home seem to retreat toward their tombs. It would be wrong to call the last scene optimistic, but it seems as though the couple may now get some rest, even if they cannot hope for regeneration. Appropriately, the light now softens. The overhead lights go out, their harsh rays replaced by filtered light from no visible source, though presumably the first signs of morning. In contrast to the opening scene, Wexler here uses variable voltage, quartz-iodine lamps, which cast an ambient light of lesser penetrating power. Sharpness is further curtailed by reflection and the use of spun-glass diffusers. As George and Martha go through their last exchange, the set looks underlit and generally appealing, in keeping with the speech itself, which suggests exhaustion more than enlightenment. But the softness is at least conducive of sleep, and the transformation of artificial light into daylight perhaps hesitantly points to somewhat more natural relations between man and wife.

While success of this order readily justifies managed illumination, there has been a pronounced trend over the past fifteen years to take light as it is found. This has been made possible by film stocks that are at least ten times (sometimes twenty) as light-sensitive as those used in the 1920s, by lenses that average three f/stops faster than their counterparts of an earlier day, by cameras that have been miniaturized for maximum mobility, and by laboratory techniques which assure acceptable resolution of the image even when the stock is "pushed" in development — i.e., developed so as to compensate for lack of light in the original exposure. These advantages not only allow new extensions of the naturalistic, daylight cinematography of the early 1920s, but also permit available-light photography of indoor subjects, in fact almost let cameramen take pictures in the dark. News photography and documentary cinema have pioneered in this area, producing imbalanced, high-contrast, grain-begrimed exposures which are the direct opposite of studio effects. At worst, this approach to lighting simply becomes an excuse for bad photography, but at best the new proponents of *cinéma vérite* fabricate images that bring us supremely close to the texture of life itself.

One of the most outspoken enthusiasts for available-light photography is Raoul Coutard, the French cameraman who got his first experience as a World War II cinematographer and sometime later went to work on the motion pictures of Jean-Luc Godard, François Truffaut, and Jacques Demy. Fond of hand-held takes and unrehearsed poses, he personifies the documentary approach to lighting transferred to the dramatic film.

In a long ruminative interview with *Sight and Sound,* Coutard describes his photographic ambitions and the revolt he led in the late 1950s against the lingering vestiges of "cinema lighting" in French studios. His watchword is simplicity. "Cameramen used to demand an absurdly long time to set up the lights for a shot," he complains, and "with the cameramen all determinedly tricking out their circus turns, the image had become pretty extravagant." [10] What the cinema needed,

---

[10] This and the following citations of Coutard are from his article "Light of Day," originally published in *Le Nouvel Observateur.* English translation copyright by *Sight and Sound.* Reprinted in *Jean-Luc Godard,* ed. Toby Mussman (New York: E. P. Dutton & Co., Inc., 1968), pp. 232–239. Reprinted here by permission of *Sight and Sound* and Georges Borchardt, Inc.

according to Coutard, was to get away from subjects that "had been carefully posed amid a network of lamps." Pitching arcs, sun-guns, and floodlights in the nearest trash heap, he would install in their place "that really beautiful overall light that is daylight." For "daylight has an inhuman faculty for being always perfect whatever the time of day. Daylight captures the real living texture of the face or the look of a man." His incomparable ability to catch the shades of gray, or to get highlights from sun flare and kaleidoscopic reflections through windshield glass, proves that he knows the ways of daylight about as well as anyone taking pictures today.

Of course the simplicity Coutard seeks is earned, not accidental. It requires knowing a lot about various film stocks and a lot more about the multifarious tones of light itself. When Godard described to this cinematographer the look he wanted for *Breathless* (1960), Coutard rejected all existing motion-picture film stocks for one designed to be used in still cameras. He and the director then spliced rolls of it together, exposed it, and accepted the responsibility of doing their own processing. Although this was a once-in-a-lifetime eccentricity (it could happen only in the company of Godard), Coutard is always scrupulous in the way he checks out the light tones of a particular location.

Paris and its environs are ideal for the somber atmosphere of Godard's films, where drab grays go well with the themes of ennui, delinquency, and prostitution. But Coutard was equally successful in applying his photographic approach to Demy's *Lola* (1960), even though the director had originally imagined this picture as a musical shot in color. The difference between *Lola* and, say, *My Life to Live* or *Band of Outsiders,* both of which Coutard shot in the early sixties for Godard, is the difference between the haze of Paris and the warmer, sun-touched tones of the French Riviera. Without the richness of the Mediterranean sun, so expertly evoked by Coutard, it is doubtful that director Demy could sustain the romantic artifice of this film. In fact, the quality of the light, always conspicuously natural in spite of its shimmering brilliance, provides just the right counterpoint to the involuted plot, the chance-directed relationships, and the intricate emotional entanglements developed by Demy's seemingly simple protagonists. Most critics agree that *Lola* is the best film Demy ever made, perhaps, I am suggesting,

AVAILABLE-LIGHT PHOTOGRAPHY. Many black-and-white films since 1960 have taken a very casual approach to lighting, as cameramen began working outside the studio and without floods or fill lights. This revolt against the studio tradition is typified in the photography of Raoul Coutard, here composing for Godard in *Vivre sa vie.* The Museum of Modern Art/Film Stills Archive.

LAFOND
AU
62
SPECIAL
MEDI
de 13h 45
IE SAINT
LEURS
LE ZO
VAU.
29.47
du 7 au LUNDI 12
RECORD D
DANNY
DOU
DU G
EN SCOPE
du MERCRE
LES PL
ARTISTE
AM
CEL
EN SCOPE
VARIETE
CROIX-NIVERT
PAUL NEWM
ARNAQUE
EN CINEMASCOP

because the astringent naturalism of Coutard saved a sentimentalist director from the further sentimentalities of technicolor.

Coutard also knows how to use low light — halos from streetlamps, swatches of light from storefronts, the cold glow of nighttime neon, the flicker of traffic along an otherwise dark boulevard. *Shoot the Piano Player* (1960), which Coutard did for Truffaut in the style of American gangster pictures, illustrates how well he handles light-deprived scenes. It also shows how different available-light photography is from the Hollywood "low key" of pictures like *Shanghai Express*. If this really were an American gangster film of the thirties, not a self-conscious imitation of one, the opening would be very different. It would be dark, of course, and a man might be fleeing from an unseen pursuer, just as in *Shoot the Piano Player*. But we would get visual clues and catch sight of an occasional detail — the white tie of a prospective robbery victim, momentarily pinpointed by headlights from a passing car, or a piece of the heroine's jewelry, or her white, fear-stricken face. Coutard gives us none of this. The film opens in virtual darkness. We know there is a chase because we hear someone running and suspect violence because there are angry voices. But the visuals tell us nothing. Coutard has provided the streetlamps from studio-made pictures, but has not seen fit to place the protagonist under them. We must wait until we get into the grubby cabaret to meet Eddie Saroyan and the other creatures of the night who inhabit the world of *Shoot the Piano Player*. It is the same at the climax of the film when Eddie's girl friend is accidentally shot. This too is done in low key, but not the key of 1930s melodrama. The dirty snow completely lacks highlights, and the flat, dull light diffused through heavy winter clouds drains from the scene all hint of romantic spectacle.

Panchrome stock, especially as upgraded in the 1940s and 1950s, has provided the speed and flexibility that allows a director or cameraman to personalize his approach to lighting. It allows a Coutard the rich mix of sihouette, sun flare, reflection, and brooding shadow that have become his trademark. But it just as legitimately allows the carefully modulated light tones of Krasker or Wexler. Capable of either smooth or rough effects, panchrome helps assure us that control and spontaneity will be complementary, not exclusionist, ambitions. Tastes will continue to vary and rival schools to debate, but the stock itself will respond agreeably whether the light is discovered on the scene or developed on the set. Its versatility is the best possible safeguard against either mechanical formalism or simplistic naturalness. Aware of the potential of the medium, most cinematographers now recognize that a scene is correctly lit, not just because the lighting is studied, nor just because it is impromptu, but because it conforms to the dramatic resonance it must support.

LIGHTING
WITH COLOR
FILM

Although filmmakers are still doing exciting things with panchrome, the most important innovation in film stock of the past quarter-century has been the development of an efficient, practicable, low-cost color process. This has turned the gray tones of yesterday's film world into the varied hues we see in everyday life. First used to lend occasional tints to black-and-white images, later called into service as gift-wrapping for confections from Hollywood's dream factory, color now claims so important a place in the repertoire of international cinema that all major directors and their cameramen have begun to explore its potential. They have found that it adds much more than an obvious and usually insignificant "realism." It enhances contrast, facilitates separation of planes, supports or conceals movement, and invites bold departures in lighting, filtration, and processing. Less directly, it may also influence such seemingly unrelated matters as a choice of lenses or a decision in the cutting room. Above all, it constitutes a further resource for the execution of a visual design.

There is no need to study in detail the complex technology of color printing in order to understand its bearing on the art of motion pictures. It is sufficient to remember that the process involves the incorporation of color dyes into a standard panchromatic emulsion. These dyes represent the three primary colors of photography (blue, green, and red), from which all hues of the spectrum are derived. Such derivation of course depends on extensive mixing and merging of primaries, as well as upon the fact that colors differ from one another not only in hue but also in saturation (the density or concentration of a particular color) and in brightness (the light reflectancy of a color). We might have, for example, a relatively "pure" red (i.e., one not adulterated by green or blue) that would be rich in saturation but low in brightness. This would be perceived as scarlet. On the other hand, another "pure" red might be low in saturation (said to be "desaturated") but high in brightness. It would be perceived as pink. The addition of other primaries complicates the pictorial rendering. Add green to red and it turns yellow; bias this mixture toward red and it becomes orange; reduce the brightness and it is degraded to brown. When blue is mixed with red we get various shades of purple or violet, while blue-green combinations yield the infinitely varied tones of this color family. A subject which reflects all the primary colors equally (and with high brightness) will record as white; one which reflects colors equally but less brightly is gray. A subject which reflects none of the primaries will record as black. Aside from these particular characteristics, color stock responds to light exactly as panchrome; the exposure is a function of the sensitivity of the stock and the color temperature of the light.

Lighting color stock is not greatly different from lighting panchrome; they have had much the same history. The first color films were shot with carbon-arc illumination, though by the late 1930s Hollywood had devised high-powered tungsten lamps bright enough to use with color stock. A more important breakthrough came in the 1960s, however, with the widespread introduction of quartz-iodine and xenon lamps. These are superintense lights which match the color temperature of daylight. Used in conjunction with increasingly more light-sensitive color emulsions, quartz and xenon units have moved color photography out of the studio and now let it compete with panchrome in pursuit of the naturalistic look in cinema.

FROM TECHNICOLOR
TO TRIPACK

Evolution of color cinematography. The role of the Kalmuses. Bert Glennon and Natalie Kalmus: Drums along the Mohawk. *More ambitious expressiveness of* Black Narcissus. *Introduction of Eastmancolor. Work of Teinosuke Kinugasa and Kohei Sagiyama in* Gate of Hell. *Further innovations of* Black Orpheus.

Color cinematography has an extensive prehistory which has left us the fossils of many defunct patents — Biocolor, Cinechrome, Prizma, and Colorcraft, to name only the first few that come to mind. These failed for various reasons, mostly related to cost, projection problems, and difficulties of duplication or maintenance. Few of them could compete successfully even against the primitive color baths and hand tints early in this century. The first modern color process derives from the Daniel Comstock patents for Technicolor, which was first marketed under the auspices of Herbert Kalmus in 1922. Though it was another full decade before the quality of this process improved enough to interest motion-picture producers, the Technicolor corporation eventually monopolized the whole industry, not only providing lab facilities but also renting the color cameras, co-opting the technicians, and pre-empting the right of directors and cameramen to determine how the stock would be used. The Technicolor process was not the final term in the evolution of color photography; but between 1935 and 1950 the Technicolor corporation created color conventions and color aesthetics that would influence world cinema long after Agfa and Eastmancolor had made the Technicolor process obsolete.

The forward-looking aspect of Technicolor was its use of the so-called subtractive process of color transmission. This has been absorbed into all modern systems of color recording. The most awkward feature of Technicolor, however, was its dependence upon a special camera (a "beam-splitting" apparatus that handled two strips of film simultaneously) as well as its severe insensitivity to light. These factors exactly fitted the Technicolor medium to the studio era; the already cumbersome Technicolor camera was further immobilized by the high light levels and intricate arrangements required for correct exposure. From these technical demands arose the same appeal to formula lighting that marked the handling of panchrome in the 1930s. As there were "high-key" and "low-key" genres for films shot in black and white, so also there were Technicolor subjects and Technicolor genres. More importantly, there was a way to treat particular hues of the spectrum, a kind of paint-by-number code of color aesthetics.

In the late thirties and early forties, color production was reserved for big-budget films, chiefly "epics" — meaning costume dramas — and musicals. *Gone with the Wind* and *The Wizard of Oz* (both 1939) reflect this strict adherence to genres. These pictures (and many others) also reflect what we might call the Kalmus key to color psychology, as promulgated in the pages of the respected *Journal of the Society of Motion Picture Engineers* and imposed upon the industry by direct insistence or oblique suasion.

During these years all contracts between the industry and the Technicolor corporation included a provision for color consultation, meaning that the producer purchased, along with his stock and his access to the camera, a color adviser whose services were obligatory and whose judgment overrode the taste of director and cameraman. The basic premise of Technicolor aesthetics is that each color has a special psychic association and that the medium requires character development and thematic articulation in these terms. Thus Natalie Kalmus (who personally handled consultation for many films of the period) tells us in an essay on "Color Consciousness" that color cinematography must "be molded according to the basic principles of art" and these, we are to understand, are always "in keeping with Nature's rules." [11]

[11] This and the further citations of Natalie Kalmus are from "Color Consciousness," *Journal of the Society of Motion Picture Engineers* (August 1935), pp. 139–147. Reprinted by permission of the Society of Motion Picture and Television Engineers.

In practice, this implies "the appropriateness of color to certain situations, the appeal of color to the emotions." No one would doubt this until Miss Kalmus makes its application more specific: "Just as every scene has some definite dramatic mood . . . so, too, has each scene, each dramatic action, its *definitely indicated color* [my italics], which harmonizes with that emotion." Take a love scene, for instance, which should always be done in colors of the red family. Then "the delicacy and strength of the shade of red will suggest the type of love. By introducing the colors of licentiousness, deceit, selfish ambition, or passion, it will be possible to classify the type of love portrayed with considerable accuracy." If we were ever to wonder what colors are most deceitful or selfishly ambitious, the further paragraphs of the Kalmus essay offer immediate guidance.

We might think that such rigidity could never yield results remotely approximating naturalness, but this is not quite the case. Some scenes which follow the Kalmus recipe succeed remarkably well, however hard it might be to find them extended artfully through an entire film.

There is, for example, a sequence from *Drums along the Mohawk* (1939) which both adheres to the Technicolor aesthetic and satisfies the needs of dramatic art, appearing neither forced nor contrived. Working in this film under the personal color consultation of Miss Kalmus, Bert Glennon shoots Henry Fonda's escape from hostile Indians in a chroma key that modulates from red and black to green and gold, or as the formula would have it, from the key of danger and death to the key of freedom and fruition. "Red," as Miss Kalmus points out, "recalls to mind a feeling of danger, a warning," while black "has a distinctly negative and destructive aspect." Hence the propriety of these colors to the opening moments of the scene, where Fonda seems about to be run down by his pursuers. A blood-red sun looms on the rim of the morning sky, enlarged by haze but too weak to relieve the countryside of darkness. The cloudscape framing the sun is torn and slashed like an open wound. Fonda and his antagonists are black silhouettes against the crimson sky, as they come over the horizon in quick succession. The hero's short lead upon his enemies emphasizes his peril. But this cut is followed by others that gradually change the scene from dawn to morning, tempering the fierce reds with bright orange, then gleaming gold as Fonda begins to outdistance the Indians. After the last brave stumbles in his failing effort to keep up the chase, the camera pans to the escaping Fonda, quietly gliding over a cheerful landscape of rich greens and warm yellows. The light values of this scene are formulaically orthodox (down to the gold glints which mean "harvest" or "reward"), but for once they seem perfectly realistic, almost inevitable.

A rather more ambitious use of color is found, at least intermittently, in a comparatively little known British film of 1946, *Black Narcissus*. Although the picture is flawed by its shopworn plot and stereotypic characterization, the color decor is sensitive, especially the treatment of interiors. The story features a convent of missionary nuns who have taken up residence in Burma in order to Christianize an essentially pagan culture. The project slowly disintegrates, as defections from within and resistances from without take their toll upon the energy of the missionaries. What is remarkable about the decor is the way it foreshadows the inevitable demise of the nuns' crusading adventure.

Upon arrival, the missionaries set about effacing the trappings of pagan culture in the palace they have converted to a convent. This involves smearing generous quantities of whitewash over the varicolored murals that cover the palace walls. But these great globs of Kalmusesque purity fail to achieve their intended result. As the film progresses, we have the opportunity to watch the color on the palace walls bleed through the newly applied whitewash. The reassertion of these strong and sensuous colors forms an exact analogy to the way the claims of the older, less repressive and more sensate-oriented culture reestablish themselves in spite of the single-minded spirituality of the nuns.

Whatever the early achievements, the decisive turn in the history of color cinematography came in the middle 1940s with the development of a class of stocks known as "integral tripack." Like Technicolor, the new stocks made use of the subtractive process, forming color images from blue, green, and red primaries. Unlike Technicolor, however, the tripacks gathered all three layers of color dye into a single emulsion. They were more light-sensitive, provided superior definition, and, crucially, they eliminated the need for a special camera. Their appearance broke two decades of monopoly on the part of Technicolor and opened a new era of experiment and individual initiative. Color ceased to be a Hollywood ornament and became an international idiom.

The precursor of tripack was Agfacolor, perfected through the Farben laboratories of Leipzig and employed in several German feature films of the early forties. Most people know the performance of this stock only from the brief color sequence in *Ivan the Terrible* (U.S.S.R., 1942–1946), shot with confiscated Agfacolor. In the aftermath of World War II, however, the impounded German patents became the basis of several new color processes now widely used in France, Eastern Europe, and the Soviet Union. During the same years, Leopold Mannes and Leopold Godowsky were at work for Eastman Kodak on a similar process, introduced commercially as Eastmancolor when first used in the Canadian Film Board's *Royal Journey* (1952). Eastmancolor soon became known under other trade names, derived from the production companies that purchased rights of use (Warner Color, Columbia Color,

Pathé Color, etc.) or the laboratories that handle the processing (Movielab, Technicolor, Color by Deluxe). But under whatever rubric, the Eastman stock, especially after further refinement in the late 1950s, quickly established itself as the prestige negative of the color era. Its preeminence has to do not only with the economic leverage of Eastman Kodak (which is considerable) but also with its fine-grain, high-color-separation characteristics.

The first major achievement in Eastmancolor is a Japanese film of 1953, *Gate of Hell*. While it modifies rather than supersedes the pictorial conventions of Technicolor, this film introduces into the color medium a precision and internal consistency unknown to the earlier era. *Gate of Hell* follows precedent in being self-consciously pretty (not for another ten years will directors or cameramen opt for the deliberately drab); it also conforms to the Technicolor practice of working chiefly with pastel shades (the 1950s may someday be called the "pastel era" of integral tripack); finally, it respects tradition by staying within the framework of costume drama (films about samurai warriors are the *Gone with the Wind* of Japanese cinema). But in delicacy and finesse the film is worlds removed from most of its predecessors. The camera is mobile, the decor functional, and the painterly mode consistent with director Teinosuke Kinugasa's effort to evoke feudal Japan. The photography of Kohei Sagiyama, the artwork of Kisaku Itho, and the color planning of Sanzo Wada are integrated with each other and unobtrusively support the dramatic line.

Though formally a picture about civil war, *Gate of Hell* is really about division within the self, conflicting personal allegiances occasioned and symbolized by political strife. Maritoh Endo is first a soldier, then a lover, finally a lover who kills in the name of love. The tragedy that overtakes him results from misapplication of the warrior's code to the courtship of a beautiful woman. Lady Kesa, the object of his affections, personifies the tension within his own system of values. Early in the film he sees her simply as booty won in battle, a trophy to which his samurai courage fully entitles him. Later, under the pressure of tortuous psychic growth, he will be forced to acknowledge her personhood, her participation in a sacred network of human relations which encompasses her home and her husband. Bewildered and humiliated, he is eventually caught in an impasse which compels him to resign from the world of action, giving up both love and war to live the life of a Buddhist monk. Moritoh's dilemma is dramatized not only in the color progression of the film but also in its close integration with more general aspects of composition.

The development of the film is marked by progressive desaturation of the colors and a gradual darkening of the scenes. On first appearance, Lady Kesa wears red, the royal disguise she dons to divert attention from a threatened princess. This is the costume she is wearing when Moritoh becomes fatally infatuated with her beauty. That she should be falsely (and a bit extravagantly) garbed is most significant, for Moritoh doesn't see her as she really is. We next find her wearing peach, a color that holds enough red to preserve thematic and pictorial continuity, but which also points up the reserve of her true nature. Eventually, even the pastels are bleached away: at her death Lady Kesa is clothed in white. As with costume, so with decor. There is richness in the color of the early scenes, closely imitated from twelfth-century Japanese painting. The battles reek of red and violet, while the harshness of these colors is balanced by bright pinks and translucent blues. These are the colors of the aristocratic culture in which Moritoh feels most at home. As he intrudes upon Lady Kesa's domain, though, the stage appointments shift to brown and amber. The light of day is also gradually extinguished. Although brightness revives momentarily in the tournament scene where Moritoh vanquishes Lady Kesa's husband, lamplight and moonlight key most of the later scenes.

These adjustments of light and color are intricately related to other aspects of composition. While the scene darkens it also grows more still. The opening sequences are charged with movement — swirling smoke, billowing streamers, flowing curtains, rushing carriages. The camera pans and tracks, following the battle formations of rival armies or the swordplay of individual combatants. Such mobility evokes the activist world of the samurai, where boldness and physical power carry the day. But as peace is restored the camera rests more quietly on its tripod while the subjects themselves lose much of their plasticity. Fixed screens and heavy drapes replace fluid curtains; columns and pillars complete the architectural backdrop. There is more sitting than standing; men walk rather than run. In this environment, Moritoh's blunt strength seems inappropriate; he hesitates, stalls, stumbles. The violence he works upon Lady Kesa is anticipated when he clumsily smashes her musical instrument. As events gather to climax, the stage is as bereft of movement as it is barren of color.

Acting in near darkness, Moritoh stabs Lady Kesa by mistake; his last "move" has proved another misstep. When he then submits himself to judgment, the low-key light reduces all hues to black and white, just as he and his unspeaking accuser are fixed in immobile postures. At this point, color, gesture, and theme are perfectly fused, wordlessly implying that Moritoh has exhausted all options but one.

While the Japanese looked further into the epic possibilities of color, the French in the 1950s put it to other purposes, still lavishly theatrical in *The Golden Coach* (1953) and *Lola Montes*, but comic and super-modernist in *Mon Oncle* (1958). One of the most important colorist efforts of this decade, however, was the musical adaptation of *Black Orpheus* (1960), which brought brief fame to its director Marcel Camus. Though still using color to designate an "exotic" subject (the setting is Rio de Janeiro at carnival time), this film is among the first to prefer bold, striking hues to the far more familiar pastels. It is an approach to color which allows the musical to carry more substance than we normally associate with this genre. The manner in which color is used supports both the mood of the picture and the Orphean myth behind it.

Transferring the legend of Orpheus and Eurydice to modern Rio de Janeiro, *Black Orpheus* depicts the cycle of life, death, and rebirth amid the gala festivities of spring carnival. In asking the musical genre to carry more freight than froth, Camus draws heavily upon the resources of color to render nuances of tone and meaning. Blending a natural setting with highly formal decor and ornament, he establishes a credible context for the magic and mystery of primitive myth.

The colors of *Black Orpheus* are deliberately garish, as if cameraman Jean Bourgoin had vowed to subvert facile harmonies for the sake of a more ambitious design. Technicolor clichés are rebuffed at the earliest opportunity as, in the opening sequence, a vivid orange kite is "mismatched" against the rich blue of Rio's sky. This substitutes the "found" colors of the real world for the manipulated chroma of the studio. And in so doing, it also foreshadows, though without a trace of artificial symbolism, the elements of contrast, paradox, and conflict which are basic to the film. The kite soars on the wind, then plunges, apparently to its death, just as the festival it represents is short-lived, and the passions the carnival engenders either dissolve into everyday routine or lead to the catastrophe of Orpheus and Eurydice. As if to imply this analogy, the camera follows the kite downward, forcing us to turn our eyes down to the city, where the fate of the lovers will now be played out.

The costumes of *Black Orpheus,* while respecting certain predictable associations, get beyond convention in relating individuals to mythic roles. Appropriate to his station as lord of light, a position his musical skills entitle him to assume in the carnival procession, Orpheus wears the color gold, which harmonizes reasonably well with the bright orange gown of Myra, his would-be fiancée and official partner in the dance. They are, the colors seem to say, suited to one another, though only at the ordinary level of shared interests and sexuality. Eurydice wears white in her first appearance, perhaps suggesting purity (as opposed to Myra's relentless passion). But the white dress of Eurydice also connects her with the moon, making her the polar opposite of Orpheus, the sun king, and fitting her to play "Queen of the Night" in the ensuing festivities. By rejecting Myra for Eurydice, Orpheus opts for the alien, the mysterious, and the nocturnal, epitomized in the blue and white scarf of zodiacal signs Eurydice brings from her native city to bestow upon her lover. When Orpheus wraps the scarf around his neck while dancing with Eurydice, its color and design seem seriously at odds with the rest of his attire, though this clash of colors perfectly expresses the strangeness and specialness she brings into his life. Another effective touch in the costuming is to clothe Eurydice's unknown assailant in black and white. He wears a skeleton suit (how obvious, yet how natural during carnival time!) whose austerity sets him apart chromatically from the rainbow hues of the other revelers.

The further color decor of *Black Orpheus* is remarkable for its strategic withholding and gradual release of the color red. Though the early scenes are replete with bright colors, there is little if any cardinal or crimson, which leaves these hues in reserve to fulfill later symbolic functions. The first strong red appears as an out-of-focus light bulb suspended in the background as Orpheus and Eurydice dance together. Changing camera angles slowly bring this lamp more directly over the heads of the lovers, associating its red glow with their burgeoning affection and the danger this ushers into their lives.

After Myra reveals Eurydice's identity to her assailant, the reds intrude more often and more ominously. Those arranged by the makeup department sometimes lack subtlety, like the bloodstains Benedito incurs trying to protect Eurydice. But there is great visual dexterity in the red fill light and red key light used for several later scenes. Red beacons enflame an otherwise dark sky as Orpheus first comes face to face with the skeleton-costumed assassin. The foreground lighting is realistic, but the skyscape background is eerie and bizarre. The death of Eurydice is done with red key light in a completely expressionistic mode; the red emergency lamps of the electric power station provide the only light as Orpheus searches fitfully for Eurydice, then accidentally electrocutes her. Red key light also sets the tone for the descent into Hades, first on the part of Eurydice, as she is carried to the morgue through the red-illumined corridors of a long tunnel, then Orpheus, as he begins his pursuit of her, winding down the deep stairwell of the Missing Persons Bureau toward the faint red blur of exit lights on the lower floors. In each of these scenes, however, the conventionally diabolist connotations of the color are muted by its assimilation into a completely credible lighting scheme. We travel to Hades and back without ever leaving the streets and stairways of Rio. Evoked with scrupulous moderation, the expressionistic reds of *Black Orpheus* tie together the mythic and the human order.

CONTEMPORARY INNOVATIONS IN COLOR

The available-light approach to color photography. Robert Surtees' "prefogging" in The Graduate. *Expressionistic color filtration in* 2001: A Space Odyssey. *Subjectivist uses of color:* Red Desert. *Various special color effects:* King Murray, Butch Cassidy, Allures.

Few films use color better than *Black Orpheus,* but in the 1960s many began to use it differently, working outside traditional genres and investigating new techniques. Alfred Hitchcock had disturbed precedent in the fifties when he turned to the color idiom for ghoulish melodramas like *Rope* (1948), but the photography of such films was not distinguished enough to set style. The new look in color films comes in the middle sixties, waiting upon faster, more fine-grained stocks and the will of imaginative directors and cameramen. The pictures of this decade are marked by more use of nonstudio settings, wider tolerance of low-key and high-contrast illumination, more dependence upon filtration, "light-fogging," and compensatory development. There is no calculated assault on the traditional color genres; they simply disappear in the presence of a more thoroughgoing naturalism.

One consequence of the new stocks (improved Eastmancolor is a characteristic type) is the effort to import into color photography the available-light approach used so effectively with panchrome in the fifties and sixties. Shooting for Godard, Raoul Coutard sought to give certain sequences of *Contempt* (1963) the same studied plainness that distinguishes *Shoot the Piano Player.* The results are interesting, though not completely satisfactory. We get grime instead of glamor, which is precisely the intention of director and cameraman. But sometimes, when it turns really dark, we may get a stronger impression of underexposure than of authentic night. Coutard seems to have confessed failure in abandoning this tack toward color in the later pictures he has shot for Godard, Truffaut, and Costa-Gavras. Probably the more fruitful treatment of low-light color is the one Robert Surtees adopted for Mike Nichols in *The Graduate* (1967). This involves two processes that are rapidly becoming standard practice in the handling of marginal light — "prefogging" and "hyperdevelopment."

Surtees brought to *The Graduate* the orthodox A.S.C. bias toward balanced, well-lit color, but he recognized that the picture might gain something by deviating from formula. "It wasn't long," he says in a recent interview, "before I realized that to put Mike's concept of the story onto film visually, many of the things that had seemed like good technique over the years would have to be cast aside.[12] General sharpness is one of the things pitched overboard, in spite of Surtees' awareness that "the standard of excellence in cinematography had come to mean the sharpest possible image and the greatest depth of field." But this recklessness with precedent was correct, since *The Graduate* isn't a "sharp" picture. It's about a mixed-up, minibrained adolescent who drifts in and out of a love affair with an older woman before finally winning a footrace to claim the girl he really cares for. In a moment of inspiration Surtees grasped how the picture should be shot: "How wonderful it would be to obtain *a sense of semi-reality* [my italics] with dramatic overtones in the photography." Right. And he gained this fuzziness of "semi-reality" by occasionally prefogging the negative.

Prefogging, or light-fogging, is a kind of double exposure. Before being used in the normal way, the negative is exposed to about 20 percent of its sensitivity either to white light or light of some particular hue. This reduces the light required in the ensuing exposure (hence its value in low-light situations), though it impairs the resolution of the image. Prefogging also color-tones the photography, since white light gives everything a kind of milky appearance while colored light alters hue in much the same way as a filter. In *The Graduate*, Surtees prefogs in both white and amber light, using the one to suggest the coldness of psychic withdrawal and the other for the warmth of renewed human contact.

White-light fog is used in the underwater sequence of *The Graduate* in which Benjamin, donning flippers and goggles, flees to the bottom of the family swimming pool, presumably to escape the overbearing camaraderie of his parents and their circle of friends. As the camera assumes his point of view, the world becomes a gloomy blur, shimmering but indistinct, agitated by the motion of the water and toned in a bilious, washed-out green. While the metaphor of diving reflects Benjamin's introversion and retreat, the color quality of the image indicates the psychic cost of his escapism. He has ducked away from the plastic gewgaws of suburbia but only to set himself adrift in a turbid world of ghastly color and uncertain shapes. We are not surprised that he must soon come up for air.

The tone of the scene at the discotheque is quite different, largely because the color key is set by the amber light fog that supports the visible sources of illumination. Here Benjamin is neither entwined in the embrace of Mrs. Robinson nor trapped at the bottom of the pool. He is with a girl of his own age and temperament, and though they do not yet see themselves as lovers Benjamin seems far more outgoing than on earlier occasions. The images are still murky — faces flash and

[12] This and the further citations of Surtees are from his interview in *American Cinematographer* (February 1968), pp. 172 ff.

fade to the pulse of strobe light. But the atmosphere is noticeably warmer, even if the dancers get lost in the shadows. By using amber instead of white light for prefogging, Surtees achieves a mood closer to romantic intimacy than narcissistic isolation.

This latter scene also illustrates the use of hyperdevelopment. Shooting in a real discotheque instead of a studio mock-up, Surtees avoids adding artificial fill light, which might destroy the naturalness of the take by reminding the nonactors that they are on-camera. To compensate for underexposure, he not only prefogs the negative but also subjects it to extra-long immersion in the developing chemicals. This process, usually called "pushing" the stock, brightens the image enough to make it legible, though again at the expense of sharpness. Hyperdevelopment works no substantial change upon color quality (except for a slight tendency to merge shades of the same color with one another) but may, as in this case, make it possible to shoot in lighting situations that would otherwise be prohibitive.

The color photography of the 1960s, as even *The Graduate* shows, is less scrupulous than formerly about absolute "correctness" in rendering color. We now expect to see the spectrum adapted to the situation and register no surprise at the lovers with orange faces in *A Man and a Woman* (France, 1966), or the green or purple-tinted rock singers of *Woodstock* (U.S.A., 1970). This is both a cause and a consequence of a new attitude toward filtration. As recently as a decade ago, it was widely believed throughout the film industry that filtered color should be avoided if possible, or used only to restore "normalcy" to exceptional lighting situations. Such thinking created a whole series of "color-correction" filters, used either on the camera or in the printing lab. There was, for example, an amber-tinted filter to match studio stock to the color temperature of daylight; conversely, there was a blue-tinted filter to match daylight stock to the tungsten illumination of the studio. There were other filters calculated to rectify imbalances in one of the primary colors — a magenta (blue-red) filter to neutralize excessive green; a cyan (green-blue) filter to control red; and a yellow (red-green) filter to suppress blue. These were intended to facilitate color matching, so that it would be possible to give every scene of a picture, whether shot at dawn or dusk, on the Pathé sound stage or in the Swiss Alps, the same look of homogeneous accuracy. Only in the last few years have colorists of the cinema begun to apply the wisdom of the impressionists, at last recognizing that normalcy in the perception of color is largely a subjective illusion. White is contaminated by yellow in late afternoon sunshine and turns blue in the open shade, especially at high elevations. And if such departures are not distortions, then perhaps the cinematographer should be free to invent his own palette as occasion dictates. This insight is what prompts such light-filtered extravaganzas as *2001: A Space Odyssey* (U.S.A., 1968).

The spectacular color effects of *2001* are chiefly the work of director Stanley Kubrick, who is a talented photographer and technician. For the last episode of the film, where the surviving astronaut penetrates the atmosphere of Jupiter, Kubrick decided to use "correction" filters not to restore normal color but to pull the colors as far as possible away from normalcy. The landscapes are known and familiar — the Grand Canyon and Monument Valley in the American West, the coast of the Hebrides northwest of Scotland. It is the unnatural light tones that give them their strangeness, their aura of magic and mystery. Snowdrifts and floating icebergs lose their true color under layers of magenta and cyan filtration. They defy recognition, just as do the canyons and crags we should recognize from innumerable westerns. But intercut with strange sunbursts of light and continuously agitated by thrusts of the zoom lens, these sights seem the contours of another planet, or perhaps the anchor points of consciousness itself.

Though a favorite of trip-hungry adolescents, this scene is more than a dazzling light show. It is the carefully orchestrated finale to a picture that from the outset has made good use of color.

We have watched a color progression that begins in the full-spectrum warmth of the prehuman world and then moves through the cold whites of space-age architecture to the deep blacks of the interplanetary void. The color scheme seems an analogue for the loss of affective life that has accompanied the development of man's technology. Astringent white walls form the backdrop for the abrupt cold-war courtesies that mark Soviet-American relations, and the astronauts, amid an even more austere color decor, seem little inclined to say anything at all. During the voyage to Jupiter, color is provided mostly by the red glow of Hal, the computer which has been programmed to register emotion and which, significantly, registers a great deal more than either of his two human companions. But after Dave ends the reign of the machine by disconnecting the computer, the energy of the unconscious comes flooding back on a tide of exuberant color. At one point, a judicious choice of angle shows us this play of lights upon the plastic face mask of the astronaut, as if they were burning through his insulating rationalism to impress themselves upon the inner core of his personality.

But not every advance in the use of color depends upon a new technology, or even the novel application of processes already available. Much innovation is conceptual, not mechanical. The colorist work of director Antonioni is a case in point. When this director first turned to color in *Red Desert* (1964), he was admittedly ignorant of technique and suspicious of what the lab might do to the colors he saw on the set. He seems hardly to have trusted even his cameraman, though in Gianni di Venanzo he had one of the best then practicing in Europe. "I tried," he tells Godard in their famous *Cahiers* interview, "to put the colors I wanted on the things themselves, on the landscapes. . . . After that, what I demanded from the laboratory was a faithful reproduction of the effects I had obtained." [13] No filters, no light fog, no special processing — just a canister of spray paint. This doesn't seem promising, but *Red Desert* is a milestone in colorist cinema, simply because its director thought of the film as a learning experience. At every stage of composition we find him reappraising the aesthetics of color: "I perceived that certain camera movements didn't always jell with it: a rapid panoramic sweep is efficacious on brilliant red, but it does nothing for a sour green. . . ." Or again: "With color, you don't use the same lenses," an offhand remark whose casualness conceals the fact that Antonioni changed his whole shooting style for this picture. For everything up through *The Eclipse* (1962), he had been an unfailing devotee of short-lens, deep-field composition. Now, working in color, he suddenly shifts to long lenses, using their lack of field depth to portray the frayed and deranged consciousness of the neurotic Giuliana. It is Antonioni the artist, not the engineer, who sees the relevance of soft-focus color to *Red Desert*.

Antonioni's use of selective focus in *Red Desert* is fully consonant with his subjectivist treatment of color. Giuliana typically does not see the intricate patterns and sharp bounding lines of the urban world because she is helplessly estranged from its precision and mechanical exactitude. It is this same frustration in the face of this incomprehensible urban tangle that causes the vegetables in the vendor's stall to turn gray as she stares at them. Ironically, the focus is clearest and the color most attractive in the scene where the heroine fantasizes herself nestled away on a South Seas island. Here, as choral singing replaces dissonant electronic noise, Giuliana is no longer afraid to let her eyes focus. What she sees, of course, is a kind of Technicolor paradise, full of rich, saturated blues, light-reflectant greens, and wet rocks that glow with roseate warmth. If only these were real! But this distraught woman, whose vision is sharp only when she dreams, must go back to confront the world of everyday, and in that world, unfortunately, the bright colors are those of poisonous gases belching from factory chimneys. Knowing this, she can scarcely keep the outlines of the modern industrial complex in steady focus. In fact, she is hardly safe in her own apartment. When she is seduced there by a business associate of her husband, the walls of the room go fuzzy and change colors to match the flood and ebb of her uncertain sexual passion. Without crossing any remarkable technical frontiers, director and cameraman in *Red Desert* managed to use color with remarkable fluidity and suggestiveness.

[13] This and the further citations of Antonioni are from his interview reprinted in *Interviews with Film Directors*, ed. Andrew Sarris (New York: The Bobbs-Merrill Company, Inc., 1967), pp. 3–11.

Now that color is becoming the dominant medium in the cinema, we can hope that directors and cameramen will feel challenged to use it purposefully and imaginatively. Just as there is no "correct" way to handle panchrome, neither is there an absolutely right approach to color. The seasick green of unfiltered fluorescent illumination works well for *King Murray* (U.S.A., 1969), where the unwholesome hue it imparts to certain sequences agrees completely with the garish pushiness of the insurance-huckster hero. The subtle bronze tints of the laboratory fit the mood of *Butch Cassidy and the Sundance Kid* (U.S.A., 1969), pulling the picture away from realism and toward the quaintness of a nineteenth-century tintype. On the other hand, the futuristic look of *Allures* (U.S.A., 1961) is caught equally well in the color tones, where the use of infrared stock turns the green of grass and trees into an utterly otherworldly magenta. These approaches suggest the range of options now available to the filmmaker who seeks a color palette in harmony with his own special way of seeing.

Unfortunately, not everyone in the medium yet appreciates this potential. Though stocks, lighting rigs, and laboratory processes have far outstripped the facilities of the Technicolor corporation, many filmmakers still think like the Kalmuses. As is so often the case in the cinema, technology is running considerably ahead of art.

List of Films Discussed

ALLURES 8 min. PYR
BIRTH OF A NATION 193 min. AUD-BRA, MMA
BLACK NARCISSUS 101 min. WRS
BLACK ORPHEUS 103 min. JAN
BUTCH CASSIDY AND THE SUNDANCE KID 112 min. FNC
CABINET OF DR. CALIGARI, THE 50 min. JAN
DRUMS ALONG THE MOHAWK 105 min. FNC
GATE OF HELL 86 min. JAN, TWY
GRADUATE, THE 105 min. AVCO
GREED 150 min. FNC
KING MURRAY 65 min. EYR
NOSFERATU 60 min. MMA, JAN
ODD MAN OUT 117 min. CON, JAN
RED DESERT 116 min. AUD-BRA
SHANGHAI EXPRESS 84 min. UNI
SHOOT THE PIANO PLAYER 92 min. JAN
2001: A SPACE ODYSSEY 139 min. FNC (restricted circulation)

4
SOUND

The synchronized sound track came late to motion pictures, forcing itself upon the achieved aesthetics of the silent screen like a raucous in-
terloper at a party of intimate friends. Eager for attention, it crowded
out all the versatile arrangements for improvised sound production that
for at least two decades had been supplied by everything from the
tinny player piano to the incomparable Wurlitzer organ. Some critics
have hardly been able to forgive this noisy technological intrusion, for
while it allowed Jolson to sing and Garbo to talk it also encouraged
countless directors to neglect the craft of the camera. But sound has its
own aesthetic, and the faults of the early sound film were lapses of
artistic judgment more than inherent limitations of the medium. Once
the camera got out of its soundproof cage and directors got over their
obsession with synchronized voices, it soon became possible to achieve
memorable effects with music, noise, and speech. Such effects involve
increasingly more sophisticated techniques of sound generation, sound
recording, sound mixing, and in some cases sound transmission.

BASIC
TECHNOLOGY

The concept of a sound score. Integration and orchestration of noise. Systems of sound recording. Disc sound. Optical sound. Magnetic sound. Sound mixing.

We tend to assume that screen sounds are "real," just as we sometimes make similarly naive assumptions about photography. Yet in each case there is an element of artifice. Obviously killers do not stalk their victims to the accompaniment of sinister bass chords, and singers can't really vocalize while they are turning handsprings. Perhaps not so obviously, plane crashes and car wrecks do not really sound like they do on the screen. They too must be shaped and organized—"scored," we might say, for volume, pitch, tempo, and duration that fits a particular scene. Even the human voice may be altered — deepened to sound more virile or lifted for a more feminine pitch — if such strategy contributes to the dramatic design.

What, for instance, is the sound sequence of an automobile accident? It involves the screech of rubber, the thud of impact, the grunt of sprung metal, and the spill of shattered glass. Each of these cues may carry over into a film to tell us that two cars have collided somewhere beyond the drawn blinds of the heroine's apartment. But with several differences. The whine of the tires is almost certain to be lengthened and the pitch perhaps raised, both to attract our attention and build up a bit of suspense. The nastiest crashes in real life occur when neither driver has a chance to touch his brakes, but those introduced by squealing tires *sound* nastier on the screen. Also, the noise of impact will be changed — muted, in fact, since the true sound level of a collision would be so loud in relation to the other secondary noises that the two sets of sounds could not be incorporated into the same recording. Even the technique of "wild sound recording," now much used in documentary, where the sound man utilizes real noises from the real world, still allows for a sound mix which will adjust the noise levels from various tracks. Just as lenses and film stocks do not have the eye's tolerance for an almost infinitely great variation in the intensity of light, so microphones lack the ear's capability to handle almost infinitely great variations in the intensity of sound.

Finally, there would have to be some reshaping of the postimpact sounds, probably raising the volume and extending the duration of the noise that represents flying glass. Even in this simple example, then, there are questions of sound generation (do we really need to crash two cars together on the set?), sound recording (at what level should the volume be adjusted to pick up each of the several noises?), and sound mixing (shouldn't there be some other street noises or perhaps apartment noises, to blend with the sounds of the crash?). When so many decisions are involved in approximately five seconds of an extremely simple sound take like this one, imagine the sound programming connected with a whole battle sequence — say, the raid on Pearl Harbor from *Tora! Tora! Tora!* (U.S.A., 1969) or the D-day landing in *The Longest Day* (U.S.A., 1962).

The most important technical factor in the sound system of cinema is the recording process. How is sound pulled out of the air and permanently fastened to a strip of celluloid? This may be done in several ways, which vary in cost, convenience, and quality. Historically, the film world has known three recording systems, two of which have now disappeared as primary recording techniques, though they still play a role in the later stages of sound reproduction. Filmmakers of today almost always record sound *magnetically*, as is the case when one uses a tape recorder. But sound can also be recorded *mechanically* (like a phonograph), as it was in the earliest days of sound cinema, or it may be recorded *photographically*, as was the case during the 1930s and 1940s, and still is today in the final stage of production when a picture is being prepared for release to the theaters. Naturally the various systems of recording have had considerable impact upon the treatment of sound in the cinema.

Mechanical sound recording — generally known as "disc sound" — didn't last long enough to give birth to any masterpieces or consolidate any artistic conventions. It was already passing into history by the time Vitaphone and Warner Brothers had finished counting the gate receipts from *The Jazz Singer* (1927). So far as fidelity is concerned, there was nothing terribly wrong with the Vitaphone system. In fact, it recorded sound in almost exactly the same manner as a phonograph, connecting a microphone to a mechanical stylus, so that incoming sound waves cut microscopically small notches in the grooves of a circular disc. This encoded the pitch, timbre, and volume of the speaker's voice or the musician's instrument. The problem with Vitaphone was that it produced a sound track independent of the film itself, in other words, a separate package which had to be shipped to the theatre along with the film, while everyone hoped that both would arrive in the same place at the same time. Naturally there are horror stories from the early days of the industry about sound tracks for sentimental romances arriving with picture tracks for gangster films, but these logistical difficulties could perhaps have eventually been solved. The problem that couldn't be solved was one of continuous in-theatre synchronization.

What happens when the stylus skips a groove on the disc while the picture is in progress? Under these circumstances it was virtually impossible to restore the interlock between sound and picture. For these reasons sound-on-disc persists today only in the intermediate stages of re-recording, where its instant replay capability gives it an advantage over all other systems of sound transcription.

Photographic sound recording — generally called "optical sound" — is a little more complicated and a little less sensitive than the disc system, but much better suited to the cinema. It is a "sound-on-film" process, which eventually joins sound track to picture track in a single 35mm release print. In this system — introduced to the industry around 1930 with Fox's Movietone and RCA's Phonophone — sound waves are transformed into light waves. The light waves make a carefully controlled exposure on a special kind of film stock known as a "sound negative." This photographic imprint can then be condensed and transferred to the picture track, where it is printed as a "sound stripe" and runs in continuous synchronization with the picture. Optical recording reclaims in convenience and economy what it inevitably sacrifices in fidelity. It was the exclusive method of sound recording and transmission for more than two decades and was the technology to which all filmmakers of the 1930s and 1940s accommodated their creative experiments. Today optical sound remains the standard means for actually putting sound into the theater, since few movie houses are equipped to handle magnetic sound tracks.

Magnetic sound recording has been since the early 1950s the primary recording process throughout the film industry. In this system, soundwaves input from a microphone (or a cluster of mikes) imprint a recording upon the magnetized ferrous-oxide surface of an acetate tape. This process achieves fidelity unknown in optical sound, hence finer definition of music as well as more careful discrimination of voice timbre or wild noise. It adds to this improved fidelity a mobility and ease of replay beyond that of optical sound. Magnetic recording also facilitates stereophonic transmission, when theater hookups allow for the use of magnetic release prints (as most do not). The richest rewards of magnetic recording, however, have been reaped in documentary filmmaking, whose renaissance since 1960 was made possible only by further breakthroughs in magnetic recording, such as videotaping and a more complex process known as "crystal-sync" recording. These various advantages seem to dictate that magnetic recording will retain its central place in today's cinema.

Unsurprisingly, the development of sound recording has a continuing effect upon related techniques of sound generation and sound mixing, two other processes that bear heavily upon the art of sound. More sensitive recording has obviated some techniques made others possible.

As to the generation of sound, the relatively crude microphones and somewhat insensitive sound negatives of the 1930s dictated that sound should be produced in the studio, giving rise to an "effects bank" that included fire noises made from crinkled cellophane, hoofbeats tapped out with hollow shells, and a rich assortment of bells, buzzers, and squeaky-door sounds. But the fine-grain sound negatives of the late thirties, the magnetic tapes of the next decade, and the supersensitive mikes of today have made many of these effects obsolete. The danger of crinkling cellophane in the presence of a first-rate recording system is that it begins to sound more like crinkling cellophane than like the Chicago fire. Loss is gain, however, since the sophistication of equipment has also allowed the sound man access to a much richer array of authentic noises. The modern effects bank puts at his disposal everything from the cry of high-flying geese to the undersea murmurs of the humpback whale. Of course, sound is still induced artificially, probably more often than the average theatergoer realizes, but now such effects are more often achieved by echo chambers, reverberators, filters, and electronic noise generators than by the thunder-and-lightning machines of the 1930s.

The last crucial feature of sound transmission is the mixer, a device which electrically merges and blends the sounds recorded by different microphones, often in completely different places or at quite different times. Even the simplest finished sound track requires a series of "mixes," which establish the proper level for each set of sounds in a particular scene. Imagine, for example, a supper-club dance. To score the scene, we will need a background of orchestral music and incidental dinner noises, each of which will be recorded separately (musicians generally not relishing the prospect of an "effects man" rattling spoons at them while they play their violins). These rival sounds must then be combined, making the plate, cup, and silverware noises strong enough to convince us we are dining in a restaurant and not a sound studio, yet not so prominent as to absolutely disturb the musical performance. At the same time, both of these incidental noises will have to be subordinated to conversational voices which presumably carry the dramatic thrust of the scene. These will almost certainly come from another sound track which must be added to the previous mix. And if other, illegible voices are to be included for the sake of realism, the sound man will again be at the mixer working out an even more delicate balance between noise, mood music, conversational static, and audible voice. The absence of mixing equipment is what forced performers in the earliest sound films to huddle around a single microphone; the sophistication of today's mixers is what allows the controlled mergence of so wide an array of ever more complex sound effects.

THE SOUNDS OF SILENCE

Role of the organ in silent cinema. Efforts to re-create live sound. Stan Kann's organ concerts for The Hunchback of Notre Dame *and* Phantom of the Opera. *Implicit sound notation in silent film:* Greed, October, Strike. *René Clair and* Two Timid People.

ilmmakers realized from the beginning that sight and sound were intimately connected and that motion pictures required implicit sound effects. They littered their comedies with broken china and mangled fenders, while the heavier dramatic pieces were invariably punctuated by the screams of distraught heroines. Sound effects such as these were typically treated in close-ups, the emphatic visual notation compensating for the absence of true sound. Remember, too, that though the screen was silent the theater was not. Live musicians improvised sound scores to mimic the crash of plates, the roar of cannons, and the high-pitched terror of leading ladies. Nor were these effects exclusively musical. The effects panels on some of the picture-palace organs could generate a repertoire of sounds almost as elaborate as the studio noise of the 1930s. They had car horns for traffic jams, train whistles for hairbreadth escapes, and could whine and swoosh as wind or wave might dictate.

Organists and orchestras of the silent era also gave the cinema its first stereophonic effects. These would not again become commercially possible before the middle 1950s, when the CinemaScope system introduced multiple magnetic sound tracks as a further embellishment to its wide-screen look. This allowed thunderstorms to begin rumbling in the back of the theater before clouds actually covered the sun, just as it let contending armies in battle exchange artillery fire from the left to the right side of the screen. Audiences marveled at this "new" realism, and sound engineers congratulated themselves on having at last overcome the handicaps of monaural, unidirectional sound. But there was nothing remarkable about such achievements when the live orchestras of the 1920s were on hand to move sound around the theater, enhancing the audience's sense of envelopment and participation. The organ, too, had stereophonic capability, since its pipes were typically arranged to the right and left of the screen toward the front, yet not quite at the front of the auditorium. Performers of the silent era had only to touch the stops of their Wurlitzers to produce noises that were quite literally

SOUND IN THE SILENT ERA. Before the age of optical or magnetic sound, which solidly anchored sound to picture, music and effects were supplied in theatre by the cinema organ, a versatile source of live, stereophonic sound. Witness the prominence of the organ in the Granada at Tooting, Mr. Sidney Berstein's 6000-seat London picture palace. The Stills Collection, British Film Institute.

off-screen. When they were sufficiently skillful and imaginative, they could use this capacity to anticipate and foreshadow events about to take place on-screen, just as is done in the magnetic stereo systems of today.

We can still get some feel for the sounds of the silent screen in the performance of musicians like Stan Kann, a "roaring-twenties" buff who has created a whole career for himself doing live organ recitals to accompany silent classics. With his concerts in the Fox Theatre of St. Louis, where he has access to a giant organ that rises up through the floor, Kann has been able to convey much of the richness and intricacy of the sound that belonged to the 1920s picture-palace era. Turning what was once merely a hobby into a serious effort at historical recovery, Kann now introduces his performances in the theater with lectures on his own musical intentions and how these approximate the sound conventions of the silent era. His repertoire includes mood music, mimetic sound, and a variety of leitmotifs associated with particular characters or situations. Although he handles everything from light comedy to Rudolph Valentino romances, Kann has made a specialty of Lon Chaney horror films and has achieved real distinction in improvised effects for *The Hunchback of Notre Dame* (U.S.A., 1923) and *Phantom of the Opera* (U.S.A., 1925).

Both the *Hunchback* and the *Phantom* have musical motifs built into the dramatic structure — the bells of Notre Dame cathedral in the one and the opera itself in the other. This makes it easy for Kann to invent musical themes which convey both the overall orientation of the respective pictures and the individual attitudes of the two Chaney-created protagonists. The *Hunchback* begins with the peal of bells, emanating of course from the church spire, and thus standing for the incongruous religious ecstasy of medieval Christendom that survives the squalor and barbarism of the streets. This paradox is extended as the organ chimes continue into the next several shots where we are introduced to the deformed bell ringer, whose fantastic gyrations and entanglements with the bell rope make possible the sonorous tones we hear. Strapped in a concealed harness that prevents his standing erect, Chaney strikes grotesque postures which are at odds with the rhythmic consistency of the resounding bells. At this point the sound calls attention to one of the film's fundamental ironies. These chimes of the organ, full of power and dissonant energy, are also incorporated into the hunchback's musical theme. Here they are used to counterpoint the smoother melodic line associated with Patsy Ruth Miller, a conventionally frail heroine for whom Chaney must eventually give up his life. Varied in their musical phrasing and mingled with other elements in the improvised score, the chimes express the full range of the protagonist's psychic life, encompassing joy, rage, anxiety, and ultimately suggesting his release from earthly bondage. Such sound is much more than mere "background music."

Kann handles Chaney's theme in *Phantom of the Opera* more as an instrument of suspense, taking advantage of the opportunity the music offers to suggest the phantom's secretive presence. Since the phantom is himself an organist and introduces himself to Christine as "the spirit of music," it is completely appropriate to represent him in musical terms. Adhering to this approach, Kann mixes elements of the phantom's "Don Juan Triumphant" theme into melodies that accompany his furtive movements in the early moments of the film. The organist also uses musical accents along with simulated noise to dramatize the phantom's acts of violence. When the managers of the opera replace the phantom's favorite Christine with a singer of more prestige and reputation, the evil genius who haunts the subterranean passages retaliates by dropping a giant chandelier upon the patrons who attend the evening performance. The crescendo of sound called forth by this melee includes not only organ-generated cries but also recognizably musical chords whose fierce dissonances again draw our attention to "the spirit of music." They also anticipate the chords that come in the climactic scene where the phantom reveals himself physically to Christine.

Lured to his haunts beneath the opera and awed by his performance upon the organ, the heroine cannot resist the temptation to unmask her unknown admirer. Her horror at the discovery of his disfigurement interrupts his improvised concert and introduces shrieking dissonances that call to mind the fall of the chandelier. The sound link thus connects the psychic violence done to the heroine with the physical violence that precedes and foreshadows it. Furthermore, the connection is symbolically functional, since the respective events express a perversion of the phantom's distinctly human need to love and be loved in return. Though it would be wrong to imagine every film of the silent era was graced with sound effects as fluid as these (many theatres, after all, had only a tinny piano) Kann's concerts remind us of the potential of the medium prior to the advent of synchronized sound-on-film.

Inasmuch as early filmmakers often had sound resources at their disposal, they were prone to write musical (and other aural) notations into their visuals. It was relatively easy, for example, to indicate the timbre suitable to a particular occasion. A cut to a trumpet instructed the local organist to use brass chords; a shot of a violin meant that strings seemed more appropriate. Such shots might either be part of the dramatic framework of the film or play a purely metaphoric role.

The sound cue is part of the literal action in *Greed,* where cameraman Daniels irises in upon McTeague's accordion while he is serenading Trina. But there is obviously no need to phase out the accordion music the moment the instrument itself leaves the screen. Clearly, its notes and timbre are meant not merely as incidental stage business but as the hallmark of the whole relationship between McTeague and the girl he is wooing. The music stands for McTeague's sentimentality, his lower middle-class romanticism, and as such it might properly be intoned through all the scenes of his courtship. Eisenstein asks for music in much the same way during one scene of *October* (U.S.S.R., 1927). Less committed to surface realism, however, he introduces harps and balalaikas without any literal motivation. The Mensheviks are speaking, downgrading Lenin and pleading for the survival of Kerensky's Provisional Government. Eisenstein wants to tell us they are woolly-headed buffoons, lacking contact with basic political realities. But instead of scripted inserts full of platitudes and clichés, we get musical cuts to instruments which symbolize unearthly idealism (don't angels play harps?) and leisure-loving rusticity. Undoubtedly, the dulcet tones and facile harmonies of this music undercut the ideology of the Mensheviks more effectively than synchronized voice could ever have done. If we actually heard speech or read script, we would be tempted to give the Mensheviks some attention. As it stands, their cause dies with the final pluck of harp strings.

The silent cinema succeeded best when speech did not seem called for and when moods or effects might be credibly assimilated into music. Hence the piano treble that tells us the heroine is enjoying her romp through the woods or the clash of cymbals that describes a comic collision. But the most imaginative directors, like Eisenstein, and especially France's René Clair, found more subtle ways to imply sound through scene.

One helpful approach is through an analogy with motion. Moving things tend to make noise; objects at rest tend to be silent. Eisenstein achieves an interesting variation upon this approach in *Strike* through shots of a factory whistle, used to call workers to the lockstep routine of their jobs. Several times in the early scenes of the picture we watch the whistle discharge its jet of steam. In addition to suggesting a shrill, unpleasant cry, the image contributes to the metaphor of pressure, the sense of pent-up hostilities that finally drives the workers from their jobs. Later, as we are invited to look at the whistle after the strike is underway, we notice its remarkable stillness. Not only are there no bursts of steam, but birds are roosting on the whistle, idly resting from flight just as the workers are casually taking their ease in the woods and fields. Eisenstein's ability to convey both the sense of sound and the sense of its extinction is surely one of the major achievements of the silent years.

There is even greater virtuosity, however, in the implicit sound effects Clair creates in *Two Timid People,* a comic masterpiece of the late 1920s. Like all of Clair's comedies this one is full of popping firecrackers and butter-fingered chambermaids. But there is also an effort to make mime and camera movement give voice to the voiceless. In one scene from this picture he renders the content, pace, and tenor of speech without recourse to a single descriptive title or a single onomatopoetic sound.

In this instance we are treated to the rhetorical performance of Fremissin, a novice lawyer defending an indefensible client. Pleading his first case the lawyer has concocted an absurdly sentimental story to exonerate the vicious wife-beater Giradoux. We know his speech is fabricated because the director has already shown us what really happened. And after the dutiful rustling of papers which hints at Fremissin's careful rehearsal, we settle back to admire his ingenuity. What follows, however, is not just the fairly predictable pseudoflashback which translates the speech into a fictitious dramatic scene. By changing the running speed of the camera or freezing the actors into immobile postures, Clair conveys both the pace of the presentation and the mental lapses into which it eventually dissolves.

With the camera running at normal speed, we see the lawyer's glowing account of the defendant's behavior. Giradoux is not a villain, he is a model husband. He smiles to his wife from the doorway, then trips graciously across the room to kiss her on both cheeks. Soon he has propped up her feet on a pillow and moved to the window to serenade her on his violin. Fremissin's speech clearly is going very well. But he is interrupted at this point by a stray mouse in the courtroom and never regains his composure. He starts the speech over, repeating each detail, but the movement is unnaturally accelerated, suggesting that he speaks with undue haste. And beyond a certain point, unhappily, Fremissin can't remember the script. We get the smile, the kisses, the pillow, but as Giradoux starts toward the window to begin the violin serenade he stalls in midstep. The speaker's memory has failed him. The scene is repeated again, this time at a still more frenzied pace, but cut short at the same point. Finally the camera is running in reverse, producing a jerky, unintelligible conglomeration of pillows, kisses, and smiles, while miming Fremissin's effort to recover the argument he has mentally mislaid. In thus sensing the communicative power of the purely visual, Clair had a substantial lead over most of his contemporaries when sound was finally added to celluloid.

THE AGE OF OPTICAL SOUND

n its nearly foolproof system of synchronic recording and transmission, the optical sound track offered the cinema an irresistible package of sound and image. Although the new technology gave up the richness of live organ or piano music, it gained the precision of the spoken word, and with it the possibility of more complex plots and more psychologically intricate motives. Yet the early talkies were not everything one might have hoped for. Lacking efficient mixers and multimicrophone hookups, the new recording system forced characters to huddle together in front of the mike, while the camera had to be so elaborately soundproofed that it lost its mobility.

Besides these technical difficulties (which were solved sooner than some people realize), filmmakers soon found that talking pictures

NOISE AS DRAMATIC INSTRUMENT.
What we hear in the cinema is often
just as important as what we see.
Action films, in particular, have
long depended upon startling sounds
like gunshots and the breaking of
glass to intensify the dramatic tempo,
as in this episode from *Jesse James*.
The Museum of Modern Art/ Film
Stills Archive.

could easily become too talkative. In the early days of the sound film, this realization encouraged the development of genres like musical comedy, which of course made some use of dialogue but which also promoted dancing and choreographic design, thus balancing the aural and visual claims of the film medium. The effort to avoid the tedium of endless speeches was also paramount in the minds of Eisenstein and Sergei Prokofiev when, with the superior sound negatives of the late 1930s, they undertook the more ambitious symphonic score of *Alexander Nevsky*.

The so-called dramatic film matured more slowly in its assimilation of sound, often resorting to overstated musical effects even when it escaped the vice of verbal declamation. In this respect films like *Zero for Conduct* (France, 1932) and *The Criminal Code* (U.S.A., 1931) are exceptions to the tendencies of the times. It was with the maturation of directors like Jean Renoir in France and, even more importantly, Orson Welles in the U.S.A. that the dramatic sound film acquired the same sophistication enjoyed in the 1930s by various musical films.

THE MUSICAL DIMENSION

The musical idiom as an extension of silent-film technique. Interest of various composers in the sound film. Vogue of musical comedy. Collaboration of Georges Auric and René Clair: A Nous, la Liberté. The symphonic film. Collaboration of Eisenstein and Sergei Prokofiev: Alexander Nevsky.

Since the days of *The Jazz Singer* music has proved one of the most dependable staples of the film sound track. Very early in the history of sound recording, the musical score ended the ill-starred reign of the "100 percent talkie," restoring through its lyrical passages the pan, the dolly shot, and the graceful swoop of the overhead crane, all of which had temporarily vanished when sound hit the screen. The centrality of music to the cinema also encouraged studios to perfect techniques of dubbing, mixing, and playback, thus liberating the camera from the tyranny of on-the-spot recording. Though not always composed with finesse or recorded with the highest fidelity, music has remained integral to the film medium, since the fluidity of its phrasing is closely analogous to the endlessly unfolding mutations of the moving image.

The importance of the musical score to sound films of the 1930s and 1940s is reflected in the number of talented composers who brought their skills to the film capitals of the world. While some made only passing contact with the new medium, others came to Moscow, Hollywood, or Paris to launch long careers. In 1930 Dimitri Shostakovitch took leave of his work as a symphonic composer to help inaugurate the Russian sound film; within two years he had completed four sound scores, among them his composition of 1936 for *Maxim Gorki's Return*. Somewhat later, he was followed into the Russian cinema by Sergei Prokofiev, whose scores for *Nevsky* and *Ivan the Terrible* challenged Eisenstein to rethink his conception of montage. In America, two of the kings of Tin Pan Alley, Rodgers and Hammerstein, teamed up quite early in the 1930s with the sophisticated German expatriate Ernst Lubitsch, contributing their music to his pioneering innovations in the sound film. Later Aaron Copeland would try his hand, as would Britain's Walter Leigh, Benjamin Britten, and Ralph Vaughan Williams. French cinema of the 1930s similarly sought the integration of music and effects with camera work, lighting, and pictorial detail. Such integration required and elicited close cooperation between sophisticated directors like René Clair or Jean Vigo and imaginative musicians like Georges Auric and Maurice Jaubert. Although these two composers excelled in various types of musical scores, none are better remembered or more revered than their contributions to musical comedy.

Auric and Jaubert both worked in the 1930s with René Clair, already a versatile director of comedy in the silent twenties and one who quickly grasped the potential of sound. Ironically, it was Clair's reservations about the new medium which made him use it tastefully and discreetly, incorporating into the sound film as much as could profitably be retained from the art of the silent screen.

Before setting out on his career as a director of sound films, Clair had the opportunity to see in London most Hollywood products of the late 1920s. He disliked nearly all of these pictures, especially ones like *Strange Cargo* (1929), faulted for its "interminable spoken scenes, boring for those who do not understand English and unbearable for those who do." [1] Nor did he approve of those sound films which avoided talk by turning to mere noisemaking, "the ticking of a clock, a cuckoo singing the hours, dance-hall applause, a motor-car engine or breaking crockery. . . ." His criticism of such effects, however, is not relentlessly negative. "We must draw a distinction," he concludes, "between those sound effects which are amusing only by virtue of their novelty (which soon wears off), and those that help one to understand the action, and which excite emotions which could not have been raised by the sight of the pictures alone." In other words, sound must be used selectively.

This is why Clair admires *Broadway Melody*, an American musical of 1929. In this picture, he says, "the talking film has for the first time found an appropriate form." The sound interprets the pictures without

---

[1] This and Clair's further remarks upon the sound film are from *Cinema Yesterday and Today*, ed. R. C. Dale and tr. Stanley Appelbaum (New York: Dover Publications, Inc., 1972), pp. 137–139.

redundantly describing events shown on screen. The music not only counterpoints human speech, but like speech arises and expands from a concrete dramatic situation. This is the same strategy that Clair calls to his service in the following year, working with Georges Auric on the much more ambitious sound score of A Nous, la Liberté (1931).

Auric first worked with Clair as an actor in the surrealist comedy Entr'acte (1924), while the musician was quite close to several avant-garde composers, including Darius Milhaud, Arthur Honegger, and the so-called Group of Six. This entire coterie, but Auric in particular, as a disciple of Erik Satie and student of D'Indy's Schola Cantorum, sought to loosen French symphonic music from its melodic, nineteenth-century moorings and connect it with the disruptive tones of dada and surrealism. This tendency of his music is what qualified Auric to do sound scores for Jean Cocteau. But Auric also respected street music and cabaret songs, which is the idiom most in evidence in his work for Clair. In A Nous, la Liberté Auric occasionally flirts with bizarre accents and consistently fractures the melody with random bursts of wild noise. But these dadaist touches are subordinated to the more popularistic accents of the total sound score. For the most part Auric's music follows Clair's libretto, adding the tonal punctuation which unifies and energizes the director's satiric assault upon industrial capitalism. A Nous, la Liberté is a difficult film, in that it combines unabashed slapstick with severe social criticism. Without the range and fluidity of Auric's sound score, it is doubtful that Clair could have held such diverse elements together.

"I realized," says Clair, "that A Nous, la Liberté would risk being absurd, if I developed it in a realistic style; . . . I had . . . to employ the form of an operetta." [2] Auric grasped the spirit of the picture perfectly and the right mixture of music, voice, and noise is always there to ease the theme forward. The musical overture immediately tells us that the tone is comic, though we sense more somber concerns in Auric's swift modulation from lilting melody to authentic noises of oppression. Such aural interchanges persist throughout the picture, tightening its otherwise episodic structure and cuing the dramatic intent of particular sequences.

The overall movement of A Nous, la Liberté is a progression from authoritarian control to anarchistic openness. This is encapsulated in the sound score as well as the visuals. Following the brief musical introduction, we hear shrill whistles and the thud of marching feet, the rhythm of prisoners ordered from workshop to cells, and back again, under the pressure of a sullen, relentless routine. The beat of their steps stands in marked contrast, however, to the one used to suggest

[2] Cited in Barthelmy Amengual, René Clair (Paris: Editions Seghers, 1963), p. 75. Reprinted by permission of Editions Seghers.

HARMONY OF MUSIC AND IMAGE. The march beat of the music reinforces the organized, lock-step movements of the human figures, pointing up the similarities between prison and factory in *A Nous, la Liberté*. The Museum of Modern Art/Film Stills Archive.

the eventual emancipation of the protagonists, not just from the prison to which society once consigned them, but from another prison fashioned out of their own narrowly commercial ambitions. As the opening of the film is organized around the drum-tap monotony of a forced march, the later climactic sequence is orchestrated by the improvised cadence of a whimsical wind. Its dominant musical note has enough of a whistle in it to remind us of the arrogant tooting from the first reel, but the whistle of gusting air is not the harsh cry of a prison guard. It is wandering, vagrant, capricious, a sound corresponding exactly to the unstructured swirl of top hats and bank notes which by this time visually dominates the scene. This noise then blends with the reemergence of the musical "liberty" theme, while the characters shake off the last fetters of arbitrary social constraint.

Auric's music also serves to distinguish one protagonist from the other. While Emile and Louis are prisoners together, they share a common fate and are not musically individuated. But once Louis has made his escape, his self-assertiveness expresses itself in musical chords of brass and drums. These are harmonized with a "phonograph theme," introduced when he founds his recording company, then repeated through successive scenes of his ascent from rags to riches. In fact, Clair makes no effort to dramatize this change of fortune, but depends simply upon the music, which accompanies Louis' acquisition of fancy clothes, a glass monocle, and an ever larger entourage of bootlicking associates. The phonograph theme, an extension of Louis' personality, also provides transitions from one brief cut to another as Clair follows the company's discs and players to different parts of the city, illustrating the expansiveness of the manufacturer's newfound empire. Eventually we are returned to the home office, where trumpets blare Wagnerian chords to announce the master's presence. At this stage of the film, Louis has chucked off his prison garb to become, in effect, a prison warden, running his factory according to the same exacting code that prevailed in the world behind bars. Clearly he is ripe for a visit from his convict-friend Emile.

Emile is the more poetic of the two characters, and his softening presence is needed to free Louis from the thrall of his entrepreneurial instincts. This is made explicit when the two men come together, and each is at first seriously embarrassed by the other's presence. Again the treatment relies heavily upon the sound score. While Louis and Emile converse in the workroom of the factory, the sound track reverberates with marching feet, repeating the prison theme of the first sequence. But as the two men, renewing their friendship, retire to the privacy of Louis' office, the march gives way to the liberty theme, first announced in the overture and periodically repeated throughout the picture. The implication is clear. Emile will rescue his comrade from the pomposities of the business world and send him back to the open road. This point is then underscored in the dramatic action, as Louis, now drunk and disorderly, begins to throw bottles at his own portrait.

In addition to anticipating the film's dramatic development, Auric's score also interlocks with the visual notation of Georges Perinal's photography and Lazare Meerson's decor. The march beat associated with the prisoners (and factory workers) is as stiff as the rigid geometry of the sets and almost as depressing as their shadow-infested corners. Yet by the time Louis dissolves his empire we have moved out of doors, into limpid, high-key lighting, bright without harshness or glare. The music of the wind generates not a march but a dance, built from spirals, curves, and arabesques which destroy the sharp rectangles of the old order. When this climactic scene begins, Louis is still trying to keep up some of his earlier pretenses, dressed in his tight-fitting suit and mouthing platitudes from his interminable speech. But the breeze blows away the last vestiges of his bourgeois mask as gracefully as it lifts the hat from his head and scatters the leaves of his manuscript.

Soon everything on the set seems in motion, answering to the wayward fluidity of the sound score. Hats, papers, bank notes, even the bankers and brokers themselves, are gathered into an incongruously salvific dance of life.

Clair's later musical comedies followed the direction he had taken in *A Nous, la Liberté*, while in America Lubitsch, with *Monte Carlo* (1930) and *The Merry Widow* (1936), also helped consolidate the conventions of the genre. In both directors, the dance and the march organize the visuals around a musical beat, just as is the case in the more elaborately choreographed spectaculars of Busby Berkeley or the vintage toe-tapping of Astaire and Rogers. In fact, the orientation of musical comedy was virtually built into the fabric of the early sound medium. It never strained the limits of optical sound recording, since it never called for the timbres or frequencies of high-fidelity orchestral music. In a pinch it could always cover up clumsy mixes with bumps, rattles, and snappy chatter. Ironically, as sound recording achieved its modern refinements, the genre fell into decline. Witness the difference, for example, between Hollywood's *Forty-Second Street* (1933), with its lyrical innocence, and the stuffy pretentiousness of *Hello, Dolly!* (1968).

Although optical sound recording did not encourage full-fledged symphonic scores, some directors were tempted to use them whatever the technical problems. The results were not always gratifying, though such scores at least avoided the dialogue-ridden monotony of photographed stage plays. The symphonic film enjoyed its greatest success in countries like Russia and Germany, which already had a strong tradition that enabled Sergei Prokofiev to collaborate effectively with Eisenstein on *Alexander Nevsky* and *Ivan the Terrible*. Prokofiev came to the cinema supremely well versed in music, and also experienced in how to adapt pace, pitch, or timbre to the physical demands of a performing ensemble. Paying astonished homage to his composer, Eisenstein says of Prokofiev that "his place is amid microphones, kleig lights, celluloid spirals of film, the faultless accuracy of the meshing sprockets of synchronization. . . ."[3] But in all probability, Prokofiev succeeded with *Nevsky* by assimilating the film into opera and ballet more than by mastering the cinema so completely as Eisenstein imagined.

Eisenstein's approach to the sound film is remarkably similar to Clair's. His silent films, like Clair's, are rich in imagined noises, from the guns of the *Potemkin* which explode in defiance of czarist tyranny to the icy stillness of the factory whistle in *Strike*. Like Clair's, Eisenstein's conception of sound was shaped by abuses of the new medium in Europe and America. In the statement of 1928, which he signed in

[3] This comment should be seen in the context of Eisenstein's tribute to Prokofiev in "P-R-K-F-V," *Notes of a Film Director*, tr. X. Danko (New York: Dover Publications, Inc., 1970), pp. 149–166.

conjunction with Pudovkin and Grigori Alexandrov, Eisenstein deplores "commercial exploitation of the most saleable merchandise, TALKING FILMS." [4] He fears that "sound recording will proceed on a purely naturalistic level, exactly corresponding to the movement on the screen and providing a certain 'illusion' of talking people, of audible objects, etc." For Eisenstein, the deeper danger of this bent is that cinema, now invested with its new technical capacity, will become a mere vehicle "for 'highly cultured dramas' and other photographed performances of a theatrical sort." In other words, the visuals will be shackled to synchronized stage voices. His solution to the problem is formulated in capital letters: "THE FIRST EXPERIMENTAL WORK WITH SOUND MUST BE DIRECTED ALONG THE LINE OF ITS DISTINCT NON-SYNCHRONIZATION WITH THE VISUAL IMAGES." Ideally, this will "later lead to the creation of an ORCHESTRAL COUNTERPOINT of visual and aural images." It was another full decade before Eisenstein had the chance to make his first sound film. But when the opportunity came he developed *Nevsky* according to the principles outlined in this early essay.

By the time Eisenstein began to collaborate with Prokofiev, the composer himself had achieved a considerable independent reputation. Educated at the St. Petersburg Conservatory, Prokofiev had studied under Rimsky-Korsakov, who brought him into contact with the whole Russian musical tradition of the nineteenth century. This includes Peter Tchaikovsky and Modest Moussorgsky, whose contributions to ballet and opera, respectively, are central to Prokofiev's development. Prokofiev also steeped himself in music of the Mediterranean world, especially after he left Russia in 1918 to travel with Rachmaninoff in Europe and America. Prokofiev's musical versatility, together with his feel for the stage and for bodily rhythm, made him ideal for the role in which he was cast with Eisenstein. The pageant opera style of *Nevsky* was entirely agreeable to Prokofiev's imagination. So were the themes of patriotism and defense of homeland, upon which the picture so extensively dwells.

Alexander Nevsky is essentially a war-propaganda film designed to brace the Russian people for an anticipated Nazi invasion of their homeland. Its hero is Prince Alexander of Novgorod, called Alexander Nevsky, a great folk leader of the thirteenth century, who met and repulsed an invading army belonging to the Order of Teutonic Knights. Sensitive to the topical analogy between the Nazis and the medieval Teutons, the picture dwells upon Alexander's awakening to his mission, his organization of a counteroffensive against the invaders, and his decisive defeat of the Knights in a battle fought on the frozen surface of

[4] "Appendix A," *Film Form and the Film Sense,* ed. and tr. Jay Leyda (Cleveland: The World Publishing Company, 1957), pp. 257–259.

Lake Chudskoye in 1225. The music of the film parallels this unfolding of themes, giving them epic sweep as well as patriotic fervor. The musical motifs come to climax in the battle on the ice, just as Eisenstein's thematic intentions are similarly fulfilled.

The sound track of *Alexander Nevsky* includes many natural noises — rhythmic hoofbeats, the clang of staves and swords against armor, the chime of bells in the lofts of churches. But it also develops an ambitious symphonic score, involving a full complement of orchestral instruments recorded through a multimicrophone hookup that at this time was new to Soviet studios. Prokofiev's skill as a composer shows itself in his ability to assimilate real noises into an intricate choral and instrumental progression. It shows, too, in his finding musical analogues of the film's imagery, thus enlarging the significance of the action through the epic resonance of the score.

Everything in *Alexander Nevsky* points to the battle of Lake Chudskoye, and Prokofiev seems to look forward musically to this climactic event from the opening chords of the film. At the outset we find Russia sluggish and slumbering, with no sense of national identity and no inclination to resist the Tatars, who have imposed upon various provinces a confiscatory system of taxation. The camera work in this sequence is marked by slow pans and tracking shots which crawl across a desolate landscape strewn with bones and skulls. Both literally and figuratively, we are in the presence of death. The musical score for this sequence is also dirgelike, handled as a *molto andante* movement which is as torpid as the camera. The phrasing is punctuated by a much repeated low C, which is struck with tuba, cello, and bass viol. Though the higher-pitched harmonies of oboe and strings hint at emancipation, their vagaries are controlled by the dominant bass rhythm which suggests bondage and lethargy. But these strains contrast absolutely with those that later dominate the film, especially in the fight at the Lake where the racing *allegretto* movement matches the gallop of Nevsky's cavalry. This latter scene was shot at 12, and in some instances 8, frames per second, doubling and then tripling the apparent speed of the charging horses. Prokofiev's music is fully ready to keep up the pace as the scoring of the opening sequence is dramatically reversed. Now the high strings lead and the bass follows, as the music mimes the new energy that Nevsky's gallantry has drawn out of the Russian people. They are now a transformed society, quickened to life by the will of a powerful leader and the support he receives from the workers of Novgorod.

The emerging national consciousness of the people is defined in several musical themes which Prokofiev introduces early in the film and modulates in various ways. Two themes are associated with Nevsky and another, antagonistic theme is used to personify his enemies, the Teutonic Knights who have crossed the Russian border and march upon Novgorod. This latter is a modal chant, an insistently repetitive, almost nonmelodic theme which is sung in Latin instead of the vernacular. It is both musically and verbally at odds with the Nevsky themes and advertises the stern, unbending fanaticism of the Teutonic hosts. We hear it as they sack Pskov, ruthlessly putting citizens to the sword and buildings to the torch. During these scenes the Teutons seem little more than mechanical engines of death, a quality echoed in the relentless incantation: "*In extremis expectavi. . . .*" Insistent dissonances of brass and muted trombones reinforce the visuals in conveying the ruin wrought by the invaders. As Pskov becomes a smoke-swept graveyard, the chords themselves suggest violation and disharmony.

Throughout the film, Prokofiev's music measures the moral qualities of the contending forces. But the progress of rival themes is brought to completion only with the battle of the Lake and Nevsky's triumphal return to Novgorod. Again we hear the modal chant of the knights, now in an accelerated tempo which accentuates its strange rigor. Ironically, however, in this context it takes on new meaning. The music which was intoned at Pskov while innocent victims were executed now is used to foreshadow the deaths of the charging Teutons, soon to be unhorsed by Nevsky's battalions. The sound of metal on metal, first heard as Nevsky's men forge weapons, now is repeated as they pound the armor of their enemy with swords, staves, and maces. The clash produces a unique orchestral timbre, dominated by irregular percussion beats but achieving new harmonies, as the attacking knights in their metal suits are forced to contribute to the music of Russian nationalism. Although the noise of combat becomes increasingly cacophonous, especially as the ice cracks in the spring thaw, there emerges from the chaos of the battlefield a modification of Nevsky's Novgorod theme, quieter now and more solemn, as if taking account of the tremendous toll taken by the Russians' patriotic commitment, yet still assertive of nationalistic claims. The reintroduction of this theme looks forward to Prokofiev's coda, articulated as Nevsky returns victoriously, himself personifying the reverence for homeland he has inculcated in the peasants and workers.

The sound score of *Alexander Nevsky* remains a major achievement in the treatment of film music. This picture was the ancestor of nearly all the "epic" films that followed in the 1940s and 1950s, from the authentically majestic *Henry V* (Britain, 1944) to the assorted Hollywood Biblical tales of the next decade, which added stereophonic embellishments to *Nevsky*'s brass, strings, and choral chants. Yet there was clearly a need for another kind of sound score, one primarily oriented to the spoken word, though taking support from the music and effects track. Such developments in dramatic sound began taking place toward the end of the 1930s in both Europe and the U.S.A.

THE VOICE-MUSIC-EFFECTS MIX

Unimaginative use of voice in the early sound film. Some exceptions: the Marx Brothers, Chaplin. Orson Welles and the impact of radio. Sound without image: Welles' "panic broadcast." Sound mix of Citizen Kane. *Extensions of technique:* The Lady from Shanghai, The Stranger.

Although music has always claimed an honorable place on the sound track, the sound medium obviously requires some attention to the human voice, usually blended in one way or another with the assortment of secondary noises that make up our aural environment. Before sound could really come of age, filmmakers had to learn how to use voice, to bring it into play imaginatively, so as not merely to give redundant information or impair the fluidity of the camera. This would eventually involve such techniques as changing the recording speed, turning up the effects track, introducing echo or reverberation, and making use of electronic sound scores. But in the beginning it simply entailed taking a few hints from the already mature art of radio.

Just because films involve speech, they need not be talk-ridden. It is a question of who does the talking, and when. Speech may simply add a caption to the picture or become an elocution exercise for the star. And so long as the sound cinema was in its infancy talk seemed an end in itself. Didn't the fact of speech let filmmakers put profound sentiments in the mouths of the performers? Didn't this improve the pedigree of movies, giving them status as high art? So goes the special pleading of Hollywood during the early 1930s. But only when voice is used contrapuntally, in throwaway lines or with special accents, or even as nonsynchronized commentary, does it become a specifically new sound resource.

Not that all nonmusical sound films of the 1930s used voice uncreatively. The Marx brothers balanced the claims of sight and sound quite nicely, with Groucho spinning off his relentless gag monologues while Harpo counterpointed visually by drawing swordfish, blowtorches, or police badges from the folds of his impossibly intricate overcoats. Even Groucho's monologues are not really an abuse of the voice track, whatever else they might abuse. His speech is such an outpouring of verbal nonsequiturs that we are hardly inclined to regard it as a communications system. It might almost be thought of as part of the effects track, of a piece with the horns, bells, and rattles that Harpo uses to annoy his adversaries. Charles Chaplin, from the security of his position as an independent film producer, also resisted the craze for dialogue. He made almost no concession to the human voice before *The Great Dictator* (1940) and then used speech in close conjunction with other elements of sight and sound. The fact that the microphones wilt in the

presence of Herr Hinkel's oratory is a visual comment upon his bom-
bastic pronouncements. Similarly, when "Our Phooey" dictates a letter
to his secretary, the typewriter condenses his multisentence maunder-
ings into a split-second whirr of keys. Apparently not even the office
machines of his private bureaucracy can resist revising what he has to
say. Such techniques of comedy effectively guarded the cinema against
the tyranny of the human voice.

These and other contributions notwithstanding, the sound cinema
took a significant step forward after the arrival in Hollywood of Orson
Welles, who brought with him much immensely valuable experience in
radio. He also had the benefit of the more fine-grained sound negatives developed in the late 1930s and comparable advances in the technology of sound mixes. Welles' experiments thus look forward to the
much more ambitious sound collages of the 1960s and 1970s.

Welles learned how to handle sound while he was working exclusively in the radio medium for the Mercury Theatre of the Air. It was
here that he originated the noise effects, the enjambed conversations,
and the media commentary that became the trademark of his films.
Forced to make sound substitute for picture (something that perhaps
doesn't come readily to someone trained for the stage), Welles medi-
tated carefully the meaning of an auto engine, a crackling fire, or a
voice that tonally conveys menace and hostility. His radio effects were
so masterful that he once persuaded most of the East Coast that an
army from Mars had landed in New Jersey. This almost legendary radio
show, "Invasion from Mars," which CBS carried on 30 October 1938,
displays particularly well how the soon-to-be film director could use
simulated news commentary for dramatic purpose, making words conjure up nonexistent images while rapid cuts from one narrator to another compress the passage of time and jounce us abruptly from place
to place. Perfectly cinematic, though done without anyone ever getting
near a camera, the sound track of Mercury Theatre's "Invasion from
Mars" looks directly forward to Welles' sound films of the 1940s and
1950s.

Scripted by Howard Koch from H. G. Wells' *War of the Worlds*,
"Invasion from Mars" dramatizes a landing from outer space and the
havoc it brings to America's Eastern seaboard. The subject is treated as
a series of emergency bulletins followed by interviews with scientists,
lawmen, witnesses, and public officials. In spite of the improbable plot
there is close attention to verisimilitude, complete with the clatter of
overturned microphones and disrupted audio connections, which often
act as dramatic bridges from one episode to the next.

The presentation begins with quick sound cuts involving three an-
nouncers. The first is a network weather reporter giving routine information about temperature, though alluding, perhaps prophetically

to "a slight atmospheric disturbance of undetermined origin. . . ."[5] He quickly signs us over to the Meridian Room of the Hotel Park Plaza in downtown New York where the Spanish rhythm of the music track tells us we have joined Ramon Racquello and his band, who introduces the first number of the evening, "La Cumparsita." The music mix then fades in strongly, only to be interrupted almost immediately by a bulletin from International Radio News. The details are unclear but the import is ominous, as the announcer mentions trails of incandescent gas "moving towards the earth with enormous velocity." The invasion is on. In these few brief sound notations, apparently from quite diverse points of origin, Welles has managed to convey the sense of shattered security. Here was a nation at its Sunday ease, indulging in a little South-of-the-Border musical escapism and worrying about nothing more serious than a slight chance of rain. Suddenly, with the speed of sound waves, the complacent radio listener must confront the prospect of annihilation at the hands of Martian invaders.

The remarkable thing about "Invasion from Mars" is the pace it sustains, especially through the first half hour of the broadcast. Looking back at the program, many students of mass psychology have wondered how so many people (literally thousands) could believe that Martians might blast off from their native planet, land in New Jersey, and destroy most of America's armed forces, all between 8:00 P.M. and 8:30 P.M. on a Sunday evening. But the key lies in Welles' ambitious sound cuts, which create the impression that much more time elapses. We are moved so swiftly from person to person and place to place that we feel we have lived through an extended military engagement. After the metal monsters emerge from their landing site at Grovers Mill, we hear in rapid-fire succession an eyewitness reporter, the commander of the New Jersey militia, the network vice president, the Secretary of the Interior, and finally the spokesmen for air force and gunnery units hurriedly called into combat. When we have been bombarded by all these reports, we are almost ready to believe in the complete aloneness of the ham radio operator whose voice closes the first half of the program:

2X 2L calling CO in New York
Isn't there anyone on the air?
Isn't there anyone . . .
2X 2L —

After such a tour de force as "Invasion from Mars," Welles' first film might have seemed anticlimactic had it been anything other than *Citizen Kane*. This picture not only set new standards in cinematography but evidenced an equally imaginative approach to sound. Working with

[5] Textual citations are from *Panic Broadcast,* ed. Howard Koch (New York: Avon Book Division, The Hearst Corporation, 1971).

sound men Bailey Fesler and James Stewart, Welles again shows his sense of timing and timbre, his ability to define a situation in terms of voice and music. At the outset of the film we are confronted with the mystery of Kane's personality and invited to penetrate it, though the sound score suggests this will be no easy task. For the first several minutes there is no voice, though the visuals cry out for explanation. Where are we? Who is this man whose relationship to the world seems summed up in the No Trespassing sign that the camera lingers upon? Voice is strategically withheld as we slowly are transported across Kane's estate and into the inner sanctum of his mansion. Suspense mounts powerfully as we approach the one lighted window, enter, and wait for the dying magus of Xanadu to pronounce the cryptic word "Rosebud." Thus situated, these two syllables are more memorable than a twenty-minute verbal exchange from *Anna Christie* (U.S.A., 1930) or *Strange Interlude* (U.S.A., 1932).

Having touched the center of the mystery, we are now pulled to its periphery with an abrupt cut to the facile résumé of Kane's life presented in "News on the March." While the lighting changes from nightmare gray to flat, newsreel clarity, the musical score shifts tempo from dissonant dirge to bouncy march. The speaking voices too are of markedly different timbre, the plaintive gasp of Kane's last utterance contrasting with the crisp, mechanical brashness of the commentator who mouths a capsulized obituary. His self-assured voice bridges over the contradictory images of Kane that now flit before our eyes. In fact, there is considerable tension in the voice track itself, since Kane has apparently made quite different impressions upon the various people who have had to deal with him. We hear from a Wall Street broker that Kane was "nothing more nor less than a Communist," while an unidentified speaker in Union Square seems sure Kane was "a Fascist." The narrator, however, feels no need to deal with these incongruities, as he trips nimbly among his facts and numbers in an elaborate inventory of Kane's possessions. Welles is careful to make both the music and commentary of this episode sound utterly artificial, so that we recognize it as a teasing exercise in nonhistory, a manufactured reality concocted by reciting journalistic formulas into a microphone.

Though he always treats voice skillfully, Welles is probably best known for his expressive noise effects. There is, for example, the famous conclusion of *The Lady from Shanghai* (1947), which comes to climax with the shattering of glass in a gigantic hall of mirrors. The scene was developed by the director through close collaboration with the sound man Lodge Cunningham and special effects adviser Lawrence Butler. Here as elsewhere, sound and picture are efficiently interlocked to give the action a symbolic dimension. The husband and wife protagonists have spent their lives in tactful evasions, each hiding his authentic personality behind multiple masks. But now these will be stripped away as the hatred each feels for the other at last erupts in open violence. The penetration of disguises, the splintering of the false image, is nicely captured when Bannister and Elsa confront one another amid fun-house mirrors, and their gunfire begins to burst the glass. The shots which leave both of them mortally wounded create fantastic echo effects in the closed room, as pane after pane of mirror glass comes crashing down to the floor. The calm which follows the exchange of fire leaves no room for delicate illusions. Elsa's last words are trite but severely honest: "I don't want to die." In the cacophony of breaking glass, we have heard the sundering of all the psychic defenses two people could muster.

Another Welles film of the forties, *The Stranger* (1946), includes several impressive sound sequences built upon the use of media noise. The plot deals with the efforts of an escaped Nazi war criminal to slip inconspicuously into the life of a quiet New England town. To this purpose he courts and marries a good-naturedly sentimental local debutante who is blind to her husband's past. Though eventually forced to recognize she has wed an internationally notorious killer, she admits this only after fierce prodding from the federal officer charged with investigating Franz Kindler, alias Charles Rankin. At one point she is obliged to see a documentary film detailing the horrors of Nazi concentration camps. Of course, she refuses to implicate her spouse in these atrocities, but the impact the report makes upon her is caught in the sound effects. After the last image passes from the screen, the projector is left running so that the film spins loosely upon the take-up reel, the leader slapping against the projector with disturbing staccato beats. As we can see from the pained expression that clouds the heroine's face, this whiplash noise symbolizes the lacerating effects these revelations have had upon the domestic loyalties of the dutiful wife.

Welles' use of sound is as ambitious as anything before the advent of magnetic recording. Competing voices, intricate mixes, and memorable background noises are an integral part of nearly all his films. His instinct is to produce not a conventionally "clean" sound track, free of every distraction or distortion, but a dense one, where materials so seemingly irrelevant as a newscast, a hair-oil commercial, or a jukebox lyric become vehicles of dramatic exposition.

Welles also showed the cinema how sound tropes could collapse time and create space. Just as earth is conquered by Martians in a matter of moments, so also does Kane's whirlwind campaign for governor come to climax with incredible speed, through an effective sound collage. Kane's campaign manager launches the gubernatorial effort with a casual speech to a handful of people, but a sound mix intervenes in midsentence and the speech is finished by Kane himself in a huge, jam-packed auditorium. Months have passed in seconds, while voice gives continuity amid changes of scene and decor. By the same token, the doings of the world beyond the camera are often brought to bear upon the characters through on-screen radios or off-screen voices. In this way the "space" encompassed by the dramatic life of the picture becomes larger than the merely pictorial space covered by the lens. Occasionally there is even a conflict between sight and sound. In the trial scene of *The Lady from Shanghai,* the camera dollies forward to the point where two characters are caught in close-up, leaving the courtroom and the judge's bench visible in the background. We then get a "voice close-up," i.e., a voice that is clearly not oratorically projected and thus would have to be heard from close range. The irony is that the voice is not that of the characters in the pictorial foreground, but comes instead from the area of the judge's bench. In order to shift emphasis in a startling way, Welles has inverted the contents of the sight image and the sound "image." We see things in one perspective but hear them in another. Without the various precedents supplied by this director, it is difficult to imagine some of the more adventurous sound experiments of later decades.

THE ADVENT OF MAGNETIC SOUND

The quality of sound recording and transmission was gradually bettered throughout the 1930s and 1940s with the introduction of sound negatives of increasingly finer grain. Mixing equipment also improved, particularly with the so-called high-level mixers and constant-impedance faders, which facilitated amplification and subsequent blending together of voice, music, and effects tracks. But the real technological breakthrough came in the early 1950s with the cinema's conversion from optical to magnetic sound. Although first marketed with the package that brought stereophonic reproduction to the theater, magnetic sound ultimately made a different and more significant contribution: its portable, compact gear revolutionized *sound recording,* while its capacity to survive numerous re-recordings without loss of quality greatly enhanced the possibilities of *sound mixing.*

Stereophonic sound rode into the cinema on the coattails of wide-screen photography, dramatizing the famous roller coaster sequence of *This Is Cinerama* with squeals of fear and joy that emanated from six separate magnetic sound tracks. Thereafter it became fashionable for a few years to make up special magnetic effects tracks to add a further aural dimension to the optical sound track already wedded to the print. This practice introduced stereophonic sound to such films as *From Here to Eternity* (U.S.A., 1953), where the multidirectional sound transmission contributed significantly to the climactic bombing of Pearl Harbor. As the sluggish peacetime American army in Hawaii is first alerted to the prospect of war, the news comes to them, as it does

PORTABLE SOUND. The development of magnetic recording and portable synchronization systems notably enhanced the mobility of the documentary filmmaker and the realism of documentary production. Along with Leacock and Pennebaker, the Maysles brothers pioneered the "wild sound" movement with such films as *Gimme Shelter*, shot largely with shoulder-mounted cameras and handheld tape recorders. *Love in Vain* (1970). Courtesy of Maysles Films, Inc.

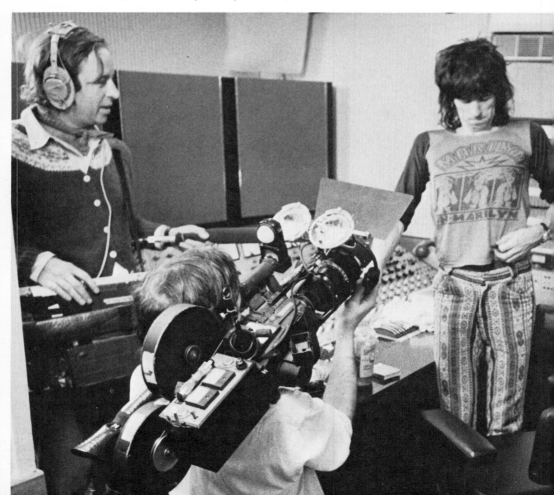

to the theater audience, in the form of off-screen noises of whining dive bombers and teeth-jarring explosions. The use of stereo outlets to pull sound away from the screen and distribute it around the theater helps generate the psychic effect of a surprise attack.

What seemed likely during the early years of stereo was the gradual outfitting of all theaters for magnetic sound. This would have spread the new technology beyond New York City and a few prestigious theaters in other metropolitan areas. Such developments were encouraged in 1953 when the introduction of CinemaScope (with its "squeezed" image) made it possible to engraft four fully synchronized magnetic tracks upon the print itself.

Stereo reproduction integrated well with the scope system in that it not only allowed off-screen sound effects to erupt from various corners of the theater but also made possible the directional treatment of screen voices themselves. Thus sound could be used to compensate for the lack of photographic selectivity in wide-screen composition, when wide-angle lenses spread out the action over a seemingly limitless expanse of space. At such moments the directionality of the sound effects could shift our attention from one character to another by shifting the voice from the left to the right, or the right to the center of the screen. The effect would be a kind of intimacy, but a "close-up" achieved through sound, not sight. Unfortunately, the rich potential of stereo reproduction was never fulfilled, since too few exhibitors were willing to make the necessary investment in multimicrophone hookups and magnetic sound projectors. As a result of these commercial considerations, magnetic sound made its force felt more as a recording system and as the basis of a new mixing technology than as a system of sound reproduction and transmission.

THE WILD-SOUND MOVEMENT

Economy and portability of magnetic tape. Market for authentic documentary in the television industry. New documentary teams: Richard Leacock and D. A. Pennebaker. Automatic sound synchronization: Primary *and* Don't Look Back. *Frederick Wiseman:* High School.

Anyone who has ever snapped the switch of a cassette recorder knows how easy it is to handle magnetic sound. Tapes are light, recording is simple, playback can be accomplished almost immediately, and the whole process is relatively inexpensive. Besides, magnetic sound holds two further advantages: the quality of the recording is very good, and the sound track can be mixed or re-recorded many times without appreciably degrading the original voice, noise, or music. Because sound tape picks up the whole aural world with great accuracy and little unwanted interference, it quickly revolutionized sound recording even though it failed to find its prospective place in stereophonic reproduction. Especially in documentary filmmaking, the portable tape recorder at last fulfilled the long-entertained hope of unobtrusive, on-the-spot reportage.

From the earliest days of sound, the documentary movement both in Europe and America had hungered for the noise of real people in a real world. In 1934, John Grierson, the father of British documentary, was already anticipating ways in which sound recording might contribute to cinematic realism. "The microphone too can get about the world," he says, and "in so doing it has the power to bring to the hands of the creative artist a thousand and one vernacular elements, and the million and one sounds that ordinarily attend the working of the world." [6] But to do so, Grierson concludes, it must be "released from the bondage of the studios," for only after it has learned to move among men can it fulfill its promise as "a collector of raw material."

So far as was possible in the 1930s, Grierson practiced the principle of direct sound recording, inspiring such colleagues as Basil Wright and Harry Watt with his own enthusiasm for realistic sound. The Grierson approach is evident in *Night Mail* (1936), where he collaborated with directors Wright and Watt to turn a film about a new London to Glasgow express train into a celebration of the modern communications network. Here authentic railway noises lend a touch of naturalism to a sound score that, with W. H. Auden's poetic narration and Benjamin Britten's music, might easily have become a little too self-consciously "arty." Actually, the high point of *Night Mail* is a sequence in which Auden's verse begins to mime the sound rhythm of the locomotive as it picks up speed. It is as if the sound track were forcing us to recognize that technology, intelligently applied, creates its own special kind of poetry.

Nonstudio sound found its way into other British documentaries of the 1930s, including Edgar Anstey's *Granton Trawler* (1934), which was also made under Grierson's inspiration. The film orchestrates sea sounds and fishermen's cries very effectively, turning storm and wave into full-fledged antagonists in this contest between man and nature. In America Pare Lorentz combined the photographic lyricism of Flaherty with Grierson's imaginative approach to sound as he directed films like *The Plough that Broke the Plains* (1936) and *The River* (1937). In this

[6] This and the following citations of Grierson are from his "Creative Use of Sound," *Grierson on Documentary*, ed. Forsyth Hardy (Berkeley: University of California Press, 1966), pp. 157–163.

latter film, the foreboding sound of dripping water hints darkly at a flood which brings disaster to the Mississippi valley, the innocence of these first noises establishing how easy it was to overlook the threat that they posed. With precedents such as these in mind, filmmakers of the 1950s and 1960s called upon the new sound technology to further extend the possibilities of direct, "wild" recording.

The 1950s ushered in commercial television and with it an almost limitless information market. This in turn gave impetus to various technological innovations, including faster film stocks, shoulder-mounted, battery-powered cameras, and (after several abortive efforts) tape recorders that would automatically synchronize the sound track with the picture. Thus outfitted, documentarists were ready by 1960 to take an impressive leap forward, leaving behind the formal narrators and speeches of an earlier generation while moving boldly into the sphere of unrehearsed dramatic sound. Several young American filmmakers who did their apprentice work in television have struck out most impressively in these new directions.

One filmmaking group to smile gratefully upon the new recording technology was the team of Richard Leacock, Robert Drew, and Donn Allen Pennebaker. In their early work for television, especially Leacock's contribution to the 1950s "Omnibus" series and their later, collective efforts on behalf of the Time-Life "Living Camera" programs, each of these men had cause to chafe at the technical considerations which excluded the filmmaker from complete participation in the events he sought to cover. Speaking of his own recording problems, Leacock says: "Having grown up in the documentary film tradition of Flaherty, Grierson, Elton, et al., I believed that we should go out into the real world and record the way it really is." But "with the advent of sound, far from being freed, we were paralyzed by the complexity and size of our equipment. We . . . went out to the real world and proceeded to destroy, by our own impact, the very thing we went to record." [7] This situation changed, however, with the fully automated, fully portable system of sound recording the team of Leacock-Drew-Pennebaker introduced in 1960 with Primary.

Primary is a documentary about the Humphrey-Kennedy contest in Wisconsin which contributed to Kennedy's receiving the Democratic presidential nomination in 1960. While not particularly significant as drama or as political analysis, the film is memorable for the intimate contact it makes with the personalities involved. Narrative comment is minimal; in its place we find the principals of this political engagement revealing themselves through characteristic phrases and gestures. Both

[7] This and the following citations of Leacock are from his interview in Documentary Explorations, ed G. Roy Levin (Garden City, N.Y.: Doubleday & Company, Inc., 1971), pp. 195–221.

camera and recorder are completely mobile, speeding from hand-shakes to impromptu orations with as much zest and ease as the candidates themselves. Gone from the recording procedure is the time-honored but awkward clapboard that banged shut to announce the beginning of a sound take and thus keep sound synchronized with picture. Here this is accomplished by a quiet electronic pulse that transmits a "beep" to the recorder at exactly the moment the camera begins to run. With justifiable relish, Leacock congratulates his filmmaking partners for introducing the sound rig by which "we got the first taste of being able to walk into a room shooting." It thus fulfilled his documentary ideal of "no lights, no tripods, no wires, no plugging in." In *Primary* the filmmakers went out to the action, instead of asking the action to wait for sound cues, cable hookups, and cumbersome overhead microphones.

The lessons of this film were learned well by Donn Allen Pennebaker (who helped with both sound and camera) and applied to the pictures he had already begun to make independently of the Leacock-Drew group. Among the best of these is *Don't Look Back* (1965), the first of several rock musicals produced in the past decade. Pennebaker's complete fidelity to wild sound recording gives this film, as well as his later *Monterey Pop* (1968), an authenticity impossible in slick, big-budget confections like *The Sound of Music.*

Don't Look Back is a stop-by-stop record of the English concert tour that rock star Bob Dylan conducted in the spring of 1965. It seeks to find the man in the music, catching his enigmatic personality, yet — says Pennebaker — remaining "musical rather than informational."[8] The challenge, he continues, was to make a "really working musical," a film that would "tell you about the mood" of the tour. But he chose a completely dramatic method, eliminating the narrator altogether and relying absolutely upon live, on-the-scene recording. Dylan thus articulates his own image, according to his own accents, his own hesitations, his occasional nervous fidgets. While the rock star does his thing, Pennebaker's sight-and-sound men hold to his feverish pace.

The slightly blurred, often echo-ridden live sound recording of *Don't Look Back* matches the studied tackiness of the Dylan image, emphasizing the rough, antimelodic qualities of his voice. It never detracts, however, from the magic of Dylan's presence, his power to catch and sway his audiences, which seems more persuasive because Pennebaker transcribes it with such complete candor. The impromptu sound effects also agree well with the completely naturalistic approach to lighting, which reduces everything in the various concert halls to highlights, silhouettes, and indistinct shapes in the distance.

Because the scenes are always underlit, the emphasis of the film shifts from sight to sound. Voice seems supremely important, the

[8] The Pennebaker interview, *Documentary Explorations*, pp. 223–270.

POSTSYNCHRONIZATION OF MUSIC. Obviously there is no need for a symphony orchestra to accompany the camera crew on its photographic assignments. Musical sound tracks are created in the studio and then matched to the image in the manner suggested by this production shot from *Airport*. Photograph courtesy of PTN Publishing Corporation.

microphone the only means to make contact with an otherwise un-known world. That's where the spotlight falls, summoned to accent and underscore the charismatic personality of the singer. In this sound-en-riched atmosphere, great barny auditoriums like Royal Albert Hall, their amplitude swallowed in shadow, become sacred precincts dedicated to whatever faith, hope, or charity is embodied in the music of Dylan. As he intones "the times they are a-changing," the light glances bril-liantly from his guitar to his harmonica, sometimes obscuring his face, but supporting our inclination to identify the man with the instrument he plays. Slight and insecure as we see him offstage, Dylan in the midst of the coterie that applauds every verse and clings to every ad-libbed phrase seems a towering figure, the prophet of a new religion. The deep shade, punctuated by unpredictable flashes of sunlight through the windows, intensifies the mystery of Dylan's magnetism, almost forc-ing us to honor the message relentlessly repeated in the lyrics of his songs.

Some small details of the musical track which lend authenticity to Dylan's portrait would certainly have been lost in re-recording. On one occasion, for instance, we find Dylan on stage addressing a microphone that fails to broadcast. For a moment the spell is broken, the voice has no electric reinforcement, and Dylan seems little more than a lonely child, unable to reach the audience that surrounds and protects him. He is saved by the stagehand who finds the loose plug and shoves it into the nearest socket, setting off an explosion of applause among the throngs gathered to salute their hero. Touches such as this, the recording "mistakes" that would be erased in a studio situation, are what give *Don't Look Back* its human depth, showing us the fragility of the Dylan myth, the tenuousness of the circuitry upon which his worldwide reputation depends.

Of course the mobile, shoulder-packed tape recorder also gleans insights into Dylan's private existence. We overhear his bantering exchanges with Joan Baez and his peevish fussing with the English rock star Donovan. We are privy to the gnomic wisdom he tosses off to an overly inquisitive reporter: "Keep a good head and always carry a light bulb." In these offstage episodes we get a fuller understanding of what music really means to the man, how it affiliates him with his friends and defends him against his enemies. Once while he is pecking away at the typewriter Joan Baez begins to sing, mostly to herself but within earshot of Dylan. He resists her momentarily, nudging the keys forward with a heavy mechanical clatter, but soon his body has taken up the beat of her music. He forgets the letter and starts to harmonize, creating the closest thing to a conversation that ever takes place between these two intimate, but basically nonverbal friends. Dylan's music is also his defense, as in the scene where another newsman pries too deeply into his psyche. Dylan's tart rejoinders are reinforced by rasping chords of guitar and harmonica, which he always keeps at hand, it seems, to enhance his verbal resources. With sound tracks such as we have in *Don't Look Back* wild recording reached a new level of maturity.

Pennebaker's inclination to avoid narrative commentary has affected the style of much recent documentary filmmaking, notably that of Albert and David Maysles, whose *Gimme Shelter* (1970) treats Mick Jagger and the tragedy of Altamont with the same uncommitted intimacy that we see in *Don't Look Back*. Others too have abandoned editorial structuring in favor of what we might call the "voice collage." With the aid of sophisticated tape pickups, we hear various dramatic voices — sometimes in conversation, sometimes in off-screen interviews, sometimes making formal or incidental announcements, but almost never reciting made-up speeches exclusively for the edification of the sound man. Together these overheard remarks give verbal focus to the imagery, replacing the editorial guide who used to tell us how to react to every situation. Although the filmmaker still controls our responses through his selection and arrangement of live voices, we get the impression that we are reaching our own conclusions independent of his prompting. This extension of realism is magnetic sound's remarkable contribution to contemporary style in the documentary.

One director specializing in this approach is the American documentarist Frederick Wiseman, whose on-the-spot recording techniques resemble those of Leacock-Pennebaker. Wiseman acts as his own sound man, while delegating the visuals to cameramen of his choice. Avoiding the staged scene and the prepared script, he has sat in emergency rooms, ridden police prowl cars, poked about at high school assemblies, and even visited maximum security prisons in order to catch the voices of contemporary American society. These come into play not as neat oral capsules, but incompletely, confusedly, competitively, a phrase and a clause at a time. His sound tracks include the impairments of unplanned background noise (quite a different thing from planned background noise) as well as the natural shyness and sometimes incoherence of nonprofessional speakers. But what is sacrificed in tidiness is recovered in authenticity. The technique allows the filmmaker to be relatively objective toward his material yet still organize the voice track so that it conveys a unified impression. Nowhere does Wiseman say that he is worried about the drift toward authoritarianism in American culture; still this theme is subtly incorporated into the voice track of all his pictures.

High School (1968) is a representative example of Wiseman's work. "I want to make films," he says, "where the institutions will be the star but will also reflect larger issues in general society." [9] To this purpose he undertakes to feel the pulse of American education through close touch with the students, faculty, and administration of a single school, North East High of Philadelphia. What emerges from the film is the sense of a collective personality, an overall impression built up from a great many fragments of speech. Wiseman's microphone roves from the cafeteria to the counselor's office to find the casual phrases that express the value system of the school.

The keynote of *High School,* frequently enunciated in the voice track, is that students must learn to obey orders, thus qualifying themselves for membership in the affluent American bureaucracy they someday will be part of. "Don't you talk, you just listen," says the gym teacher to a student who seems reluctant to wear the right gear. "We're out to establish that you can be a man, that you can take orders," says the Dean of Discipline to another who balks at regulations. "Have you got a pass?" asks the hall monitor of someone strolling in the corridor. Gradually these threads of speech come together in a tight weave. No one is brutalized at North East, but by the same token no one is ever

[9] *The New Documentary in Action,* ed. Alan Rosenthal (Berkeley: University of California Press, 1971), p. 69. The remark should be read in the total context of the interview, pp. 66–75.

released from paternalistic bonds. "It's all right to be individualistic," says a counselor, "but. . . ." Even the typing class, where the students are simply performing a routine assignment, echoes the same spirit of benign regimentation. "The two men went with me down the long road," reads the teacher, then waits for the feverish burst of mechanical clicks that mark the student "response." Lest anything be overlooked, she also reminds her charges of appropriate places for commas, spaces, capitals, and paragraph indentations. Though this is no doubt the obvious way to handle dictation, it seems in the context of the other remarks we have heard to help characterize the prevailing mentality of the school: everything at North East is done "correctly," down to the last comma, space, and capital letter.

Only on two occasions in *High School* is the question of paternalism directly broached. "The policy of North East is to avoid controversy," complains a social science student, not talking to the camera so much as debating the issue with his classmates. Then, in the assembly scene that closes the film, a school official reads a letter from a former student, now a Vietnam veteran, who represents himself as "only a body doing a job." The conformist sentiment of the letter moves the reader at the microphone to editorialize upon its significance for the rest of the student population: "When you get a letter like this — to me it means we are very successful at North East High School." North East, in other words, is devoted to producing warm bodies that do the jobs assigned to them. Since these are the last words spoken in *High School*, they are apt to be invoked as its theme. But the force they have is cumulative, coming from the casual verbal notations on dress, manners, and deportment which make up the total sound envelope of the picture.

WORD AND IMAGE: EXPERIMENTS IN COUNTERPOINT

Other applications of magnetic recording. Fictitious sound: Divorce Italian Style. *Ironic and allusive sounds:* Contempt. *Sound and the moving camera:* Targets. *Sound as voice-over commentary:* Diary of a Mad Housewife.

One consequence of magnetic recording was the handy portable gear that banished know-it-all narrators and introduced the voice collages of Pennebaker and Wiseman. Another equally important result of the magnetic revolution, however, was the economy and ease of reproduction which inspired more imaginative combinations of word and

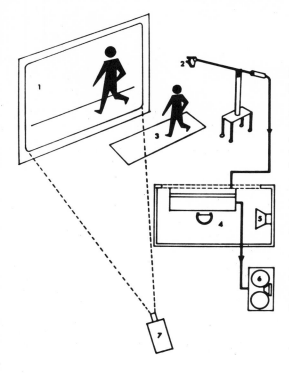

POSTSYNCHRONIZATION OF EFFECTS. Contemporary studio procedure also calls for the rerecording of sound effects in order to avoid interference and unwanted noise (a jet plane overhead, for instance) that often accompany "wild" recording. Here footsteps are being rerecorded. (1) Screen. (2) Recording microphone. (3) Various surfaces. (4) Sound recordist in monitor room. (5) Monitor speaker. (6) Recording machine, carrying a virgin loop of magnetic film. (7) Projector running the picture loop. From *The Technique of Film Cutting Room,* revised second edition, by Ernest Walter, copyright 1973 by Focal Press, Ltd., by permission of the American publishers, Hastings House, Publishers, Inc., New York.

image. While documentarists of the early 1960s sought a system of synchronization allowing complete authenticity in on-the-spot reportage, the fiction film of this period moved away from synchronized speech toward more exciting audiovisual counterpoint.

Italian cinema helped lead the way, since it had at its call a cadre of technicians expert in handling sound. The fact that Italy has no standard dialect (Romans have difficulty with the speech of Sicilians, for example) had long encouraged the practice of dubbing one voice in the place of another, so as to artificially standardize the speech of Italian screen stars. The increasing drift of the industry toward international co-production made this practice mandatory by the end of the 1950s. Hence Mexican-born Anthony Quinn won fame as the Zampano of Fellini's *La Strada* (1954), even though he speaks only enough Italian to approximate the lip movements of a native speaker. Fellini used Quinn's face and body, but got his voice from a professional studio dubber. Given this reservoir of professional skills, moreover, they could be used for more startling innovations than putting Italian words into the mouth of French-speaking Anouk Aimée or American Broderick Crawford. This environment, in fact, was highly conducive to the innovative handling of nonsynchronous sound we find in Pietro Germi's *Divorce Italian Style* (1961).

Divorce Italian Style is the severely ironic tale of a pleasure-seeking Sicilian baron who tires of his sagging, overtalkative wife and begins to lust after his much trimmer, twenty-year-old niece. Divorce being forbidden by churchly and legal prescript, he decides to dispose of his spouse by more drastic means, i.e. murder. But since not even a nobleman can exterminate his wife absolutely with provocation, he needs an appropriate motive, an ethical elixer that will change crude hostility into gentlemanly honor. He finds his pretext, of course, in the male-chauvinist love ethic which allows a husband to take the life of a spouse who has defiled the marriage bed. But as the baron plots his wife's demise, the sound track is imaginatively used to debunk the Sicilian sexual code.

The baron's plans crystallize as he hears a lawyer defend a legal transgression just like the one he is considering. The client has killed his wife in a fit of husbandly jealousy, but the attorney quickly resolves all moral ambiguities of this act in favor of the outraged husband. Why should we punish this man, he chides us eloquently, when what we should see in him is a model of Christian uprightness? Such acts should put us in mind of a stalwart Christendom marching against the heathen in the holy Crusades. As we listen to the defense lawyer's pious sonorities, we watch the baron's face brighten and know that he has found the attorney who will handle his own case. What we do not anticipate is the further use to which Germi will put this particular speech. For after the baron has returned to his palazzo and begun to stage his "crime of passion," the lawyer's voice lingers in his thoughts, bolstering confidence in his diabolic arrangements.

While he lays the trap calculated to force his wife into adultery, what we hear on the sound track is not the busywork of the baron but the voice of the lawyer, again reminding us of the holy Crusades and the godliness of the just man's wrath. This use of the sound track does more than point up the discrepancy between supposedly overwhelming rage and the baron's cruel calculation. The voice of legal authority here advertises the complicity of officialdom in this obvious miscarriage of justice and the effect is to widen Germi's indictment of Sicilian culture. We are brought to see not simply the cunning of a middle-aged roué but the perversity of a whole social system, which would rather excuse murder than bend from its "principles" to permit divorce.

Divorce Italian Style is contemporary with the early work of Jean-Luc Godard, a French director who also takes a lively interest in sound effects and sound collages. Utilizing a technology that allows him to always work on location, Godard has instructed soundmen Jacques Maumont and René Levert to give him tracks on which radios blare, sirens whine, and metros rumble, denying his protagonists the privacy of studio-recorded conversations. Such abortive communications as do take place in Godard's world must go on amid the clatter of pinball machines, the roar of construction equipment, and an occasional burst of machine-gun fire.

Sometimes these sounds are obviously symbolic, as in *Two or Three Things I Know about Her* (1966), where the pounding of drills and hammers stands for the destruction of French culture through American-istic "modernization." Sometimes Godard's sounds are more subtly symbolic, however, as in the complex, allusive sound effects of *Contempt*.

Contempt is a film about filmmaking, specifically the effort to make a film of the *Odyssey* under the auspices of international co-produc-tion. It becomes a vehicle for Godard's complaints against commercial-ization of the cinema and the heavy hand of Americanism in European cultural affairs. The antagonists of *Contempt* are an American producer, played by Jack Palance, a former gunslinger of cowboy movies, and a European director, played by Fritz Lang, a filmmaker who left Germany in the 1930s rather than bow to the political will of the Nazis. The pub-lic past of each man is relevant to the role he plays in the film and to the way Godard orchestrates the sound score. In one scene, for ex-ample, the Palance character tells the man hired to script Lang's con-ception of the *Odyssey*, "Everytime someone says 'culture' I reach for my checkbook." This paraphrases a comment popularly attributed to Nazi Propaganda Minister, Joseph Goebbels: "Everytime someone mentions 'culture' I reach for my revolver." The allusion clarifies a point central to the film — as far as the arts are concerned, the Ameri-can checkbook now does the work of the Nazi revolver, threatening Lang's understanding of the *Odyssey* in the same way Lang's right to make films in Germany was once threatened by Goebbels. The allusion is tightened by memories of Palance as the fast-draw villain who ruth-lessly gunned down the good-natured homesteader in *Shane*. But in case anyone has forgotten Palance's earlier career, Godard has the American star begin kicking film tins around the room right after he tosses off this line. The noise resonates like revolver shots, pressing home the connection between the checkbook and the six-gun, Goeb-bels and Hollywood.

Godard's approach to the sound track, as well as the earlier inspira-tion of Welles, has notably influenced the young American director Peter Bogdanovitch, whose *Targets* (1968) makes good use of illusive and symbolic noise. The film is about a psychopathic killer who com-pensates for feelings of inferiority and insecurity by committing ran-dom assassinations on a Los Angeles freeway, later at a drive-in movie. While the distraught protagonist gradually slips into his destructively aberrant behavior, cryptic media messages, unsynchronized with the visuals, hint at his personal problems and foreshadow the film's terrify-ing denouement.

Early in the film we casually overhear a radio announcement for Otto Preminger's *Anatomy of a Murder*. Since the camera is paying attention to other matters we might be inclined to dismiss this advertisement as incidental static, though the word "murder" would almost certainly continue to ring in our ears. The allusion, however, is more fully coherent with the thematic progression of *Targets* than one would first suppose. For anyone at all well informed about American film history will remember that Preminger's *Anatomy* dealt with a man who was "seized by an irresistible impulse." And naturally this impulse was homicidal, as is the one that afflicts the handsome, clean-cut protagonist of *Targets*. Hence before we have any clear evidence of how desperately he will act, we already have cause to fear his frustrations may take a violent turn.

In another scene we hear from the television set, as the grotesque cacklings of a comedy show point up the protagonist's feelings of inferiority. The young man with problems has just returned home from another unrewarding day to a father who bullies him, a mother who babies him, and a wife who never feels like discussing their difficulties. The family is watching TV, and the set flickers at the edge of the frame through a few moments of perfunctory conversation. Then the protagonist leaves the room and walks alone into an adjoining hallway, the camera following. Here the jokes of the television comic are no longer audible; instead we hear only the laugh track, with its giggles, chortles, and occasionally loud guffaws. Since there is no visible source of laughter and no intelligible prompting of its rhythmic bursts, we get the impression that somehow the world at large, some huge glob of humanity from beyond the camera, is repeatedly laughing at the lonely figure who lingers in the underlit corridor. This sound take perfectly dramatizes the feelings that cause him to pick up his rifle and go gunning for his tormentors.

Another form of contrapuntal sound is used in *Diary of a Mad Housewife* (U.S.A., 1970) — a combination of freeze-frame photography with "voice-over" comment. The scene takes place at the end of the picture, after Tina — a much put-upon housewife — has fled from the victimizing demands of her ambitious husband into a love affair with a natty, but equally exploitative would-be writer. Their amour is now over, and Tina is tentatively reconciled with her husband, though still deeply confused, disoriented, and unsatisfied with the solution circumstances seem to force upon her. In this frame of mind she consults a psychiatrist who apparently recommends group therapy. As we follow her through one of these sessions, however, the match between sight and sound makes us realize there can be no easy way out of Tina's quandary.

The scene settles quickly into a tight close-up of Tina, gleaning the response of those who have heard her describe her infidelity, its motives and extenuating elements. She is obviously trying to extract guidance from the chorus of voices that quarrel, cajole, or simply maunder.

But suddenly her expression is fixed by freeze framing into a look of bewildered anxiety. After the image has been frozen, naturally the voices continue, repeating their admonitions and observations. But the immobility of Tina's face shows us she is beyond their reach and that their comments, while clearly audible, might just as well be mere static. Such interaction between word and image effectively debunks conventional "solutions" to domestic entrapment and marital disaster. Since the advice to Tina proferred in the voice-over commentary may compare closely with what the theatergoer himself would be tempted to suggest, this conclusion to the film denies the spectator the solace of his stock response.

TRICKY MIXES, NEW NOISES: DISTORTED AND ELECTRONIC SOUND

The mix and the moving camera; mixing in voice collage. Possibility of creatively reshaping everyday sound. The effect of off-speed recording: Throne of Blood. *Filtered sound:* The Long Day's Dying. *Electronic noise:* One Day in the Life of Ivan Denisovitch. *A new dimension in sound:* The Conversation.

Though the point might escape immediate notice, most imaginative instances of audiovisual integration require a rather complicated sound mix. In a voice-over sequence, for instance, one speaker's voice must fade and a second rise to prominence, while the rumble of human static in the background remains at pretty much the same level. If the visuals happen to be a freeze frame, as in *Diary of a Mad Housewife*, then the technician in charge of the mix can concentrate on sound alone, and his task is to some extent simplified. But the moving camera and the fluid image, so very prominent in contemporary cinema, introduce new demands. Take, for example, even something so simple as a zoom-in. Suppose the camera is threading its way among the guests at a political reception, its lens observing the crowd of dignitaries from a wide-angle setting, its overhead mike picking up the bits and pieces of many conversations. Suddenly, a disturbance in the corner of the room causes the camera to pan left, and the lens is zoomed toward its telephoto setting so we can see what's going on. Naturally, as we travel optically toward the faces of the two disputants,

OFF-SPEED SOUND. The garbling of the protagonist's voice in the climactic scenes of *Throne of Blood* emphasizes his slipping to the animal level of grunts and snarls. It is fully in keeping with the sound track that he should be represented visually as the victim of the hunters' arrows. © 1974 Toho International.

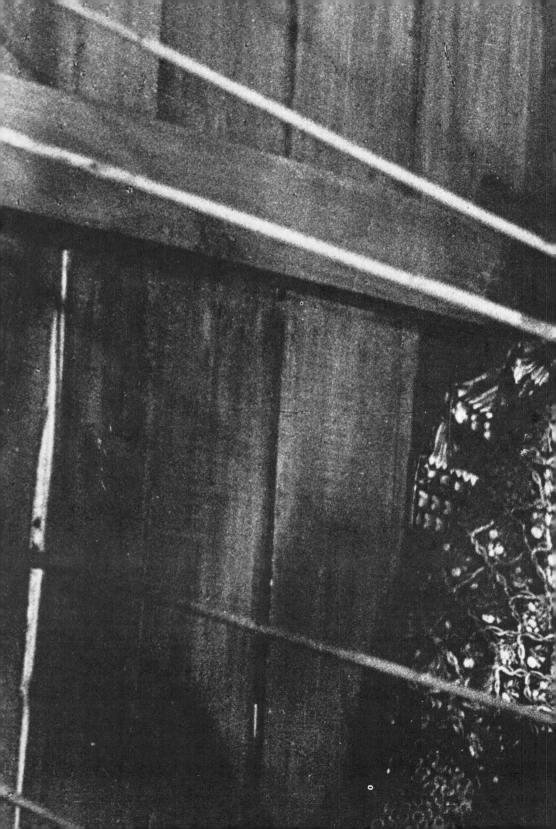

we expect to hear their voices get louder, more distinct in relation to those of the other speakers in the room. But since there's no such thing as a zoom microphone, these expectations will have to be satisfied in the rerecording process, where the principal voices may be dubbed in, programmed for increasingly ample volume, and finally timed or otherwise adjusted to the competing noises on the premises. All this is accomplished in the mixing console. The rule of thumb in these matters is simply: the more complicated the camera gesture, the more intricate the sound mix.

To anyone who knows the ABCs of the sound studio, the effects of rerecording and mixing are everywhere apparent in today's cinema. But the more startling instances are surely the more noticeable. When, for example in *The Three Musketeers* (Britain, 1973), Raquel Welch begins speaking with a man's voice, we know we are hearing dubbed sound, which in context produces a comic yet dramatically appropriate effect, since the falsification of sound conveys information to the audience. We know that her words have been overheard by a political informer, who is now passing them along to his superiors. Rerecording may produce other deliberately unnatural effects, as happens, for instance, when sound filters are used, or a tape is run through the console backwards, or perhaps just mixed at the wrong speed.

This possibility for "off-speed" sound mixing has already been used to good advantage in the cinema, not for comic "Donald Duck" effects as one might suppose, but as tragic irony in *Throne of Blood* (Japan, 1957), Akira Kurosawa's effort to make an Oriental version of *Macbeth*. Abandoning any effort toward a "faithful" adaptation of Shakespeare, the director opts instead for a calculatedly antirealistic style, where the actors use coiling, exaggerated gestures and the sound score mimes the strange notes of classical Noh drama. Of particular consequence is the gradual deformation of the voice track. Lord Washizu (the Macbeth figure) at first speaks in a perfectly natural manner. But as he dips his hands deeper and deeper into the blood of his countrymen during his illicit rise to power the recording of his speech is progressively slowed until it assumes an inhumanly gutteral tone. The intent is to suggest Washizu's degeneration, marking his decline from noble warrior to violent animal. In the last scenes of the picture his grunting efforts at speech tell us he has become a wild beast no longer capable of human behavior.

Deliberate distortion is also effectively used in *The Long Day's Dying* (Britain, 1968), where sound filters operate in conjunction with dramatic voice-over. These techniques produce a very convincing form of subjective monologue.

The Long Day's Dying is an antimilitarist film which studies the dehumanizing effects of warfare from the perspective of three paratroopers in a no-man's land between their lines and the enemy's during World War II. As they wait in vain for a sergeant who never joins them, we are given the opportunity to study the psychic impact of continuous threat upon their behavior. Even though they are an elite corps, a cadre of modern centurians (the American Green Berets are the obviously intended analogue), their expertise gradually fails them, going lame in the face of unexpressed, but powerfully felt anxieties. The sensitive voice-over monologue, which allows us to eavesdrop upon one mind after another, is the crucial element in the transmission of insight into character under the extremities of stress.

In these endlessly explaining, excusing, self-justifying monologues, we comprehend the desperate effort to maintain sanity in a madhouse world. Sometimes the individual qualities of a voice are clearly recognizable as is that of would-be humanist David Hemmings, who keeps repeating "I believe in the human spirit. I do. I do." And here we are expected to connect a particular thought with a particular man. In other cases, however, the individuating tone of the voice is modulated by sound filters, making it less easy to pin the thought to the thinker. This then suggests a kind of collective impression, a reservoir of responses that the three men share in common because of the training, discipline, and indoctrination each has undergone. Depending upon these variables, the monologue technique either isolates the protagonists from one another or fuses them into a lethally efficient team.

The camera also interacts with the voice track in producing director Peter Collinson's thematic controls. Often the long lens of Brian Probyn glides in and out of selective focus, successively sharpening the face of each character while a continuous voice-over records the hopes, memories, and moment-by-moment resolves that protect him from mental breakdown. At one point this manipulation of focus operates with particular irony. One of the paratroopers who is guarding a German prisoner mentally sentences him to death in dialectal English: "You're gonner die." But as the lens shifts focus to sharpen the face of the German, we hear another voice, presumably that of the prisoner, who offers a rejoinder to the unspoken threat of his captor. An imposing battle of wills is thus joined without any stock "what-we're-fighting-for" speeches, in fact without either of the characters even moving his lips. Voice-over effects have rarely been used with more delicacy than in *The Long Day's Dying*.

While much has been done in the last two decades with the symbolic reshaping of everyday voice or noise, the cinema has also begun to use electronic-effects generators to achieve a completely new chorus of effects. These machines can simulate almost all the timbres of music as well as most wild sounds, from raging wind to running water. But we are more likely to remember their bleeps, whistles, and whines, which are at the moment the most modish thing in film sound scores. They are already a cliché in science-fiction films, yet their potential is sometimes shown to better advantage, as in *Red Desert,* where the unfamiliarity of the sound underscores the disorientation of the heroine in the presence of contemporary, industrial culture.

One Day in the Life of Ivan Denisovitch (Britain, 1971) is similarly a step in the right direction as to the treatment of electronic effects. Here too the intention is to disorient us, as we are drawn in the opening shots into the world of a forced-labor camp somewhere in Siberia. At first we see no more than a mysterious circle of lights, hanging hauntingly in the distance as we slowly approach, apparently from the air. There is nothing in this long "establishing shot" to really establish anything — nothing to say where we are, what time it is, what sort of structure we are advancing upon. The sound track is equally cryptic, frustrating our curiosity with the static of tiny bells and buzzes. This approach to sound is much more suggestive than conventional "suspense music," with its predictable dissonances and chromatic chords. The effects disturb us profoundly, not because they mean "danger" but because they mean nothing, because they speak from a world beyond our experience. Instead of shocking us, they delay our shock, making the stark realism of the dramatic treatment more imposing, as we cease our unexplained nocturnal wanderings and descend into the midst of prisoners hidden away in this arctic wasteland.

The contemporary possibilities of sound, however, are perhaps more fully exemplified in *The Conversation* (U.S.A., 1974), where we find complex fades and mixes, deliberate distortions, ironic replays, and protracted mismatches of sound and picture, all of which are functional and expressive. The film is about a professional snoop who accidentally gets involved in a murder, and it is from the haphazard sound collage picked up by his recording equipment that we get our only insight into the crime he has (one might say) "overheard."

The substance of the film is a fragmentary conversation between a young man and a young woman, apparently lovers, but really accomplices to a murder plot. Sound expert and private investigator Harry Caul, "the best bugger on the West Coast," has been hired to spy on them, for which purpose he invades the privacy of their noontime walks with a "Mission Impossible" conglomeration of tape decks, amplifiers, and supersensitive mikes. With this technology he can snatch up the asides they whisper as they mingle among crowds, or sort out covert remarks made against a background of music and street noise. But to do so Caul must continually replay and re-monitor his globs of sound tape, patching together different tracks, cutting into and out of nonsequential exchanges, damping the static and scramble that effaces the human voice. This creates an almost expressionistic collage of fast-forward gibberish and squealing rewind noises. It also brings us all our information indirectly and ambiguously, without a firm context and without supporting visuals, a technique which leaves us, like Harry Caul, groping for the sound cues that might give meaning to the verbal ruminations we have eavesdropped upon.

If there is a "key" to the meaning of The Conversation, it lies in the phrase "he'd kill us if he had the chance," a line whose importance is underscored by the difficulty Caul experiences in picking it up. The couple dodges into a dense sound envelope before the statement occurs, and it is only after three failing efforts that Caul, using special electronic boosters, manages to separate the verbal signal from the surrounding noise. Aside from the suspense this creates, however, there is the more important question of interpretation (Caul's and ours). Soon we hear this phrase echoing through the detective's own mind, subtly altered in aural emphasis ("he'd *kill* us if he had the chance") by the sense of responsibility Caul has begun to feel. We then project Caul's interpretation upon the more neutral accents of the phrase as intoned upon the original tape. This means, in effect, that we come to regard the couple we have heard talking as threatened by a jealous husband who will probably murder them when he gets the evidence to prove they are lovers. This handling of the sound track thus sets up the ironic reversal upon which the plot of The Conversation depends.

In attempting to rescue the endangered couple, Caul eventually discovers that they are the murderers, not the victims. At this point the crucial phrase again sounds in the protagonist's mind, now with what is apparently the correct emphasis: "He'd kill us if *he* had the chance." In other words, the point is not whether there will be a killing but who will kill whom. What Caul has construed as the young man's fear that he would be killed is actually that man's justification of his decision to help kill someone else. By its ingenious promotion of sound over sight, The Conversation makes a point not only about the doubtful reliability of electronic evidence. It also touches upon the problem of knowing human motives and intentions in our increasingly more fragmented and impersonal world.

Although partners for half a century, sound still tends to compare badly in imagination and dynamism with the photography it accompanies. The technical potential is there, since magnetic sound has already revolutionized recording, greatly facilitated mixing, and still holds out the possibility of stereophonic and now even quadratic transmission. But for every ten directors with a refined visual sense it is hard to find one with an equally sophisticated ear. And unlike the now prestigious directors of photography, the sound men and sound editors never emerged from the studio bureaucracies with enough independence or authority to initiate anything on their own. Hence the persistence of musical clichés and recitations into the camera. But films like *The Conversation* suggest that voice and noise are now being approached more experimentally than ever before. Perhaps the cinema's wave of the future will turn out to be a sound wave.

List of Films Discussed*

A NOUS, LA LIBERTÉ   87 min.   CON
ALEXANDER NEVSKY   107 min.   AUD-BRA
CITIZEN KANE   119 min.   AUD-BRA, FNC, JAN
CONTEMPT   103 min.   AUD-BRA
DIARY OF A MAD HOUSEWIFE   94 min.   TWY
DIVORCE ITALIAN STYLE   104 min.   AUD-BRA
DON'T LOOK BACK   95 min.   LEA
GREED   150 min.   FNC
HIGH SCHOOL   75 min.   ZIP
HUNCHBACK OF NOTRE DAME, THE   90 min.   FCE (musical
     sound track), TWY
LADY FROM SHANGHAI, THE   87 min.   AUD-BRA
LONG DAY'S DYING, THE   93 min.   FNC
OCTOBER (TEN DAYS THAT SHOOK THE WORLD)   105 min.
     AUD-BRA, MMA
ONE DAY IN THE LIFE OF IVAN DENISOVITCH   not presently
     available
PHANTOM OF THE OPERA   75 min.   AUD-BRA, FNC, TWY
PRIMARY   54 min.   TIME
STRANGER, THE   95 min.   UAS
STRIKE   90 min.   AUD-BRA, MMA
TARGETS   90 min.   FNC
THRONE OF BLOOD   105 min.   AUD-BRA
TWO TIMID PEOPLE (LES DEUX TIMIDES)   90 min.   CON

* See p. 329 for key to film distributors code.

5
STORY AND SCRIPT

Film is primarily a visual experience sustained by the cameraman and the director. It is also an aural experience, a constantly changing mix of music, voice, and noise. But most films also require the services of a writer. Though a few pictures may simply be found, most of them are thought up, plotted out, and written down. Robert Gessner perhaps betrays too great a bias on behalf of the script when he speaks of films as the work of a "writer-director," yet his emphasis on the scenario is a worthwhile corrective to the critics who have ignored it altogether.[1] And Robert Richardson clearly argues to the point when he claims that film, like literature, is essentially a "storytelling" art.[2] Presumably, whatever a film has to say is somehow implicit in the story that it tells.

This story may be the work of a single scenarist or a screenwriting team. It may originate *ab ovo* from the mind of its author, or it may be, as is more often the case, developed and revamped from a novel, a memoir, or a play. Sometimes the director scripts the film himself, out of completely original material; this is the customary practice of Jean Cocteau and Ingmar Bergman, both professional playwrights. On the

[1] From the book *The Moving Image* by Robert Gessner. Copyright © 1968 by Robert Gessner. Published by E. P. Dutton & Co., Inc. and used with their permission.
[2] *Literature and Film* (Bloomington: Indiana University Press, 1969).

other hand, a director like Jean Renoir often pulls the plot of a picture out of his head but generally leaves the dialogue to a writer such as Jacques Prévert or Charles Spaak. The Anglo-American cinema has always leaned heavily toward adaptation, a skill which brought fame to scenarist Dudley Nichols in his work with John Ford and which more recently has added a further dimension to the independent reputation of Harold Pinter. In some instances, the film story has been a more impromptu thing, as in Italy during the neorealist era, where a whole ensemble of scenarists might get together to put words in the mouths of the characters. But here there would always be an "idea man," like Cesare Zavattini or a firm-handed director like Michelangelo Antonioni to see that the narrative was kept on a meaningful course. Whether the product of one or several hands, a film story must always have a dramatic shape.

Dramatically effective scripts always involve two interrelated elements — speech and structure. The scenarist must give the characters both something to say and something to do. He must have a good ear for dialogue, but he must also know how to create conflict, sustain suspense, and achieve resolution. He must develop what is usually called a "film treatment," i.e., a line of action and a set of interdependent scenes. What words are needed to define an attitude? Will a one-line retort suffice, or must there be an extended exchange? What stage business is right to sum up a situation? Slamming a car door? Attempting a kiss? Drawing a gun? Whether the writer's identity is single or collective, his role is substantially the same. He must sort out the dramatic possibilities of the material, so as to focus the conception that inspired the film.

Naturally both speech and action must unfold in relation to a visual design. The story ought not depend too heavily upon either verbal exchange or abstract structure. Dialogue and discourse must always interact with movements, light accents, and sound effects. We can't be talked out of what we have seen or talked into things the camera has overlooked. Hollywood writer Stirling Silliphant, author of screenplays for such films as *Nightfall* (1956), *The Slender Thread* (1965), and *In the Heat of the Night* (1966), makes a cogent point about the relationship of word to image and the responsibilities this relationship entails. "Everything I see," he says, "I see only in the visual sense, not the literary sense. I only think in terms of frames of film. Everything I see is a composition of arrangements, of elements within a photograph." [3] This would hold true of every talented scriptwriter, from the subjectivist and psychoanalytical Ingmar Bergman to the ironic Charles Spaak or Jean Renoir.

[3] *The Screenwriter Looks at the Screenwriter*, ed. William Froug (New York: The Macmillan Company, 1972), p. 300. Copyright © 1972 by William Froug.

Though film scenarios differ widely in shape, subject, and tone, there are three tendencies that seem marked with relative clarity. The first, perhaps for want of a better word, I would call a "rhetorical" tendency in scriptwriting. Writers of this persuasion try to encode much of the plot into dialogue and handle conflict as verbal exchange, even debate, among the various protagonists. Often, as in the films of Renoir, this impulse goes hand in hand with rigorous consolidation of the action and a tendency to organize the dramatic energy into a minimal number of relatively extended scenes. Although there is ample physical movement and sometimes expert camera work, the scenes build toward climactic speeches in which the thematic concerns of the film are articulated and resolved. Scenarists of this school often take inspiration from the theater, a fact particularly obvious in the scripts of Jean Cocteau and Ingmar Bergman.

On the other hand, there are writers who fabricate much looser structures, characterized by a much freer use of physical space and more emphasis upon dynamic action. Dialogue is sparser and more wayward, less fully charged with the thematic import of the film. Such scripts might best be called "picarseque," after a type of prose fiction that records a series of loosely related adventures. Genre pictures like the western and gangster film call for this approach to writing, as was well appreciated by Hollywood scenarists such as Dudley Nichols, Ben Hecht, and James Agee. This conception of script is also basic to Italian neorealism.

Recently there has evolved still another tendency in scriptwriting. This I have called the "anti-story," since it is characterized by very loose plotting and by a calculated refusal to resolve the issues that it raises. Sometimes such films make do with comparatively little concentrated speech, as is true of Antonioni's films from the Italian-made *Il Grido* (1957) and *L'Avventura* (1960) to the English-language *Blow-up* (1966) and *Zabriskie Point* (1969). On the other hand, the scripts of Jean-Luc Godard show the same disaffection for tight, fully intelligible story lines, yet they typically use a quite expansive rhetoric. Such scripts force us to redefine the motive and meaning of speech.

Rival tendencies in scriptwriting have been with us since the beginning of the sound era. They express the preferences of writers and directors more than the demands of the prevailing technology. This point notwithstanding, the impulse toward consolidation and coherence was once more substantial than it is today. While there is no solid link between technology and the film scenario, the acceptance of looser, more impromptu scripts has developed along with available-light photography and nonstudio sound recording. Here, as in so many other situations, the machinery of the cinema has applied pressure beyond its own sphere.

RHETORICAL STRUCTURES

The fully articulated script really emerged with the coming of the sound film. Before that there had been some heroic efforts at plot making, as the epic structures of D. W. Griffith testify, and in Germany such would-be scenarists as Thea von Harbou, with her very detailed titling for the silent films of Fritz Lang, had tried doggedly to expand the role of the writer. Furthermore, scenarist Carl Mayer had also left his impress upon German cinema, helping to shape the directorial work of Robert Wiene and F. W. Murnau. These facts notwithstanding, the centrality of script to the cinema was finally assured by the "talkies," which demanded that actors have fixed lines to read, rehearse, and recite. Since the investment in sound recording prohibited the extensive improvisation possible before 1925, the initial impact of this technological innovation was to produce closely plotted, heavily rhetorical films. But while some scenarists were thus pushed into verbal prolixity, others — like the remarkable group of writers who gathered around Renoir, Marcel Carné, and Julien Duvivier — found in the sound film the opportunity to create dense, compact, and meaningful argument.

THE ARGUMENTATIVE APPROACH TO SCRIPT

Jean Renoir and the problem-oriented scenario. The "October Group." Renoir and Jacques Prévert: The Crime of Monsieur Lange. *Prévert's capacity for consolidation. His poetic and allegorical tendency. Renoir and Charles Spaak:* Grand Illusion. *Primacy of the spoken word and the complete scene. Persistent interest in argument and social analysis.*

The films of Jean Renoir, particularly his best-known pictures from the late 1930s, nicely exemplify what a tight plot and rich dialogue can contribute to the cinema. They show equally well how a director and his scenarists can borrow from the theatre without binding the cinema unduly to the conventions of the stage. Renoir's plots always have the rigorous cohesion of a good play, and the dialogue, whether by Renoir himself *(Rules of the Game)* or one of his prime collaborators (Charles Spaak, *Grand Illusion;* Jacques Prévert, *The Crime of Monsieur Lange*), is invariably organized into an argument about the current ills of European society. Like every competent playwright, he prefers psychic revelation to physical adventure and consigns battles or street brawls to the reports of messengers from offstage. Still his films never lack cinematic energy, since his spacious multilevel sets encourage movement, while short lenses and a mobile camera enhance every movement we see. His characters become spokesmen for their class or their generation without ever seeming stiffly allegorical figures, and his plots are smoothly rounded without ever seeming facile.

Renoir's first great creative period began in the middle 1930s under the inspiration of the so-called October Group, a small collection of politically active artists eager to form a united front against fascism and capitalism. These shared interests set him to collaborating with another member of this group, poet Jacques Prévert, and the result was *The Crime of Monsieur Lange* (1935). Like most political advocacy in the arts, this picture is built to support a thesis. But its sense of pace and climax, its imaginative integration of visual and verbal metaphor, raise the film well above the crudely propagandistic plane.

Monsieur Lange is meant to impress upon us that even murder is justifiable when it represents the self-defense of society's underlings against capitalist exploitation. We are asked to excuse the "crime" of Amedée Lange, who shoots his former employer, Batala, after the latter tries through legal trickery to recover the publishing business he had abandoned and which has now passed into the hands of a socialist co-op. So that we will better understand the argument of the film, the entire story is told in flashback. Undertaking to escape after the murder, Lange is identified and cornered in a small border village before he can slip across into Spain, at that time a socialist country. Under threat of being turned over to the authorities, Lange is forced to explain his shooting of Batala, i.e., justify his behavior before an informally constituted jury of his peers. The fact that the entire narrative unfolds as a defense of Lange against these accusers strikingly focuses the moral issues of the film. The organization is as tight as a lawyer's brief that pleads the relevance of extenuating circumstances and a "higher law."

The flashback device in *Monsieur Lange* was part of the original shooting sketch Renoir turned over to Prévert for elaboration. More consequential for the film, however, was the decision Renoir apparently made only after consultation with his scenarist, i.e., the agreement to situate as much of the action as possible in the large courtyard, which serves as a kind of master set. Here we find not only Batala's publishing house but an ensemble of shops which house a representative cross-section of lower-middle-class French society. Because of this unity of setting, we tend to see individual acts as part of a clearly defined social world. We note how Batala cheats and intimidates the whole neighborhood, how his petty arrogance overflows into even his most casual relations with other people. By the same token, this group of near neighbors gives us the communal nucleus that generates the co-op, created after Batala flees to avoid prosecution for fraud. Whether the thought came from Prévert or Renoir, the decision to prune away various other setting stipulated in the first script was clearly a good one, promoting tightness and interaction.[4]

Prévert's stage business and dialogue also enhance thematic connections barely hinted at in Renoir's early sketch of the plot. One instance is Lange's fantasy of himself as "Arizona Jim," the cartoon character he draws for Batala's illustrated weekly. Renoir's proto-script suggests some association of Lange with the wild-west hero, recommending at one point that the illustrator be costumed "with a cowboy hat on his head" and shown "testing his aim with a bow and arrow." But only in Prévert's final script is this motif developed in a manner symbolically integral to the plot. Here "Arizona Jim" becomes Lange's full-fledged alter ego, and his frontiersman's ethic moves Lange to act against the nefarious Batala. As the dialogue cooperates with the camera to show us Lange's increasingly close identification with Jim (the shots of posters and the cartoons themselves are relevant here), we come to sense an almost mythic antagonism between Lange and Batala. Lange is the people's champion, the custodian of "natural right"; Batala, particularly when he returns to the scene disguised as a priest, is the archetypal villain, the avatar of deceit and simulation. His stolen clerical robes costume him in black, completing the symbolic pattern of hero versus devil. In gunning down Batala with his revolver, Lange lives out the role imposed by his fantasy life, accepting his mission as the straight-thinking, straight-shooting cowboy whose six-gun cleanses the world of perverted authority.

The Crime of Monsieur Lange also demonstrates the cooperation of director and scenarist in the pacing and management of individual scenes. The characters are often talkative but never when the camera work demands their silence. In the climactic scene where Lange shoots Batala, word and image work in perfect harmony. First there is a great silence as Lange seeks out Batala, moving visibly from room to room of the huge set, bent on an act we fully anticipate and need not hear discussed or described. But after the shooting we are offered a long, unexpected soliloquy from a drunken old man who was once in the

---

[4] The first draft of the shooting script for *Monsieur Lange* is reprinted in André Bazin, *Jean Renoir,* tr. W. W. Halsey II and William H. Simon (New York: Simon and Schuster, 1973), pp. 159–171. © 1973. By permission of Simon & Schuster, Inc.

French foreign legion. His rambling, booze-inspired wit has nothing to do with the story, but the tone of his monologue helps restore the seriocomic balance which has hitherto prevailed. The further function of his loquacity is to delay the discovery of the crime, to distract us from our own demand that the corpse turn up and the pursuit of Lange begin.

If the speech were less brilliant, we would immediately be disturbed by this deliberate directorial stalling. As it stands, however, the interruption of the action seems perfectly natural and Lange is provided with all the time needed to make his escape dramatically plausible. Although Renoir soon turned to scenarists who gave him less baroque dialogue and decor, he had no cause to regret what Prévert had provided for *The Crime of Monsieur Lange*.

Renoir's collaboration with Charles Spaak in *Grand Illusion* (1937) brought a plainer style to the dialogue and greater simplicity to the design. But the scenarist of Jacques Feyder's *Carnival in Flanders* (1936) and Renoir's *The Lower Depths* (1936) brought gifts of his own to *Grand Illusion:* a keen sense of verbal irony and a capacity to imbue plain speech with symbolic implications. Above all, he brought a sense of order and a capacity for consolidation which proved perfectly coherent with Renoir's personal instincts toward plot. Hence we see in *Grand Illusion* a structure quite typical of nearly all Renoir's films. The events are confined to a few fully articulated arenas of action; one scene is carefully balanced against another; even the characters are symmetrically paired, so as to throw into high relief their advocacy of conflicting value systems. Like Prévert, Spaak helped Renoir compress the dramatic action and achieve verbal precision.

Unlike most "war pictures," *Grand Illusion* is very sparing of action. The main characters are fliers, but we never see an airplane, let alone aerial combat. All of Europe is in the trenches, but we know of World War I only through posters, newspapers, and conversation. Even the stage business normally associated with prison camps is minimized. The mode is rigorously analytical. The extent to which Spaak refined Renoir's tendency in this direction can be seen in his revision and compression of several early scenes.[5]

Renoir intended that *Grand Illusion* should show the emergence of the French democratic spirit from the social upheaval of World War I. This spirit is personified in Captain Maréchal, whom Renoir introduces in his early script suggestions as "a rugged character without polish, a mechanic by trade." Though "the fortunes of war and his own merits have brought him his commission very quickly," he remains temperamentally the exact opposite of Captain de Boeldieu, who with his "monocle in place" and "riding crop in hand" typifies the traditional French aristocracy. Renoir suggests that the first scenes establish the

[5] *Ibid.*, pp. 172–182, gives the first-draft version of *Grand Illusion*.

extreme class consciousness of Boeldieu and hint strongly at his antagonism toward Maréchal. It must be shown, says Renoir, that "Boeldieu and Maréchal are of the same rank, but not of the same world."

To make these introductions, Renoir recommends the following treatment. Boeldieu, a cavalry officer, should approach Maréchal "with a touch of arrogance and impertinence," asking the pilot to "take him on a reconnaissance flight." Once airborne, however, "Boeldieu cannot see anything because of the clouds. 'Horses,' he says, 'we'll go back to them eventually. Nothing like them for reconnaissance.' " As if confirming Boeldieu's worst expectations about airplanes, the engine then stalls, forcing them to land behind enemy lines and provoking Boeldieu to describe the whole episode as "annoying." While the thrust of Renoir's suggested exposition is perfectly clear, it lacks smoothness and concentration, perhaps even plausibility. From this standpoint we can see how much it profits from later revisions, where Spaak's dialogue reveals Boeldieu more subtly while eliminating (without loss) both the flight and the crash.

As we now know the film, it opens with Captain Maréchal bending over a phonograph record. In the first close-up, he repeats its romantic lyrics, "Frou-Frou, Frou-Frou." The shots tell us Maréchal is a rather reluctant warrior, utterly different in dress and manner from Captain de Boeldieu, to whom he is almost immediately introduced. Though Boeldieu's interest in horses will appear later, Spaak suppresses his connection with the cavalry and gives him no obvious suspicion of airplanes. Presumably, the rather facile playing off of horse versus machine proved too contrived a metaphor of the class antagonism between the two officers. Besides, speech and professional bearing are sufficient to distinguish the man of inherited pedigree from the promoted mechanic. As they discuss a particular reconnaissance photo, their differences become precisely marked.

As Boeldieu first confronts Maréchal, there is immediately a businesslike atmosphere, a coldness on Boeldieu's part that excludes any sort of informal pleasantries:

Boeldieu:	I say, Monsieur Maréchal, do you know this photograph?
Maréchal:	Oh yes, Captain . . . Ricard took it when he was with me.
Boeldieu:	And is Monsieur Ricard around?
Maréchal:	He's on leave.
Boeldieu:	Of course! [6]

The distance between the two men resonates powerfully in Boeldieu's ironic "Of course!" While Maréchal finds it perfectly natural that a

[6] Textual citations are from *Grand Illusion*, tr. Marianne Alexandre and Andrew Sinclair (New York: Simon and Schuster, 1968). Translation copyright © 1968 by Lorrimer Publishing Limited. Reprinted with their permission.

fellow officer should be away from the front (he himself has just been talking about a trip to Epernay to see his girl friend), Boeldieu is clearly irked by the part-time soldiering of the new French army. He is, naturally, resigned to this change, as to all the others that are sweeping away the heroic world of the past.

Another quality of Boeldieu's character is skillfully incorporated into the exchange that continues, as Boeldieu, Maréchal, and Captain Ringis examine Ricard's problematic photo:

Boeldieu: It's that gray spot that worries me. . . . There, below the road.
Ringis: It's not a road, it's a canal.
Maréchal: Is it? I thought it was some railway lines.
Boeldieu: What touching unanimity! . . . This precise detail gives one a fine idea of the perfection of our photographic equipment.
Maréchal: Well, it was a misty day.
Boeldieu: I would like to resolve this enigma.

Boeldieu's fretting over "that gray spot" of course expresses his wholehearted commitment to his professional tasks. But the phrase has an ambiguous ring, suggesting that his demand for absolute clarity may be less a matter of military urgency than an expression of his personal fastidiousness. Just as he would never tolerate a smudge on his uniform or allow a hair of his head to go uncombed, so he will not accept a photograph that blurs under the scrutiny of his ever-present monocle. Here he has the advantage of the exchange, since both Maréchal and Ringis seem lazy and slipshod about their duties. But Maréchal's casualness gives him greater flexibility than Boeldieu, a point terribly important to the further development of the film. What we notice about this scene is that Spaak, while transcending caricature, has succinctly defined Boeldieu's aristocratic hauteur, taking account of both its positive and negative qualities.

As the narrative unfolds, Spaak's dialogue continues to define the shifting relations between the characters. In the long episode at Hallbach prison, where Maréchal first begins to displace Boeldieu as the moral center of the film, the verbally central conversation is an exchange upon the nature of patriotism. Asked why he wishes to escape from prison, Maréchal responds as we would expect: "I just want to do like everyone else. . . . Besides, it gets me down to be here while the others are all getting knocked off." The first comment reveals the same unreflectiveness we have seen in Maréchal before; obviously duty to country is not something he has spent much time brooding over. But his voice becomes more energetic in the second sentence, and his motives seem spontaneously generous, even though romantically vague. Boeldieu, on the other hand, has everything clearly worked out: "As far as I'm concerned, the question does not come up. . . . What is the

THE WELL-MADE PLOT. The script of Renoir-Spaak for *Grand Illusion* is organized into rather extended scenes allowing rich rhetorical orchestration, such as is exemplified in this conversational exchange between Boeldieu (Pierre Fresnay) and Rauffenstein (Eric von Stroheim). Photograph (*left*) courtesy of Janus Films and The Museum of Modern Art/Film Stills Archive.

At the same time, however, the verbal elaboration is always complemented by the visual, as when Boeldieu's ascent to the parapets of Wintersborn draws the prison's searchlights after him. Courtesy of Janus Films.

purpose of a golf course? To play golf. A tennis court? To play tennis. Well, a prison camp is there to escape from." Cool and apparently uninterested in his comrades (significantly, he is framed in a one-shot as he speaks), Boeldieu never touches the human in describing his loyalties. Escape is an exercise in private gymnastics, a response to what Renoir in his next film would describe as "the rules of the game." Boeldieu's metaphor of the gamesman, however, has a further reference point in *Grand Illusion*. It looks forward to his death on the towers of Wintersborn.

Boeldieu's last patriotic game is played for the benefit of his two fellow prisoners, Maréchal and Rosenthal, so that they may escape from the impregnable fortress of Wintersborn. Having concluded that his elegant world cannot survive the war, Boeldieu resolves upon the only gesture that holds meaning — the grand death scene, accomplished with poise and wit. Dying, he extends life to a new class, a pariah Jew and an ex-mechanic, whom Commandant von Rauffenstein correctly sees as "the legacy of the French revolution." But though the German Commandant fiercely resents the interlopers who are replacing the Rauffensteins and the Boeldieus, the Frenchman gaily summons his own tumbrel, apparently enjoying the spectacle his passing creates. Effectively enmeshed with other cinematic effects, the language of Boeldieu's death scene becomes an impressive memorial to the death of the class he represents.

The most interesting aspect of the scenario at this point is the way von Rauffenstein is drawn into the death of Boeldieu. Although national barriers divide these two officers, they share caste and tradition

in common, which is why von Rauffenstein so often seeks the company of Boeldieu in preference to that of his fellow countrymen. Now as Boeldieu makes his seeming attempt to escape, von Rauffenstein is immediately on the scene, pleading with him to come down from the battlements. The stage business is nicely managed, completely isolating Boeldieu from the German soldiers who pursue him from below. But the crowning touch is the verbal exchange in which von Rauffenstein, suddenly speaking English instead of German as he addresses Boeldieu, symbolically separates himself from his German comrades in a desperate effort to save the escaped prisoner. When Boeldieu also forsakes his native tongue to reply in English, the privacy of this well-bred gesture, emblematic of their cosmopolitan outlook, momentarily brings the two formal enemies psychically together. Each has more in common with the other than either has with his own countrymen.

Before the exchange begins, the camera follows Boeldieu while he climbs the massive walls of Wintersborn, tootling his ridiculous flute to draw the guard's attention. Soon we hear alarms and excursions, and the pounding of military boots is followed by the sweep of the searchlight that seeks out Boeldieu. Then an officer shouts a curt command in German: "If he passes the limits of the camp, fire at will." But after a brief volley of shots, the scene is interrupted by von Rauffenstein, shouting in English, "Boeldieu, listen."

The verbal exchange between them involves both recognition and betrayal:

Rauffenstein:	Boeldieu, have you really gone insane?
Boeldieu:	I am perfectly sane.
Rauffenstein:	Boeldieu, you understand that if you do not obey at once and come down, I shall have to shoot . . . . . I dread to do that. I beg you, man to man, come back.
Boeldieu:	It's damn nice of you, Rauffenstein, but it's impossible.

Von Rauffenstein's shift to a foreign tongue is more than an effort to speak confidentially to Boeldieu, although he could hardly have said "I *beg* you" to a runaway prisoner in German. But in addition to the matter of secrecy, this speech represents von Rauffenstein's final attempt to remind Boeldieu of the richness of their common heritage, the verbal fluency that advertises the good education and easy internationalism of Europe's prewar elite. Boeldieu shows his own mastery of this heritage when he answers in perfectly idiomatic English, "It's damn nice of you." But of course the answer is a refusal, a blunt avowal that what Rauffenstein seeks is "impossible." Betrayed in this disguised appeal to class loyalties, von Rauffenstein reluctantly fires on Boeldieu, knowing that his doom is also sealed in the fall of the hypercivilized Frenchman. The beauty of Spaak's dialogue in *Grand Illusion* is that it has both surface realism and psychological depth.

SYMBOLIC AND ASSOCIATIVE STRUCTURES

Alternative conceptions of structure. Ingmar Bergman as scenarist. His symbolic and subjectivist orientation. Symbolic language in The Seventh Seal. *Associative structure of* Wild Strawberries.

The scripts of Renoir-Prévert, Renoir-Spaak, or Renoir alone in *Rules of the Game* represent one approach to the handling of structure and dialogue. The motivation is clear, the exposition is logical, and the orientation is toward the world of public problems. The rhetoric is designed to put these problems in perspective, to make them intelligible, though not necessarily soluble. In this respect Renoir, Prévert, and Spaak all participate in the French dramatic tradition of the 1930s, which was dominated by argumentative playwrights like Jean Giraudoux, himself an acquaintance of Renoir. But there is another conception of script, which while remaining pronouncedly rhetorical is more subjective and symbolic in tendency. This orientation is manifested in scenarists such as Sweden's Ingmar Bergman, who wrote before he directed, and who came to cinema steeped in the antirealist dramaturgy of August Strindberg.

Though radically different from Renoir in theme and tone, Bergman shares with him an esteem for rhetoric and close-knit organization. "Film has nothing to do with literature," [7] he says, but we can see from his further remarks this does not rule out close attention to the scenario. For the goal of the filmmaker, he comments in another interview, is "to transfer rhythms, moods, atmosphere, tensions, sequences, tones, and scents into a readable or at least understandable script." [8] In doing so, he continues, "the vital thing is dialogue," since "the written dialogue . . . is like a score" by which the director and the performers are guided to an interpretation of the film's dramatic life. Like Renoir, Bergman realizes that filmmaking involves far more than rhetorical sophistication. Yet his inclination is to "squeeze . . . into my film scripts" as much atmospheric and tonal detail as possible. Bergman differs from Renoir and his associates in the interests that have inspired his best efforts. While Renoir looks outward toward the social world, Bergman is a deeply introverted artist, drawing his themes from the

---

[7] This comment is from Bergman's preface to *Four Screenplays of Ingmar Bergman*, tr. Lars Malmstrom and David Kushner (New York: Simon and Schuster, 1960). All citations of *The Seventh Seal* and *Wild Strawberries* are also to this text. © 1960. By permission of Simon and Schuster, Inc.

[8] This and the further citations of Bergman's personal writings are from his "Each Film Is My Last," *Tulane Drama Review*, Vol. 11, No. 1 (T33) (Fall 1966), pp. 94–102. Reprinted with permission of the author. Copyright 1966. All Rights Reserved.

tortuous vagaries of the individual psyche. Quite naturally, these differences of orientation dictate a different approach to plot. Whereas
Grand Illusion has the cogency of a well-argued debate, Bergman's
scripts deal more with reverie and dream. His ideas for a film originate
with "split-second impressions that disappear as quickly as they came,
forming a brightly colored thread shaking out of the dark sack of the
unconscious." Yet, dreams that deny him rest.

The Seventh Seal is the story of a man's eleventh-hour efforts to
make sense of his frustrating and largely painful life experience. Given
a medieval setting, apparently to justify the exceptional iconography,
the film is built around the psychic crisis of Antonius Block, a disillu-
sioned Crusader who returns to his homeland after ten years of futile
warfare in the name of Christendom. The land is plague-ridden, a fact
which contributes further to Block's anguish in the face of life's inexplicable torments. Under these stresses the erstwhile Crusader is confronted by Death, a psychic projection of his own feeling of despair.

Rather than surrender to the ghostly visitor, Block challenges him to
a game of chess. Thereafter the film develops through the interplay between highly realistic action and the symbolically staged mental processes of Bergman's groping protagonist. The import of the chess match
is first suggested through superimposition. As the two players advance
their kings' pawns, a dissolve impresses the geometrically exact patterns of the chessboard upon the fluid, asymmetrical surface of the sea.
The camera gesture thus implies Block's search for a logically structured philosophy which will order the seemingly purposeless flux of
experience and refurbish his shattered faith. The match with Death, we
realize at this point, will progress in a manner directly analogous to
Block's struggle against the spirit of negation that threatens his moral
universe. Throughout the film, Bergman's rhetoric reminds us of the
continuing connection between the chessboard and the world.

In one of the first rhetorically crucial scenes of the film, Block enters
a church, kneels in front of a small altar, and begins to blurt out his
problems in an impromptu confession. His confessor listens, making
curt replies and implicitly inviting Block to speak further. The doubts
pour out — his dissatisfaction with the "half-spoken promises and unseen miracles" of religion, his gnawing fear that "all is nothingness,"
his impatience with a God who will not "stretch out his hand toward
me." But in the end Block attempts to rally his spirits, commenting on
his chess match with Death and his plan for victory: "I use a combination of the bishop and the knight which he hasn't yet discovered. In the
next move I'll shatter one of his flanks." It is at this point that Death
reveals himself as Block's confessor and makes a note of the strategy
the Crusader has devised.

These particular words fulfill several dramatic purposes. They immediately suggest that Block isn't much of a chess player, since the "com-

THE RHETORIC OF SYMBOLIC DRAMA. Unlike the scripts of Renoir-Spaak, those of Ingmar Bergman are strongly oriented toward allegory and symbol. This demands a rhetoric that integrates abstract philosophical metaphors into the unfolding of realistic detail. The image of the chessboard from *The Seventh Seal* accurately exemplifies this approach. Photograph courtesy of Janus Films.

bination of the bishop and the knight" is one of the most conventional attack formations and relatively easy to blunt. But Bergman is not interested in playing chess critic, and the significance of the remarks lies elsewhere. Not only is this combination of moves an unimaginative game plan; it is equally unimaginative philosophy. The cooperation of knight and bishop figuratively represents that synthesis of temporal and spiritual power which characterized medieval culture and which sent Block on his misadventure in the Holy Land. The fact that he is still thinking of solutions involving knights and bishops advertises how little intellectual liberation he has thus far achieved. It also explains why Death should surprise him in church and be accorded the privilege of hearing his confession. For the priestly worldview he still implicitly endorses is the chief source of his guilt and despair.

Block's quest for values goes better after he leaves the church and finds his way into the open fields with Jof and Mia. They are contented Bergmanian innocents charged with a simple faith that requires no proofs. Traveling with their small son of whom great things are expected, they resemble the holy family, with Mia as madonna figure. When he sits down with Jof and Mia to a meal of milk and wild strawberries, Block seems rejuvenated by their youth and announces a kind of covenant between himself and the natural world: "I shall remember this moment. The silence, the twilight, the bowl of strawberries and milk, your faces in the evening light . . . I'll carry this memory between my hands as carefully as if it were a bowl filled to the brim with fresh milk. And it will be an adequate sign — it will be enough for me." The metaphor of the hands is noteworthy, in that Block — who once yearned for God's touch — now feels privileged to have handled simple human nourishment.

Inevitably we return to the chessboard, where Block now attacks his adversary. By unexpectedly sacrificing his knight, i.e., by casting off the image of himself as Christian Crusader, Block temporarily baffles Death and announces "check." But his exuberance is premature, as Death hints in observing, "You're rather arrogant." The next time they sit down at the table Death will exclaim, "I take your queen," and his dazed opponent can only reply, "I didn't notice that." This change of fortune, however, is encoded in the scenes that immediately precede.

Block loses the chess match because he can't maintain the moment of epiphany he experienced with Mia. The queen of the sunny fields must forsake him, and he must return to the dark brooding of every Bergmanian intellectual. When we hear him tell the supposed witch Tyan that he wants to meet the devil "to ask him about God," we should know that he could never rest comfortably in the world of strawberries and fresh milk. All he can do is upset the chessboard, allowing Jof and Mia to escape. Like so many others in *The Seventh Seal,* this is a symbolic act which carries noteworthy literal consequences, Bergman again moving gracefully from one plane of reality to another. By skillfully managing both word and act at the chessboard, the scenarist here controls the unfolding of a dense and complicated human drama.

Bergman's scripts often involve some conspicuous symbolic nodal point whose influence radiates outward in all directions. In this respect the chess match of *The Seventh Seal* is of a piece with Vogler's magic show in *The Magician* (1958), the arcane ceremony of *The Ritual* (1970), and the amateur theatricals of *Through a Glass Darkly* (1961). In such episodes, the typically expansive rhetoric of the play or performance always obliquely reflects the concerns of the film as a whole, usually giving these themes a mythic or allegorical significance. Bergman's alternative paradigm for a script is the associative structure of *Wild Strawberries*, in which everything flows out of the opening soliloquy of the aging protagonist Isak Borg.

Just before nightmare images begin to crowd every corner of the screen, the seemingly amiable narrator of *Wild Strawberries* makes a speech to himself about what his life amounts to: "At the age of seventy-six, I feel that I'm much too old to lie to myself. But of course I can't be too sure. My complacent attitude toward my own truthfulness could be dishonesty in disguise, although I don't quite know what I might want to hide. . . ." This self-satisfied characterization continues, but there is already ample material to call forth Bergman's most adept visual counterpoint. Phrases like "I'm much too old to lie to myself" are immediately reversed in images of horror, leaving to the remaining ninety minutes of the film the task of reconciling contradictions between the verbal (or we might say self-conscious) and visual (or subconscious) description of Isak Borg.

There is no speech (indeed no sound) in the dream sequence following Isak's soliloquy, but the imagery generates further action and dialogue, as Borg tries to solve at the conscious level problems posed in the cryptic language of his nightmare. He sees himself wander silently through empty streets, where shuttered windows and locked doors speak eloquently of all the things he has closed himself off from. The human figure he approaches disintegrates at his touch, perhaps a metaphor for the disappointments that have driven him into embittered privacy. Whatever its meaning, the next image makes clear the psychic consequences of Borg's withdrawal, since the old man now confronts a corpse in a coffin and finds that the dead man is himself. Yet this last detail carries a hint of resurrection and renewal, for the coffin lurches out of the funeral carriage, like a child springing from the womb, and the corpse itself seems determined to climb from the coffin, having clutched Isak's arm in its fierce grasp. As if impressed by this message from his unconscious, Isak arises early and begins to deviate from his normal routine. This is the first clue to the viewer that the film will unfold as Isak's effort to find the suppressed dimension of his own personality.

To reclaim the affective life he has long neglected, Isak will eventually have to converse with a dream girl, be mocked by his dead wife, and endure inquisitorial examination from a man who almost killed him on the highway. But the thread that connects these startling and wayward episodes is the theme introduced in the opening monologue. Isak is indeed "too old to lie" to himself, and thus cannot be allowed to go on believing that "all I ask of life is to be let alone." In all its intricate turns of plot, *Wild Strawberries* is moved forward by the simple opposition of verbal and visual we find in the opening scene. Isak's unconscious mind refuses to tolerate his official view of himself. Though always an accomplished rhetorician, Bergman here uses Borg's soliloquy to illustrate convincingly the sometimes total unreliability of the spoken word.

PICARESQUE STRUCTURES

hile one approach to script builds thematic progression around the spoken word, another approaches language in quite a different way. In contradistinction to the compact rhetorical scenarios of Renoir or Bergman, we have films whose voice track wouldn't provide much information about plot or character. Such genres as the western or the thriller traffic in explosive adventure, leaving relatively few opportunities for characters to sit down and talk. Sometimes even more meditative films, such as those emanating from Italy during the neorealist period, also play down the spoken word. In such instances we find more use of improvised dialogue, more evocation of inanimate objects, and less inclination to organize dramatic life around the fully played scene with a recognizable beginning and end. Here the word by no means vanishes, but becomes a different cinematic vehicle.

ACTION GENRES: SCRIPTS FOR SPIES AND COWBOYS

Collaboration of Dudley Nichols and John Ford. Nichols' conception of script. His scripting of The Informer. *Primacy of the visual. Ford, Nichols, and* Stagecoach. *Relatedness of language to the action structure.*

Dudley Nichols is a Hollywood scenarist whose reputation rests upon his handling of action-oriented scripts. His name of course is closely linked with John Ford's, since he did much of his best work for this director. They collaborated well together because of Nichols' skill in adapting the word to the needs of the camera, surrendering a phrase or a speech wherever necessary to give the director a freer hand with the visuals.

Generalizing from his experience in adapting fiction or drama to the screen, Nichols thinks of cinematic form as evolving from literary form, losing many of its rhetorical trappings along the way. In "The Writer and the Film" he says:

A motion picture undergoes a series of creations. First it is a novel, a short story, or a conception in the mind of the screenwriter. That is the point of departure. Next the filmwriter takes the first plunge towards the finished negative by building the story in screenplay form. This rough draft, at least in the case of the present writer, will undergo two or three revisions, each nearer to the peculiar demands of cinema. With luck the director, who must have an equal sympathy for the drama to be unfolded, will be near at hand during the groundwork, contributing cinematic ideas here and there, many of which will not appear in the script, but will be remembered or recorded in other notes to be used when the time comes.[9]

As the scenarist continually revises the script to bring it "nearer to the peculiar demands of cinema," he presumably makes it progressively less verbal, more visual.

This assumption seems borne out by Nichols' description of how he handled the scripting of *The Informer* (1935), the first of his vintage scenarios for Ford. In translating O'Flaherty's novel into film, Nichols found that his principal problem was a method "by which to make the psychological action photographic." Confronted by this difficulty, Nichols speaks of following Ford's lead and "catching his instinctive feeling about film." Under this inspiration the scenarist "sought and found a series of symbols to make visual the tragic psychology of the informer." Hence "the whole action was . . . played out in one foggy night, for the fog was symbolic of [Gypo's] primitive mind; it is really a mental fog in which he moves and dies." Nichols, according to his further account, also chose other stage props to take the place of words: "A poster offering a reward for information concerning Gypo's friend became a symbol of the evil idea of betrayal, and it blows along the street, following Gypo; it will not leave him alone. It catches on his leg and he kicks it off. But still it follows him, and he sees it like a phantom in the air when he unexpectedly comes upon his fugitive friend."

This sense of the symbolic potential of objects allows Nichols to be quite sparing in his use of dialogue. That skill is important, since the slow-witted, nonverbal hero of *The Informer* could hardly be expected to verbalize the guilt and pain he feels.

Ford's *Stagecoach* (1939) called for substantially the same approach to script. Working from the Ernest Haycox story which first appeared in *Collier's*, Nichols allegorized the original narrative, conforming it to Ford's view of the American West. In so doing, he also expanded and loosened up the dramatic action. This resulted in a film with a highly coherent theme, but one that is delivered in largely nonrhetorical terms.

The allegory of *Stagecoach* involves the Ford-Nichols conception of the American frontier, that morally ambiguous region where we feel the conflict between savagery and civilization. Each is rendered in all its complex variety. Civilization is the U.S. Cavalry, with its orderly

[9] This and the further citations of Nichols are to his preface to *Great Film Plays*, edited by John Gassner and Dudley Nichols. © 1959 by Crown Publishers. Used by permission of Crown Publishers, Inc., New York.

ranks, careful dress, and scrupulous protocol; savagery is Geronimo's Apache legions, with their long hair, fierce cries, and random battle formations. Yet the discrimination of rival forces by no means ends with these simple antinomies. Savagery is also the Plummer brothers, Lordsburg gunslingers who shot the father of the Ringo Kid, and Ringo himself, the hero of the film, who has an element of savagery in his own nature. Having retaliated against the Plumbers, Ringo must take refuge in Mexico to avoid "the blessings of civilization" (as Doc Boone puts it) and the penalties of the law. Civilization is Lucy Mallory, educated and articulate wife of a cavalry officer, whose trek westward to join her husband symbolizes the taming of the frontier. But civilization is also Ellsworth Gatewood, the banker who flees from Tonto with stolen funds, and Hatfield the gambler, a would-be Confederate gentleman who treats "ladies" with unctuous elegance yet has been known to shoot his enemies in the back. Besides these, there are other figures like Dallas and Boone, whose interior conflicts reveal the moral confusion that marks the frontier environment. While Dallas yearns to be a "lady" and struggles toward social respectability, Boone has turned his back on polite society, alcoholically muttering a few lines from Marlowe's *Dr. Faustus* as he departs. Together these constitute the rich mix of character types who personify the evolving American nation.

Though *Stagecoach* argues a thesis with close coherence, it does so in a manner entirely different from *Grand Illusion* or *Monsieur Lange*. Even in the shots that go over the credits, we have already been pulled beyond the rhetoric of Haycox's short story:

> This was one of those years in the territory when Apache smoke signals spiraled up from the stony mountain summits and many a ranch house lay as a square of blackened ashes on the ground and the departure of a stage from Tonto was the beginning of an adventure that had no certain happy ending. . . .[10]

Stagecoach opens with a nonverbal collage that implies a much more general alignment of forces. We see a stagecoach moving away from the camera, penetrating the wild and forbidding butte country of Monument Valley. Its littleness in wide-angle perspective tells of the boldness of its venture. The next image is of the stage protected by a cavalry troop, as if the risk implied in the first shot had created the security system visualized in the second. Now we see the Apaches riding furiously toward the camera, their direction in space making them the antagonists of those who ride the stage. This is the Apaches' country and they rush out from the midst of it, in direct contrast to the stage which has been shown pressing into it. The movement of the Apaches

---

[10] "Stage to Lordsburg," *Collier's Magazine* (April 1937). Reprinted in John Ford and Dudley Nichols, *Stagecoach* (London: Lorrimer Publishing Limited, 1971). This text is also used in citations of Nichols' script.

SPEECH AND THE MOVING CAMERA. Dudley
Nichols' dialogue for *Stagecoach* depends less upon
fully articulated debate than upon memorable
phrases uttered while the camera is hurrying to
meet some further visual obligation. The scene in
which Dallas is escorted out of town provides a
characteristic example. Courtesy of J. E. D. Productions Corporation.

also seems to make them our enemies, as if their forward thrust threatened both the camera and the audience. But in spite of the power and grandeur suggested by the Apache charge, the outcome of the struggle is foreshadowed in the last shot of this sequence. The stage rolls on, no longer escorted by troops, as day dawns behind the huge buttes. These few shots pictorially condense the whole epic of western settlement, reducing to irrelevance the explanatory overtitles which follow.

The verbal elements of *Stagecoach* are woven into this fabric of action. Riding, walking, and drinking are as significant as speaking. Witness the first scene, set in the streets and shops of Tonto where various parties gather for the trip to Lordsburg. While the stagecoach remains the focal point, the whole town is the arena of the action, the setting where introductions take place, loyalties or antipathies are suggested, and further events foreshadowed.

After the camera attends to the arrival of the stage, we first meet the passengers already aboard, in particular Lucy Mallory, whose primness is underscored when Buck corrects his speech on her behalf: "You folks might as well stretch your legs . . . your limbs, ma'am." Hatfield, another representative of the cultured elite, is introduced as he momentarily makes eye contact with Lucy, inviting Lucy's friend Nancy to identify him as "a notorious gambler." A moment later we recognize him in the Oriental Saloon, where he salutes Lucy as a "gentlewoman" and boards the stage to get better acquainted with her. The other character drawn into the scene by the arrival of the stage is Gatewood, a further specimen of polite society, who stands behind the counter of the Miners' and Cattlemen's Bank and waits for the payroll. We are reminded of his relationship to the stagecoach in photography that shows this vehicle reflected in the windows of the bank. Just as the visuals foreshadow a theme yet to be developed, so too do the verbals. There is a hint of things to come when Gatewood self-servingly announces that "what's good business for the banks is good business for the country." And the Wells Fargo agent's comment, "It's good business for you, Mr. Gatewood," carries even clearer prophetic overtones.

After this dynamic roll call of affluent, though not completely respectable, citizens, the camera turns toward the social undesirables of Tonto, introducing them as vagabonds and creatures of the street. Before Dallas has a chance to speak, we see her with her luggage, moving furtively forward, just ahead of a solid wall of black-clad ladies who represent the Law and Order League. The composition tells us she is being pushed out of town, boarding the stage by order, not choice. She is introduced in the same take that first shows us Doc Boone, evicted from his quarters for nonpayment of rent. They are both wastrels, yet not without significant differences of personality. While Dallas is weak and plaintive ("Can they make me leave town?"), Doc is full of irony and hauteur. He too is carrying his belongings (his Union army jacket and the sign from his office), but more as if to rescue them from contamination than to save them for himself. Like the doomed Sidney Carton to whom he likens himself ("Take my arm, Madame la Comtesse! The tumbrel awaits."), Doc thinks himself morally superior to those who exclude him from their midst. To the sheriff's curt admonition, "Doc, you're drunk," he has a patrician reply, "I'm glorified, sir." He quickly buoys up Dallas with his cheerful cynicism, "Come, be a proud, glorified dreg like me."

Though social distinctions loom large in the opening scene, the stagecoach plays the role of leveler, crowding all travelers together and eventually forcing each to fight for the survival of the others. The Law and Order League tries to discourage Lucy from traveling with Dallas ("that creature"), but the army wife decides to board anyway. With that decision, the proprieties gradually begin to slip away. Lucy at first welcomes the solicitations of Hatfield (sipping water from his silver cup) and moves delicately away from Dallas at the rest stop. But mutual dependency is built into the frontier situation. Before the trip is over, Doc Boone (who according to Tonto's ladies "couldn't doctor a horse") delivers Lucy's baby and Dallas takes charge of her recovery. Meanwhile, the Ringo Kid, an outlaw that Curly officially takes into custody, must protect the stage from hostile Apaches. During these sequences the pedigree peddling of Hatfield and the carping of Gatewood ("I don't know what the government's coming to.") seem increasingly out of touch with the situation. The crest from Ringfield Manor can't save Hatfield from Apache rifles and Gatewood must finally submit to the crude hands of a deputy sheriff. Thus does the West, epitomized in the jostling stagecoach, democratize American society. The pace of this film allows little time for expansive speeches, but Nichols' words are well chosen and in context fully adequate to carry the burden of argument.

THE NEOREALIST SCENARIO

Redefinition of structure in neorealism. Role of Cesare Zavattini. His collaboration with Vittorio De Sica. Harmony of speech and movement in The Bicycle Thief.

In a film such as *Stagecoach* we see how well the picaresque script is suited to a conventional action-oriented genre like the western. The world of cowboys and six-guns readily lends itself to tight-lipped heroism and bristling adventure. But Italian neorealism, which followed fast upon the havoc wrought by World War II, evidences another kind of departure from rhetorical structures. Here, as in the American western, we note a shift of emphasis away from consecutive dialogue, and toward the symbolic use of open space or large-scale movement. Tanks, crowds, and storefronts are all drawn into the drama. In contrast to the western, however, films like *Open City* (1945), *Shoeshine* (1946), *The Bicycle Thief* (1948) and all the 1950s works of Fellini tend to abandon the well-made plot with its relatively predictable climaxes. *Stagecoach* ends with the inevitable shoot-out in which Ringo outguns Luke Plummer and his two brothers; *The Bicycle Thief* also concludes on a note of high-pitched action, but not with an event that follows so obviously from the conventions of a particular genre. The contribution of Italian neorealism was to establish a much looser, a more subtle conception of structure than prevailed in the Hollywood action genres of the 1930s.

The greatest literary personality of postwar Italian cinema was Cesare Zavattini, who helped a whole generation of Italian film directors to a new conception of film form. In different ways, Visconti, Fellini, and Antonioni are all in his debt. Zavattini's closest collaboration, however, was with Vittorio De Sica and their collective imagination generated such landmarks of neorealism as *The Bicycle Thief, Umberto D,* and *The Roof* (1956). The first of these films typifies Zavattini's approach to script; it incorporates intense social concern into a seemingly unarranged and random plot.

The emphasis upon randomness in Italian neorealism derives in large measure from Zavattini's avowed hostility to the theater. His *Sequences from a Cinematic Life* opens with a blistering polemic against the stage: "I . . . say it is wrong to attach any importance to the episodes people are told in the theater, to people waiting behind those little curtains." Instead, cinema should strip down "those little curtains"; the film-maker should "set up the camera in a street, or a room" for in that way he shall help us "train ourselves in the contemplation of our fellow man in his elementary actions." [11] When making these pronouncements, Zavattini was alive to the peculiar historical situation of Italy in the middle 1940s. The actors had been conscripted into marching armies, the theaters leveled by British and American bombers. The "white telephone" films that aped the stage seemed ridiculous and inauthentic. "Today," Zavattini wrote in 1944, "a destroyed house is a destroyed house; the odor of the dead lingers. . . ." In this environment, what need for sets or costumes? "Our stupor and fear are whole," he continues, "it's as if we could study them in a test tube. Our cinema must attempt this documentation, . . . collect within the spectator's pupil the multiple and the diverse. . . ." The condition for achieving this

---

[11] Page 7 from the book *Zavattini: Sequences from a Cinematic Life* by Zavattini. © 1970 by William Weaver for translation and © 1967 by Casa Editrice Valentino Bompian. Published by Prentice-Hall, Inc., Englewood Cliffs, New Jersey.

THE THROWAWAY LINE. Speech in *The Bicycle Thief* does not always achieve the status of conversation. The pressure of crowds creates the murmur of half-heard phrases, a scattering of rhetorical fragments that gather meaning only from their collective effect, as in this scene, where Ricci is beset by hostile accusers. Courtesy of Lorrimer Publishing Limited.

new honesty, Zavattini believed, was that the cinema give up "its usual narrative methods." [12] Such was the mind-set of the man who conceived of *The Bicycle Thief*.

As in *Stagecoach*, movement and pictorial openness are implicit in *The Bicycle Thief* from the very beginning. We are made to feel the pressure of crowds, the competition for jobs, the absence of personal contacts in the Roman streets. The film analyzes the problem of unemployment, yet not by debating it in extended exchanges so much as by reporting the helter-skelter scramble of desperate people in search of gainful tasks. At the outset the camera follows an overfilled bus through its approach to a tacky-looking government housing project; the bus stops and disgorges its passengers, many of whom swarm across the street and clatter up the steps to a largely walled-in govern-

[12] *Ibid.*, p. 27.

ment employment office. Without formal introductions we have just met what Marx called the army of the unemployed. As yet we have not made the acquaintance of Antonio Ricci, the unheroic hero who will prove the ultimate victim of the creaking social system we see depicted. This man is first no more than a name read from a long list of job seekers. "Ricci, Ricci, where's Ricci?" shouts the official who presides over the bureau, briefly unclamping his teeth from a half-smoked cigar.[13] A moment later this chant is taken up by a friend in the crowd, who rushes through several shots of the open streets, still crying, "Ricci, Ricci." At last collected and brought to the office, Ricci discovers that he has a job as a bill poster, provided he can appear for work with the bicycle he must reclaim from a pawnshop. Ricci confusedly assents to the demands of officialdom, then slips quickly away from the crowd we have just joined. Everything in this scene is hurried, strained, precarious — presentiments which set the tone for everything that follows.

In keeping with this highly kinetic mode, organized rhetoric is held to a minimum. Significantly, Zavattini did none of the dialogue, and De Sica supervised the creation of individual lines in a remarkably relaxed way. For the actual content of speech in the film isn't all that important; what is important is the continual presence of a set of choral figures whose most casual remarks remind us of the continuing problem.

In the scene where Ricci gets his job, for instance, we are confronted with the frustration of all those who didn't. "What about me," shouts one; "I'm a mason, must I die of hunger?" "What about me," chimes in another, not bothering to identify a special skill. We also hear the bureaucratic voice of officialdom, with its numerous defensive ploys: "What can I do? It's not my fault there aren't enough jobs." The lines are not individually memorable but swell to an impressive chorus of pleas and protestations. Already this collage of voices has turned the anonymous crowd into a powerful enemy of Ricci's personal hopes: "Hey, I've got a bike. . . . Give me the job"; "So have I. . . . Come on, give us your job."

Once the film is launched, director and scenarist continue to communicate by nonrhetorical and nontheatrical means. The bicycle becomes not only a symbol of the competitive advantage Ricci has gained over his work-hungry comrades, but also of his efforts to restore his personal dignity and brighten up his marriage. There is nothing but plastic lyricism in the bike ride that Ricci and Maria take through the streets, yet the gentle tinkling of the bell on the handlebars tells us a lot about the improved relations between man and wife. Similarly, while

---

[13] Textual citations are of *The Bicycle Thief*, tr. Simon Hartog (New York: Simon and Schuster, 1968). Translation copyright © 1968 by Lorrimer Publishing Limited. Reprinted with their permission.

Ricci has his bike, he commands the respect of his young son Bruno, whom we see diligently polishing the fenders and frame. Bruno is clearly proud of his father's new occupation as together they glide about the town with the son perched on the handlebars. Along with these images of psychic rehabilitation, however, conflict is maintained in unspoken suggestions of threat. The trams Ricci passes en route to work are desperately overcrowded, and the buses continue to spill oceans of human derelicts out into the street. Though Ricci's trip to the pawnshop has returned him his most valuable possession, the camera silently records the fact that few are so fortunate. We see rows of unclaimed bicycles, piles of bed linen, the pitiful old man who mutely gives up his binoculars.

The structure of *The Bicycle Thief* is relatively tight, and several elements bind the beginning to the end. During his first day on the job, Ricci has his bicycle stolen; at the close of the film he makes a failing effort to steal one for himself. The victim of theft thus succumbs to thievery, giving us through this structural analogy a new sense of the relationship between crime and social legitimacy. What emerges from the comparison is a severe indictment of social injustice, made keener by the meaningful contrasts between the two episodes.

The robbery which deprives Ricci of his bike is the work of professional thieves and shows careful planning. As one culprit jumps on the bicycle and rides away, an accomplice rushes forward to block Ricci's pursuit. Moments later, after Ricci has hailed an automobile to chase the thief, the accomplice leaps on the opposite running board shouting deliberate misdirections. As a result the thief escapes, the bike is dismantled, and all hope of its recovery is quickly lost. The bureaucracy to which Ricci appeals for redress is as bumbling as the one that can't find jobs for skilled workers. The police don't even promise an investigation, announcing flatly, "We'd need an entire mobile brigade to find your bicycle." Clearly the thieves will go free. It is otherwise, however, when Ricci tries to save his job by stealing someone else's bike. Basically honest, he lacks the smoothness of a professional criminal. Instead of using his son Bruno as an accomplice, he sends the boy away, embarrassed to admit that he must resort to robbery. Instead of carefully sizing up his prospects, he leaps aboard the bike just as its owner returns. Too distraught to make evasive maneuvers, he is easily run down and captured. Ironically, he must then bear the epithets that could be more appropriately spent upon those who had stolen from him: "thief," "scoundrel," "bugger."

This reversal makes a point about the misorganization of society. Since there is no justice, shrewdness and opportunism have become the only avenues to success. Furthermore, as we see in a second scene that also compares closely to the climactic episode, criminality is a way of life that fosters a peculiar kind of trade-unionist solidarity. Thus when Ricci appears to have tracked down one of the thieves, cornering him in a local brothel, the entire neighborhood rises to the defense of the young man he has chased to these quarters. The licensee tries to prevent Ricci from entering the premises, several women chime in with threats or insults, and outside a massive crowd gathers to keep Ricci from claiming his prisoner. Even the policeman Ricci summons is intimidated by the mob and begs off weakly with, "All those people are witnesses for him." Frustrated and despairing, Ricci sulks away to become a criminal himself. The difference, however, is that he steals without consensual sanction, exposing himself to physical assault as he is run down on the street. His act is no worse than the one that went unpunished, but he has no coterie of henchmen to save him from reprisals.

This structure carries the argumentative line of the film: the social and political system conspires against the man who tries to lift himself out of poverty by honest effort. But in spite of the studied articulation of this thesis, many episodes of the film bear only indirectly and obliquely upon it. Ricci is a victim of social injustice, but he is also a narrative convenience, a passive figure whose presence allows De Sica–Zavattini to survey the life of the streets. Sometimes the camera loses interest in the protagonist, and strays to a street urchin who is trying to beg money from a well-heeled pedestrian. Presumably there is another story in this anecdote, just as important as Ricci's. Or again, there is the fragmentary scene where Bruno encounters the homosexual who tries to entice him with an expensive toy. No effort is made to attach this event to the structural axis of the film; it is introduced merely as a random element in the social scene. Even the near-drowning that Ricci happens upon is treated with the utmost casualness, without a hint of explanation or interpretation. Some shouts are heard from a bridge, a man is fished out of the Tiber, and Ricci hurries off to reclaim the affections of his son. It is in anecdotal touches of this sort that Zavattini finds "the reality buried under myths . . . ; a tree, an old man, someone eating, sleeping, weeping. . . ." [14]

In *The Bicycle Thief* we find a clear-minded perception of social reality, but fewer formal controls than were historically characteristic of the fiction film. There is a simple plot, expanded and enriched by a number of peripheral incidents. The protagonist is not the sole point of interest and his story is frequently intersected or interrupted. Naturally the digressions are not completely irrelevant or tangential, yet neither do they constitute anything so conventionally coherent as a subplot. They serve to document the more general malaise of the community, but never to specifically comment upon the fortunes of the protagonists.

[14] From the book *Zavattini: Sequences from a Cinematic Life* by Zavattini. © 1970 by William Weaver for translation and © 1967 by Casa Editrice Valentino Bompian. Published by Prentice-Hall, Inc., Englewood Cliffs, New Jersey.

THE ANTI-STORY

lthough the spirit of neorealism eventually was absorbed into other cinematic currents, the thinking of Zavattini and his disciples has had an enormous impact upon contemporary conceptions of script and structure. In encouraging the use of anecdotal material, the neorealist orientation has led to dangling conversations and even looser threads of plot. When such a revolution in scriptwriting receives further reinforcement from current experiments with disjunctive editing, we are forced to rethink basic questions of dramatic motivation and artistic coherence. Must a story have an "ending"? Must the doings of a character "make sense"? These are the issues raised by such director-scenarists as Michelangelo Antonioni and Jean-Luc Godard. For just as Vladimir Nabokov and Alain Robbe-Grillet have given us the so-called anti-novel, so these filmmakers have brought the "anti-story" into the cinema.

THE REJECTION OF "PLOT"

Michelangelo Antonioni as disciple of Zavattini. Deliberate violation of expectations as to structure. L'Avventura as inversion of motifs in the "adventure story." Rejection of the climactic. Substitution of alternative values.

The creed of Zavattini has found its most far-reaching applications in the career of another Italian film director, Michelangelo Antonioni. This director, a major force in world cinema since 1960, does his own scripting, though always in collaboration with other writers, usually Elio Bartolini and Tonino Guerra. In the pictures that evolve from these scripts we find the looseness and apparent aimlessness of life itself. They are replete with unfinished quarrels, unconsummated love affairs, unsolved mysteries, unexplained encounters. Yet the care beneath this seeming carelessness has established a new pattern in scripting, beholden neither to rhetorical structures nor to the conventions of the genre film. His plotting somewhat resembles that of *The Bicycle Thief* or *La Dolce Vita,* but without the element of climax that associates even these pictures with traditional concepts of structure.

Antonioni went through his cinematic apprenticeship while neorealism was at its zenith, getting his start as a writer for two of its most notable directors, Federico Fellini and Alberto Lattudua, both personal friends of Zavattini. Antonioni's ties with the movement are clear from his contribution to films like *Love in the City* (1956), an assemblage of short pictures which brought together most of the great names of the neorealist era. Since these years, he has never abandoned the drifting, curiously critical gaze that Zavattini had first applied to the waifs, pensioners, and bicycle thieves of De Sica.

Antonioni first attained international recognition through the film trilogy he began with *L'Avventura* and completed with *La Notte* (1960) and *The Eclipse* (1962). These pictures, unlike typical films of the neorealist period, all deal with the thinness and sterility of upper-middle-class culture. They anatomize the behavior of well-to-do people who

THE RHETORICAL NON-SEQUITUR. Rhetoric in the films of Michelangelo Antonioni is not "continuous" in the conventional sense of the word. Here Claudia in *L'Avventura* is moved to an extraordinary emotional pitch by an "irrelevant" conversation she has overheard in an adjacent compartment of the train in which she is riding. Courtesy of Rizzoli Film S.P.A., Rome, distributors of the film.

have found no outlet for their energy or talent. But it was not this departure from neorealist precedent that set critics to hissing when *L'Avventura* was first exhibited at the Venice Film Festival. It was rather that this film, like so many Antonioni would make later, seemed to lack a story, in fact seemed almost to parody the idea of a story.

Just as *Blow-up* is a "murder story" without a murderer, so *L'Avventura* is a "mystery story" in which no effort is made to unravel the mystery. A girl vanishes while vacationing on an island off the Sicilian coast, and her friends, fearing accident or suicide, undertake a search for her. That's simple enough. But naturally we expect before the end of the film to get either a corpse or an explanation. Antonioni offers neither. Instead he gives us a cunning analysis of how human energy and emotion is futilely exhausted. While there is a connecting thread that unites the various episodes of *L'Avventura,* the picture frustrates all our stock responses about plot. The effect is to force us toward a new definition of film structure.

Such pressure follows directly from Antonioni's antagonism toward traditional conceptions of script. Speaking of his own efforts at screenwriting, he complains of "forcing words into events that refuse them." [15] In his view, words should merely hint at moods, not attempt to explain themes. But structure, in the traditional sense, also explains themes, as the transformation of class consciousness is argued through the juxtapositions of *Grand Illusion* or the character of the frontier situation is analyzed in the organization of *Stagecoach*. For better or worse, Antonioni will have none of this. Instead he looks with favor upon "the turn being taken by the other arts . . . such as music and painting," which now seem "inexorably headed towards freer forms." It is this movement toward liberation that he hopes the cinema will emulate. He sees some evidence that this process has already begun, since "screenplays are on their way to becoming actually a sheet of notes for those who, at the camera, will write the film themselves." In other words, he would prefer to see both rhetoric and structure largely improvised. This ideal naturally carries over into his own films.

Although every director expects to modify the script in the process of shooting (witness even so plan-conscious a director as Bergman), Antonioni typically "modifies" the conception of his scenarists so much as to virtually reimagine and reshape the whole experience. "It's only when I hear dialogue from the actor's mouth itself," he says, "that I realize whether the lines are correct or not." But even more revealing is this further remark: "It's only when I press my eye to the camera and begin to move the actors around that I get an exact idea of the

---

[15] Antonioni's remarks on his craft are from his introduction to *Screenplays of Michelangelo Antonioni*, tr. Roger J. Moore (New York: The Orion Press, Inc., 1963), pp. vi–xviii. Textual citations of *L'Avventura* are from the same publication. Reprinted with the permission of Michelangelo Antonioni.

scene." No wonder, then, "there is always a critical moment during the arrangement of scenes when it seems as though the story won't hold up and everything has to be done over again." When this happens, says Antonioni, "I start reconsidering the film, thinking about its features and the way I came to discover them during the preparatory phase on location." Clearly for this director, a film is conceived as "visits to certain places, conversations with people, time spent at the very spots where the story is said to take place, the gradual unfolding of the picture in its fundamental images, in its tone, in its pace." By comparison to this, "the arrangement of scenes" is only "an intermediate phase, a necessary, but transitory one." Scripting does not mean fastening together a heavy frame; it means recalling "that emotion, those feelings, these figurative intuitions."

This conception of structure underlies *L'Avventura,* scripted by Antonioni in collaboration with Bartolini and Guerra. The film subverts our expectations at every turn. While it seems to be about a missing girl, it might be much better described as a series of variations (in the musical sense) upon the theme of fidelity. How if at all, *L'Avventura* asks, can permanent affections survive in the twentieth century, where they must withstand the mobility and diffusive energy of an ill-organized technocratic society?

Movement and change, given to us in a steadily unfolding succession of concrete images, relentlessly compete against the psychic loyalties of the various characters. "I am positive," says Antonioni, "that the world today is filled more with dead feelings than with live ones. I would like to know more about the residues." Apparently, such tradition-sanctified concepts as "love," "trust," "duty," belong among this collection of residues. *L'Avventura* seeks to test their vitality by setting them at odds with the machinery of the modern world, and in this frame of reference the central activities of the picture form a coherent pattern. Boarding a train; cruising on a motorized yacht; racing about rural Sicily in a late-model car: amid this constant hustle from one vehicle to another, Antonioni's characters must ask themselves whether their "principles" continue to be meaningful. And since the arrangement of incidents obliges us to maintain the same fretful pace as the overtaxed protagonists, we directly experience their psychic fatigue, their emotional limpness.

Fidelity, sexual or otherwise, is a constant concern of *L'Avventura.* In the first scene we hear the voice of tradition in Anna's father, who scolds his daughter for taking on a lover, reminding her that "that type will never marry you, my child." We expect this man to have little force in the film, however, since he is already confessing to Anna "the fact of my retirement, not only as a diplomat, but also as a father." Yet Anna herself is more her father's child than she would like to admit. Through the episodes prior to her disappearance, she worries endlessly about the stability and permanence of her relationship with Sandro, the young architect who enjoys her affections. "Aren't we already the same as being married?" she asks him, apparently seeking a guarantee of perpetual fidelity. Such questions spring from her own lack of security, as is clear from one of her asides to her close friend Claudia: "Really it's difficult to keep an affair going when one is here and another is someplace else." Hence the desperation in her aggressive lovemaking with Sandro and the prophetic element in her exclamation: "The very idea of losing you makes me want to die." Anna's hunger for emotional absolutes seems to be what occasions her flight, or perhaps her suicide.

Following Anna's abrupt departure, her place in the dramatic structure is filled by Claudia, confidante of the missing girl. Claudia shares some of Anna's anxieties, but is a more complex character, content neither to retreat into traditional codes nor to run from her friends and acquaintances. She is looking for a way to conserve personal integrity yet still handle the contemporary world. The role Claudia will play is foreshadowed in a brief episode immediately before Anna vanishes, when she gives Claudia one of her dresses, announcing, "It looks better on you than it does on me. You keep it." Having slipped comfortably into her friend's wardrobe, Claudia spends much of the rest of the picture wondering if she might move with equal ease into an affair with Anna's lover, Sandro. At first she is deterred by loyalty to Anna, later by an aloofness that is perhaps a form of psychic defense. When she finally consents to a liaison with Sandro, it is apparently on terms that safeguard both her self-image and the principles she entertains. In the last analysis, however, these guarantees prove illusory and the idea of fidelity is left completely exploded.

While Claudia remains central, *L'Avventura* (like *The Bicycle Thief*) is remarkable for the number of incidental episodes that bear obliquely upon the theme. Overheard conversations, casual street encounters, rigorously compressed vignettes; these are as important to the structure as the fortunes of Claudia. In fact, they illumine the heroine's sensibility by comparison and contrast, placing her failing efforts to define a personal value system against a much broader background of shifting manners and mores.

There is, for instance, the sleazy little seduction scene that Claudia and Sandro overhear on the train, while Claudia is deciding whether or not to encourage Sandro's overtures. As the rail carriages clatter toward their destination, we hear a man in one of the closed compartments making an approach to a new-found acquaintance: "They told me that you were a very nice girl and that you always mind your business." After a few nonsensical remarks about Chinese radios, the man's small talk quickly becomes more bluntly erotic: "But for you, what comes

first, music or love?" And when the woman's response is less than enthusiastic, he presses the point all the more strenuously: "For me, love
comes first. I'm a man and I know what's what: first love, and then
music." Claudia listens in fascination to this exchange, taking a sort of
vicarious pleasure in it. But the crudity of the invitation offends her,
and she is thus persuaded to resist Sandro, whom she feels has urged
his romantic claims with similarly untoward ardor. The scene closes
with her forcing him to get off the train.

In this instance, the analogy works to the advantage of moral tradi-
tionalism, moving Claudia to repress her amorous impulses and hold
out for the promise of a more permanent relationship. But in another
scene, with further analogical implications, the butt of Antonioni's
irony is the institution of marriage. Here we find Claudia and Sandro,
reunited through their search for Anna, interrogating a couple who
claim to know something of her whereabouts. Soon it becomes apparent that husband and wife have nothing to say about Anna but much
to reveal about each other. The entire scene is fraught with mutual
loathing, he for his wife's nagging, she for her husband's continuous
womanizing. The interview is constantly interrupted by the ongoing
quarrel between husband and wife:

Sandro:	How was she [Anna] dressed?
Husband:	I don't quite remember. Seems to me she wore a black dress.
Wife:	He doesn't look at dresses, he looks at what's under them.

After being verbally lacerated by her husband, the wife turns to Claudia
with a plaintive "I don't like it here very much." And to Claudia's
"How long have you been married?" she responds, "Three months."
Visibly shaken, Claudia hurries away, wondering how a love relationship — made officially permanent in marriage — could disintegrate utterly in so short a time.

Lacking authoritative guidelines, Claudia makes provisional arrangements, accepting Sandro after he has given some evidence of steady
affection. She won't let him speak of love, "because then I'd force you
to swear to it, I'd force you to tell me an indefinite number of things
... and that wouldn't be right." Yet she hopes for something like love
between them. This is why the last turn of the film is such a crushing
disappointment. For exactly when their relationship seems to have become most stable (the prospect of finding Anna having all but disappeared), Sandro arbitrarily betrays Claudia for a woman he casually
meets at a cocktail party. Though his infidelity comes as a stunning surprise to Claudia, it is well motivated in terms of Antonioni's dramatic
preparation and more precisely defines the problem of sexual fidelity.

To understand Sandro, we must be aware that his sexual caprice
springs from professional disappointment. He is a potentially talented
architect who has surrendered to the lure of easy money. At one point

in the development of their friendship, Sandro tells Claudia, "I would like to go back and start working on my own projects again." And then, to Claudia's question about why he put them aside, Sandro responds:

> Once they gave me a job to draw up an estimate for the construction of a school. It took me only a day and a half to finish it and I got paid six million lire. Ever since then I've been doing estimates for other people's designs.

While Claudia responds sympathetically ("I'm sure you'd be able to design some very lovely things."), she doesn't sense the depth of Sandro's personal guilt feelings. We see them, however, when we follow Sandro into a courtyard of noteworthy design where he comes upon two students, excitedly talking about the architecture. Ghostly reminders of his younger and more idealistic days, they seriously upset him by the ardor of their interests. He leaves the courtyard quickly, thereafter becoming moody and aggressive. He returns to the apartment and roughly tugs Claudia to the bed for "a new kind of adventure." This is the detail that links sex to frustrated ambition, making plausible the betrayal of Claudia that soon follows. When sex is only a narcotic, one woman is as good as another.

Sandro's behavior, though explicitly a sexual delinquency, really raises the concerns of the picture beyond the sexual level. It suggests that the problem of fidelity includes more than love relations and that the sexual disorientation we have seen in the film is part of a much larger pattern of social dysfunctions. Burdened with a "residue" of false feelings and unable to formulate a new set of values, Antonioni's characters are all caught up in aimless "adventures" that provide temporary relief from their comfortable but spiritually unsatisfying situation. Anna, the first victim of the disease that infects them all, simply runs away, either over a cliff or down some other road. But ironically her tragic flight simply intensifies the bewildered spasticity of her friends. Ostensibly they set out to find her, yet really only to lose themselves in another round of hopping, skipping, and jumping. The style of L'Avventura was expressly devised to record this meaningless profusion of activities.

Antonioni's loosely structured scripts, in which neither a dialogue nor a scene ever seems conclusively rendered, are completely congruent with the way he perceives the world. Voices are lost in the roar of the wind or smothered by street noises of the modern city. Lovers stray far from each other, held in the same frame only by the immense inclusiveness of much-used wide-angle lenses. The action is hurried forward in speeding cars while human effort is dwarfed by the massive stone of contemporary high-rise architecture. In keeping with this atmosphere, speech is never conventionally "significant," summarizing the import of an incident or situation. It drifts and wanders like the characters, who follow wayward whims and refuse to be guided by the logic of traditional dramatic exposition.

RECONCEPTIONS OF SPEECH
AND ACTION

Jean-Luc Godard as scenarist. Renewal of interest in the verbal. Dependence upon improvisation. The Brechtian use of dialogue in La Chinoise. *Interest in extended monologue. Verbal dimension of* Weekend.

While Antonioni has exploded conventional structures with scripts which avoid dramatic climax and linear plot development, the scenarios of Jean-Luc Godard have proved innovative in other directions. In the casualness of his conversations and the open-endedness of his situations, Antonioni has achieved the ultimate illusion of reality; Godard, on the other hand, seeks no illusion of reality. He wants to advertise the fact of illusion, the element of artifice basic to all the endeavors of art. Unlike Antonioni or the neorealists, he borrows unabashedly from literature and theater, though he rejects the formal organization and thematic coherence we ordinarily associate with both stageplay and novel. He too is an architect of anti-stories.

The immediately striking thing about Godard's scenarios is that though they make much use of talk they are never properly "rhetorical," i.e., the talk is never integrated into an overriding argument, as in Spaak, Prévert, or even Bergman. In Godard's films, speech is not used to define character, supply motive, generate suspense, or solve problems. This is why he doesn't mind if the characters improvise their dialogue. Sometimes Godard's speakers, like Ionesco's in *The Rhinoceros* or *The Bald Soprano,* seem to be just jabbering, as when Yves Johnson is interviewed by the computer Alpha 60 in *Alphaville* (1965) or the intrusive narrator in *Band of Outsiders (1964)* extemporizes nonsensically about opening and closing parentheses. More often Godard's dialogue resembles that of Bertolt Brecht's plays, where characters are allowed to momentarily put off their stage personalities and make ironic remarks about the theatre, the audience, or the world in general. Godard is not kidding when he tells us he confronts his actors "as an interviewer faced by an interviewee." [16] In *La Chinoise* (1967) he interrupts the unfolding of the story (such story as there is) to conduct an interview with Veronique, one of the characters from the film. And when she tells us she would like to "go dynamite the Sorbonne, the

---

[16] *Godard on Godard,* ed. and tr. Tom Milne and Jean Narboni (New York: The Viking Press, Inc., 1972), p. 177.

Louvre, the Comedie Française," [17] we can't be sure whether she speaks as a fictional creation of the screenwriter or as a real-life human agent. Such are the ambiguities of Godard's language.

The curious ambivalence of Godard's scenarios is pointed up in another passage from *La Chinoise*, where Guillaume, an actor committed to Maoist principles, engages his comrades in a dialogue about film aesthetics. While Guillaume speaks "in character," it is fairly clear that he also speaks as a stand-in for Godard:

> Guillaume: Your ideas about movie documentaries are all wrong. It is said that Lumière invented documentaries while, during the same period, there was a guy named Méliès, whom everyone says made fiction films. They say that he was a dreamer, that he filmed phantasmagoria. And I think just the opposite was true.
>
> Everyone: Okay, prove it.

Already the subject seems a bit esoteric for a cadre of Maoist revolutionaries, although several are university students with backgrounds and interests in the arts.

The further exchange, moreover, takes us still deeper into the specialized concerns of Godard, as we know them from his personal writings:

> Guillaume: All right. Two days ago I saw a film at the Cinematheque, a film on Lumière. . . . And this film proves that Lumière was a painter. By that I mean that he filmed exactly the same things that the artists of that period were painting—people like Pissarro, Manet, or even Renoir.
>
> Veronique: What did he film?
>
> Guillaume: He filmed parks. He filmed public gardens. He filmed the gates to factories. He filmed people playing cards. He filmed the tramways.
>
> Veronique: He was one of the last great impressionist painters of the period?
>
> Guillaume: Yes, yes exactly. He was a contemporary of Proust.
>
> Henri: Well then, Méliès was too. He did the same thing.
>
> Guillaume: But no, that's just it. What was Méliès doing at the time? Méliès was filming *A Trip to the Moon*. Méliès was filming *The King of Yugoslavia Visits President Fallières*. And now, from the vantage point of our distance in time, we realize that these were really the current events of that epoch. Ah yes, you may laugh, but it's true. He was making documentaries. They may have been reconstructed documentaries, but they were real documentaries. And I'll go even further than that. I would say that Méliès was Brechtian. We mustn't forget that Méliès was Brechtian.

Aside from the allusion to Brecht, which seems particularly appropriate to an actor, these comments might just as easily have come from any

---

[17] The textual citations of *La Chinoise* are from the screenplay excerpts reprinted in *Jean-Luc Godard* by Jean Collet, translated by Ciba Vaughan. © 1963 by Editions Seghers, Paris. Used by permission of Crown Publishers, Inc., New York.

one of several other characters, Veronique, for example, or even Henri. The impression we have of their being arbitrarily assigned to Guillaume is strengthened by the fact that Godard makes no effort to extend this interest in Méliès as a device to further characterize Guillaume. At the end of the film we find him doing a kind of door-to-door theater, perhaps Brechtian in tendency, but certainly having nothing to do with the respective merits of Lumière and Méliès.

What we have here is something quite different from the familiar case of a director who uses a character as his spokesman. Godard doesn't subtly insinuate himself into the fictional persona, as does Renoir, say, in *Rules of the Game,* taking care not to violate the internal motivation of the character himself. Rather, Godard takes over Guillaume as one might seize a microphone, making such a racket that we cannot help noticing his presence.

But once he has caught our attention, what does he say? Unlike most bits of directorial propaganda, Godard's commentary is so oblique as to seem almost unintelligible. Yet in the last analysis we find he is making an observation upon his own aesthetics, and upon the form of *La Chinoise.* Like Méliès and unlike Lumière, Godard conjures "documentaries" out of his own fertile imagination, dispensing with the surface phenomena, such as we find in television news, or even *cinéma vérité.* Instead he "reconstructs" the "current events" of his epoch with a prophet's sense of what "from the vantage point of [further] distance in time" will seem the central concerns of the age. In other words, Godard is endeavoring to explain why his "Chinese" are actually Frenchmen, why his revolutionaries are film buffs, rock singers, and pop artists, and why his films of proletarian consciousness are beyond the reach of the proletariat. As if to underscore this last point, Godard has Yvonne, the only authentically proletarian character in *La Chinoise,* ask at the end of Guillaume's preachments, "What's an analysis?" But Godard is not embarrassed by this irony because his aesthetic is calculated to take account of it. He knows he makes revolutions out of celluloid just as Méliès made rocket ships out of studio stage props. He seeks only to remind his audience that the fact of artifice does not exclude the imagination of reality.

Even when Godard relates speech to character in a seemingly more normal way, his use of language is still far from conventional. Like Bergman, he is fond of the monologue or the dialogue heavily weighted toward one party, and lets his characters do recitations in front of the camera. But while the Bergmanian monologue serves either as psychic disguise *(Wild Strawberries)* or reluctant revelation *(Persona),* the monologue in Godard takes on a more formalistic quality. The speeches of Godard's characters may tell us more about the tone of the film than the personality of the speaker. *Weekend* (1967) provides a case in point.

THE SUBJECTIVE MONOLOGUE. Although the films of Jean-Luc Godard have a deserved reputation for visual complexity and vibrant action, they may also be characterized by lengthy, vagrant conversations that approach the stream-of-consciousness style in modern fiction. *Weekend* provides a representative example. Courtesy of Lorrimer Publishing Limited.

Weekend is a study of self-destructive tendencies in French bourgeois culture, epitomized in reckless highway carnage that becomes in the course of the film ever more bloody and surreal. But before the series of motorway massacres leads us from civilization to barbarism, there is a quiet scene at the beginning of the film consisting almost entirely of talk. Corinne, diabolic heroine of the roadside nightmare to follow, is secluded in the apartment of her friend, lover, and analyst, to whom she describes in great detail an extended sexual adventure, or perhaps an extended sexual fantasy. Although at the literal level this experience has nothing to do with the later action, it sets the tone for everything that follows, marking a drift toward degeneracy in the culture and suggesting at the same time Corinne's perverse mastery of her associates. In this scene camera and stage business collaborate, meaningfully but minimally, with a mode of articulation that is primarily verbal.

The first question we might ask of this scene is why Godard has elected to tell, not show, the action. For the exchange between Corinne and her analyst is deliberately static, the characters freezing in their initial postures and the camera making itself scarcely more mobile. But the point of the scene is not Corinne's promiscuity, which could easily be rendered more dynamically. What interests Godard is her insistence upon re-creating and reexperiencing her sex life as a kind of psychic masturbation. The other, equally crucial element in the scene is the way Corinne's analyst is drawn into her narrative, taking erotic stimulation from his patient's personal relations. From the standpoint of these concerns, speech is preferable to action. In fact, the implicit schizophrenia of leisure-class culture is remarkably well expressed in this static image of a well-bred couple sitting quietly in a comfortable study, while one tempts and teases the other with lurid outpourings of sexual self-indulgence. Godard's approach is the right one, and he makes the most of it.

Although Corinne's recitation does not literally duplicate anything that follows, it sets up a pattern of progressive deviation from normalcy that anticipates the overall movement of *Weekend*. According to Corinne's account, her sexual orgy began rather innocently as "we necked for a long time in the parking lot." [18] But after a long drive (paralleling the trip to the country later in the picture) Corinne treks to an apartment where the sex play becomes more ardent. It now includes her Lesbian involvement with Monique as well as the male lover's use of both women as instruments of his sexual whims. Most noteworthy, however, is the fact that all attachments are narcissistic, culminating in masturbation. In the car Corinne had told her partner that she "fancied him," but in the apartment there is not the slightest mention of personal affection. (Even the identity of Corinne's male partner is slightly obscure — is he the man she was with earlier? or Monique's husband? or was Monique's husband also the man in the car?) What stands out in the scene is not personal relations at all, but how the depersonalized sexual acts of licking and sucking look forward to the overt cannibalism toward which *Weekend* eventually moves.

Nor can Corinne's language be isolated from its effect upon her analyst, since her narrative is also an exercise in seduction. The analyst's responses change markedly between the beginning and end of the scene. As first there is professional distance and a note of authority in his voice: "Begin at the beginning, when did it happen?" Here the camera is focused upon his face, relegating Corinne to a weak off-camera position as she begins to speak. When the camera pulls back to include her in a two-shot, it seems more to reveal her nervousness (she fidgets with her hair) than to suggest command of the situation. But she apparently draws strength from her recollected or fantasized sexual experience, for as she talks about petting in the car the camera closes in on her face, gradually excluding her companion from the shot. It is his off-camera voice that sounds weak as he asks, apropos her lovemaking, "Were you thinking of me too?"

Thereafter the camera movement is interlocked in a more complex way with the behavior of the characters, though its ultimate function is to promote Corinne. It backs away from her as she brings the first episode to a close, then crowds in on the face of her analyst as he, tantalized, discovers that she has more to tell. By this time, even though he

[18] The textual citations are from *Weekend* and *Wind from the East*, tr. Marianne Sinclair and Danielle Adkinson (London: Lorrimer Publishing Limited, 1972).

is featured in close-up, Corinne continues to control the scene. The most expressive camera gesture is an unbalanced two-shot which shows Corinne commanding two-thirds of the picture space and her analyst clinging to the edge of the frame. His queries of "What next?" and "What for?" show how complete a participant he has become. Corinne's nervousness has now transmuted itself into sexual teasing as she runs her hands through his hair, then breaks off the narrative with, "Don't you have any American cigarettes?" When the camera again composes upon Corinne in extreme close-up, the low angle gives her absolute dominion. Her conquest of her would-be counselor is then verbalized, as he (tentatively touching her legs) exclaims, "I adore you, Corinne; come and excite me." With this voyeuristic surrender to perverse impulse, the concept of moral normalcy vanishes from *Weekend*, opening the way to the more violent excesses that will soon transpire.

With his strong literary background and polemicist leanings, Godard may some day be credited with "reverbalizing" the cinema. But it can never be said that he has simply repeated the scripting procedures of the past. True to his affection for Renoir and the classical French cinema, he is always conscious of the literary dimensions of film, including posters, billboards, and self-made signs in his shots even when his characters are silent. Yet he is very sensitive as to how he assimilates rhetoric, knowing the respective merits of irony, absurdity, poetry, pomposity. His harmonization of these rhythms is something new to the cinema, as is his deliberate refusal to tell tales with a beginning, a middle, and an end.

List of Films Discussed

AVVENTURA, L'   145 min.   JAN *
BICYCLE THIEF, THE   87 min.   AUD-BRA
CHINOISE, LA   95 min.   LEA
CRIME OF MONSIEUR LANGE, THE   90 min.   AUD-BRA
GRAND ILLUSION   111 min.   JAN
INFORMER, THE   91 min.   AUD-BRA, FNC
SEVENTH SEAL, THE   96 min.   JAN
STAGECOACH   96 min.   STA
WEEKEND   105 min.   GRO
WILD STRAWBERRIES   90 min.   JAN

6
ACTING
AND STAGING

Acting, like scripting, is another professional discipline normally indispensable to the cinema. The actor's gesture adds dynamism to the image, while his voice etches the script upon the sound track. Whether he appears as his full-bodied self or only as a face, a foot, or a speck on the far horizon, his physical presence completes the decor and often his personal performance adds a significant new dimension to the director's intentions. John Wayne's walk is conspicuous from well beyond pistol range and constitutes a characteristic feature of Ford's films. Chaplin's fingers are uniquely expressive, whether they are holding onto the floor in *The Gold Rush* (1925) or flipping bank notes in *Monsieur Verdoux* (1947). Voices too have their special pitch and timbre. A pompous tone may debase an otherwise eloquent statement, while the right inflection may redeem a verbal cliché. Dialectal speech also extends or alters expression, as Godard's use of actors with recognizable accents (Jean Seberg, Anna Karina) abundantly proves. In a few cases, the availability of a certain performer has changed the whole shape of a picture. Jean Renoir and Charles Spaak let Erich von Stroheim substantially expand the role of von Rauffenstein after they talked him into taking over that part in *Grand Illusion*.

Occasionally the actor is a nonprofessional person fetched up from the street or the farm to play one part exactly suited to all his previous experience. Eisenstein's sad-eyed peasants may well be sad-eyed peasants, recruited almost at random to pull their ploughs in front of Tisse's camera. These completely convincing character types may have spent up to half a century rehearsing the roles they play in *The General Line* and *Que Viva Mexico.* Sometimes too, the nonactor with instinctive theatrical gifts can distinguish himself in a major speaking part, as documentarists from Grierson to Pennebaker have discovered to their pleasure. Yet for the most part, the cinema requires trained personnel capable of dramatic simulation. Their aim is to step out of their own personalities and into the world of make-believe. At the same time, however, acting for films is quite different from acting on the stage. Orson Welles, Ingrid Thulin, Louis Jouvet, and Marlon Brando (not to mention many others) have mastered both media, but cinema and theatre ask for essentially different skills.

THE ACTOR
AS
ICON

Special nature of film acting. Effects of framing upon performance. Interaction of the actor with decor and ensemble. Bergman's treatment of the actor: The Passion of Anna. *Alternative approach to framing in Antonioni. Antonioni and Monica Vitti. Variation in the iconography of the film frame:* Glenn Ford and Sidney Poitier in Blackboard Jungle.

Although stage training may be highly useful to the screen actor (as might professional skill in gymnastics, modeling, or ballet), the fact of technological mediation changes the performing conditions of cinema. We all know the obvious differences. The film actor plays without the benefit of a live audience to which he can pitch, perhaps even adjust, his rehearsed behavior. He performs disjunctively, doing a thirty-second take five times in quick succession, then waiting two hours for the lights and camera to be set up for the next shot. He also plays his scenes out of dramatic sequence, doing the interiors one day, the location footage another. This often disturbs his feel for the part and upsets his effort to build his emotions to their appropriate climaxes. Yet even these circumstances might be thought of as barriers to theatrical performance, rather than something that alters its essential nature. The more fundamental difference between stage acting and screen acting is that in the cinema the actor is always one part of a photographic frame.

This point may seem almost self-evident, but the fact of framing really has far-reaching implications. In any theatrical presentation, there are three principal elements: the actor himself; the ensemble with whom he interacts; and the decor or architecture of the stage itself. These persist in the cinema, but are markedly altered by the mediation of the camera. First of all, the *variability of the space within the frame*, controlled by the range of the camera and the focal length of the lens, bears importantly upon how the actor performs. Secondly, the *variability of the angle from which he is seen*, altered from shot to shot as well as by tracking, panning, or zooming within a shot, continually changes his relationship to his partners and to the set itself. Finally, the *boundedness of the frame*, the exclusions implicit in the restrictedness of the film rectangle, give the camera the power to bind and to separate, thus visually establishing connections which in the theatre would require the performer's effort and refusing to recognize other relationships which on stage could hardly escape recognition. These factors must be given due weight in any description of film acting.

Unlike the unvarying dimensions of the space behind the proscenium arch, the area in which the film actor performs is adjusted to the style of a particular director and the dictates of a particular shot. This space may be no wider than the actor's cheekbones, in which case, gesture becomes a very specialized and subtle thing. Sergio Leone revolutionized the conventions of the cowboy film in *Once Upon a Time in the West* (Italy-U.S.A., 1969) simply by pointing an extremely long lens right into the baby-blue eyes of Henry Fonda. Our sense of the genre tells us that villains are always dark, and we are startled by the effrontery of his fair complexion. As for Fonda, little more is required of him than that he keep his eyes open in a hard-steely glare. Magnified to the proportions of a wide-screen format, they are sufficient unto themselves, and even an untimely blink might be construed as overacting.

The way in which an actor's manner is adapted to the area granted him by the camera's range and lens is evident from any of the more recent films of Ingmar Bergman. Working with veterans of Stockholm's Royal Dramatic Theatre, he has always had at his disposal a thoroughly professional cast, headed by such stalwarts as Max von Sydow, Gunnar Björnstrand, Ingrid Thulin, and Bibi Andersson. They came to Bergman's pictures with a full command of histrionic skills, which he used quite fully in his films of the 1950s. But in the last decade he has imposed upon himself a more severe discipline, often restricting himself to shots of the human face, "in order," he says, "to give the greatest possible strength to the actor's expression."[1] Consequent upon the directorial decision, his performers must give up many staples of the actor's craft — carriage, hand movements, the manipulation of costume.

Yet this minimizing of the actor's effects has not reduced the expressiveness of Bergman's films. The telephoto lens that pries into the faces of his protagonists hàs its own particular way of advertising their physical resources. The rounded cheeks, smooth complexion, full lips, and flowing hair of Gunnel Lindblom seem pronouncedly different from the bonier, more angular facial contours of Ingrid Thulin: this physical iconography immediately transmits the right character impressions for *The Silence* (1963), which builds its theme upon the split between sense and spirit personified in the two sisters, Anna and Esther. The restrained elegance in the face of Liv Ullmann sets her similarly at odds with a shallower-looking Bibi Andersson in both *Persona* (1966) and *The Passion of Anna* (1970). When the framing is consistently so tight, the slightest flexing of a muscle seems charged with meaning. Gunnar Björnstrand coughs and sniffles through *Winter Light* (1962) with enormously telling effect, his throat spasms bursting like explosions upon the screen. Bergman's concentration upon the face of Max von Sydow not only emphasizes his deeply expressive eyes, but magnifies the import of his occasional squinting and furrowing of the brow. The modern *angst* that this actor has come to personify in Bergman is caught by such simple theatrical touches as these.

Since Bergman's characters live so utterly in a world of faces, any space that is opened up to them is always graphically significant. Hence at the opening of *The Passion of Anna* we see Max von Sydow framed tightly against a background of open sky. He wears a neutral expression, his eyes show concentration, and in this pictorially attractive environment he seems at peace with himself and the world. But as the camera gives us a little broader view of his bodily situation, we note that he is perched somewhat precariously upon a roof and that the bucket in his hand tends to unbalance him. While his movements are not really labored as he slides his torso forward, he lacks the stability and surety we first associated with the face against the sky. If the earlier shot suggested the perfect adjustment of Rousseau's "natural man," what follows conveys a disconcerting impression of aloofness, of awkward isolation, which the dramaturgy of the film will go on to explain. As we would expect, von Sydow plays the scene with characteristic un-

[1] Bergman, "Each Film Is My Last," p. 99. Reprinted with permission of the author from *Tulane Drama Review*, Vol. 11, No. 1 (T33), Fall 1966. Copyright 1966. All Rights Reserved.

THE ACTOR IN CLOSE-UP. The role of the actor depends in large measure upon his place in the frame as a whole. The composition favored by director Ingmar Bergman, here typified in a shot of Max von Sydow from *The Passion of Anna,* assigns overriding importance to the actor's face. The shadowed eye-sockets and veins visible at the temples thus become important elements in establishing situation and character, while background detail (the tree, the sky) is of lesser, though not negligible, significance. Courtesy of Aktiebolaget Svensk Filmindustri, Stockholm.

derstatement. Without theatrical gestures, the rhythm of his body in the unfamiliar task of climbing is sufficient to suggest the slight unsteadiness that the role requires.

The consequences of wider framing are obvious when we turn from Bergman to a completely different sort of director like Antonioni. Here the actor's torso is almost always relevant to his performance, indeed demanded by the director's preference for short lenses.

Perhaps it is not accidental that Antonioni began to attract attention as a director only after he found Monica Vitti to play his leading female roles. For her carriage and bearing seem wonderfully well suited to express his conception of contemporary disorientation and ennui. Her body is completely pliable, seemingly almost incapable of calculated movement. Her arms float in space, her back relaxes into a perpetual slouch, her fingers dangle loosely, her head turns carelessly at the top of her spine. Sometimes her limbs and appendages seem to obey laws of their own, refusing the claims of a central nervous system. Adrift in one of Antonioni's typically spacious frames, Vitti wanders hesitantly,

THE ACTOR IN WIDE-ANGLE PERSPECTIVE. In contrast to Ingmar Bergman, whose composition involves extensive use of the actor's face, Antonioni typically shoots actors at long range, with relatively short lenses, and amid what seems to be a decor chosen at random. Notice in this scene from *The Eclipse*, however, that the actors are very carefully arranged within the space of this expansive "stage." The framing draws the eye toward them, even though they do not loom large in relationship to the set. From this range, of course, posture and body language mean more than voice or facial expression. Courtesy of Michelangelo Antonioni and Paris Films.

clinging to walls, curling around tables or autos, draping herself over beds or couches, threading her way among invisible obstacles to forward progress. Paired with the athletic Alain Delon, as in *The Eclipse*, or the husky, heavily muscular Richard Harris, as in *Red Desert*, her movements appear even more unhinged and wobbly. While Vitti's face is also expressive, we are more likely to remember her as a figure isolated by her lax posture from the stone and aluminum severity of postwar Italian architecture.

As we describe the behavior of actors and actresses, we quickly notice how difficult it is to treat their talents without reference to the set and the ensemble. This continuous interaction with the decor, while analogous to theatrical staging and blocking, is greatly intensified by photographic framing. We all have seen enough Ibsen and O'Neill to know that bookworms sit at oversized desks, heroines carry vases of rosebuds, and free spirits collect around open windows. But while such symbolic notation easily becomes manneristic on the stage, the cinema handles it much less conspicuously, just by varying the content of successive frames. Since the camera can track a character, shoot him from different angles, pare away irrelevant detail with a slow zoom, or even get up on a boom to frame him against the intricate elegance of an Oriental carpet, the total decor of the set is always available as material for metaphor. Since such things as selective focus are also well within the available technology, the director can also determine how intensely aware of the decor we should be at any particular moment.

Even Bergman's tightly squeezed framing does not exclude the extensive use of symbolic decor. In *The Passion of Anna*, though we see little more than faces, each is complemented by an appropriate stage prop. The Bibi Andersson character, steeped in romantic and religious sentimentality, is several times framed in immediate proximity to a lighted candle. When the candle is excluded from the shot, its effect lingers in the orange glow of the partition against which the actress' face is framed. The Max von Sydow character, on the other hand, is at one point bound into the same shot with a poorly shaded desk lamp which blanches his face and reflects unpleasantly from his glasses. In another outdoor scene, the cropping of the frame balances von Sydow's head against the lighted, rotating turret of a police car, visually sounding a note of warning and impending disaster. Antonioni's decor is of different proportions, as befits his much more expansive frames. While Bergman associates his characters with objects that can be framed with a 200mm lens, Antonioni's stage props are the burned-out volcanoes of *L'Avventura*, the high-rise apartments of *The Eclipse*, the factory interior of *Red Desert*, the imposing sand dunes of *Zabriskie Point*. Whatever their scale, however, the principle is the same: the performer and some highly relevant segment of the background fuse in a single image.

Such symbol making, of course, is fluid and temporary. The object loses its special status as soon as the camera stops giving it close attention. There is a scene, for instance, in *Blackboard Jungle* (U.S.A., 1955) where Glenn Ford, playing a conscientious high school teacher, quarrels with Sidney Poitier, a capable, but alienated, black student who thinks that the teacher is manipulating him on behalf of the educational bureaucracy. Richard Brooks staged their confrontation on one of the school stairways, a piece of the set to which we would not normally assign any particular significance. But as the stairway is isolated in the framing of this exchange, it becomes a metaphor of the relationship between the two men. Ford's solid, stocky build betokens his authority, as does the suit and tie, badges of his professional status. Surely, however, these details of physique and costume merely confirm the impression we have from the position of the two figures on the stairs. The guardrail which slants diagonally across the frame emphasizes Ford's higher place on the stairway, i.e., his superior importance in the academic hierarchy. To reach him, Poitier must stretch his body, perhaps occasionally rise on his toes. Ford, on the other hand, leans forward in a slight crouch, taking a posture that seems condescending even though intended as an effort to meet the student on equal terms. In this case, the decor both symbolizes the relationship between the characters and prompts each toward posture and gestures that further articulate it. Once the stairway has done its work, however, the camera casts its glance elsewhere, allowing this particular prop to dissolve into the set as a whole.

This treatment of decor is paradigmatic of all cinematic staging. The archway that frames an intruder, the bed rail that divides quarreling lovers, the bottle on the bar that represents the alcoholic's lapse into old habits: these momentarily become anchor points of visual design, supports to an actor's delivery. But then the character moves, the camera follows, and new elements are called upon to organize the film rectangle.

EMOTION HEIGHTENED BY A PROPERTY. The stairway adds tension to the composition of this scene in *Blackboard Jungle* between Glenn Ford (*left*) and Sidney Poitier. Courtesy of Metro-Goldwyn-Mayer Films, copyright © 1959, released through Allied Films, distributors.

FOUNDATIONS OF FILM ACTING: GESTURAL STYLE

Since the film actor owes a deep debt to the camera, there should be no surprise in the close connection between cinematic technology and acting style. Normally the actor is trained for the stage, but the hardware of the filmmaker may well determine how much of this training is relevant to the screen. This fact determines, I should think, the tides of taste that through the years have promoted one approach to the actor's craft over another. What we have is a process of selective absorption in which the technology of the cinema works as a filter: it admits to the screen only those elements in the performer's repertoire that suit the needs of a particular historical moment. Naturally, the first need of the cinema was for actors who had mastered the art of expressive gesture. But from this ideal of body control developed concepts of expression which would adapt the performer's posture to the ensemble, and both to the architectural facade. Responsive to its own interior logic, the silent cinema thus evolved the styles of physical comedy, biomechanics, and expressionism. In turn, the elaboration of gesture in these several modes of film acting laid the foundations for all that would follow in the sound cinema.

THE STYLE OF PHYSICAL COMEDY

The art of Charles Chaplin. Centrality of body gesture: The Idle Class, The Immigrant. *Ingenuity with costume:* The Gold Rush, Shoulder Arms. *Increasing importance of decor:* City Lights. *Involvement of both decor and ensemble:* Modern Times. *Alternative orientation of Buster Keaton. Keaton's more elaborate gymnastic skills. Capacity to extend and modify a routine:* College, The General.

Before the cinema developed a voice, the filmmaker necessarily required actors whose face and figure would tell a story. Fortunately, they could be found, fully trained and eager for new tasks, in the vaudeville, music-hall, and circus acts that constituted the most interesting strain of popular theatre at the turn of this century. Behind the escapades of these performers stood the much older conventions of comic mime first systematized in Italy's *commèdia dell'arte*. Out of this tradition came the Chaplins and Keatons, the Langdons, Lloyds, and Keystone Kops of the silent era. Far more than their comrades from the "serious" stage, these performers were able to win a debate with the arch of an eyebrow or upend social pomposity with the flick of a cane. Their agility and grace compensated perfectly for the physical sluggishness of the early cameras, while their command of gesture and timing made explanatory titles superfluous. As the conventional stage actor struggled to find substitutes for his hard-earned verbal skills, the mime from vaudeville persisted in the routines he had learned in childhood, grateful that the special features of cinema had given new flexibility and emphasis to his style.

Early in the history of cinema, the style of gestural acting achieved classic refinement in the subtle harlequinade of Chaplin and the broader gymnastic skills of Keaton. Though neither immediately sat in the director's chair, each was allowed almost from the beginning to control his own routines. These involved primarily the mastery of personal body gesture. Later Chaplin and Keaton broadened their conception of style to include more meaningful use of the ensemble and the set.

Chaplin's art in particular is bound up with his own body. The cane, the shoes, the baggy pants are merely extensions of his person. In his dependence upon personal gesture, he is a true child of the English music hall and the Fred Karno mime troupe, which gave him his theatrical start. But unlike the clowns and mummers of the English stage, he individuates his gags very skillfully, not only avoiding pantomimic clichés but developing new jokes out of the violation of stereotypic expectations.

The quivering torso routine of *The Idle Class* (1921) and *The Immigrant* (1917) are cases in point. As a theatrical cliché, the trembling body ordinarily suggests deep psychic or physical disturbance. Chaplin knows this and plays upon it carefully as the alcoholic millionaire of *The Idle Class*. In one scene the camera peers over his shoulder while he looks down at a letter from his wife, which informs him she is leaving until he gives up drinking. As he reads the letter, we notice that his body begins to shudder and shake. We assume, prematurely, that he is seriously upset by his wife's impending departure. Yet we should have known better. When Chaplin turns toward the camera after a well-timed interval, we discover the true cause of his quivering. He is busily mixing a cocktail. He had used the same gag in *The Immigrant* four years earlier. The arriving passenger leans over the side of the ship, apparently wretching from seasickness, poor man. But the sentimental cliché is again exploded, as the immigrant suddenly straightens up, hoisting the fish he has just hooked and landed.

The same capacity to transcend the predictable is evident in the way he keeps bringing new gags out of his costume. Take the baggy trousers, for example. We would expect him to have to hitch them up now and then, probably in embarrassing situations when he is forced to choose between his dignity and his decency. Hence the routine in *The Tramp* (1915), where he improvises a belt out of a stray rope, holds no surprises, though it manages to be funny just the same. But who could have predicted the much more skillful elaboration of that routine in *The Gold Rush,* where the stray rope happens to have a stray dog tied to the other end? The working of the routine into a dance sequence adds to the humor by widening the circle of confusion, and Chaplin's reluctance to help his canine friend chase the cat is the final touch. So rich in possibility are the objects attached to Chaplin's person that we are left constantly wondering which of them he will call into life. The belt he wears in *Shoulder Arms* (1918) is positively mind-boggling, since from it dangles not only the soldier's ordinary accoutrements but such refinements as an eggbeater and a cheese grater. Passing over these, he builds his routine with his rifle, but the other gadgets continue to tantalize us.

It is symptomatic of Chaplin's emphasis upon personal body skills that he spent much of his career defining and developing the persona of the Tramp. Chaplin is probably correct in claiming that this character appealed widely because he "brought to the surface . . . the irresponsible joy of life possessed by the nomad and the ne'er-do-well." [2] But the Tramp was also a formal vehicle ideal to exhibit Chaplin's talent for pantomime. The ill-fitting costume concealed exquisite grace that would magically leap forth with every deft kick of a cigarette butt. The situation as social outcast was perfect to motivate those innumerable escapes which required ducking between the legs of an overstuffed bartender, sidestepping the clutches of an irate butler, or outrunning a whole brigade of Keystone Kops. The precariousness of the Tramp's economic status also meant he had to catch meals when he could and sometimes attempt jobs he was unfit to handle. This invited Chaplin to boil shoestrings, swallow confetti, launch half-built ships, or do a few rounds as a prizefighter.

Though Chaplin's mimicry tends to be self-contained, using other people only as something to bounce off of or wriggle around, he is capable of meaningfully interacting with the set, converting the stage into a symbolic artifact. The best examples come from his later films, made after American physical comedy had come into contact with other traditions.

---

[2] "Development of the Comic Story and the Tramp Character," *Focus on Chaplin,* ed. Donald W. McCaffrey (Englewood Cliffs, N.J.: Prentice-Hall, Inc., 1971), p. 46.

COSTUME, GESTURE, AND DECOR. Though American silent comedy evolved without an elaborate framework of stage theory, mimes like Chaplin were always sensitive to the decor and the ensemble. Note in still *above* how the bend of the leg reinforces the line established by the curve of the wheel behind, and *below* how the wrenches associate the performer with the assembly line, even while his manic dance undercuts all the values of mechanized industrial society. Photographs from *Modern Times*, courtesy of rbc films.

In Chaplin's early pictures the decor is just marginally relevant, providing an open manhole to fall into or a giant rink in which to whirl giddily about. But the stage trappings at the opening of *City Lights* (1931) offer more than a gymnasium for stunts and pratfalls; they immediately suggest the theme of the picture. As the curtains part at a public unveiling ceremony, we find the Tramp asleep in the arms of "Peace and Prosperity," a ridiculous ensemble of statues. Already there is a powerful contrast between this marble emblem of social pomposity and the urban vagabond whom society seems to have denied bed and board. In this context, the Tramp's antics figuratively express his relationship to the affluent world that has gathered to congratulate itself on this ceremonial occasion. Though he will be driven from the precarious refuge he has achieved, he withdraws only after forcing upon the society an insight into its own pretenses.

The establishing shot which opens this sequence is held long enough to point up the contrast between human beggary and marmoreal elegance. Thereafter, we sense a further irony that the reign of Peace and Prosperity has begun by rousing a man from his slumber. Once awake, the Tramp's movements create emphasis and dramatic progression, carefully shifting our attention from one detail to another so as to further explore both the set and the situation.

As Chaplin begins his routine, further ironies quickly emerge. Trying to gracefully retreat from the public eye, he finds that Peace (or is it Prosperity?) brandishes a drawn sword, on which he inadvertently catches his baggy trousers. While he might have reason to take offense at the statue's apparent hostility, he shows no malice whatsoever, even tipping his hat to the crowd, in keeping with the festive spirit of the unveiling. When the band strikes up a patriotic piece, the Tramp's face registers respect for king and country, even though his torso remains shackled to a sword blade. Difficulties continue to multiply, but he still wants to be friends. After he carelessly sits in the face of Prosperity, he tenders a quick apology with a nod of the head and tip of the hat brim. It is only when these natural courtesies are rebuffed that he begins to fight society with its own weapons. At this point he puts his face up to one of the great stone hands, using its sculptured massiveness to complete a grandly enlarged gesture of nose thumbing.

Modern Times (1936) further extends Chaplin's capacity for interaction. The famous assembly-line disaster involves him with both the ensemble and the decor. Though his individual moves create most of the belly laughs, these gestures set up kinetic force fields among the other performers as well as call into play all the apparatus of the set itself. Few scenes show to better advantage the genius of Chaplin's timing and his instinct for controlled variation.

In this scene from *Modern Times*, each routine builds upon the one that precedes, incorporating new stage props, widening the number of comic participants, adding new motifs and slapstick gestures. There is comic tension from the beginning, as the Tramp's duck-waddle walk is so seriously at odds with the exacting tasks of the assembly line. He interiorizes the discipline quickly, however, tightening so many bolts that he can't stop twitching at lunchtime. But the bolt-tightening tick that knocks over a co-worker's soup is nothing when compared to the great sneeze which initiates a series of farcical catastrophes.

Once the first hints have been given, Chaplin gives the routine a chance to build. At first the Tramp is just a little behind in his work, keeping pace by leaning over into his co-worker's territory. Next he must jostle this man aside in a frantic effort to get his wrench on a bolt that eluded him. A moment later a whole row of assembly hands is disturbed as Chaplin leaps onto the conveyor belt, forcing urgent rescue operations which fail to prevent his being sucked into the machine. After weaving among gears and wheels for a fairly extensive interval, Chaplin allows himself to be extricated and begins an ambitious variation of bolt-tightening caper.

Once the Tramp is again on his feet, we note the presence of a new musical theme and with it a substantial modification of Chaplin's walk. No longer a duck, he now moves like a ballerina, though the grace of his footwork is completely at odds with his deranged behavior. Suddenly insane, he is pirouetting around the factory, pausing on the beat of the music to tweak the nose of a colleague with one of the giant wrenches he still carries. Though he has lost all touch with the assembly line, he is still beset by the urge to tighten things up. When he spies the manager's secretary he immediately concludes that the buttons on her dress require a twist of the wrench. Although this romantic contretemps carries the action outside, where Chaplin finds a much burlier and stuffier-looking woman to tighten up, we are soon returned to the factory, where an extended finale has been prepared.

In the last turn of this sequence, Chaplin spreads the chaos he created at the conveyor belt throughout the whole factory, progressively involving more people, more stage props, and more extravagant behavior. First the Tramp interests himself in switches, watching momentarily while the expert does it, then undertaking to throw a few himself. Soon he is snapping things on and off with complete abandon, while electric circuits around the factory begin to pop and crackle at his caprice. Inevitably the switches get larger, and the last one he tackles partly lifts him off the floor. Still the mayhem persists, and when an official tries to curb him, the Tramp whips out a long-necked oil can and cuts down the enemy with a single squirt. Surrounded by irate workers who close in upon him, he relieves pressure on both flanks by restarting the conveyor belt, a move that immediately sends his antagonists back to their jobs. Still outnumbered and beleaguered, he has one more strategem in his repertoire, a Douglas Fairbanks maneuver negotiated while swinging from a long chain. Here, like the swash-buckling pirate of a thousand adventure stories, the Tramp does battle while wheeling through space, thrusting at his adversaries with his oil-can rapier. By this time the routine has gained and spent all its comic momentum, requiring that Chaplin gradually slow it to a graceful close.

Chaplin's mastery of physical comedy is unsurpassed, though closely rivaled by that of his Hollywood contemporary Buster Keaton. But there is no need to promote one of these men over the other, since each has his own idiom and repertoire. Chaplin's reactions are often registered in his face — where a smile twinkles, the mustache slides sideways with a quirk of the lip, or a beetling black eyebrow leaps to attention. Keaton, by contrast, is typically "the great stone face," decorated by almost no makeup and renowned for its look of dour stoicism. Chaplin wiggles every appendage as he walks, swaying his hips, bowing his legs, letting his arms fly askew. Keaton tends to maintain a uniform posture, confronting the world as if he were always leaning into a strong breeze. Only in the crises of hairbreadth escapes and wild misfortunes do his muscles flex and his arms fly. While Chaplin gets his most remarkable effects from his personal belongings (a cane, a shoelace, a piece of silverware), Keaton is most at home with larger stage props. He loves locomotives, giant balloons, even ocean liners, and only when these seem unavailable will he settle for horse carts, riverboats, and floating logs. In short, Chaplin's pantomime is the art of the music hall, while Keaton's belongs to the circus.

Although Keaton is no funnier than Chaplin, he sometimes seems to have a better sense of form. This accounts for the controlled repetition of gesture which we find in his best comic efforts. Irrespective of the-matic concerns, which he could not in all cases determine or direct, Keaton invariably imposes a purely physical organization upon his films, his stances constantly reminding us of those he has struck in other contexts.

Notice, for example, his gift for burlesque in *College* (1927), a spoof of campus rah-rah pictures. Keaton spends most of the film displaying his incompetence in all forms of athletics, so that he can brilliantly re-verse this pattern in the last scene.

Taking each sport in season, Keaton systematically fails at football, track, and baseball, while coaches and players gasp at the genius with which he subverts their brave attempts to train him. But when his girl friend is snatched away by the campus bully, we see how seriously we have underrated the hero's athletic prowess. Returning in haste from the regatta, he outdistances the crowd like an olympic miler; he then high-hurdles over a series of hedges, high-jumps a huge clump of bushes, and broad-jumps a further impediment to his progress. Since his sweetheart is entrapped in a second-floor apartment, nothing could be more natural than his pole-vaulting through the upstairs window. Confronting the villain face to face, Buster bashes him with china bowls hurled discus-style across the room, then wards off retaliation with line drives from an improvised baseball bat. When the rival tries to escape, he is downed with a flying tackle, and finally speared on the run with a lamp-pole javelin. While this scene would be funny even without the previous context of athletic clowning, the richer humor arises from meaningful repetition. Having seen how badly Keaton could do with the proper gear, we find doubly charming his conversion of household whatnots into tools of the sportsman's trade.

An even more careful integration of comic gesture is noticeable in *The General* (1927). It is in the slight but memorable coherences of this film that Keaton shows his complete control of the mummer's art. While the roundtrip journey of the locomotive organizes the plot, Keaton invents gags that are inseparably associated with the train.

Let one example suffice. Early in the film, Keaton courts his girl friend but finds his suit rejected when he is unable to enlist in the Confederate army. Dejected, he goes off by himself and sits down on the driveshaft of his locomotive. Suddenly the engine starts up and he is carried ridiculously out of the frame, riding helplessly up and down on the driveshaft. This visual anecdote is both a charming piece of comedy and an effective representation of the way Buster has lost control of his personal destiny. Later, after he has won a commission in the army and collected the girl as his bride-to-be, this shot is repeated, but with significant variation. Buster is now sitting on the driveshaft of the same locomotive, not alone but with his girl. His change in military status is advertised by the fact that half an army is now marching past him, and every man feels obliged to salute the young lieutenant. We would almost expect the wheels of the train to turn again, carrying the lovers off to some beyond-the-screen sanctuary where Keaton could kiss his girl in privacy without having to return the endless salutes from comrades in arms. Instead, however, the gag is altered, so that Buster can kiss his girl on-screen while fixing one hand in a posture of permanent salute. This small touch is visually eloquent. It tells us that the hero is now completely in charge of his own affairs and requires not even the comic muse to come to his assistance. He remains anchored in the center of the frame, handling his problems as they come.

The contribution of Chaplin and Keaton lies first in establishing the actor's physical presence. They extended the ambience of this personal impact, however, in many different ways. Their costumes inevitably tangled them up with their partners, while their own movements in space pressed upon them an awareness of the need to choreograph the

THE COMIC GESTURE. Buster Keaton is highly adept at gesture which achieves both repetition and variation. Here in *The General,* the salute he delivers while seated on the drive shaft of his locomotive is a measure of the control he has gained over his own destiny. Photo courtesy of Raymond Rohaur

behavior of the whole ensemble. In *Cops* (1922) Keaton handles both the set and the ensemble brilliantly, pulling antagonists from their off-camera sanctuaries at just the right moment to leap wildly at the giant teeter-totter on which he is suspended. Chaplin interacts effectively with the factory workers of *Modern Times*, using their stiff, lockstep rhythm as counterpoint to his own highly eccentric gyrations. But what the American clowns were attempting in their ever more ambitious use of set, choreography, and decor was also the impetus for experiment on the European stage and screen. From these issued several avant-garde movements with a distinct bearing upon gestural style.

BIOMECHANICS AND CONSTRUCTIVISM

Theories of Vsevolod Meyerhold. Interest in Chaplin. Promotion of the acting ensemble above the individual performer. Innovations in stagecraft and design. Meyerhold's influence upon Eisenstein. Potemkin *and* Strike. *Eisenstein's demands upon the actor. Testimony of Nicolai Cherkasov. Cherkasov's performance in* Alexander Nevsky *and* Ivan the Terrible.

While vaudeville and the music hall gave film its first authentic style of acting, the interest in mime extended well beyond the sphere of physical comedy. From the beginning of the century theatre directors in Europe had seen the grace and discipline of stylized gesture as an effective antidote to the verbal grandiloquence of nineteenth-century melodrama. The Russian experimentalist Vsevolod Meyerhold added a revolutionary note, holding up the acrobat and the circus clown as figures the Soviet theatre might take inspiration from as it extricated itself from bourgeois conventions of stagecraft. When the Soviet cinema was born, its midwives, Eisenstein and Pudovkin, paid close attention to Meyerhold's theories of staging and acting. This extended into film two overlapping movements known in the theatre as biomechanics and constructivism.

Meyerhold, like Eisenstein, personally admired the work of Chaplin, finding in it the mastery of "maximally expressive motion." [3] In "Chaplin and Chaplinism," the Russian proclaims: "We must learn from Chaplin how to place our bodies purposefully in space." This might be construed as the starting point of biomechanics: the belief that posture, rhythm, and muscular tension are inherently more dramatistic than traditional stage rhetoric. But if the individual actor were to become a gymnast and an acrobat, what implications would this hold for the stage on which he would perform? How might his gestures affect the choreography of the whole ensemble? How should he interact with particular props? These questions lead directly to the "constructivist" movement in stagecraft and into the films of Eisenstein.

What separates the Russians' approach to staging and acting from the American style of physical comedy is the collectivist emphasis. Although Meyerhold applauds the contribution of Chaplin, he is hostile to the mystique of the star. In "The Actor's Role" (1922), he represents theatrical talent as nothing more than rigorous discipline: "A person who possesses the necessary ability for reflex stimuli can be or can be-

[3] This and the immediately following citations of Meyerhold are from his "Reconstruction of the Theatre," and "Chaplin and Chaplinism," both reprinted in *Tulane Drama Review* (Fall 1966), pp. 186–195.

come an actor; he can fulfill one of the roles in the theatre in accordance with his natural and physical talents." [4] Distrustful of individual genius, which might turn the performer into a prima donna, Meyerhold emphasized the ensemble, the resources of the entire theatrical company. While certain figures might momentarily step to front-center of the Meyerholdian stage, it was the mass of performers, the expertly regulated crowd, that this director expected to fulfill the kinetic design. These lessons of Meyerhold's "First Theatre of the R.S.F.V.R." were not lost upon the Soviet cinema.

Meyerhold's experimental theatre also broke with the "peepshow illusionistic stage" of the bourgeois period. Stripping away curtains, draperies, and backdrops painted in simulated perspective, Meyerhold radically simplified the set, peeling the flesh of incidental ornament down to its skeletal structure. His *Coco the Magnificent* (1922) was staged on boards swept clean of naturalistic bric-a-brac and against a backdrop of unplastered brick walls. Without conventional props to stumble against, the actors were free to swing and stretch their own limbs. But Meyerhold's so-called machine for acting gradually acquired a new kind of symbolic apparatus — poles and trapezes, cunningly contrived panels, giant rotating disks. As these mechanical engines assumed a life of their own, the performers were forced into interaction with them and into new relations with each other. This is the dimension of constructivism that carries over into the films of Eisenstein and Pudovkin.

In his lectures at the Soviet Institute of Cinematography (1934), Eisenstein contrasts Meyerhold's "external" approach to acting with the "internal" system of Constantin Stanislavsky, which asked the actor to personalize the emotions he exhibited on the stage. While Eisenstein calls for a synthesis of the two conceptions, his own leanings are toward Meyerhold, since he finds that Stanislavsky's "method reflects the point of view of the introverted individual moving towards mysticism." [5] Stanislavsky's "is a very dangerous theory," which when applied in the Moscow Art Theatre "developed some pathological elements and . . . escaped from reality." Better to follow Meyerhold, thinks Eisenstein, since movement can create feeling, not only in the audience but also in the performer. Besides, adds Eisenstein, "there are moments when movement must be divorced from psychology and emotion." In granting this divorce between outward form and inner feeling, Eisenstein definitely affiliates himself with Meyerholdian assumptions.

[4] Nikolai Gorchakov, *The Theatre in Soviet Russia,* translated by Edgar Lehrman. © 1957 by Columbia University Press.

[5] This and the following citations are from the notes of Marie Seton, as recorded in *Sergei Eisenstein* (New York: Grove Press, Inc., 1960), pp. 486–493.

This affiliation was strongest in the days immediately after he had worked as Meyerhold's designer at the Proletkult Theatre, Moscow. Here Eisenstein got not only his basic orientation to stagecraft but the cadre of Meyerholdian actors he used in his early films. Whatever their difference of approach, Eisenstein's staging follows Meyerhold in its curtailment of individual performances, its intricate coordination of collective movement, its emphasis upon muscular stress and gymnastic display, its feel for machinery and stark, functional architecture.

Consider *Potemkin*. The performance is collectivist in inspiration; actors like Grigori Alexandrov are rarely separated from the flow of communal dramatic life. The movements of the ensemble are carefully programmed, so that the great crowds on ship or shore never fail to fulfill an explicit plastic design. The Odessa steps is a giant constructivist set, denuded of conventional decor and confronting us as a grim skeletal outline. The crew of the *Potemkin* relate themselves to the gears, gauges, and guns of the cruiser in a manner resembling the relationship of Meyerhold's actors to the machines on his variously contrived stages. Even the progression from the sagging limpness of the sailors in their hammocks (their flesh awkwardly bulging the canvas, their arms hanging clumsily askew) to the powerful muscularity they later exhibit is a further Meyerholdian touch. True to the principles of biomechanics, their bodies enact with swift and decisive strokes the psychological transformation they experience.

Constructivist design and biomechanical gesture often merge in Eisenstein, as in a short sequence from *Strike* featuring a group of anti-czarist organizers. In planning their moves against the factory directors, they are apparently compelled for the sake of secrecy to rendezvous upon the anchor of a ship. Yet privacy is only a pretext for Eisenstein's choice of this unlikely trysting place. The real reason is his interest in the anchor, which not only has strong symbolic overtones (the stable component in a revolutionary situation, etc.) but also furnishes an austerely impressive constructivist set. The playing of the sequence soon resembles a trapeze performance, since one by one the members of this revolutionary cadre emerge from the water and climb upon the anchor. Their moves are careful, catlike; though distinguished by noticeable muscular stress. Hands join in tensive camaraderie, bodies extend and complete a design suggested by the anchor itself. As with Meyerhold, there is an ironic political dimension to the circus style of the acting and stagecraft. When the anchor becomes overcrowded and slightly topheavy, we get the suggestion Eisenstein has intended — that of a would-be revolution organized upon too narrow a sociopolitical base.

BIOMECHANICAL ACTING. The Meyerholdian conception of the actor as gymnast finds expression in the choreography of Eisenstein's *Potemkin*. *Above* the fatally wounded Vakulinchuk accidentally entangles himself in the ship's rigging, the stressful posture of his body thus becoming a metaphor of the tension and difficulty implicit in revolutionary activity. *Below* his would-be rescuers enact movements reminiscent of trapeze artists as they illustrate Eisenstein's vision of revolutionary energy and moral solidarity. Courtesy of the Rosa Madell Film Library.

The most famous actor who worked with Eisenstein was Nicolai Cherkasov, hero of *Alexander Nevsky* and *Ivan the Terrible*. Trained in both mime and dance, first at the Academic Opera and Ballet Theatre and then with the Meyerholdian "Experimental Ensemble," Cherkasov would seem to be an ideal vehicle for Eisenstein's biomechanical endeavors. In his *Notes of a Soviet Actor,* Cherkasov comments enthusiastically upon his early work as a mime, relishing how, as a seaweed in Rimsky-Korsakov's *Sadko,* "I twisted and turned as if swaying in water," and how other roles "taught me to gesticulate with plastic expressiveness and in time with music."[6] But by the time Cherkasov entered the Leningrad Institute of Stage Art (another citadel of Meyerholdism), he was beginning to have reservations about a style of acting he thought too exclusively based upon rhythmics and acrobatics. "We were taught," he remarks, "how to walk, run, assume the most intricate poses, dance in groups upon sharply sloping platforms, cubes, and squares." Yet while Cherkasov credits the Leningrad Institute with "developing our physical abilities," he eventually became convinced of the "utter untenability" of biomechanical premises. This constellation of attitudes helps explain both his contribution and his difficulties in performing for Eisenstein.

Cherkasov's reflections upon his work with Eisenstein provide an interesting commentary upon the strengths and weaknesses of biomechanical acting. For while Cherkasov accepted Eisenstein's guidance he did so with some qualms and reservations. Though he was ready to grant Eisenstein's absolute mastery of design and *mise-en-scène,* he was less convinced that he fully appreciated the individual talent. He felt, perhaps rightly, that even the roles of Nevsky and Ivan could not be invested with much psychological subtlety, given Eisenstein's Meyerholdian attitudes. Speaking of the Nevsky role, Cherkasov observes: "At times it . . . seemed to me that Alexander Nevsky was being drawn somewhat abstractly, that he was not human enough, and that his true image evaded me."[7] In spite of these reservations, however, he trusted Eisenstein's guidance: "In acting, just as in any other art, he told me, one should pay attention to the whole, the general, the main. And it was in this direction that Eisenstein insistently led me, teaching me to seek the general and widely understandable in my role, to keep within a strictly defined style, and in this case particularly within the epic plan of the production." In the end, Cherkasov was quite happy with the results: Eisenstein, he concludes, "not only taught me a great deal

[6] *Notes of a Soviet Actor,* tr. C. Ivanov-Mumjiev and S. Rosenberg (Moscow: Foreign Languages Publishing House, n.d.), esp. pp. 20–41.

[7] *Ibid.* The remarks on *Nevsky* and *Ivan the Terrible* are pp. 102–106.

about how to portray epic characters, but also taught me a good deal about spacing, the use of gestures and movements."

Cherkasov, however, was less well pleased with *Ivan the Terrible,* where the biomechanical approach was applied with even greater exactitude. "Carried away by his enthusiasm for pictorial composition," says Cherkasov, "Eisenstein moulded expressive, monumental mise-en-scène, but it was often difficult to justify the content of the form he was trying to achieve. In some of his mises-en-scène, extremely graphic in idea and composition, an actor's strained muscles often belied his inner feelings. In such cases, the actor found it difficult indeed to mould the image demanded of him." What seems to have most disturbed Cherkasov was the problem of conforming psychological attitudes to a rather limited set of bodily postures: "Eisenstein never seemed to tire of setting me intricate tasks in movement and action. . . . He not only demanded highly emotional acting, but sharply defined outer plastic form, often shackling me by the rigid line of his graphic and artistic thought." While Eisenstein could surely say something in his own defense, Cherkasov's problems indicate reasonably well the burdens that Meyerhold's system imposes.

Both biomechanics and constructivism are, in effect, modes of theatrical simplification. They lead logically either to caricature or epic enlargement, rather than toward psychologically exact portraiture. In keeping with the total system, the actor becomes a self-propelled marionette whose gestures suggest external precision more than internal depth. The voice is less important than the face, the face less important than the body, and the body is significant not so much in itself as in relation to the whole stage. Eisenstein's films of the 1920s, especially *Strike* and *Potemkin,* adhere almost exactly to constructivist and biomechanical principles. The later pictures, however, most conspicuously *Ivan the Terrible,* still reflect Meyerholdian inspiration, but follow the theatre director's prescripts much more loosely and selectively. The stretching and straining of Ivan is biomechanical, but the decor is much more elaborate, the lighting much more painterly, and the costume much more self-conscious than Meyerhold would typically have allowed. In complaining of *Ivan,* Cherkasov apparently thought he was censuring Meyerholdism, but what he perhaps recognized was Eisenstein's drift toward another style of staging and performance. This is the style of expressionism, a theory of gesture, decor, and choreography that first evolved in the silent era, but survived with various modifications well into the sound period.

EXPRESSIONISM AND ITS DERIVATIVES

The school of Max Reinhardt. His sensitivity to lighting, costume, decor. His disciples in the cinema: Paul Wegener, F. W. Murnau, Fritz Lang. Expressionist impact upon Josef von Sternberg. Sternberg's work with Emil Jannings and Marlene Dietrich. Reinhardtesque performance and choreography in The Blue Angel.

Even before Meyerhold had launched his revolutionary "October in the Theatre" movement in Russia, other European directors were also attending closely to questions of stagecraft and acting. Of these, perhaps the most important was Max Reinhardt, whose thinking underlay the development of expressionism in the German theatre. Although politically the antithesis of Meyerhold, Reinhardt also schooled his actors in stylized body gesture and gave much thought to the renovation of stage architecture. While there was a place in his scheme for the actor's personal gifts, he too insisted that they be subordinated to the ensemble and to the achievement of harmonious plastic form.

A religious conservative and an admirer of Wagner, Reinhardt sought a style of production that would reassert the actor's connection with priesthood and ritual, while reassociating the theatre itself with magic and myth. Reacting against the vogue of Ibsen, he sought not only to bring symbol and allegory but also music, dance, and spectacle back to the stage. This meant, in effect, a much greater emphasis upon what we might call "stage atmosphere" as well as close attention to the actor's posture and bearing. To achieve this atmosphere, he sought highly expert effects of light and shadow, while he conformed the actor to the stage environment through careful costuming and choreography. The theatre of Reinhardt is thus a spectacle of flowing capes and shimmering gauzes, set in motion by performers perfectly sensitized to each other's gesture. Although Reinhardt's influence was immediately registered in films like Paul Wegener's *The Golem* (1920) or Fritz Lang's *Destiny* (1921), his theories of stagecraft and performance eventually spread well beyond Germany.

For the two decades after he became director of the Kleines Theater in Berlin (1905), Reinhardt was perhaps the leading force in European theatre. His work at the Deutsches Theater (from 1906) gave him experience in the treatment of intimate psychological drama, called *Kammerspiel*. Here the sophisticated acoustical facilities made possible the experiments with sound he encouraged his actors to make: changes in the quality, strength, and pace of the spoken word; cackling laughter, suppressed cries, drunken bawling; and sometimes a long, unexpected hush. At the same time his experiments on vast outdoor stages, like the cathedral square in Salzburg, refined his skill in the handling of spectacle. It was here, in 1920, that he staged Hugo von Hofmann-sthal's *Everyman*, using the natural change from early to late twilight to symbolize the darkening of emotions in the play. Later, the climactic scenes are played in the chiaroscuro of flickering torchlight while cries resound from the lofts of nearby buildings. Although the cinematic potential of such stagecraft is immediately evident, Reinhardt bound himself even more directly to the new art form. By 1913 he had diverted some of the training programs of the Deutsches Theater to the preparation of film actors, and soon several members of his acting ensemble — Lubitsch, Murnau, and Wegener — would undertake careers as film directors. While modifying some of Reinhardt's values (especially his religious interests), his disciples in the film world spread the formal characteristics of his style throughout Europe and to America.

Though always a man of the theatre, Reinhardt did not want the cinema shackled to the stage. "The film," he insists, "must create its own new adequate mode of expression. It must open up new springs of composition, performance, and music, must live on its own soil, without borrowing. . . ."[8] It did not always live this independent life in the days of German expressionism, yet occasional excesses of staginess implicit to this filmmaking mode did not prevent the Reinhardt-trained actor from attaining real distinction. He learned to make abrupt, startling gestures which suppressed the smooth transitions we think of as "normal" behavior; he learned to conform his physique to the lines of the set, fixing himself in space with ramrod straightness when the frame was dominated by verticals but leaning at abnormal angles when the composition was diagonal. He learned to bring his eyes, his arms, his step into harmony with the ensemble, so that crowds would sweep across the stage as an absolutely integral unit, a mass that moved as a single man; he learned to make his costume disguise his thematically irrelevant movements and exaggerate those associating him with the decor and the role. Witness Conrad Veidt, veteran of Reinhardt's Deutsches Theater, in his performance for Murnau and Robert Wiene. Witness, too, the Reinhardtesque choreography of Fritz Lang's *Metropolis* (1926).

Reinhardt was also influential beyond the slightly too specialized mode of German expressionism. He substantially affected the directorial style of America's Josef von Sternberg, who recognized him as "the ablest of all men it has been my good fortune to know."[9] When Sternberg visited Germany in 1930 to make his only German-lan-

[8] "On the Film," *Max Reinhardt and His Theatre*, ed. Oliver M. Sayler, tr. Mariele S. Gudernatsch (New York: Benjamin Blom, Inc., 1968), pp. 63–64.

[9] *Fun in a Chinese Laundry* (New York: The Macmillan Company, 1965), p. 47. Copyright © Josef von Sternberg 1965. Reprinted by permission of The Macmillan Publishing Co., Inc. and Kurt Hellmer.

EXPRESSIONIST STAGECRAFT. The sets of *Metropolis* offer a classic illustration of the approach to the actor and the stage that prevailed in Germany during the 1920s. Lighting and chiaroscuro effects are extremely important (note the gradations of light tones in the treatment of steam and smoke), while the stage architecture tends to control, almost overwhelm, the performer. Note how the set determines the placement of the actors, not only by restricting each to his particular stall on the upper tiers of the set, but also by driving the more randomly distributed members of the ensemble into a kind of pyramid between the two giant cylinders in the foreground. Courtesy of Janus Films.

guage film, *The Blue Angel,* he was ready to create a truly cinematic version of Reinhardt's *Kammerspiel,* tailoring the expressionistic style to the more naturalistic demands of the nascent sound film. Predictably, he was supported by two classic presences from the Reinhardt stage — Emil Jannings and Marlene Dietrich.

Jannings joined Reinhardt at the Deutsches Theater in 1914, where he quickly perfected those controlled hand and wrist movements ideal for a small auditorium. These he naturally brought with him to the cinema, since they accorded so well with the photographic intimacy of midshot and close-up. Dietrich submitted herself to Reinhardt's coach-

EXPRESSIONIST COSTUME. While costume in the cinema almost always has a symbolic dimension, the expressionist approach runs heavily toward the exaggerated and the grotesque. Here director Josef von Sternberg checks Emil Jannings' costume and make-up for the scene in *The Blue Angel* in which the protagonist goes mad. Note particularly the oversized collar, miscombed hair, and undersized hat as emblems of derangement and psychic disturbance. The Museum of Modern Art/Film Stills Archive.

ing a few years later, having first trained for a musical career at the Berlin Konservatorium. Dietrich and Jannings first played together in the middle 1920s as the mismatched pair of *Love's Tragedy,* to some extent rehearsing the roles they would play together in *The Blue Angel.* The exact integration of their talents, along with Sternberg's skill in devising an appropriate decor, is what makes this film one of the cinema's masterpieces. Hovering delicately on the edge of exaggeration, Dietrich and Jannings call upon a wide range of acting skills to evoke the destructive fascination that binds the professor to the cabaret girl. Dress, voice, and gesture are all applied in strikingly relevant ways.

The early scenes of *The Blue Angel* establish the professor (Jannings) as a stiff, introverted specimen of German academic bureaucracy. His clothes seem to weigh him down as well as bundle him up, and the cape thrown over his shoulders emphasizes their roundness. Jannings senses the import of his costume and walks with a weary gait, always slightly stooping. Time too seems to hang heavily upon the professor's hands, an impression we get from the way Jannings stalls and protracts every action, even the most trivial. The slight overstatement of gesture seems intended to emphasize certain select elements of decor. Sitting meticulously at the kitchen table, Jannings crooks his elbow eccentrically as he picks up a cream pitcher, then holds a lump of sugar in his hand for an astonishingly long time. Such bits of stage business, together with the gestures that underscore them, bring out a sentimental strain in the protagonist's character we might not otherwise so quickly notice. In this breakfast table ritual of the German burger, Jannings' short steps beyond realism give commonplace activities a slight symbolic touch.

We also see early in the film that the professor's personal disposition is somewhat at odds with his professional bearing. In the classroom he is an academic bully, intimidating the students with his niggling authoritarianism. Again the handling of minor stage props contributes importantly to the presentation. As he instructs the students in English pronunciation, Jannings' pencil becomes a spear threatening his delinquent charges, once probing at the mouth of a student who can't say "th." When there is no pencil, a finger, an arm, or a cane is called into play to create the same aggressive gesture. As the hands grow still the head leans forward sternly, prodding and haggling. But these authoritarian gestures are complicated by others that suggest nervousness and vulnerability. Jannings' head often seems to bob about on his torso, while he constantly touches and adjusts the cuffs of his shirt. From Jannings' enactment of these early scenes, the professor emerges as an insecure man who protects himself by browbeating his students. He is also represented as a lonely man, more affectionate toward his bird and his crockery than toward any man or woman. The stage is thus set for his contact with the temptress, Lola.

Dietrich, as Lola, is in all ways the antithesis of Jannings. He is wrapped up, almost huddled inside his vest and jacket. She is virtually unclothed, flaunting her bare thighs as she strikes her famous cabaret girl's pose. She stands erect, solidly, like a piece of erotic sculpture. Her voice is deep, but melodious, and significantly we first hear her as a singer, not a speaker. While Jannings' voice rasps and carps, the husky bass of Dietrich suggests the firmness and control by which she soon subjects and humiliates the professor.

As the professor falls under the spell of Lola, his classroom gestures are memorably transformed. The head, which once bobbed in annoyance with uncooperative students, now becomes mobile with imperfectly repressed sexual excitement. For the first time the tight lips open in a thin smile. At last, as if in surrender, Jannings' head slides forward to rest on hands and elbows, while the eyes reveal how completely he is beguiled by Lola's charms. Naturally the atmosphere of the cabaret scene is entirely different from the imposed silence of the schoolroom. Screechy music, drunken shouts, and animal cries — familiar elements in Reinhardt's stagecraft — foreshadow the degradation of the protagonist.

Once the professor has given up his academic position in order to marry Lola, Jannings extends the gestures he has already used to suggest infatuation and subservience. His fingers thread their way through Lola's hosiery as he helps her get ready for her act. The sexual symbolism here is well handled, as is the suggestion of erotic fetishism. Jannings' voice also acquires new properties. On the day he weds Lola, the professor crows like a rooster, mimicking the clown act which is part of Lola's cabaret routine. Ironically, the man who once winced at a mispronounced "th" is now making animal noises. The cause of this transformation is obvious, however, since the crowing is a response to the "cluck-cluck-cluck" of Dietrich. This unusual handling of voice nicely conveys the sense of the professor's being sucked into the animal world. Already too, Dietrich's voice has taken on the teasing, wheedling quality which so convincingly expresses her role as temptress.

Robbed of both his dignity and his livelihood, the professor quickly degenerates into Lola's plaything, and once their relationship has lost the attractiveness of its novelty Lola begins to deliberately taunt him, carefully inventing new devices of humiliation. Eventually he becomes part of the clown act (with a change of costume that powerfully underscores his demeaned position) and is then obliged to perform the crowing act he first did spontaneously on their wedding day. The ultimate humiliation is their return to "The Blue Angel," the cabaret where the professor first met Lola and where he must now play the clown in front of his former students. This is too much for him, and he slips into madness. The scene of this psychic breakdown combines the histrionic skill of Jannings with Sternberg's inventive handling of light, choreography, and decor.

Preparing to go on stage, the professor sits dejectedly at the makeup table, as if resisting the greasepaint which signifies his bondage to Lola. The fact that he is impervious to the swirl of activity about him marks his drift into an almost catatonic state. After he is pushed onto the stage, he still seems completely removed from the actors, repeatedly missing the cues which should tell him it is time to crow. When the sound finally bursts forth, it is a new note, announcing that another psychic threshold has been crossed — this time the one that leads from sense to madness. Once the actor has taken the initiative, Sternberg furthers the theme with various visual effects. Rotating shadows swirl wildly upon the cabaret wall, the outward sign of the professor's inward state. Moments later the professor himself is crazily gyrating, these movements the complete opposite of his circumspect steps in the opening scenes. He is eventually entangled in gauze curtains (an extension of the feminine image represented by Lola's hosiery); in addition to its symbolic implications, this piece of stage business widens the circle of pictorial confusion that Jannings' turns and pivots first introduced. The expressionistic, chiaroscuro lighting of the final scene is the last visual complement to the actor's performance. Jannings stumbles amid nightmarish lights and shadows as he wanders in madness back to the classroom he once willingly abandoned.

Like Sternberg, Reinhardt asked of the actor something rather different from the requirements of Meyerhold. There was a place for voice and ornament, as well as an opportunity for a Jannings or a Dietrich to exercise considerable personal initiative. Though she was always a creature of dark veils and slinky gowns, Sternberg's favorite actress was much more than an exquisitely upholstered puppet. Furthermore, the gestures and stage movements Reinhardt encouraged were more calculated to extend the boundaries of realism than to absolutely overthrow natural deportment. Jannings bows a bit too deeply, swings his arms in arabesques that are a bit too elaborate, fondles the stage props a bit too lengthily, yet never with such completely stylized or formalized movements as characterize biomechanical acting. In decor, too, the departures from realism are only relative. The clown masks, the poses, and the flickering lights carry us into the realm of symbol, but without leaving behind plausible motives and manners.

In all these respects, Sternberg's *The Blue Angel* demonstrated that Reinhardtesque techniques could be modified to fit the sound film. This was an augury of substantial moment, since the new sound technology was clearly the wave of the future.

STYLES
IN
TRANSITION

Before 1930 the cinema had developed several co-herent styles of acting largely founded upon body gesture. With varying emphases, each of these extended a role to the individual player while accommodating his behavior to the ensemble and the set. But the sound revolution upset the signals that had evolved during the silent era, forcing a thorough reappraisal of choreography and performance. Stage movement was influenced by the placement of microphones; written scripts brought with them more complex plotting; makeup and gesture were affected by the shift to panchromatic film stock and tungsten lighting that was contemporaneous with the coming of sound. Most importantly, however, the fact of voice gave the actor a radically new resource, already explored and exploited by Sternberg in his treatment of the husky tones of Dietrich. Henceforth there would always be this new element in the actor's expression and delivery. For some a curse, for others a blessing, sound touched the art of every performer.

In no sense did the sound film completely destroy existing styles of acting and staging. Physical comedy survived and may even have enriched itself, in the Marx brothers of the 1930s, in Chaplin's European disciples, Pierre Etaix and Jacques Tati, who emerged in the 1950s, and perhaps most recently in Woody Allen. These performers have not only successfully mixed sight gags with verbal humor but, like Chaplin and Keaton, have learned to think of the comic gesture in relationship to the set and the ensemble. The school of Meyerhold has had a less obvious continuing impact upon the sound film, though traces of its substance surface from time to time. What could be more Meyerholdian, for example, than the scene in *The Great Dictator* (1940) where Chaplin and Jack Oakie compete for supremacy by jacking up their barber chairs toward the ceiling? The jerky, puppetlike movements of the performers, the centrality of a machine that determines the choreography, and the translation of every detail of the business into political satire: this is almost the essence of biomechanics and constructivism, though surely not intended as imitation of Meyerholdian theory. For the most part, the post-1930 cinema reflects the interests of constructivism in a more diffuse way — in an attention to careful crowd choreography, for example, or in the use of starkly modernistic sets. Staging films aboard ships and in factories, so as to include wheels, pipes, gauges, and guns in the decor, by no means ended with *Strike* and *Potemkin*.

The same mutations are notable in the aftercourses of German expressionism. Lon Chaney, Jr., and Boris Karloff are directly in the tradition of expressionist performance, while Marlene Dietrich in *The Scarlet Empress* (U.S.A., 1934), letting her stately figure glide among the grotesque statues and paintings of the czarist court, conforms more closely to the expressionist mode than in *The Blue Angel*. But these are somewhat exceptional cases. For the most part the impact of expressionism is visible in the more self-conscious use of lighting, costume, and stage decor very evident in both French and American studios after 1930. This influence, of course, did not prevent the modification of acting styles. And here, in spite of these significant continuities, the sound film did force the actor to simplify or compress his gestures, promoting first a more functionalistic delivery and eventually a greater interiorization of the performer's motives.

THE HOLLYWOOD STUDIO STYLE

Functional and pragmatic tendencies of Hollywood studio style. Testimony of Henry Fonda. Personalization of stereotypic roles: Humphrey Bogart. Possibility of greater theatricalism: George Cukor's handling of Greta Garbo in Camille. *Alfred Hitchcock's emphasis upon minimal performance:* Joseph Cotten in Shadow of a Doubt. *Changes wrought in the 1950s. Contrast of acting styles in* The Tin Star.

The effects of the sound film upon acting were first noticeable in Hollywood, which the new technology turned into the world's cinematic capital. The big studios of the 1930s became a kind of theatrical melting pot, where performers schooled in various traditions acquired a functional and pragmatic orientation to their craft. Garbo came from Stockholm's Royal Dramatic Theatre, Dietrich straight from Reinhardt, Maurice Chevalier from Paris; Henry Fonda, Katherine Hepburn, Spencer Tracy, Bette Davis, and Humphrey Bogart emerged from widely different American roots. But all adopted variations of what we might call "the Hollywood studio style." This means, basically, a role-centered approach to acting which combines stereotypic appearances with personalized speech and manner.

The myth persists that Hollywood actors of the thirties and forties never exactly acted; no one contributes more to that impression than these actors themselves. Since many of them developed their talents outside of a carefully structured theatrical tradition, they tended to be suspicious of acting theory. Having listened for most of one evening to a debate about the merits of Stanislavsky, Spencer Tracy is said to have announced his own simpler secret of great acting: "Learn your lines." [10] Some carry simplification even further: John Ford and Frank Capra are notorious for their resentment of actors who show signs of having rehearsed their parts. Henry Fonda claims he learned his lesson about film acting the day director Victor Fleming accused him of "mugging." Shocked and hurt, he says, "I then realized that I was giving a stage performance that I had been giving for months in New York." [11] After that, apparently, Fonda knew that in film acting, "You do it just like in reality."

But do you? In the same interview, Fonda makes an interesting remark about Ford that perhaps gives a better look at the Hollywood studio system. Noting that in *The Grapes of Wrath* he had no chance to rehearse the lines of his good-bye scene with Jane Darwell, Fonda observes: "[Ford] knew that we knew our lines and he knew that we were ready — that's where Ford is. Like other directors *he'll cast for what he knows he can expect* of the actors. I guess *he knew what he could expect* from Jane Darwell and me. *We'd both worked for Ford before* [my italics]." This idea of fulfilling "expectations" — those of the director, those of the studio, and perhaps those of the actor's public — is the key to the classical Hollywood style. It means the accommodation of personal talent to a received stereotype, but this does not necessarily work to the detriment of performance. In fact, it makes the actor's behavior seem utterly "real."

Take as a case in point the screen image of Humphrey Bogart. What was the relationship between the myth and the man? Bogart didn't turn into Sam Spade or Philip Marlowe the moment he set foot on a Hollywood sound stage. The role grew over the course of a decade, being trimmed and adjusted until he could walk around in it with absolute ease and comfort. It developed from the stereotype of the Hollywood "heavy," the anti-hero of melodrama who gets his kicks from bullying respectable people. This was the slot into which Bogart dropped when he arrived at Warner Brothers in the early 1930s, his craggy looks and raspy voice apparently disqualifying him for "star" parts. What specialized his situation, however, was that Warners, to avoid direct competition with highbrow, Europeanized Paramount and big-budget MGM,

---

[10] Quoted in Garson Kanin, *Tracy and Hepburn: An Intimate Memoir* (New York: Bantam Books, Inc., 1972), p. 7.

[11] This and following citations are from the interview with Fonda in *Take One* (March–April 1972), pp. 14–17. Reprinted by permission of *Take One*, Unicorn Publishing Co., Montreal, Canada.

was tailoring its product to a working-class audience, which might conceivably identify with a sympathetic heavy. Hence the opportunity to experiment with the role, to introduce redemptive touches and let the invective against "dames" flow somewhat good-naturedly off the tongue. It was this Bogart, a performer personalizing a long-standing stereotype, that John Huston and Howard Hawks discovered in the 1940s and further developed through astute direction.

This refinement of a role was not achieved without many missteps. Not all the heavies Bogart played were susceptible to his own kind of personalization. When he played in *Bad Sister* (1931) for Universal Studios, his image as heavy won him the role of Valentine Corliss, a clever fraud who leads the impressionable Marianne astray. But the neatly pressed suit, slicked-back hair, and starched white collar give Bogart little to build from. We see him once in a blooming, studio-built bower, inventing completely artificial gestures as he toys fondly with the fingers of Marianne's hand. Here he is surely the stereotypic villain, but the role doesn't encourage any of Bogart's individuating mannerisms. Neither does the casting in *The Return of Dr. X* (1939), where Warners pushed him into playing a zombie. Trussed up in a tight black coat and smothered with lip rouge and eye makeup, Bogart again fails to fulfill the Bogart character.

It is otherwise when he plays Duke Mantee in *The Petrified Forest* (1936), again for Warners. Suddenly the image is more authentic. The stubble beard emphasizes the deep lines of his face, the hair seems parched by the desert wind, and the soiled, sweat-soaked open collar leaves him free to move naturally. Bogart's muscles seem to unlimber, he feels free to let his shoulders slump and his legs reach out in long strides. This is the Bogart image that Huston would take over and use almost to the exact detail in *The Treasure of the Sierra Madre* (1948) and *The African Queen* (1952).

Once Bogart had found the visual basics of his screen character, he elaborated the details with great skill. In his films of the 1940s, his face becomes very pliable, hovering between a grin and a grimace. It is the vehicle of his wary irony, his love-hate relationship to the world. The annoyed Bogart puts his tongue behind his lower lip, pushing it slightly forward while the mouth as a whole pouts. A more ambiguous facial gesture is the one with the teeth slightly apart and the lips drawn back tightly. This seems modeled upon the snarl of a dog, though it often means no more than perplexity or unavoidable pain. It can soften into a smile, if the right cues come from his acting partner and the problematic issues are resolved. As Bogart acquires mastery of his poses, the costume diminishes in importance, though the carelessly attached tie remains as a symbol of incomplete civility, just as the cigarette suggests frayed nerves and long hours on the job. Interestingly, however, by the

HOLLYWOOD FUNCTIONALISM. The Hollywood studio style of the 1930s and 1940s did not so much require of the actor the right sort of "performance" as the right sort of look. Humphrey Bogart, as "tough guy" in *Treasure of the Sierra Madre,* classically typifies the Hollywood actor who varied and sophisticated a predictable role. Courtesy of United Artists.

time he performed in *Casablanca* (1943) his slightly seedy image was so well established that he could come on in a white dinner jacket and everyone would see it as a psychic disguise. We all knew that Rick, the love-starved American expatriate, would have to strip off this badge of unsullied political aloofness and get into the war before the film was over.

The Hollywood style does not exclude a more orthodox thetatrical performance, when the star, or even a character actor, has a taste for such tasks. Greta Garbo always "acted," not only with her exquisitely mobile face but also with great rolling body gestures that took full advantage of MGM's elegant costumes. She too worked out of a Hollywood stereotype but personalized and varied it so skillfully with her accent-ridden voice and arc-lamp eyes that audiences could almost forget she was always a version of the conventional "fallen woman." Far from frustrating her directors, Garbo's theatrical initiative deeply gratified such *metteurs en scène* as Lubitsch, Rouben Mamoulian, and George Cukor.

"I accomplish things through the actor," says Cukor in a recent interview on American television, "through the actor's gift." [12] Nowhere is this more evident than in the scene from *Camille* (1937) where Garbo in a brief moment captures all the ambiguities of the heroine's personality. She stands at the piano while an old admirer (Henry Daniell) entertains her; suddenly Armand Duval (Robert Taylor) appears at the door, his arrival signaled by imperious chimes. But Camille has decided to jilt him, so that her courtesan's reputation will not stain him for life. She must therefore cling to Daniell while secretly treasuring the affection of the young innocent who calls for her. Cukor plays the camera almost exclusively to Garbo, assuming, quite correctly, that the whole scene can be carried by her personal performing skills.

The scene begins with an exchange between Daniell and Garbo, in which her broad-smiling remark, "You play beautifully," brings the retort, "You lie beautifully." Garbo then takes control of the scene, demonstrating in the strained-for camouflage of her true emotions the absolute correctness of Daniell's comment. Garbo's controlling gesture in the ensuing action is a continuous tossing back of the head, each time to a more extreme angle. The effect in Cukor's tight, close-up composition is to exaggerate the prominence of the heroine's throat, its naked softness functioning not as an erotic enticement but as a sign of her extreme vulnerability. At last, after she has tilted her head to the furthest possible extent in successive slow lifts of the chin, she brings her face forward and down, with a crashing movement that suggests a more general psychic collapse. The pitch of the head is so extreme as to approach physical deformity. These gesticulations are accompanied by wild laughter, intended to feign reckless gaiety but unmistakably showing nervous hysteria. The mingling of Garbo's voice with the chords of the piano and the chimes of the door nicely indicates the divided loyalties driving her to this climax of emotional stress. Such a

[12] The program was aired on KETC, St. Louis, Mo., 25 November 1973. It originated with WNET 13, New York.

scene illustrates the outer limit to which Hollywood functionalism might go in assimilating a more histrionic mode.

Although the studio style could absorb even Garbo, the typical way to do this kind of scene would be without the grand gesture from the star. Instead of continuous concentration upon the leading lady, there would be close-up attention to several faces, cut together in such a way as to build up an equivalent emotional charge. The heroine would then be required to strike one or two convincing poses rather than use her facial mask to organize the whole transformation of mood. Alfred Hitchcock, who typically downplays the actor, would almost certainly have handled the material in this fashion.

Alexander Knox, a Canadian veteran of both stage and screen, once complained that film directors "in Hollywood and elsewhere" too often reduce acting to mere "behaving." [13] He thought Hitchcock a particular offender, since this director is so prone to pull the film away from the performer. Knox objects especially to a scene in *Spellbound* (1945) where Hitchcock seems to deny Ingrid Bergman the right to react to her first kiss from Gregory Peck. Instead, Hitchcock used a montage of opening doors, presumably suggesting a kind of release, or perhaps the perception of new possibilities in their relationship. But, says Knox, "I have complete faith in Miss Bergman's ability to convince me that doors in her soul are opening, if she is given adequate material to do it with, and, frankly, I'd rather look at her opening doors than see Mr. Hitchcock do it." Beyond this jurisdictional dispute between actor and director, there lies an important point about the nature of functional style, here classically exemplified by Hitchcock. It may truncate the actor's gesture, in order to extend to the camera the opportunity for a gesture of its own.

Hitchcock's emphasis upon minimal performance is illustrated by his handling of a scene from *Shadow of a Doubt* (1943), which might easily have allowed more explicitly theatrical behavior. This is the sequence in which Joseph Cotten, the seemingly affable Uncle Charlie, first begins to reveal his psychopathic hatred of women. The family is gathered together and the conversation is innocently trivial until a slight shift toward the gutteral in Cotten's voice signals the arrival of a more sinister mood. At this moment traces of a grimace appear in his face, though his mannerisms change relatively little as he starts to soliloquize upon the hideousness of money-grasping widows. What impresses us is an act of the camera. It dollies forward, carrying the key light much nearer Cotten's face, and naturally bleaching his features to a harsh, pasty white. The framing also disturbs our composure, since the tight-

[13] This and the further remarks of Knox are from his "Acting and Behaving," *Hollywood Quarterly* (Spring 1946), pp. 260 ff. Reprinted by permission of the University of California Press.

ening of the close-up robs the speaker of his hairline and the bottom of his chin. At the conclusion of the dolly shot we are left with the fragment of a face, a chalky blob of speaking flesh that lacks fully human form yet reveals to us every one of its blemishes and imperfections. Cotten doesn't have to do anything nasty. He already looks about as nasty as anyone might.

For at least two decades, this functionalist approach to performance prevailed in Hollywood, though stretched to its elastic limit by Garbo, Dietrich, Bette Davis, Orson Welles, Katherine Hepburn, and others. In the 1950s, however, the contract system of the studios changed, giving greater independence to the actor, while the genres themselves were powerfully altered by the impact of television. This changed casting in a significant way and eventually brought a new kind of talent to Hollywood, not better, certainly, but pronouncedly different. In certain films of the 1950s it is possible to see both styles on the screen together, as when Henry Fonda plays opposite Tony Perkins in Anthony Mann's *The Tin Star* (1957).

On the screen, Henry Fonda is a typical functionalist actor — deadpan face, controlled torso, a distinctive voice, but not one with a wide range of inflections. In *The Tin Star* he plays a professional bounty hunter who reluctantly takes on the task of showing Tony Perkins how to be sheriff. While Perkins seeks to interiorize his role, working out the personal psychology of the greenhorn sheriff, Fonda molds his part to the studio stereotype of the inarticulate westerner, remembering no doubt his own performances in *My Darling Clementine* (1946) as well as the precedent of Jimmy Stewart in *The Naked Spur* (1952), not to mention any number of films starring John Wayne or Gary Cooper. Though noticeably different, the two styles do not clash but meaningfully counterpoint one another, since Mann skillfully fits each to the role in question.

The framing in *The Tin Star* is contrived to take advantage of the physical presence of Fonda while giving Perkins the opportunity to interiorize the psychology of the role. Fonda does relatively little explicit performing. He is often caught standing sturdily erect at the edge of the frame, where his vertical stance is reinforced by the bounding line of the picture itself. This position is significant not only in graphic terms, but also emphasizes his peripheral yet powerfully supportive role in relation to Perkins. Further, it clears the frame for Perkins himself, who then has plenty of room to pace the floor, fidget with his hands, or bob up and down between one chair and another. When Mann seeks to strengthen Fonda's image on the screen, he normally does so through composition rather than the actor's gesture. A case in point is the scene where Perkins and Fonda argue over who is best qualified to track the renegade McGaffeys to their hideout. During this sequence, which culminates in Fonda's knocking Perkins down, the preparation for this gesture is accomplished in shots which show Fonda with a blazing fire behind him. The raising of the emotional pitch is accomplished not so much through the obvious (and slightly inexact) fire-rage equation as through the plastic energy of the pictorial form. With smoke swirling and flames leaping at his back, Fonda inevitably seems the stronger, more aggressive character.

The few things Fonda does with his body are followed assiduously by the camera. He gives Perkins a lesson in how to draw a pistol, which is covered in tight close-up to underscore Fonda's smooth hand and finger coordination. We watch him lift the gun delicately out of its holster, then slide his thumb to the left, so that it hooks over the hammer and cocks the pistol. This close-up treatment of the hands is accompanied by an assured off-screen voice which urges the would-be sheriff always to take his time. That is the one thing Perkins can't do, as the camera again shows us when the stage rolls into town carrying one of the outlaws' victims. As the vehicle slows to a stop, Perkins races up to it, arriving before there is anything specific to do. He dances around, rubs his hands together, and spits out his lines in precipitous bursts. Meanwhile Fonda approaches the stage much more slowly, not hesitantly, but just taking his time. This allows the camera, which has tracked Perkins, to pick up Fonda with a face and chest shot as he advances with sure strides. Though Fonda does nothing more than put one foot before the other, his forward thrust in space is all that's necessary to take control of the action in cinematic terms. This type of performance represents functional style at its best.

THE IMPACT OF STANISLAVSKY

New sources of theatrical talent. Elia Kazan and Lee Strasberg at the New York Actors Studio. Their indebtedness to Konstantin Stanislavsky. Their emphasis upon the interiorization of a role. Kazan, Marlon Brando, and On the Waterfront. *Rod Steiger as Actors Studio performer. His role in* The Pawnbroker. *His personal testimony.*

In contradistinction to Fonda, Tony Perkins' performance in *The Tin Star* is in a style we have come to associate with the New York Actors Studio and, more distantly, with the name of the great Russian theatre director, the polar opposite of Meyerhold, Konstantin Stanislavsky. Usually described, though not quite correctly, as "method acting," it is the style of Marlon Brando, James Dean, and Paul Newman as well as that of slightly lesser-known actors like Anne Bancroft, Keir Dullea, Jane Fonda, Steve McQueen, Patricia Neal, Eva Marie Saint, Rod

Steiger, and Joanne Woodward. It is the style that Elia Kazan and Lee Strasberg refined for the Broadway stage, in order to handle the psycho-analytical concerns of playwrights such as Arthur Miller and Tennessee Williams.

Though Stanislavsky's conception of acting is hard to summarize (since it grew slowly from his practical stage experience), his central concern was with the performer's personal inspiration. Unlike the Meyerholdian actor, who might simply be an agile puppet, or even the Chaplinesque mime, gifted in adding one gesture to another, the actor whom Stanislavsky sought had to feel the role that he played. The world of the stage, Stanislavsky decided, depends upon a magic "as if" by which the actor temporarily identifies his own emotions with those of the character he is impersonating. As endorsed by the New York Actors Studio, this search for personal emotion substantially altered the functionalist style of Hollywood acting. No longer could one attach one's behavior to a prevailing stereotype; every role must have its personal psychic coherence.

The founding of the Actors Studio in 1947 represents the full unfolding of an interest in Stanislavsky which began in America in the early 1920s. It was then that Richard Boleslavsky and Maria Ouspenskaya, both disciples of Stanislavsky, left Russia for the U.S.A., where they immediately began teaching and directing for the American Laboratory Theater. Their work was then incorporated into a nativist American tradition by such theater directors as Lee Strasberg, whose work with the New York Group Theater of the 1930s anticipated the orientation of the Actors Studio. It was not until the days of television, however, that the American cinema began searching for a more intimate, more interiorized performing style which emerged out of the training program of Strasberg and Kazan. They introduced the American public to a group of actors highly astute in conveying complex psychological responses. Unheroic yet forceful, sympathetic yet unsentimental, they were well suited to the American cinema at the moment when it was absorbing Italian neorealism and dipping into controversial social issues.

The early impact of the Actors Studio upon the cinema came through films directed by Kazan. Such pictures as *A Streetcar Named Desire* (1951), *Viva Zapata* (1952), *On the Waterfront* (1954), *East of Eden* (1955), and *Baby Doll* (1956) not only introduced members of the Actors Studio like Woodward, Brando, Steiger, Saint, and Dean, but also placed these figures in ensembles and amid stage arrangements that similarly smack of Stanislavskian naturalism. The most notable of these films, *On the Waterfront,* is not only vintage Brando but also a typical example of Kazan's choreography, stagecraft, and treatment of the supporting cast (Steiger and Saint). The stammering, T-shirted earthiness of Brando is much in evidence in *On the Waterfront,* but comes through more powerfully because it is effectively counterpointed by the slimy good grooming of Steiger on the one hand and the delicate firmness of Saint on the other.

Brando's role in *On the Waterfront* is of a piece with the rest of his career, perhaps with his basic personality. He specializes in oblique self-revelation, displaying remarkable ingenuity in the invention of physical mannerisms and in controlling the tone, timbre, and accent of his voice. Paradoxically he is always the same yet always different, fabricating an astonishing array of ethnic accents while playing the surly proletarian who suspects every smell of middle-class decorum. Cast by Kazan in *On the Waterfront* as a dock worker who develops a conscience, Brando immediately transcends the outward gestures that made him the archetypal vulgarian of *A Streetcar Named Desire.*

In *Streetcar* Brando evidently built the part around his sense of Stanley Kowalski's animal aggressiveness. Sometimes this is innocently canine, as when his incessant scratching of back and belly reminds us of a dog going after fleas. But the Kowalski character is also destructive, as we are told in Brando's use of the mouth: he chews fruit with loud crunching noises, munches up potato chips with the same relentless jaw muscles, washes beer around in his mouth and then swallows it with physically noticeable gulps. These two Brando-generated metaphors come together in the scene where Kowalski rummages through Blanche's trunk, his clawlike hands burrowing furiously and throwing velveteen dresses and fake fox fur back over his shoulders with fierce determination. These apparently insubstantial bits of stage business prepare us for the climactic scene in which Kowalski, having worked havoc upon Blanche's wardrobe, at last destroys the woman herself, devouring her futile illusions of Southern gentility.

But if the Brando hero of *Streetcar* is a study in pure animalism, the role of Terry Malloy in *On the Waterfront* requires from the outset a suggestion of higher capabilities. His costume of lumberjack shirt and leather jacket is as clearly lowbrow as Kowalski's sweat-soaked bowling jersey, but there's a shyness and detachment about Brando's Malloy that marks him as capable of reflection and judgment. The ease with which Brando slips in and out of something resembling a boxing stance is also a nice touch, since it reminds us of Malloy's abortive career as a prizefighter and also expresses his combative approach to the world. As in *Streetcar,* Brando's mouth is again mobile, but here it nervously massages a wad of gum (looking forward to *The Last Tango in Paris*) instead of swallowing up everything in sight. What emerges from Brando's approach to the role is the portrait of an inarticulate but sensitive young man betrayed into the service of a waterfront hoodlumism by slum education and the misdirection of his older brother Charlie

(Steiger). The portrayal is subtle enough to suggest both Malloy's allegiance to the waterfront gang and his ultimate ability to transcend its code.

The first scene presents Malloy as a figure isolated through his own introspection while he sits in a bar among his fellow longshoremen. He is obviously worried about his implicit part in the murder of Joey, a co-worker who was killed when he threatened to testify in court about criminal practices within the waterfront union. Brando's vague irritability in this scene suggests more the prick of conscience than unmotivated nastiness. Already he is at odds, even in terms of physical choreography, with the union boss (Lee J. Cobb) whose contrived friendliness is strikingly different from Malloy's honest despondency. Cobb sweeps casually through the barroom, unifying the group through the serpentine arcs of his walk and singling out certain favorites for back-patting, finger-poking affection. Through the scene he harps incessantly upon loyalty to the organization, the occasional bumps of his fist on the tables adding emphasis and a hint of threat. As Cobb's movements upon the set bind the men together against whatever might challenge their interest, we can see in Brando's unresponsiveness his doubts about what the organization stands for.

In Terry's brother Charlie we see the fruits of loyalty to the gang. His camel's-hair coat testifies to the creature comforts that flow from unquestioning allegiance, but his boot-licking subservience to Cobb advertises the moral price of the clothes he wears. As Terry begins to question the acquisitiveness that makes murder an instrument of trade unionism, Charlie's fear and fury erupts in hands and arms that fly out from his body as he shouts frantically, "Shape up." Brando is less expansive with his hands than either Steiger or Cobb, using them to cradle his chin and inching them up nervously to cover his face (another skillful reference to his boxing days). Brando's hands open out slowly in his first lengthy conversation with Edie (Eva Marie Saint), the sister of the murdered Joey and eventual custodian of Malloy's conscience. Amid repeated shrugs of the shoulders, Brando's hands struggle toward human contact, hesitantly at first but with more conviction as the scenes progress. His embracing Edie is naturally the last term in this development of gesture. Before the conflict between them can be resolved, however, Malloy must confess his unwitting contribution to the murder of her brother. Kazan here challenges the performers very effectively. The sound of a whistle (an obvious but effective metaphor for the release of pressure) drowns the dialogue of the confession scene, forcing the actors to handle their emotions in pantomime. Brando strains every muscle of his face and neck (a level of stress worthy of Meyerholdian biomechanics), as he tries to shout over the whistle; Saint responds with a lightning transformation of looks, marking successively her disbelief, horror, and rage.

The scenes with Saint also find Brando extending his hands toward the animal world in gestures of simple affection and symbolic suggestion. Before his death Joey had tended pigeons, an interest that functions in the film not only as a symbol of tenderness but also of care and concern. This role is taken over by Malloy as he and Edie visit Joey's coop together. Brando's fingers thread their way through chicken wire to reach the birds in spite of intervening barriers, and this gesture works effectively to establish Malloy's discovery of his innate gentleness and decency. The other external stage prop that Brando leans upon is Joey's jacket. It is first passed to Duggan, another wharf-hand who agrees to cooperate in the exposure of labor racketeering. Then, after Duggan is also murdered, it is offered to Malloy. As he accepts it, he also accepts the role of victim-redeemer toward which the film as a whole has pointed him. Here Kazan's stagecraft merges with Brando's intuition to complete the thematic articulation of *On the Waterfront*.

While Brando in one sense epitomizes the Actors Studio performer, his intuitive approach to the psychology of his roles is a slightly specialized variation upon Stanislavsky. Perhaps the methods of "method acting" are better illustrated in the career of Rod Steiger, who has many times put aside his own personality to think his way into an alien psyche. Often a gangster, as in *On the Waterfront, The Harder They Fall* (1956), and *Al Capone* (1959), he is also a quite convincing cowboy in *Jubal* (1956) and an unforgettable Mississippi sheriff in *In the Heat of the Night* (1966). That Steiger seeks an intellectual penetration of his roles is clear from his remarks on how he played Napoleon in Sergei Bondarchuk's *Waterloo* (Italy-U.S.S.R., 1972):

> My concept of Napoleon is really based on a report I got from the American Medical Association of Chicago. . . . I decided to find out what his physical condition was at the age of 45, which was his age at the Battle of Waterloo. . . . I got a translation of his autopsy as well as a document on his medical history and I found out that from the age of 45 until his death at 51, Napoleon was afflicted by primary cancer of the stomach, but also by partial blockage of the urinary canal, perforated ulcers, a liver disorder, and hemorrhoids. Out of this came the conception of a man whose body was decaying but whose mind refused to die. And I started from there.[14]

Whether or not such research actually improved his performance, it demonstrates how strongly Steiger feels his obligation to be informed about a character's psychology. It is difficult to imagine Marlene Dietrich studying Catherine the Great with the same intensity before impersonating her in *The Scarlet Empress*. In this respect, the Actors Studio is at odds with both Hollywood functionalism and the school of Reinhardt.

[14] Steiger is quoted in Ann Guerin, "Rod Steiger's Napoleon: A Self-Defeated Man," *Show* Magazine (May 1971), p. 30.

Although Steiger's conception of character might begin at the abstract level of a medical report, it eventually extends down to the last detail of dress, manner, and speech. What he does with the German-Jewish accent in *The Pawnbroker* (1965) illustrates this point.

Normally the ethnic accent in either theater or cinema is done only in general terms, so as to sound vaguely "foreign." This is the logic that casts Garbo as a Polish patriot in *Conquest* (U.S.A., 1938). While her vowels are not Polish, neither does she sound like a native speaker of English. The other alternative is to reduce foreign speech to an ethnic stereotype, as Peter Sellers does with the Germanized English of Dr. Strangelove.

Steiger, however, goes after and achieves an authentic reproduction of ethnic speech. He takes pains in the early moments of the film to establish that Nasserman handles the sounds of English reasonably well, avoiding the clumsily Germanic "d" for "th" substitution as well as the equally telltale "v" for "w." Where he errs is in articulating the subtler sounds of English, as a German "d" slips into his speech when he tells his Puerto Rican assistant, "You take a little acit." The same comparatively minor errors creep into his conversation with the social worker, to whom he once retorts, "You must be joking," giving the "j" a strong "ch" sound. Having mastered the ethnic accent to this extent, Steiger can use it as a dramatic resource. Hence it noticeably worsens each time the protagonist is distraught, as in his last conversation with the black boss who uses the pawnshop as a front for his dealings in prostitution. Nasserman's excited outburst, "I vant no more to do with you," is stereotypically Germanized English, but in context it suggests the disintegration of another defensive facade. Just as Nasserman's soul is buried in Nazi Germany, so his speech — at the deepest psychic level — is still rooted in Germanic phonemes.

Because Steiger works so hard at the roles he plays, he resents the refusal of some directors to let an actor make a point in his own way. The hurrying of effects arouses his particular ire: "American directors especially are desperately frightened when nobody's talking. If nobody's talking, he'll [*sic*] cut away like mad. He'll photograph whoever's talking, which is the antithesis of acting. Acting is basically reacting. You build up a lovely moment and that moment is the moment after you stop talking, but when you see it on the screen, they cut away. And the whole moment is gone." [15] This is a continuing problem for actors of the Stanislavskian persuasion.

Like so many others from the Actors Studio, Steiger also has problems with the film medium itself. He resents postsynchronization of

[15] This and the following citations are from Steiger's interview with the editors of *The Seventh Art* (Winter 1963), pp. 9 ff.

THE MAGICAL "AS IF." The impact of Stanislavsky and his disciples has moved the film actor toward more thorough psychological exploration of the roles he plays. Rod Steiger, here as the expatriate Jew of *The Pawnbroker*, typifies the versatility and professional discipline which Stanislavsky's approach seeks to inculcate in the performer. Copyright © 1965 by The Landau Company, reproduced courtesy of IOTA Entertainment, Inc.

dialogue and regrets that scenes must be filmed discontinuously. This is the normal, almost inevitable reaction of a man trained for the stage, especially when he has been educated to revere personal inspiration and integrity of feeling. It is difficult to feel inspired while alone in a glass-enclosed sound booth dubbing your own voice. Steiger, however, has no regrets about his theatrical background, insisting that his training has added to his range and skill: "I think it's better to have a theatrical background and then go into films because the actor has learned, since once the curtain goes up in the theatre he's on his own, to handle himself in those circumstances and to be responsible for what he's trying to do. I think it's best to have that command and ability." He is prepared to recognize that film acting can sometimes be competently handled by untrained persons, but quickly adds: "What non-professionals do not give (which to me is the whole essense of acting) is their personal exploration of a particular piece of life they are asked to portray. Because they have no means of exploring it. But the actor, a sensitive, talented person who is trained to be an actor, can bring illumination." Such emphases go to the core of the Stanislavskian inspiration and epitomize what his disciples have given to the cinema, not just in the U.S.A. but in England and on the Continent as well.

IMPROVISATION, FORMALISM, AND CONTINUING EXPERIMENT

Other conceptions of "naturalism": Stanislavsky and V. I. Pudovkin. Handling the nonprofessional actor: Deserter. *Pudovkin and Italian neorealism: Roberto Rossellini and* Paisan. *Fellini and François Périer in* The Nights of Cabiria. *Continuing interest in formalistic approaches to acting: Peter Brook, Ken Russell, and Glenda Jackson.* Marat/Sade *and* Women in Love.

Although Stanislavsky has sired numerous progeny, the personal interiorization he encouraged has by no means replaced all other approaches to acting. There is another species of naturalism which advocates the use of nonprofessional actors or sometimes invites professional players to improvise their roles. This we know from Italian neorealism and its derivatives. In addition, we can also see on today's screens somewhat more formalistic conceptions of the actor's craft, distantly related to both Meyerhold and Reinhardt, though more immediately dependent upon renewed interest in the French actor and critic, Antonin Artaud, who in the 1920s and 1930s was close to the surrealist movement and founded the "theater of cruelty." Glenda

Jackson, especially when directed by Peter Brook or Ken Russell, is probably the most noteworthy practitioner of the Artaudian performing style.

While Stanislavsky was preaching the furthest refinement of simulation, the Soviet film director V. I. Pudovkin was considering how much of this method could be applied to the cinema. Unlike Eisenstein, Pudovkin viewed Stanislavsky sympathetically, yet felt that the essential difference between stage and screen made some of his suggestions unworkable. In their place Pudovkin put an approach to performance that stressed the actor's motivation but avoided Stanislavsky's demand for total psychic participation in the role. Pudovkin thought it possible to guide the actor at crucial moments rather than to depend upon him to have absolutely digested the part. Hence even the nonactor might play a crucial role (something unthinkable in Stanislavsky) and there would be a place for spur-of-the-moment improvisation after the cameras had begun to roll. Such thinking became the basis of another kind of naturalism, different from either the functional style of the Hollywood studio or the analytical psychologizing of Strasberg and Kazan.

Pudovkin cites an instance from his *Deserter* (U.S.S.R., 1933) as a model for dealing with nonprofessional performers. It involves the director's provoking a feeling instead of letting the actor consciously build it for himself.

There is a scene in the last reel of this picture where a teen-age nonactor must play the role of the Young Communist who is unexpectedly elected to preside over a huge assembly. When the time came for the young man to act out these emotions, says Pudovkin, "the atmosphere of shooting and his anticipation of the requirements the director was about to make of him combined to render him excited, self-conscious, and tie him generally in knots." [16] But instead of asking him to "rethink" the scene, i.e., to perform the Stanislavskian "as if" and pretend there was no camera, Pudovkin proceeded with the shooting, heightening, not damping, the young performer's embarrassment. "I purposely strengthened and increased the atmosphere that was making him self-conscious," says Pudovkin, "because it gave me the necessary colouring." For "when I made him stand up in response to applause, and then began to praise his acting unstintedly and flatteringly, the youngster, much as he tried, was unable to hold back a tremendous smile of complete satisfaction, which gave me . . . a gorgeous piece."

"Certainly," concludes Pudovkin, what was achieved here "was not the acting of an actor, *for the element of conscious creation was not*

[16] *Film Technique and Film Acting*, tr. Ivor Montague (New York: Grove Press, Inc., 1970), pp. 337–338. Originally from *Film Technique and Film Acting* by V. I. Pudovkin, translated by Ivor Montague: Memorial Edition, 1958, published by Vision Press Ltd., London. Reprinted here by permission of Grove Press, Inc. and Vision Press Limited.

present [my italics] in the lad who portrayed the Young Communist."
Yet "in this case all the real conditions of shooting did in actual fact
happen to coincide with the conditions that later invested the scene on
the screen. They fitted both the confusion of the Young Communist on
being unexpectedly elected to the presidium of a huge meeting, and
his uncontrollable pleasure when the huge meeting greeted the announcement of his name with unanimous applause." In other words,
the circumstances of production were here employed in prompting the
untrained actor to make a response he was presumably incapable of
thinking out for himself. Pudovkin himself had supplied the Stanislavskian "as if."

Such strategies of motivation are clearly at work in the neorealist
directors of the 1940s. In *Paisan* (1946), Rossellini uses the language
barrier between English and Italian-speaking performers to generate a
mood of confusion and distrust. This is then incorporated into a scene
where a group of American soldiers, operating as a scouting party for
the Allied forces in World War II, infiltrate a small Sicilian village in
search of the retreating German army. Though there is not an actor
among the villagers, they perform very convincingly, shying away from
speakers who mystify them and from weapons that are unaccounted
for. We note, too, the authenticity of the thaw in relations that begins
the moment one of the Americans shows knowledge of the native
tongue. Here neither the fright nor the reassurance was "acted"; it was
inherent in the structure of the social situation Rossellini had deliberately created.

Occasionally this same approach can be brought to bear upon professional acting. François Périer, the male lead in Fellini's *The Nights
of Cabiria* (1956), recalls an instance from this film where the director
used the actor's physical fatigue as a means to the effect he sought:
"During my big scene with Giulietta [Giulietta Masina, the Cabiria
figure], we took, both she and myself, much too quick a rhythm. Without reproaching us in any way, Fellini asked us to begin again. . . . He
tired us out completely and after several takes we were forced to relax
the precipitious pace we had both adopted: we had to slow down. It
was just what he wanted. I understood it only after the scene had been
filmed!" [17] Played at the pace Fellini at last achieved, Périer's assault
upon Giulietta seems less actively malevolent than the actor himself
had intended it to be. And when circumstances finally overrode the
performer's conscious intentions, the director had presence of mind
enough to shout "print it." Given the camera's exacting scrutiny of

---

[17] The comments are reprinted in *Federico Fellini* by Gilbert Salachas, translated by
Rosalie Siegel (pp. 207–210). © 1963 by Editions Seghers, Paris. Used by permission of
Crown Publishers, Inc., New York.

every detail, accident and improvisation will always be part of the "naturalness" so much esteemed in cinematic performance.

At the opposite pole, however, stands the formalist tendency of acting and stagecraft, which remains an important part of the screen's gestural, vocal, and stylistic heritage. Mask, makeup, and exceptional costume; violent, protracted, or eccentric movement; shrieks of delight, gasps of pain, or other specialized inflections and accents: all these belong to the inventory of formalist effects. Although often mistakenly associated only with avant-garde experiments, such approaches run deep in the popular cinema. Construed in the broadest sense, the formalist style embraces everything from the expressionistic costumes of Vincent Price to the dancing and gesticulating ape-men of *2001* or the "Planet of the Apes" series; it should also be thought of as including the black Hercules antics of Robert Roundtree (or his stand-ins) of the "Shaft" series, the karate exhibitions of the Chinese-decorated "kung-fu" films, and even the film presence of many rock singers — from the strutting and prancing Mick Jagger of *Gimme Shelter* to the leaping and bouncing Who in *Woodstock*. Contrary to what many people seem to believe, the contemporary American gangster film is not highly naturalistic but virtually surreal: *The Seven Ups* (1973) or *Magnum Force* (1973) do not so much document the problems of urban law enforcement as display the routines of highly accomplished stunt men performing Meyerholdian acrobatics. In all these instances we would be perfectly justified in seeing a style that Artaud, the mage of French surrealism, intended for his theater of cruelty.

A more conscious indebtedness to Artaud is manifest, however, in the work of directors and performers who have sought histrionic means to portray abnormal psychology. Peter Brook undertook this task in *Marat/Sade* (Britain, 1967), a film adaptation of the Peter Weiss play that studies political ideology through the eyes of the inmates of an asylum. Both the theme and the style are true to Artaud, Brook's sets, makeup, and choreography contributing equally to the impression of cosmic disorder and derangement. While short lenses deform structural perspectives and exaggerate the visual unsettlement of a stage full of swinging trapdoors, the actors cavort with manic gyrations, linking themselves together in hideous rocking movements or simulating whiplash effects with furious swishing of the hair.

Glenda Jackson, as the fanatical Charlotte Corday, fits perfectly into this Artaudian frame of reference. Her long tresses and white robe mark her as a lovely innocent until the camera gets close enough to pick up the grotesque contortions of her mouth. These are in keeping with her speech, which distorts normal utterance by deliberately shifting accents from the right to the wrong syllables of key words. As she lifts the knife to murder Marat, her manner tells us that what first

THE PERSISTENCE OF FORMALISM. No single performing style can be expected to monopolize the motion picture screen. In Peter Brook's direction and the Royal Shakespeare Company's execution of *Marat/Sade*, the tendency toward truncated, antirealistic gesture powerfully reasserts itself. Notice in the stiffened arm and obscured face of Glenda Jackson, as well as in the rigidly triangular arrangement of figures in the frame, a partial return to the stagecraft of expressionism. Courtesy of United Artists and Glenda Jackson.

seemed grace is really a kind of insane somnambulism distancing her completely from the normal human world. Jackson's Corday portrait is surely one of the cinema's most plausible representations of lunacy.

Jackson's talents are less idiosyncratically expressed in *Women in Love* (Britain, 1970), though Ken Russell's stagecraft, choreography, and photographic framing are still worlds removed from naturalism. While we are no longer entrapped in an asylum, the characters derived from D. H. Lawrence's novel, like those from *Marat/Sade,* continue to show physical signs of mental disturbance. In staging the action of this film, Russell depends a great deal upon such Reinhardtesque techniques as changes in the actors' body rhythms. There is a scene, for instance, in which Elinor Bron (Hermione), Jennie Linden (Ursula), and Glenda Jackson (Gudrun) join in a pretentiously costumed ballet. In context, the baroque poses of this dance exemplify the labored, self-conscious culturedness of Hermione, which is the direct opposite of Rupert Berkin's (Alan Bates) authentic vitality. Hence, when the women are interrupted by a jazz beat that sets Bates bouncing around the set, this clash of rival body rhythms physically sets forth the antagonism of personalities that dominates the film.

As the cast goes through such gyrations, often intensified by the framing and angling of the camera, Jackson performs within the ensemble, making no particular effort to individuate herself with highly specialized gestures. But in the climactic moments of the film, as quick cuts associate her with the destruction of Gerald Crich (Oliver Reed), the serpentlike uncoiling of her neck adds exactly the right symbolic detail. Such virtuoso endeavors as these are sufficient to show that acting and staging have not congealed into any single cinematic orthodoxy. The sound medium has now been digested into the actor's craft, so fully, it seems, that many feel free to experiment again with one of the various modes of physical mime.

List of Films Discussed

ALEXANDER NEVSKY   107 min.   AUD-BRA
BLACKBOARD JUNGLE   101 min.   FNC

BLUE ANGEL, THE   94 min.   CON, JAN

CAMILLE   65 min.   FNC

CITY LIGHTS   87 min.   RBC

COLLEGE   70 min.   AUD-BRA

DESERTER   not presently available

GENERAL, THE   90 min.   AUD-BRA, SWA, TWY

GOLD RUSH, THE   81 min.   JAN

IDLE CLASS, THE   20 min.   RBC

IMMIGRANT, THE   20 min.   AUD-BRA, SWA, TWY

IVAN THE TERRIBLE I AND II   96 min. and 90 min.   AUD-BRA

MARAT/SADE   115 min.   UAS

MODERN TIMES   85 min.   RBC

NIGHTS OF CABIRIA   110 min.   AUD-BRA

ON THE WATERFRONT   108 min.   AUD-BRA, SWA

PAISAN   not presently available

PASSION OF ANNA, THE   99 min.   UAS

PAWNBROKER, THE   114 min.   AUD-BRA

POTEMKIN   67 min.   AUD-BRA, MMA

SHADOW OF A DOUBT   109 min.   UNI

STRIKE   90 min.   AUD-BRA, MMA

SHOULDER ARMS   30 min.   RBC

TIN STAR, THE   93 min.   FNC

WOMEN IN LOVE   132 min.   UAS

7
EDITING
AND ASSEMBLY

Editing is the last refinement of the filmmaking process. It is also, paradoxically, the simplest and the most complex of these processes. It may consist merely of cutting strips of film and splicing them together; on the other hand, it may involve all the laboratory skills that go into the making of wipes, dissolves, freeze frames, superimpositions, or intricate mattes and inserts. In either case, editing is the process that orchestrates a motion picture, giving rhythm, pace, and sometimes new meaning to what we see and hear. The two basic questions of editing are always these: How long should a particular shot be held? And by what visual logic can one move from this shot to the next? The use of editing to build this rhythm of shots is usually referred to as the creation of a "montage" — an imaginative, well-timed progression of images.

BASIC PRINCIPLES OF EDITING

Editing as a source of motion and metaphor. Cuts and dissolves. Superimposition: Psycho, The Birds. *Editing in conjunction with composition, lighting, color:* Easy Rider, Last Year at Marienbad, War and Peace. *Editing with respect to sound:* Topkapi. *Putting together a sequence:* High Noon. *Editing in its historical context.*

To understand editing, we must simply remember that motion pictures move. Individual images whir through the projector at 24 f.p.s. This means that if we insert into the projector a filmstrip 24 frames long, the image recorded there will remain on the screen for one second. If the strip were 48 frames long it would last two seconds, while a 72-frame shot would take up three seconds of screen time. Cutting shots in this way creates movement; naturally, such cuts also create motive and metaphor. When a passage has been skillfully edited, we are allowed to see the subject from different angles, at different ranges, with different light accents, and against different (sometimes completely artificial) backgrounds. Editing is thus the cinema's principal source of visual dynamism as well as one of the filmmaker's chief instruments of interpretation. So pervasive is the power of editing that most serious-minded directors do a great deal of it themselves.

The two simplest editorial transitions are the cut and the dissolve. In a cut two strips of film are spliced together; in a dissolve the two strips are allowed to overlap each other, so that one image is gradually faded out and another faded in. Sometimes this results in a superimposition of images, which may last a split second or several seconds, depending on preferences of the editor and director. While the cut is swift and straightforward, the dissolve is oblique, protracted, hesitant. Each has its own peculiar psychological resonance.

Beyond the cut and the dissolve, there are other visual juxtapositions — perhaps less obvious ones — also achieved through collaboration of the director, the editor, and the "special-effects" department. Something like continuous superimposition is a case in point. This is a highly specialized editing technique which involves laying images back to

back, instead of end to end. In other words, the strips of film, especially prepared by a process called "matting," are placed on top of
each other and then recopied, thus superimposing the images. The
matting process makes it possible to float ghosts and specters through
someone's nightmares five feet above the bedroom floor. It is also the
source of subtler special effects, as in many of Hitchcock's films. This
director resorts to superimposition in *Psycho* (1960), to send storm
clouds scudding across the sky at an unnaturally rapid rate. The trick
is a simple one. The skyscape is shot at 8/f.p.s., while the visitors to the
old dark house are photographed at the normal 24/f.p.s. speed. The
two images are then matted together (i.e., superimposed), so that the
clouds move three times faster than normal, as they are incorporated
into the scene with the people and the house. Hitchcock also uses superimposition in *The Birds* (1963) to gradually introduce more hostile
seagulls than could ever conceivably be brought before a single camera. Again we have cinematic chills fabricated through editorial options. Unlike the floating specters, however, Hitchcock's terrors are the
more authentic because of their seeming realism.

Editing affects every aspect of filmmaking, from composition to acting. What happens, for example, when a series of short-lens shots are
grouped together, as in the scene from *Easy Rider* (U.S.A., 1969) where
Billy and Captain America are experiencing the effect of drugs. Such a
sequence achieves a cumulative visual impression that could not possibly be gained by one or two shots. In this instance, the combination
of startling perspectives (the inevitable effect of a short lens) and rapid
cuts dramatizes the hallucinative state of the characters, the more so
because much of this picture was shot with long lenses and comparatively few cuts. As in composing with lenses, so in composing with the
camera: the place of editing remains crucial. If the camera is dollying
forward in the first cut, can it be brought to an abrupt halt in the
second, and then again mobilized in the third? Perhaps — if the dramatic situation warrants so exceptional an approach. But ordinarily,
such a cutting technique will have the same effect as stopping an auto
with a fierce squeal of brakes, then struggling to restart the engine.
Cuts with a moving camera have to be matched together as carefully
as they are in the opening passages of *Last Year at Marienbad* (France,
1961).

The question of matching comes up in other connections, most obviously with respect to lighting and color. We expect the exposure to
remain the same as we move from establishing shot to midshot, just as
we expect a sky that was blue in a facial close-up to remain so in a
shot of the whole landscape. Once established, however, these expectations can be violated where plausible motivation is supplied.
Abrupt cuts to overexposed footage have by now become almost an

editorial cliché. We now find, too, that scenes sometimes open in black and white, then shift to color, or vice versa. While this device often seems pretentious, it occasionally gleans meaningful effects. In *War and Peace* (U.S.S.R., 1967), for example, the glory-hungry Pitya begins his saber charge in color but dies in black and white. It is hard to conceive of a more effective commentary upon the emptiness of military splendor.

As sound is added to picture, the editing choices become more challenging. The easiest way to avoid this challenge is simply to match voice to lips and produce what many filmmakers call "photographed drama," a mere filmed play. Another conventional evasion is musical, which gives us a reverberating gong when the camera visits San Francisco's Chinatown, then castanets while we visually tour the Spanish district of the same city. Most travelogues offer an A to Z encyclopedia of such musical clichés. There are times, however, when sound and picture are cut together with much more imagination. In *Topkapi* (Britain, 1964), for instance, the thrill of suspense is punctuated by an absolutely brilliant sight-and-sound cut. A would-be jewel thief is lowered by rope through a skylight so as to avoid activating a very sensitive alarm system. As he drops nearer the floor, the sound track becomes almost mute, while every ear in the theater strains for the bells and buzzers that might go off at any moment. Suddenly we hear a clamorous noise and suppose that the thief has touched the alarm. Yet a fraction of a second later we learn the truth in a visual cut: the noise is not the alarm system but the shouts of spectators at a bullfight we have unexpectedly joined. The information we are receiving is not about the robbery at all; it tells us what's happening around town while the robbery is in progress.

We can see the whole process of editing more concretely as we turn from these rather generalized examples to the famous sequence from *High Noon* (U.S.A., 1952), where Gary Cooper, the threatened sheriff of a small western town, must face the outlaws who have come to kill him. Rhythm, continuity, emphasis, and some quite complex instances of cutting to movement occur in a summarizing montage.

First we see the sheriff himself in a relatively long take whose extended duration establishes his centrality to the action. He has just made his last will and testament, marking his awareness of impending disaster. This image is accompanied by the ticking of a wall clock, whose hands draw near to noon, the time when the last of the gunslingers will arrive by train. Having finished his will, Cooper picks up his revolver and swings it at arm's length in front of his body. Cut. The next shot is of the gunmen. It is matched to the preceding shot by position, movement, and dramatic logic. Though we travel in this cut from inside Cooper's quarters to the train station where his enemies have gathered, there is no problem of continuity because of the strong visual and psychological bond between the two shots. In both there is a revolver in the foreground; in both it is centered in the frame; in both it is swung through space at arm's length from the body. Since the arm swinging the gun in the second shot is the outlaw's, the cut effectively introduces the sheriff's antagonists and points to their lethal confrontation. While maintaining this tight continuity, the cut also introduces variations which contribute to dramatic progression: the outlaws immediately begin to walk, generating dynamism; they have their backs to the camera, a dehumanizing note; and the shot is held less long than the shot of Cooper, thus quickening the tempo of the sequence.

The ensuing cuts of this short sequence are what we might call "suspensive"; they delay the inevitable meeting of sheriff and gunmen. They also extend the significance of the struggle, since they refer us to other townspeople implicated in its outcome. The cuts come faster now, as is appropriate to the gathering energy of crisis, and their relationship to each other is looser, though not disruptively so. Faces figure prominently — a close-up of the distraught wife who has tried to keep her husband from accepting the gunmen's challenge, a close-up of the Spanish woman who had once taken a romantic interest in him. In these portraits of intense concern we still sense the psychological continuity that binds the sequence together. This is reinforced in the sound track which has now picked up the "High Noon" theme at an *allegro* pace. The strength of the sound track allows further complication of the visuals, as in the wide-angle shots of the saloon, which functions as a symbol of evasion. But after this retrospective glance at the townspeople we are returned to the beginning of the montage loop with further shots of the outlaws and the sheriff. The sound of a train whistle calls the gunmen to greet the arriving member of their gang; the sound echoes in the sheriff's quarters, reminding him that the appointed hour has come. The sound cut to this whistle, shrill by comparison to the musical line that precedes it, is the final note of editorial punctuation, the cry that anticipates the coming battle.

Like the disciplines of scripting and acting, the editing process has been powerfully influenced by film technology, though never so strongly as in the case of camera, lighting, and sound. At first filmmakers had only picture to handle, together with the task of deciding where to introduce explanatory titles. For options they had few besides the straight cut, since dissolves, wipes, and superimpositions were technically difficult. Before 1920 even the dissolve was somewhat rare, as most filmmakers changed scenes either by fading to black or making transitions with iris shots. The first significant movement in editing, therefore, was to refine and perfect the art of the straight cut. This work was begun in America by D. W. Griffith, then extended by Pudovkin, Kuleshov, and Eisenstein. The Russian directors, of course, also at-

FINDING THE RIGHT TAKE. At its most basic level, the editing process involves choosing from several "takes" of the same scene the one that best conveys the relationship of the performers to each other and their place in the frame as a whole. For *Alice's Restaurant*, editor Dede Allen and director Arthur Penn chose "take 3" (far right) over the two other possibilities shown here. In compositional terms, was this choice a good one? Reprinted from p. 63 of *Show* Magazine, January 1970, by permission of Arthur Penn and *Show*.

tempted the more intricate optical effects made possible by wipes and dissolves.

The coming of sound for some years seriously disturbed the development of editing skills, since it introduced problems of synchronization and voice cutting that no one previously had had to cope with. Unfortunately this complication of the editor's task occurred exactly at a time when the big studios were emerging, and producers began to substitute easy formulas for imaginative extensions of the film medium. While the Eisensteinian conception of montage, so painstakingly developed in the silent cinema, never completely disappeared, its use was severely restricted, often limited to brief transitional passages in a feature film. Naturally, however, some genres proved more hospitable to the art of cutting than others, as the careful editing of Hitchcock's suspense films demonstrates. And by the 1950s the interest in editing had reawakened in both Europe and America, as evidenced particularly in the theorizing of France's "New Wave." This was soon to crest in the work of Resnais, Godard, and Truffaut, as well as that of slightly less renowned figures like Chris Marker and Henri Colpi.

For approximately the past decade, the cinema has been struggling to assimilate technical innovations that promise further enrichment of the editing process. These include new types of editing equipment which make it possible to store and find footage more swiftly, achieve voice-picture synchronization more easily, and compare available pictorial options more effectively. Even more important are the animation rigs, laboratory processes, and electronic mixing systems which reduce the cost and widen the range of what is usually called special effects. It is these that encourage freeze framing, split-screen printing, multiple imposition, and many other visual effects we are beginning to take for granted as part of our cinematic heritage. Here the short film has often provided the most meaningful arena for the venturesome imagination.

MONTAGE IN THE SILENT FILM

From our present vantage point it appears obvious that films must be edited. We find it hard to conceive of a picture without close-ups of heads and hands intercut with wider shots of whole families or armies going about their special business. We have equal difficulty imagining a film that lacks multiple camera setups from which a single continuous action is shown. As a column of tanks moves toward us, we expect to see them from an eye-level position slightly to the left of the road they travel, then from a second position slightly to the right of the same road. When they draw nearer, there may well be a third cut from a low angle and almost directly centered, where we seem to see their tractor treads roll over us. The possibility of such cuts is what allows the filmmaker to keep the tanks on the screen long enough to make a strong visual impression. But the strategies of presentation we now take for granted were by no means self-evident to the first filmmakers. In fact they often resented any tampering with the continuous flow of the imagery, assuming that any interruption of this sort would violate both our sense of drama and our sense of realism. It was a few bold spirits like D. W. Griffith who first took the initiative with splicing, and his Russian successors Lev Kuleshov and V. I. Pudovkin who systematized the editing process.

To some extent the reservations that early filmmakers entertained about editing were well founded. Neither in real life nor on the stage do we see someone step into a hotel elevator and then immediately exit on the nineteenth floor. Nor do we ever see a pair of disembodied legs ascending a flight of stairs. If the cinema should attempt such visual shorthand, wouldn't the effect be laughable? The answer to this question is more complicated than it might first seem. Anyone who has screened the first efforts of student filmmakers knows that a cut can provoke unintentional laughter. How do we establish whom the disembodied legs belong to? How do we make clear that the lobby and the nineteenth floor are part of the same hotel? In short, how do we maintain visual orientation while eliminating irrelevant and uninteresting footage? These are the problems that the editors of silent cinema first faced. Their solutions fall into two classes: one that invokes the principle of "continuity," another that thinks of editing in terms of "collision."

THE CONTINUITY PRINCIPLE

Lev Kuleshov as analyst of the editing process. Results of his experiments. Pudovkin as disciple of Kuleshov. Conception of montage in Mother. *Matching of motion. Contrasts of size. Interaction of objects. Complex intellectual montage.*

Although the first consequential film editing was done by D. W. Griffith, it was in the "Experimental Laboratory" of Lev Kuleshov that the art found its theoretical basis. Once a designer at the Khanzhanov Studio, Kuleshov acquired his interest in the cinema while handling newsreels for the Red army. After the war he connected himself with the State Film School, where his "workshop" became, essentially, an editor's cutting room. Though he made several efforts as a director, it was as editor that he established a place for himself in the annals of cinema. Though overshadowed now by both Pudovkin and Eisenstein, Kuleshov was himself expertly adept at cutting and splicing.

Working on what he once called "films without film," Kuleshov discovered how the rearrangement of shots could project new meanings into the same image. In his most famous editing experiment, he selected several minimally expressive facial close-ups of the Russian actor Mosjukhin which could be intercut with other shots. He then made up three short sequences, each using almost identical facial expressions but followed by three different images, so that in every case the actor seemed to be reacting to something different. When he showed these sequences to his audience, he proved the point he expected to. In each instance members of the audience imagined they could see in the actor's features the emotion called for by the adjacent image. What they failed to realize, of course, was that the effect had been created by the editor, not the performer. The facial mask had not significantly changed, only the context in which one might see it. From this Kuleshov concluded that meaning could be made and unmade in the cutting room, and that filmmaking consisted of "linking" one image to another.

Kuleshov passed along this "continuity principle" to Pudovkin, who used it as the ground plan of his own editing. Having had his Kuleshovian impulses reinforced by the example of Griffith, Pudovkin declared boldly for the primacy of editing. "The expression that a film is 'shot,' " he says, "is entirely false and should disappear from the language. The film is not shot, but *built*, built from the separate strips of celluloid that are its raw material. . . ." [1] In this building process, the director continues, individual shots have no meaning until they are incorporated into an intelligible design. Like Kuleshov, Pudovkin firmly believed that the same images might make totally different impressions, just as the same stones might be used for a temple or a railway terminal. Naturally this feeling for the editing process carries over into Pudovkin's own works, the most famous of which is *Mother* (U.S.S.R., 1927).

Mother is a virtual textbook of editing techniques, ranging from the simplest continuities to complex exercises in crosscutting and symbolic montage. The increasing complexity of the editing follows the growing intricacy of the narrative, which traces the development of revolutionary consciousness in a relatively conventional woman of the late czarist period. Pudovkin endeavors to show, mostly through his editing, how a drunken husband and a politically active son gradually draw the mother of the family ("Mother Russia," undoubtedly) into the revolutionary struggle, finally making her a martyr to the cause.

---

[1] Introduction to the German Edition, *Film Technique and Film Acting*, p. 23.

From the first scene of the film, Pudovkin looks for ways to remind us that the picture is about the mother and that all other roles are subsidiary. Hence the camera follows her alcoholic husband into the family home, but soon leaves him after he gets there. We watch him take note of an ornate clock in the corner, which he evidently imagines can be sold to buy more drink. As soon as he takes one step toward it, however, Pudovkin cuts to the face of his wife. The cut is both technically and psychologically well timed. The direction of the husband's stride is perfectly matched by the movement of the wife's head as she follows his steps across the room; this is what later generations of editors would call "thrust matching." We don't see the husband again until he has begun to rip the clock from the wall, but the eyes of the wife have already told us precisely where we are going to find him. The effect goes beyond formalistic neatness. The cut shifts our attention from husband to wife, who is by far the more dramatically interesting of the two characters. His face, if shown, would register only the besotted monomania we are already familiar with. Hers registers puzzlement and then anguished alarm as she realizes he is going to steal or destroy the last token of family respectability. This deprivation, of course, provides the pressure toward revolutionary involvement.

Pudovkin also takes great care in the matching of facial close-ups. His technique is shown to advantage in the scene where the mother asks a czarist officer not to arrest her son. The strategy here is to make her seem weak and naive, readily victimized by czarist tyranny because of her lingering faith in its rectitude. As the mother makes her plea, the treatment consists almost entirely of alternating facial close-ups, the mother's and the officer's. The two are not alike, however. The mother is shot with a head-and-shoulders take which leaves considerable open space in the frame; the officer, on the other hand, is shot with a somewhat longer lens (or at closer range), so that we see only his face and it fills at least 30 percent more of the frame. In this arangement of cuts, size figuratively expresses power. The woman seems dwarfed by the arresting officer whose judgment determines the fate of her son. The last turn of this sequence is a cut from the officer's face to his two gloved hands, methodically stroking each other. Since the son rests in these hands, it is fitting for us to notice how carefully covered they are, how thoroughly protected against what the officer evidently regards as the slime of maternal sentiment.

Pudovkin's feel for inanimate objects also finds a place in the editing of *Mother*. This should come as no surprise, since his personal writings remind us that in the cinema all human emotions must be translated into "action connected with objects." [2] Hence in the scene of the son's

---

[2] "The Plastic Material," *Film Technique and Film Acting*, p. 58.

trial we first see the massive columns of the Hall of Justice, shot slightly atilt to suggest law corrupted by czarist expediency. Then there is a close-up cut to a soldier guarding the building. The framing of the shot shows us only his booted leg, stiff and rigid as the columns shown in the previous cut. The editorial juxtaposition creates an expressive analogy: the men who defend czarism lose their humanity (the soldier's facelessness, fleshlessness, etc.) and become depersonalized instruments of the system. Since the system is figuratively represented by a piece of architecture, Pudovkin chooses aptly when his cutting assimilates the guard into this architectural metaphor.

Other objects, like running water, are associated in the cutting with the workers who finally resolve to resist the system. First we see a sizable body of angry demonstrators walking toward the camera. Then comes a cut which takes the camera to a slightly higher angle. We now have a shot that shows the workers moving in the same direction as the flow of a small stream, apparently created by the spring thaw. The next cut returns us to eye level but shows the shadows of the workers reflected in the rippling stream. Thus the connection of the workers with the spring thaw becomes more intimate. Having forged this bond between workers and water, Pudovkin cuts to ice breaking up on a river, assuming — quite correctly — that most viewers will immediately catch the figurative relationship. As nature rouses herself to life in the spring, so the working class rises up against the cold chill of political oppression. The last cut of the sequence carries the visual analogy still further: the camera itself is now in motion over the ice, as if in search of fissures and cleavages.

The most complicated montage of *Mother* is reserved for the conclusion, in which the heroine, now solidly identified with the strikers, is killed while leading a demonstration. At this juncture, Pudovkin wishes to show that, though she loses her life, her spirit prevails in the eventual triumph of the revolution. He does this by calling upon several metaphors he has already introduced, extending their meaning with elaborate dissolves and superimpositions. The sequence begins with a head-and-shoulders shot of the mother carrying the revolutionary flag. This yoking of the banner to the woman is essential to what follows. We get several cuts of the woman herself as Pudovkin concentrates for the last time upon her individuality and humanity. Immediately before she is killed, however, Pudovkin cuts to the flag, here saturated with light from the spring sun. The flag-sun relationship motivates a further cut to cracking ice, shot at such close range and from such a low angle that it resembles some kind of geological upheaval. At this point the editorial arrangements become completely abstract and intellectual. Superimposed shapes (similar to the ice fragments) slide past one another on the horizontal axis, shortly giving way to further shapes that move vertically. The thaw has become a kind of earthquake, which is then developed as a metaphor of cultural transformation. Out of this profusion of visual detail emerges a shot of the Kremlin with the revolutionary banner flying from its dome. The last cut of the film frames the flag in isolation, again drenched in sunlight, virtually repeating the shot intercut with the mother's martyrdom. Without commentary and by purely editorial means are all the strands of the film thus brought together. Pudovkin had obviously learned well the lessons that Griffith and Kuleshov taught.

THE COLLISION PRINCIPLE

Eisenstein's differences with Pudovkin. Emphasis upon maximum conflict: Old and New. *Use of superimposition:* Strike. *The moving figure and the moving object:* October, Strike, *and* Potemkin.

The technique we see in the closing movement of *Mother* is less typical of Pudovkin than it is of another famous theorist of editing, Sergei Eisenstein. As in almost every other area of the cinema, here too Eisenstein had his own unique contribution to make. While agreeing with his compatriots on fundamentals, Eisenstein took issue with Kuleshov and Pudovkin on what he regarded as their too conservative view of editing options. This issue is broached in "The Cinematographic Principle and the Ideogram," where Eisenstein criticizes Pudovkin for unduly limiting the editor's choices. Pudovkin, says Eisenstein, thinks of editing only as "a *linkage* of pieces" which are "arranged in a series to expound an idea."[3] But "from my point of view," he continues, "linkage is merely a possible *special* case" of editing strategy. Deeply interested in cubist painting, caricature, and Japanese picture writing, Eisenstein argues for a more complex style of editing formulated around his favorite word "montage." He wants jarring transitions from cut to cut, in other words, "collision." The upshot of this approach is to emphasize the implicit tension between one shot and the next. Like Pudovkin, he builds an effect through a succession of cuts and dissolves (hence, "montage" — mounting). Yet he goes much further than Pudovkin in his search for building materials. With Eisenstein the editing of silent cinema reached the peak of its evolution.

Unfortunately Eisenstein's films offer several classic examples of farfetched cutting that are sometimes taken to epitomize his editing theory. At the end of *Strike* the assault on a band of defenseless work-

---

[3] This and the further citations of the same essay are from *Film Form and the Film Sense*, pp. 28–44.

ers is cut together with the butchering of cattle. In *October* Eisenstein mocks the anti-Leninist Provisional Government by intercutting images of Kerensky with shots of an ornamental peacock. In *Potemkin* the figures of several stone lions are cut quickly together to create a short animation sequence in which the lion seems to leap to its feet. Though such tricks undoubtedly express a certain tendency of his imagination, they probably do not constitute his greatest contribution as an editor.

We can get closer to Eisenstein's concept of collision editing by noting how he treats so familiar an image as the human face. In *Old and New* (U.S.S.R., 1928), for example, we have a situation where a peasant woman, confronted by new agricultural technology, is torn between a belief in progress and an inclination to hold by the old folkways. She watches the performance of a cream separator while the camera watches the reaction she registers. The ordinary way to cut this shot would be to show gradual changes of facial expression illustrating the hesitant transition from doubt to belief. But Eisenstein cuts it differently, splicing together shots that sharply contrast the woman's conflicting moods. As he himself explains: "I have eliminated the intervals between the sharply contrasting polar stages of the face's expression. Thus is achieved a greater sharpness in 'the play of doubts' around the new cream separator. Will the milk thicken or no? Trickery? Wealth? Here the psychological process of mingled faith and doubt is broken up into its extreme states of joy (confidence) and gloom (disillusionment)." Deliberately violating the principle of continuity, Eisenstein has arranged a series of cuts to generate the greatest possible plastic impact.

The same conception is typically applied to Eisenstein's dissolves. Instead of using this device to smooth and soften transitions, as many editors before and after him would do, Eisenstein frequently holds a dissolve long enough to achieve superimposition, thus augmenting the possibility of collision and conflict. There is a memorable example in *Strike* where the military police raid the tenements of the strikers' families. We first see a screen-filling facial close-up of the police chief who orders the attack. His gaping mouth, wide open as he shouts orders to his subordinates, already makes him grotesque, a study in tyrannical hysteria. But to carry this image of deformity still further, Eisenstein holds the image of the police chief on the screen as he dissolves to the sequence showing the fulfillment of his orders. This scene is introduced by a wide-angle shot of the entire tenement with its balconies full of frightened residents. As we contrast the size of the superimposed face with the proportions of the tenement dwellers, the police chief seems a nightmarish monster whose huge mouth is about to swallow the whole building. The superimposition also relates him to his minions, the military horsemen who assault the tenants. When the cavalry unit tramples women and children trapped on the ramps and

EISENSTEIN AND MONTAGE. The concept of collision montage, as defined by Eisenstein and illustrated here from *Strike*, implies not only abrupt changes of time and place but also changes of camera angle and visual perspective in the fulfillment of more conventional continuities.

Here we begin with a conventional mid-shot (a) showing an affluent capitalist as he entertains his managerial cronies who have come to discuss the response they will make to their workers' demands.

As the scene progresses, the carelessness of the affluent requires the summoning of a servant (b) to clean up the table and the floor. The cut from normal to wide-angle perspective emphasizes the cavernous distance separating master from servant class.

The cut to a high angle after the servant's arrival (c) not only gives us a functionally important view of the table and the floor (the servant's domain, so to speak) but also emphasizes the laziness of the elite in showing the almost recumbent posture of the brandy-sipping executive to the right.

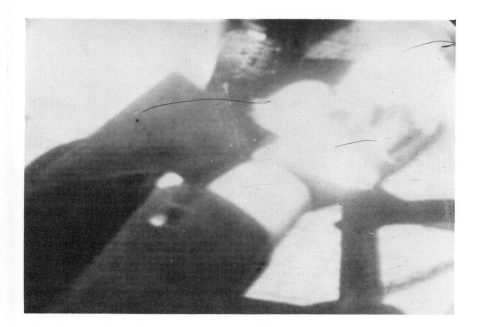

The climactic close-up (d) summarizes the servant's humiliation in the image of the dutiful hand that sweeps garbage off the managerial shoe. The slicing away of the body which accompanies the hand furthers the metaphor of a depersonalized, dehumanized working class. Courtesy of the Rosa Madell Film Library.

balconies, the rage-contorted face of the police chief remains continually present, apparently urging — even demanding — the worst acts of cruelty. Pudovkin, remember, convicted czarism of injustice by analogizing a guard into a stone pillar. Eisenstein delivers his indictment of the Romanovs by much more daring means of plastic expression.

Eisenstein's unsurpassed sense of physical relationships is the key to his genius as an editor. Shape, movement, scale, light — all figure into his conception of matching and building. In *Strike* the editing charges fire hoses with menace; in *Potemkin* gears, dials, and hands speak of proletarian awakening; in *October* the assembly of a crown-capped wine bottle symbolizes Kerensky's love of luxury and power. In the last of these three films, Eisenstein adds light and movement effectively to his montage in a passage which ironically applauds Kerensky's Provisional Government. The written title "Long Live the Provisional Government" is followed by quick cuts of priests swinging giant incense thuribles and blessing congregations with heavy and ornate gold crosses. The thuribles swing diagonally through the picture space, right to left in one cut, left to right in the next. Each gleams as it catches the light and emits great clouds of smoke as it sweeps back and forth. Here the association of Kerensky with spiritual obscurantism is obvious. But what makes the image memorable is not so much its simplistic symbolism as its plastic density. The motion itself — of crosses, thuribles, smoke spirals — is so oblique and confusing that it seems to mime the circuitous rationalizations Eisenstein seeks to debunk.

In composing this interplay of moving objects, timing is of highest importance. While the pace of the cuts is usually swift, so that the eye never rests from active attention, Eisenstein also holds certain cuts longer, deliberately introducing irregularities into the beat of what he calls "rhythmic montage." Generally speaking, the close-ups occur rapidly since the eye can quickly assimilate their content. The wide-angle takes will typically get more time on the screen because there is more detail to sort. But aesthetic and thematic factors also control the pace of the cuts, as in the scene from *Strike* where the captains of industry gather to discuss the claims of the striking workers.

The scene begins with a wide-angle establishing shot held long enough to give us a feel for the relevant decor. The waste space in the foreground suggests separation from the world of the workers, while the massiveness of the walls and columns underscores the security of the ruling class. The next cut brings the camera closer to the conference table, acquainting us with the group of executives who have gathered. Once these introductions are completed, Eisenstein is free to play more intricately with individual faces, as he does in the numerous close-ups soon to follow. These cuts break up what would otherwise be tediously long explanatory titles citing the workers' terms. As each sentence is read and recorded in a title, there is a cut to a face, usually grinning in amusement at the audacity of the demands. Since each face is distinguished by its special look (the gold tooth of the host, the smoking cigar of the fat straw boss), conflict and counterpoint are sustained even in the movement from face to face.

To avoid losing momentum in this sequence, Eisenstein arranges several surprises that justify more extensive cutting. A wooden panel immediately in front of the host unfolds to reveal a bottle and a set of wineglasses. This motivates further facial close-ups that register astonished pleasure. Next the host reaches for a lemon squeezer, which we must see close-up in order to identify. As he begins crushing a lemon to flavor the drinks, his fists clench in close-up and his grin grows more grotesque. By this time the tempo of the cuts is swift, and the collision of images is intensified by cuts to events outside the conference room. The host's hand presses downward on the handle of the lemon squeezer, and this shot is answered by a cut to a horse rearing upward with its rider. The two movements match like synchronized strokes of a piston, and this matching is thematically congruent, since we are watching the military assemble to suppress the workers.

Further intercuts of this gathering of forces are edited into the conference scene before Eisenstein begins to relax the tempo and draw the sequence to a close. When it comes, this reduction of tension is managed in a return to wide-angle composition. A lemon peel falls to the floor, spotting a guest's shoe, and a servant must be called to pick up the garbage. The take here is with a short lens as, without a cut, we watch a servant march down an endlessly long flight of stairs to answer the master's needs. He bows deeply in close-up before retrieving the offending lemon peel and reascending the stairs in another extended wide-angle cut. Every image in this scene supports Eisenstein's parable about the rulers and the ruled. Yet the editing is immeasurably complex, providing for titles, crosscuts, and stinging caricature.

Eisenstein's montage is further enhanced by the finesse of his transitions from general to particular. His drama always involves the activation of great masses, but the individual never gets lost in the crowd. In the Odessa steps massacre from *Potemkin*, we remember the basic visual antinomies of the scene — the methodical advance of the military regiment and the hysterical gyrations of the victims. But the editing fixes upon a few well-chosen figures who personalize the fate of the anonymous mass. The bespectacled woman is memorable because her attempt to climb the steps contrasts directly with the general flow of the action; the untended baby carriage catches the eye because its helter-skelter bouncing down the steps is so markedly out of step with the soldiers; even the stump-legged cripple is isolated by movement as well as physical appearance. The cuts in which he is featured show him whirling diagonally through the crowd instead of simply responding to the dominant thrust. Although the volatility of these objects and characters was first captured in Tisse's photography, Eisenstein's editing is what continuously accents the movements the camera has recorded. With Eisenstein, the art of editing achieved a level of sophistication it would not recover for many years to come.

MONTAGE
IN THE SOUND
FILM

I n 1929, after outlining in detail what he calls "the principle of optical counterpoint," Eisenstein spoke prophetically of the future: "let us not forget that soon we shall face another and less simple problem in counterpoint: *the conflict in the sound film of acoustics and optics.*" But the sound film did not immediately meet the challenge to editing the Russian director foresaw. Its failure in this sphere again draws our attention to the way technology impinges upon artistic enterprise.

STUDIO SPECIALIZATION
AND ITS CONSEQUENCES

Shifts of directorial emphasis. Introduction of the "montage sequence." Formulaic versus imaginative montage. Contribution of Slavko Vorkapitch: Viva Villa *and* The Good Earth. *Use of the symbolic dissolve in Sternberg and John Huston. The special case of* Fantasia.

There is no absolute reason why the editing of a sound film cannot be as subtle and imaginative as anything in the silent cinema. But by 1930, and for most of the following decade, there were several practical reasons why the art of editing declined. With the emergence of large studios like Pathé or MGM, production grew more bureaucratized, separating the art of the director from the mere "busywork" of editing. Griffith, Pudovkin, and Eisenstein all sat at the cutting bench, if not always splicing, at least closely supervising every detail. Such absolute involvement ceased to be practicable in the film factories of the thirties, though this differentiation was not itself fatal to montage. The director need not handle his own celluloid, so long as he remains interested in how it is handled, offering suggestions to both his scenarist and his editor as the film idea evolves. But the vogue of the sound film shifted the emphasis of directing. The director existed not to shape the celluloid but to coach the writers and help the stars come to grips with the microphone. Editing thus lost its prestige. Montage seemed an anachronism that lingered from silent days, when the flow of the narrative had to be interrupted by explanatory titles or information cuts. And since no provision for optical counterpoint was made in the early stages of production, the film reached the cutting room in a form not at all susceptible to editorial reworking. The sound was locked so tightly to the image that Eisensteinian crosscuts or juxtapositions would leave the narrative scrambled and unintelligible.

Given this climate, editing ceased to be an integral function of filmmaking and became an occasional adventure, an excursion into the visual baroque. The editor — or the "montage expert" — was called upon to produce elaborate transitional effects instead of a continuing cinematic rhythm. Some editors specialized in "coming of spring" sequences; these might consist of successive dissolves from one tree branch to another: the subject first encumbered with snow, then wet with melted frost, finally swelling into bud and bursting into leaf. Grand-tour sequences were also a specialty, whereby the hero, endeavoring to recover from disappointment in love, might in the course of fifteen seconds land in London (aerial shot of Big Ben), push on to Paris (dissolve to Eiffel Tower), stopover in Venice (gondolas), and return to New York (the Empire State Building). Editors of less ornate imagination might conjure up spring by tearing pages from a calendar or send travelers abroad with no more than train wheels, steamship whistles, and taxicabs. In either case, the restriction of the editor's sphere promoted the emergence of visual clichés.

During these early years of sound, there were many talented people in the cutting rooms of Hollywood and Paris who often redeemed these short montage sequences from tedium. Slavko Vorkapitch, for example, who would later become an inspiration to American experimental filmmakers, was a cutter for MGM in the 1930s. He assembled the revolution sequence from *Viva Villa* (1934) in a manner reminiscent of Eisenstein, and his famine montage from *The Good Earth* (1937) is also remarkable for its energy. Vorkapitch's insistence upon what he calls "a visual-dynamic language independent of literature and theatrical traditions" [4] was always fulfilled in his own editing. The only problem is that his hands touched so little of these pictures that they don't really bear his personal stamp. In *Viva Villa* we find the oil of Vorkapitch's genius floating in random pools upon the water of Hollywood hackwork.

We can find cases, on the other hand, where such sequences are suited to the general tenor of a film. The visually striking dissolves of *The Scarlet Empress* (U.S.A., 1934) come to mind. Although the picture is largely a vehicle for Dietrich's theatrical talent, the sets of Van Nest Polglase and the lighting of Bert Glennon give this film the quality of an eerie nightmare. Director Josef von Sternberg's prescriptions for the dissolves cohere completely with this mood. Early in the film, as young princess Catherine learns she is to marry the Russian czar, she decides to familiarize herself with the history of Russian court politics. The intention of the sequence is to contrast the childhood innocence of Catherine with the dark history of the family into which she is about to marry. While the passage begins tritely, with a dissolve from pages of a book to visuals showing its apparent contents, the progression of images in further dissolves becomes ever wilder and more bizarre. Scenes of grotesque torture are piled upon each other with fantastic virtuosity, the last showing a man being beaten to death as he is swung back and forth on the clapper of a giant bell. This shot is then slowly dissolved to an image of Catherine moving through exactly the same arc in a garden swing. The force of this juxtaposition prepares us for the further violations of her innocence which she will meet at the Russian court.

Protracted dissolves were used throughout the 1930s and 1940s in cinematic spheres far removed from the gothic imagination of Sternberg. Normally they just marked the passage of time, easing a transition from one month to the next or the beginning of an adventure to its end. Sometimes, however, a director or an editor would sense the symbolic potential of these optical effects, as is done in *The Treasure of the Sierra Madre* (U.S.A., 1948). Here we find a slow dissolve that both designates elapsed time and also creates a metaphor. In one sequence we have a campfire that is slowly faded out; in the next we shift to a daylight shot of a rugged old prospector who imagines he has found gold. For a moment the two images are superimposed, so that the fire seems to burn in the hands of the prospector as he clutches his find. By a process unique to the cinema, what was only a campfire an instant earlier has suddenly become a symbolic flame, a mark of the lust for gold that still burns in the spirit of the old man. Although dissolves

---

[4] "Toward True Cinema," *Film Culture* (March 1957), p. 14. Reprinted by permission of *Film Culture*.

frequently lack the energy and thrust of a straight cut, here the choice was obviously the right one. The dissolve establishes a relationship that would never have existed had the shears been used instead. Such moments as these compensate for the many editorial transitions that are made unthinkingly and in purely formulaic terms.

Although it is comparatively easy to find isolated examples of bold editorial work, these tend to stand somewhat apart from the pictures in which they occur. Comedy, which had once been vigorously edited, now became the preserve of gagmen. Buster Keaton gave way to Bob Hope. The musical preserved elements of montage more successfully than comedy, but the sight-sound mix of these pictures was not always sustained by strictly editorial means. The most ambitious adaptation of montage effects to music is found in films like Disney's *Fantasia* (1940), where the use of pure animation makes possible absolute control of the sight-sound relation. But the results are somewhat disappointing. Though the cutting of abstract shapes to a musical beat looks forward to the editing of Ed Emshwiller and Norman McLaren, too often the conception of *Fantasia* leads nowhere beyond simplistic illustration. Halo-bedecked monks march from darkness to dawn to the strains of Schubert's "Ave Maria," and dinosaurs do battle amid the dissonances of Stravinsky. Truly successful montage requires something more than program music. As the genres of the sound film crystallized in the 1930s only one showed continuing respect for the editing process. This was the mystery story.

EDITING WITHIN THE GENRES: THE THRILLER

Susceptibility of the thriller to dynamic cutting. The example of M. Hitchcock's interest in editing. Collaboration with Alma Reville. Pace and rhythm in North by Northwest. *Continuity of movement:* Foreign Correspondent. *Dissolves and superimpositions:* Shadow of a Doubt, The Wrong Man. *Treatment of sound:* Notorious. *Mood and suspense:* Psycho.

The suspense film is generally conducive to imaginative editing. Suggestion and surprise are its essence, meaningful concealment its *modus operandi*. Its plots almost invariably require sleuthing, chasing, and fighting — ideal material from which to build visual tropes. Editorial inserts are the inevitable means of picking up overlooked clues, revealing deadly weapons, or tracking the limousine of runaway kidnappers as they seek to escape the screeching sirens of the police.

Already in *M* (Germany, 1931), that early classic of the suspense genre, we can see integral sight-and-sound montage exceptional for the 1930s. The young girl Elsa has been kidnapped and murdered by a criminal psychopath; her disappearance on the way home from school is treated in a highly imaginative series of cuts. The mother's voice reverberates down a flight of empty stairs, "Elsa, Elsa." The girl's lunch grows cold on the kitchen table. Cuts to the world outside the home show us places the girl once frequented and now visits no more. Finally there is a shot of the balloon she carried as she came from school. When we see it entangled in overhead electrical wires, we require no further clarification of her fate. The story has been told with economy and subtle indirection.

Of all the filmmakers who have opted to work in the suspense genre, surely the most noteworthy is Alfred Hitchcock. Often assisted by his wife, Alma Reville, he has spent a lifetime in film refining what are essentially editorial skills. Though still at the peak of his power (witness, *Frenzy* — 1972), his training goes back to the silent era and includes a studied effort to assimilate the use of sound. Furthermore, he brought to the sound film a rather exceptional disposition. Speaking of *Psycho* he confided to François Truffaut: "I don't care about the subject matter; I don't care about the acting; but I do care about the *pieces of film and the photographs and the sound track* [my italics] and all of the technical ingredients. . . ." [5] By and large this statement holds true of every Hitchcock picture. While other directors carefully rehearsed the lines of the leading lady, Hitchcock worked on detailed drawings that provided the ground plan for camera setups and editing strategy. Though he lacks the wide-ranging intellectual interests of Eisenstein, his draftsmanlike approach resembles that of the Russian director, just as it resembles the cartoon and the animation film, two realms of cinema where editing reigns supreme.

Hitchcock still relishes the experience he gained from silent pictures. They were, he says, "the purest form of cinema" and their limitations "did not warrant the major changes that sound brought in." Even today, he insists, films suffer from excessive dialogue, which produces "photographs of people talking." His own advice runs in another direction: "We should resort to dialogue only when it's impossible to do otherwise. I always first try to tell a story in a cinematic way *through a succession of shots and bits of film in between* [my italics]." [6] Hitchcock learned the cutter's art while working in the editing department of Paramount's overseas branch in Islington, England. He never forgot, apparently, that in the cutting room "one could really do anything — take the end of a picture and put it at the beginning — anything at

[5] *Hitchcock*, ed. François Truffaut (New York: Simon and Schuster, 1967), p. 211. © 1967. By permission of Simon and Schuster, Inc.

[6] *Ibid.*, p. 42.

all." [7] Consequently, the pre-production planning of his own films always gives an enormous amount of attention to the placement of cuts.

In an essay on "Direction" written in 1937, Hitchcock spelled out the working method that carried over into his later sound films. Although he seems to give priority to the scenario, it is clear from context that his conception of "script" includes the complete editorial ground plan of a picture:

> With the help of my wife, who does the technical continuity, I plan out a script very carefully, hoping to follow it exactly, all the way through, when the shooting starts. In fact, this working on the script is the real making of the film, for me. When I've done it, the film is finished already in my mind.

Thus he adds:

> Usually . . . I don't find it necessary to do more than supervise the editing myself. I know it is sometimes said that a director ought to edit his own pictures if he wants to control their final form. For it is in the editing, according to this view, that a film is really brought into being. But if the scenario is planned out in detail, and followed closely during production, editing should be easy. All that has to be done is to cut away irrelevancies and see that the finished film is an accurate rendering of the scenario. [8]

Although in his great films of the 1950s and 1960s Hitchcock was ably assisted by his favorite cutter George Tomassini, these remarks suggest that the director has an editorial expertise of his own, exercised at whatever stage of production. Naturally it figures in the building of suspenseful or horrific effects. Hitchcock needed only to wait until he had the full resources of Hollywood's technology in order to carve his present reputation.

Hitchcock's English period (1922–1939) represents a significant apprenticeship to filmmaking, which includes the production of two of his most ingenious thrillers, *The 39 Steps* (1935) and *The Lady Vanishes* (1938). But it was after gaining access to the American laboratories of Fox, RKO, and Paramount that he realized his full potential as a director. There he could not only practice the careful cutting that distinguishes his pictures of the thirties but could also experiment with the intricate mixes, matte shots, and superimpositions that mark his mature style.

The force and skill of Hitchcock's cutting can perhaps be best illustrated by a passage from *North by Northwest* (1959). The scene is the attempted assassination of Roger Thornhill, mistaken for an American

---

[7] *Ibid.,* p. 19.

[8] *Footnotes to the Film,* ed. Charles Davy (London: Lovat, Dickson and Thompson, Ltd., 1937), p. 5.

intelligence agent. As if to make his task difficult, Hitchcock schedules the assassination in bright daylight in the middle of an open prairie. There are no doors to squeak, lights to flicker, or spring knives to draw from secret pockets. Thornhill gets off a bus and seems almost alone; we would hardly notice the airplane circling in the remote background were it not for the casual remark of a passing farmer. But naturally this airplane is the assassin's instrument. We get our first clue to its menace as Hitchcock increases the volume of the effects track, so that the high-pitched whine of the engine becomes noticeable before the plane itself is visually prominent.

In the first cut of the developing action sequence, the plane swoops down upon Thornhill, forcing him to dive to the ground. Then, while the drone of the engine supplies the sound of continued threat, the plane returns in the next significant cut for another attack. The timing of the cuts doesn't change but their character does. This time Thornhill is running before he dives, and the pass at him is punctuated by gunfire. As the plane maneuvers to do further mischief, Thornhill tries unsuccessfully to flag down a passing car; the cut at first seems non-functional, but it draws our attention to the highway, highly significant a moment later. Next Thornhill takes cover in a cornfield, and as he crouches we hear the plane roar overhead. A skillful delay, an apparent reprieve. The next set of cuts almost repeats what we have just seen, except that the plane drops crop-dusting chemicals, adding smoke to the visuals and Thornhill's gasping cough to the sound track. Flushed from his cover, the victim races back to the highway, desperate to stop a gasoline truck that bears down upon him. Crosscuts between Thornhill's face and the truck show how its approach creates a different kind of threat. We almost forget the assassins as the hero is carried under the bumper. Yet true to the best traditions of action serials, Thornhill emerges unscathed as a well-timed facial close-up tells us. The sound track then recalls our attention to the airplane, wheeling into another assault. This time, however, the pilot has dipped too low and crashes the plane into the gasoline truck. Amid billowing smoke (already anticipated in the crop-dusting cuts) and booming explosions, the sequence concludes.

This scene is so well assembled that we hardly notice it makes almost no sense. Why this place as an assassination site? Why the decision to run a man down with an airplane? Why is there no gunfire on the first pass? Why in a completely open arena can't the pilot avoid the gasoline truck? The point is, however, that the pace and timing of the sequence catch us in its inexplicable terror. Furthermore, the editing feat is the more remarkable when we remember that the action involves extensive matting. Most of the sequence was shot in the studio with the doings of the plane added by superimpositions.

In this sequence Hitchcock has used what we might call the "additive principle": each shot injects a new note of threat until, with a final twist at the end, two threats cancel each other, the aircraft exploding the tank truck. Although the passage is not particularly rich in plastic energy, we may notice that most of the cuts involve movement toward the camera (Thornhill running, the plane diving, the truck advancing) and that lateral movement (presumably intercut for the sake of variety) disappears altogether at the climax. Then, in a complete reversal of these directional arrangements, Thornhill makes his escape from the scene in a truck that moves away from the camera. These repeated thrusts into the forespace seem to implicate the cinema audience more deeply in the action. Only as the energy finally begins to flow in the opposite direction are we persuaded that the threat has finally been relieved.

Hitchcock's appreciation of movement is felt in the cutting of all his famous chases, from the rooftop chills of *Vertigo* (1958) to the fall of a Nazi agent from the Statue of Liberty in *Saboteur* (1942). But there is an almost Eisensteinian energy to a certain sequence from *Foreign Correspondent* (1940), where Hitchcock builds a memorable montage from the rotation of a windmill. Set in Holland at the outbreak of World War II, the film depicts the increasing involvement of an American journalist in the situation that is pressing Europe toward war. The windmill functions as a symbol of this involvement. As we would expect, it is also handled in such a way as to take full advantage of its plastic potential.

First we get an establishing shot of the windmill, held long enough for us to share reporter Jonny Jones' discovery that there is something abnormal about it. Soon we learn, in another cut, that it sometimes moves against the wind, thus signaling an airplane to land. Having in this fashion connected the windmill with political espionage, Hitchcock then moves Jones closer to this impressive stage prop, as the reporter endeavors to unravel the mystery he has almost accidentally turned up. A moment later, when we find Jones trying to listen in on a secret telephone conversation, the windmill remains part of the composition through a series of well-made cuts. In each shot, sails or shadows of sails slash the picture space at odd angles, keeping the set constantly in motion, as if the broken arcs and circular windings of the mill were meant to match the perplexity and confusion of the hero, who cannot completely decipher the conversation he overhears. Sight and sound are exceptionally well interlocked, since the turbulent visuals seem to symbolize the incomplete revelations of the sound track. The cuts of the mill also prepare us for the further action, where the gears of the mill catch the reporter's coat, making the machinery a threat to his personal security. The progression of cuts is thus persuasive in both visual and thematic terms. Once Hitchcock has established the mill as an instrument of political conspiracy, he maintains its centrality to the cutting until Jonny Jones is caught up in its gears. It becomes then a highly relevant image of his own enmeshment in the action, a reminder of how unlikely it is he can remain neutral and unscathed.

Hitchcock's editing style, like that of the suspense film in general, depends more upon cuts than dissolves. Yet he uses dissolves effectively, sometimes to achieve an almost subliminal montage, as in the opening passages of *Shadow of a Doubt,* sometimes to protract an effect for explicitly ironic purposes, as in *The Wrong Man* (1957). In *Shadow of a Doubt,* shots of an elegant waltz are intermittently projected over a sordid scene of a bridge and a slum. For brief instants dancing figures whirl in the space around and above the bridge, then vanish, then reappear. At this stage the dissolves are totally disorienting, since we have no context for interpreting the incongruity. They later become intelligible, however, as Hitchcock introduces us to one of his most complex characters, Charlie Oakley. One of a large gallery of Hitchcockian murderers, Charlie is unique in his combination of psychopathic behavior with social grace. The dissolves thus foreshadow the ambiguity of Charlie's personality, which fits him both for grimy alleyways and elegant ballrooms.

The scene from *The Wrong Man* is optically more conventional but no less successful. This picture deals with a case of mistaken identity, where an innocent but inarticulate man, Manny Balestrero, is arrested and tried for robbery. All the circumstances work against him and it appears that he will eventually be convicted. He is a religious man and as things grow more desperate we find him standing in church before a votive candle, praying, it seems, for a miracle. Hitchcock then arranges this miracle in a lengthy dissolve. Manny's face remains a close-up in the foreground, but this is superimposed upon a wide-angle shot of a dark street, where an unidentifiable man slowly walks toward the camera. Suspense mounts as he advances into the foreground, since in size and build he resembles Manny. Though we can see his face, it is rather dark and he is too far away for us to read his features. But naturally he continues to come forward, until his face exactly fills the picture space still showing the close-up of Manny. It is now apparent that the stranger resembles Manny enough to be his double. After this hint at solution, Hitchcock erases Manny with a cut, sets the real robber to the task of committing another crime and, after his capture, allows the mystery to be unraveled in the normal way. As in *Shadow of a Doubt,* the dissolve optically anticipates a narrative and dramatic movement not yet undertaken.

Frequently when Hitchcock edits in a visually expressive way, he makes only a minimal, though effective, use of sound — the overheard telephone conversation of *Foreign Correspondent*, the fall of the foot-steps in *The Wrong Man*. Sometimes, however, the sound has a more direct bearing upon the unfolding of images. In *Notorious* (1946), for example, it pulls two people together, the American intelligence agent, Devlin, and the woman whose cooperation he seeks, Alicia Huberman. The daughter of a Nazi espionage agent, Alicia is valuable to American intelligence as someone who might penetrate a German spy ring now getting organized in Brazil. The trick will be to get her consent in this operation.

Devlin begins with a direct approach, appealing to Alicia's "patrio-tism," a word that provokes her rage. She seems politically of the same stripe as her father. Then, after Alicia and Devlin have gone to separate rooms, there is a cut to Devlin's hands as he sets a phonograph record going.

The record is a conversation between Alicia and her father, which now becomes the dominant force in the scene. Ironically, Alicia's re-marks on the record reinstate the values she has just scoffed at — love of country, fidelity to America, etc. In an emotion-charged argument, she insists to her father that she wants no part in "your dirty schemes." As this voice dominates the scene, Devlin takes two steps forward in a one-shot, while Alicia rounds the corner in a matching one-shot. A second cut holds on Alicia while she stands still, but Devlin, still walk-ing circumspectly forward, slowly penetrates the frame. She has tried to avoid him, but the record has given him moral leverage against her. This point is underscored in the ensuing two-shot, where both parties, instead of looking at each other, turn and face the phonograph to-gether. Alicia makes a further effort to escape, pulling the camera with her as she tries to hurry out of the shared frame into the isolation of another one-shot. But the panning camera fails to absolutely exclude Devlin, who remains present at the far right of the frame while Alicia makes her last verbal evasion: "I want lots of good times with nice people." But Devlin's return to centrality in the frame tells us visually that the issue is already decided. Any lingering doubts are resolved in a final one-shot where a silly-looking, would-be yachtsman pops into the room and invites Alicia to go cruising. Since this is apparently what "good times with nice people" amounts to, it is evident that Alicia will reject them.

Surely Hitchcock's most energetic editing is to be found in *Psycho*. The cuts, the sound tropes, the matte shots: all attain a new level of intricacy and artistic integration. The stabbing of Marion Crane in the shower has already become one of the touchstones of cinematic hor-ror; so have the subliminal cuts matching the face of Norman Bates to the corpse of his grotesquely embalmed mother. In the shower scene, according to Hitchcock, there were seventy camera setups for forty-five seconds of footage, which makes possible the lightning-fast cuts of the

SIGHT AND SOUND IN CONCERT. Once sound has been added to picture, the two media must be coordinated, as illustrated in the cutting strategy of *Notorious*.

The sequence (below) is introduced by a phonograph record which Inspector Devlin (Cary Grant) plays for Alicia (Ingrid Bergman) in order to remind her of patriotic sentiments she now denies ever having felt.

The cut to a tighter shot of Devlin (bottom) while he moves forward gives him plastic momentum in the sequence just as the record of Alicia's patriotic testimonial gives him leverage in his argument with her.

The reintroduction of Alicia (opposite page, top) becomes the next logical step in the unfolding editorial design, since she is drawn back toward Devlin by the pronouncements of her own voice on the record.

The new meeting of minds is plastically represented in a two-shot (center), although the composition is intentionally unkind to Devlin, whose shadow and shoulder seem to intrude upon the already slightly bewildered Alicia.

As Devlin turns toward the camera, however, the two-shot takes on happier overtones of reconciliation and accord (bottom). Significantly at this point Alicia is facing the phonograph stand and Devlin has begun to turn back toward this instrument which inspired their new-found understanding of each other. The continuities are simple ones but executed with typical Hitchcockian professionalism. Courtesy of A.B.C. Films, American Broadcasting Company.

attack. The montage is remarkable, however, for more than the whipping rhythm generated by its pace. Look, for instance, at the treatment of the victim's face. She wears an expression of open-mouthed delight as the water first pours down over her; this matches almost exactly her facial expression when she is stabbed. The mouth is still open, though the size of the close-up has been enlarged and the sound track punctuated with cries of terror. These facial close-ups are also expertly integrated with torso shots of the stabbing. After knife thrusts that carry unmistakable sexual connotations, the face of the dying woman, no longer able to struggle, relaxes into an expression resembling erotic submission. The macabre and the metaphoric are thus fused in the editing process.

In contrast to the furious rapidity of the cutting in this scene, other sequences from *Psycho* are done with exceptionally long takes, as the narrative strategy dictates such an approach. Once it was necessary to show Bates carrying his mother to the cellar and at the same time avoid showing that this woman is an embalmed corpse. This required a special angle of coverage, which the camera must gain without calling attention to what it is doing. Here Hitchcock rejected cuts in favor of a complicated continuous take supported by off-screen sound. The director explains: "I didn't want to cut, when he carries her down, to a high shot because the audience would have been suspicious as to why the camera has suddenly jumped away. So I had a hanging camera follow Perkins [the Bates figure] up the stairs, and when he went into the room I continued going up without a cut. As the camera got up on top of the door, the camera turned and looked back down the stairs again. Meanwhile I had an argument take place between the son and his mother to distract the audience and take their minds off what the camera was doing. In this way the camera was above Perkins again as he carried his mother down and the public hadn't noticed a thing." [9] These are the moves of a director who has completely mastered the editing process. Perhaps the hardest thing to learn about cutting is when not to cut.

Through a half-century in the cinema, Hitchcock has rested comfortably within the conventions of the suspense film. The genre provides him with all the framework he needs to study the human anxieties provoked by a coldly bureaucratized world. Essentially nonpolitical, he cares very little whether his villains are Nazis, Communists, or American police officers. Since he trusts no solutions, it doesn't worry him that his films never succeed in defining the sociopolitical relations he loves to play games with. What is real for Hitchcock is the knife behind the shower curtain, the face watching at the window. These concerns

[9] *Hitchcock,* pp. 208–209.

receive continuing emphasis from the editor's shears even while his plots creak with cloak-and-dagger clichés. From a crassly commercial standpoint Hitchcock is father of James Bond; but whatever his connection with 007 he has always been part of the cinema's avant-garde.

EDITING BEYOND THE GENRES

Relationship of editing to the conventions of the genre film. New approaches to cutting by Fellini: I Vitelloni. *Subjective and disjunctive editing in the French "New Wave." Collaboration of Henri Colpi and Alain Resnais. From* Guernica *to* Hiroshima, Mon Amour. *Interweaving of past and present; interrelated montage of sight and sound. Influence of Resnais-Colpi upon Truffaut and Godard.*

As to rhythm and pace, shock or surprise, Hitchcock has done almost everything that can be done with a moviola. He has also absorbed most of the new technology as it has come along. But there are areas of the cinema to which his editing style is quite alien. Suppose there are no chases, no cries of panic, no poisoned cups of tea? Or further, suppose there is no plot in the conventional sense — no routine introductions at the beginning, no curtain calls at the close? What place might montage hold in films of this sort? And how might the inner world of fantasy be dealt with editorially, perhaps incorporating today's refinements in lighting or laboratory technique? These are concerns that emerged after World War II, first penetrating the neorealist movement in Italy and later dominating the interests of the French New Wave.

In a sense, the genre films of the 1930s, 1940s, and early 1950s almost invited a stereotypic approach to cutting. Gangster films, heavily charged with action, could be cut to an *allegro* beat; love stories should be *moderato,* so that the boy-meets-girl transaction would not take place with unseemly haste; religious films, being full of moral profundities, would almost certainly be *andante,* especially after cinema made it possible to include so much detail in a single shot. Beyond these general conventions, there were also formulas for cutting particular scenes. The hand-holding close-up should precede the first kiss; the fleeing stage and the pursuing bandits should always be shown passing the same landmarks. If the plotting of pictures were to change, what would happen to these standard cutting-room ploys? Here Zavattini and the neorealists were a liberating force.

Although the theoretical writings of Pudovkin were instrumental in the launching of neorealism, imaginative montage did not at first figure prominently in the products of this movement. In fact *La Terra Trema*

(Italy, 1948) might well lay claim to being one of the most sluggish films ever made. With films like *Umberto D* and *I Vitelloni* (1953), however, we notice the Italian cinema challenging the editorial options which had prevailed since the beginning of sound.

Handbooks of editing generally advise caution in handling shots done with a moving camera. This makes sense, because moving images are harder to match with one another than static ones. At the end of Fellini's *I Vitelloni,* however, we get a series of cuts in which fast tracking shots are matched very effectively. The picture tells the story of young Moraldo's emancipation from the values of his adolescent companions, and the cuts at the close make the final comment on this development.

The keynote of the last scene from *I Vitelloni* is a train pulling away from a station. Moraldo is boarding it and, in so doing, saying good-bye to the town he grew up in, the friends he knew there. In the course of the film we too have grown well acquainted with Moraldo's friends — Leopoldo, the bookish would-be playwright; Ricardo and Alberto, two pleasant do-nothings; and Fausto, who is finally getting reconciled to married life. Fellini gives us a last look at these several characters in cuts that represent Moraldo's parting thoughts.

As Moraldo arrives to take an early morning train, we are aware that he has said no formal good-byes. Only little Guido, the railroad boy, realizes Moraldo is leaving. And to the question "Weren't you happy here?" Moraldo can make no reply. Obviously he finds it difficult to break his ties with the world of childhood, even though he tells Guido, "I have to leave."

The train then starts to roll and the camera assumes a subjective viewpoint. The next cut is a tracking shot of houses and buildings left behind, the literal sights Moraldo would see. The next cuts, however, go beyond literalism, showing us the movements of the young man's mind. First we visit the bedroom of Leopoldo, who sleeps with an open book on his pillow, as if exhausted from the effort to make himself learned; next we see Ricardo, embracing his pillow, as if dreaming of a love affair that in real life has never materialized; we also see Alberto, snoring; finally, there is Fausto, resting comfortably with his wife and baby beside him. Throughout these cuts the feel of the railway journey is preserved; the sound of the train echoes in the bedrooms, even though it could not literally be heard there. Moreover, the tracking shot used as the train left the station is also repeated now with metaphoric implications. In each case the camera rushes away from the bedside of the sleeper, the unexpectedness of this movement emphasizing the psychic wrenching involved in the protagonist's sudden departure. At last we are back on the train, watching the town disappear in the distance. As a result of this complex crosscutting, we more fully appreciate the spiritual import of Moraldo's leave-taking.

Fellini would later perform further editorial experiments, cutting more intricately from a moving camera in *The Temptation of Dr. Antonio* (1962), then undertaking the ambitious light and color matches of *8½* (1963) and *Juliet of the Spirits* (1965), respectively. But between *I Vitelloni* and *Juliet* there intervened developments in the French cinema with worldwide implications for editing technique. This was the decade which produced the directors and editors prominent in the French New Wave, notably Henri Colpi, Alain Resnais, François Truffaut, and Jean-Luc Godard. They not only reinstated the basic elements of Eisensteinian montage but added many new strategies to the editing process.

As editor and director, respectively, Henri Colpi and Alain Resnais presided over two of the most boldly edited pictures of the postwar period, *Hiroshima, Mon Amour* (1959) and *Last Year at Marienbad* (1961). Both are films of dream and memory, where the past is conjured out of the present and the present loses itself in the past. They are "editor's films" in the sense that their mixture of fantasy, recollection, and experience gains coherence only through very dexterous cuts and dissolves. Colpi once complained in his "Debasement of the Art of Montage" that, given the drift of the sound film in the 1950s, "soon there will be no place left for the moviola and the splicer." [10] But this indictment surely would not apply to his work with Resnais, a director just as sensitive to the editing process as Colpi himself. On the contrary, these films provide the best possible demonstration of Colpi's claim that "montage is the most fundamental and unique means by which the cinema has succeeded in attaining such a high degree of effectiveness."

Colpi made an ideal partner for Alain Resnais. This director had entered filmmaking by way of the editor's bench, training at L'Institut des Hautes Etudes Cinematographiques. The editing process satisfied his urge to achieve in cinema those curious disjunctions that had once attracted him to comic-book drawing and time-lapse photography. The first test of his own skill came in the late 1940s when he made films out of paintings and pieces of sculpture, simulating movement in these static subjects through cutting and splicing. The best known of these, *Guernica* (1950), is built from photographic fragments of Picasso's canvas, rearranging in time the elements that the painter had first organized in space. As his talents matured Resnais came to see editing as a means to convey the perception of time that Bergson had described philosophically and Proust had articulated in fiction. In Resnais' films, as in Proust's novels, distinctions of "here" and "there" utterly vanish while time as measured by clocks or calendars becomes quite mean-

---

[10] This and the immediately following citation of Colpi is from *Cahiers du Cinéma* (December 1956), pp. 44–45.

ingless. In *Hiroshima, Mon Amour,* the first of his feature-length films, there is only the flow of a character's mental processes, made intelligible by montage. Since Resnais insists that in a good film "everybody is responsible for everything," it is pointless to argue about who guided the shears in a particular cut. Resnais and Colpi seem to have been of one mind about editorial procedure.

The opening of *Hiroshima* marks a cinematic revolution. The editorial style, in its bold associations and feel for abstract shapes, harks back to Eisenstein; yet the preference for dissolves over cuts is a departure from Eisenstein, as is the whole conception of sound. The most unique feature of this passage, however, is what might be called its "inductive" approach to editing: the material is given to us without context or orientation. This must be built up from the total experience of the film. All we have at the outset is what Colpi, in his reflections on this picture, describes as an "extraordinary . . . agglutination of image-script-music." [11] Their interaction, as the editor further notes, produces the impression of a state "midway between dream and waking." Since *Hiroshima* is about a set of horrific associations, it is appropriate that it should begin by forcing us into the human sensorium.

The first shot on the screen is an abstract image of entangled flesh, which gradually becomes recognizable as a man and woman making love. Before this shot calls up conventional erotic stereotypes, however, the image dissolves and is replaced by flesh and forms mangled in the Hiroshima raid. Later the image of writhing bodies periodically recurs, still with an exclusive concentration on torsos and without explanation of what connects Hiroshima with sexual love. The only guide is a female voice, off-camera, telling us that while visiting Hiroshima she has seen "the hospital," "the museum," "the reconstructions," "the news-reels." [12] Apparently this experience is being explained during love-making, though we never get the lip-synced shots of faces which would make this absolutely certain. But the more burdensome riddle, clearly, is the mental process which associates sexual intimacy with deformity, derangement, and destruction. Only much later do we discover that the woman's first sexual partner, a Nazi soldier, was killed in France during World War II and that she, as a collaborator, was subjected to torments analogous in her own mind to the atrocities of Hiroshima. The footage from the Hiroshima raid, for all its newsreel authenticity, is actually a cryptic sign of personal terror, the symbolic disguise under which private trauma presents itself.

[11] This and the immediately following citation of Colpi is from "Musique D'Hiroshima," *Cahiers du Cinéma* (January 1960), pp. 1–14.

[12] The textual citations are from *Hiroshima, Mon Amour,* tr. Richard Seaver (New York: Grove Press, Inc. 1961). Reprinted by permission of Grove Press, Inc. Copyright © 1961 by Marguerite Duras.

Another noteworthy element in the montage is the extent to which the sound track resists the images. The French woman's Japanese lover seems inclined to talk her out of her own experience as he keeps repeating, in defiance of what the alternating dissolves show us, "You have seen nothing in Hiroshima, nothing." Although at this point motives are still opaque, the images are so horrifying it is immediately clear why the male speaker wishes to save the woman from the nightmare vision that haunts her. We also now perceive, as the entangled bodies return to the screen, that the physical behavior we are seeing is kind of a psychic struggle in which two people contend for mastery. The lover must emancipate the woman from her personal Hiroshima, else she remain like the living dead of the newsreels, unable to respond to stimuli from the world beyond the bomb. At this point the woman's absolute removal from time present is underscored in a voice track resembling a musical chant. Her lover must pursue her down the echoing corridors of her own mind in order to create the conversational tone that will eventually prevail between them.

The course of the struggle continues to unfold in a highly unconventional way. Image and sound continue to compete, though the terms of this competition are never fully defined. What we notice, however, is that while the off-camera debate persists the imagery suddenly shifts from shots of Hiroshima devastated to shots of the city restored (tour buses, advertising posters, high-rise buildings). As if anticipating the new flow of the visuals, the woman acknowledges, "I know what it is to forget." A few seconds later, dreamy incantation gives way to normal speech and, absolutely without preparation, we get the first cut of the woman's face. In spite of the unrelenting opacity of the theme, the strategy of the cutting is clear. While she completely identified herself with the victims of Hiroshima, she was simply a fragment of flesh, whose posture might be said to resemble the death agonies of the bombed. Only as she admits her separateness from the past does she acquire a face, a smile, and a voice, becoming (at least temporarily) a person. But this first note of recovery, because it amounts simply to the lifting of a disguise, cannot be the last term in her psychic development. She has yet to relive the experience that produced the trauma, as soon becomes apparent when she begins to be mentally transported away from Japan and back to her childhood home in Nevers.

The memory sequences of *Hiroshima* are handled with the same editorial boldness that distinguishes the opening passage. The "jump cut," a kind of visual *non sequitur*, is the normal means of transition. The first memory shot occurs when Reva, standing on the balcony while her Japanese lover sleeps, looks back into the room, noticing one of his arms and hands. In the next cut we are looking at another hand in the same posture, but situated against an entirely different background. The cut to the woman's pain-clouded face tells us this is something from her personal past, and moments later we see her kissing the lips of a man with a bloody face. Without warning, we have been made witnesses to the death of her Nazi lover, which took place fourteen years before. This image of the German soldier becomes more intrusive as the film progresses. Once, in a memorable superimposition, he crowds between Reva and her new lover as they lie together on the bed. Eventually the presence of the dead soldier hangs so heavily over the film that the city of Hiroshima vanishes, giving up its place to Nevers.

As memory jostles with here-and-now experience, strange things happen to both sight and sound. "You are dead," Reva tells the Japanese just before we get a cut of the German dying in a quay in Nevers. Though the Japanese submits to this role of ersatz lover in which she casts him, he cannot break the spell that her former love still holds over her. She and the Japanese meet on the boulevard where he makes his last strenuous effort to claim her affection. In a two-shot we see him catch up with her and plead, "Stay in Hiroshima with me." But when she doesn't reply, he drops back several paces, gradually losing more ground as she walks on. The next cuts are from a moving camera which has taken the woman's viewpoint while she walks face-forward along the boulevard. First the scene is Hiroshima; then suddenly it is Nevers. Though the ensuing series of jump cuts are visually startling, they are psychologically lucid. Walking away from her new lover, Reva is walking back into her past. The next lines between her and the Japanese are inevitable:

He: Maybe it's possible for you to stay.
She: You know it's not.

This answer is already foreshadowed in the cuts of Hiroshima and Nevers that precede the verbal decision.

The landmark contribution of Resnais and Colpi was to make the contemporary cinema more ambitious in its use of editorial apparatus. The freeze-frame technique that Truffaut made famous in the conclusion of *The 400 Blows* (1959) had been anticipated by Resnais, Colpi, and Chris Marker with their inclusion of photographic stills in *Night and Fog* (1955). The cuts based on light and decor which enabled Fellini to maintain thematic coherence in *8½* closely resemble those Resnais and Colpi had used in *Last Year at Marienbad*. Though the color cutting of *Muriel* (1962) proved less successful (was the absence of Colpi a factor?), Resnais had by the middle 1960s securely established his place among the shapers of contemporary cinema. Even

Godard, now the better known of the two directors, owes much to his influence. The fragmentation of the human form, so conspicuous in the cutting of Godard's *A Married Woman* (1964), finds both technical and psychological analogues in *Hiroshima*. So does the Godardian treatment of cityscapes, which seems always to hark back to those radically disjunctive cuts of Hiroshima and Nevers. Such things as the introduction of negative footage (in *Alphaville*, for instance) are almost uniquely Godardian, though they are grounded in the same visual logic that dictates the jump cuts of Resnais. If, as Godard claims, editing is "the beating of a heart," [13] we may be sure that his own films beat with the same calculated irregularity we find in *Night and Fog, Hiroshima, Mon Amour*, and *Last Year at Marienbad*.

THE SHORT FILM

Following his vigorous attack upon the "debasement" of editing in the 1950s, Henri Colpi conceded that montage "has found its refuge in the short film." In this genre, he concludes, "the film is still made in the editing room. Here the image has not become the slave of the sound track. Here the image . . . determines the length of the music, of the sounds, and of the text." [14] He might also have added that we find in the short film the fullest possible application of contemporary technology, especially the new "process cameras" and "optical printers." It is these that generate new themes through the restructuring and recombination of old images. The available techniques, analogous to animation and cartooning, have promoted two genres of film, not new, but newly reconceived. One is the compilation film, which implies the reassembly of old footage; the other is the lyrical film, which is achieved purely by the flow of image and sound.

[13] "Montage, Mon Beau Souci," *Cahiers du Cinéma* (December 1956), p. 45.

[14] "Debasement of the Art of Montage," p. 45.

THE COMPILATION FILM

Nature of the compilation film. Compilation as documentary and propaganda: Frank Capra. New turn in the compilation film: Night and Fog. *Short compilation film in America: Charles Braverman. Braverman's editorial innovations:* American Time Capsule, The World of '68, The Sixties. *The compilation film as parody: Bruce Connor and* A Movie. *As jazz improvisation:* Cosmic Ray.

The compilation film, by which old images are recombined to generate new impressions, has a long and distinguished history as documentary and propaganda. In the 1920s H. Bruce Woolfe developed several documentaries of World War I, editing together newsreel footage and fictionally reconstructed scenes. The more famous example, of course, is Frank Capra's "Why We Fight" series, which used footage of Fascist military aggression to raise American spirits to heights of patriotic fervor. And countless times since the 1940s, newsreel material from World War II has been recut to tell yet another story of its causes, course, or consequences. While these efforts by no means lack editorial distinction, they do not represent the last frontier in this genre. For lately the compilation film has taken a turn toward greater compression and intensity, as evidenced by work in both France and America. The pace of the cuts is quick, the interpretative commentary minimal, the sound track as dense and ambiguous as the images themselves. The intent is not so much propaganda as high-impact, direct experience.

The ancestor of the contemporary compilation film is Resnais' *Night and Fog,* which incorporates into its meditation upon Nazi concentration camps much newsreel and archive footage from the World War II period. But while Resnais moved from this work to his features of the 1960s, a school of American cinema committed itself exclusively to resorting images from film and television. Within this group figures of such diverse sensibility as Charles Braverman and Bruce Connor have found common ground in the impulse to wrest new images from old. These filmmakers work at an animation stand, with what is called a "process camera," a machine designed not to do photography, in the conventional sense of the word, but *rephotography.* Here the original image is cropped, frozen, zoomed, accelerated, color washed, or altered in any way desirable. The images thus generated are then edited to fit a new sound track and fulfill a new design. Such films represent the purest possible exercise of editorial skill.

Charles Braverman's first film, a three-minute short called *American Time Capsule* (1968) is an animation film which retells American history through paintings, drawings, and photographs. The film, however, does much more than simply reproduce preexisting graphics. The cuts come faster than the eye can assimilate the detail (the average length is four frames, i.e. one-sixth of a second), hence producing new configurations of images. The original pictures are also affected in other ways, by such devices as zooming in and out on the stills. At one point, to suggest the westward migration, Braverman programs the process camera to zoom back from a still of several covered wagons. This naturally creates open space in the foreground and simulates the effect of the wagons pulling away from the camera to begin their westward trek.

By the time he made *The World of '68* (1968), Braverman was applying the same technique of flash cutting and reanimation to television news footage. This provided the training for his lengthier and more substantial film, *The Sixties* (1970). Here the eye is dazzled by a profusion of images that compacts the history of a decade into a twenty-minute visual tour de force. Everything is there — the Kennedys, the Beatles, the Berlin wall, the Cuban missile crisis, the civil rights struggle, and the Woodstock festival. The challenge is to bring order out of such heterogeneous and inchoate material. Avoiding conventional commentary, Braverman undertakes to organize the data by purely editorial means. The verdict on the decade is delivered in a high-impact sight and sound montage.

The Sixties begins with the voice track of a Nixon speech celebrating "the great silent majority," the constituency of white middle-class voters who brought him to power and whose values, in Braverman's judgment, have shaped the decade. The use of echo and reverberation protracts the phrase "silent majority," so that in garbled form it accompanies images of suburban sprawl, impacted traffic, bowling alleys, laundromats, and finally tombstones. This imagery furnishes an ironic comment on Nixon's rhetoric, yet also has its own interior organization. Though the progress of dissolves goes too fast for us to submit every detail to scrutiny, we have in all cases an impression of crowded frames overstuffed with highly uniform objects. Nor is the order and tempo of the transitions in any way arbitrary. The haste with which images melt and merge give us a sense of what Alvin Toffler calls "future shock," a state of ever accelerating growth and change. There is also perhaps the implication that the American way of life requires this rush from home, to auto, to bowling alley or laundromat, and finally to the grave. It is in this cultural environment, says Braverman by implication, that Nixonian values prevail.

If middle-class conservatism triumphs, however, it is only after extended competition with another value system, more idealistic and less completely oriented toward creature comforts. The image clusters here

COMPILATION FILM MONTAGE. The careful re-editing of familiar images can achieve radically new meanings through unexpected juxtaposition. This principle is forcefully illustrated in Charles Braverman's *The Sixties*. Photograph courtesy of Pyramid Films, Distributors.

gather around John Kennedy in the early moments of the film, then later are associated with Robert Kennedy and Martin Luther King. The Kennedy presidency is wittily introduced as Nixon, preparing for a television debate with the Democrat candidate, suddenly begins to hear his rival's inauguration address. It is as if Nixon were taken by surprise, before he had consolidated the forces that would put him in the White House. The presentation of Kennedy is followed by a short montage attempting to capture the optimism generated in the early 1960s. Strict chronology is violated as, after Kennedy announces the space program, the trip to the moon is shown as completed before the President is struck down by an assassin's bullet. The strategy here goes beyond political partisanship. The moonshot personifies the idealism (possibly misplaced or naive idealism?) of the Kennedy years, when the promise of interplanetary exploration carried a positive resonance it later lost.

As American society is polarized in the mid-sixties, Braverman's editorial style becomes more turbulent. He gives up dissolves for straight cuts, shortens the length of shots, disregards calendar time, reduces the opportunities for orientation, and selects footage marked by more violent movement. The civil rights sequence is opened by the serene voice and image of King whose physical composure personifies the orderliness of his efforts on behalf of American blacks. But this cut almost immediately gives way to the scene of his assassination, coupled with shots of black riots and white retaliation. The ideal of integration becomes a metaphor of social coherence, against which is measured the forces of disintegration that tear the fabric of American culture. The story of Watts, Detroit, and the "white-power" riots of Chicago, 1966, is told in flash cuts which leave individual faces and scenes unintelligible. Visually, however, the formal integrity of the film is maintained amid this portrayal of confusion.

Braverman organizes the imagery so that, even when the cuts last as little as two frames (one-twelfth of a second), larger patterns emerge to prevent visual chaos. As an unidentified voice repeats, "You've got to be left, or right; you've got to be left, or right," the masses within the fleeting frames shift rapidly from one side of the picture space to the other, creating the visual tension the sound track describes. Police, crowds, rioters, soldiers: all mix and lose their exact identity. Only under the moviola is it possible to isolate pictures we would remember from newspapers or television — the balcony where King was shot, Carmichael shouting to a group of his followers, bloody faces and swinging clubs. There is also a significant use of color in this section of the

film. Red tints, supplied by a color wash, begin to appear as occasional flashes and streaks in the cuts depicting racial polarization. These foreshadow the fully legible images of burning and bombing from the 1968 riots, which saturate the screen with stark reds. The cutting of this sequence illustrates Braverman's peculiar skill in structuring marginal perceptions. We come to understand America's racial confrontation, not from the standpoint of a professional historian, but as one who has imperfectly digested its details. Names and dates get lost; even events (like one riot and the next) blur into one another. Only the sense of rageful energy comes clear.

The last turn of the film, which links the race problem in America to events in Africa and Asia, is also accomplished by a skillful editorial transition. The cuts move us from domestic riots to warfare in Vietnam, and they come so swiftly as sometimes to create the impression that the Viet Cong might be fighting on the outskirts of Chicago. After assaults on homefront demonstrators, General Westmoreland announces, "We have a significant advantage in firepower." The remarks are apropos of the Tet offensive, but the editorial context gives them a more general application. American blacks and radical activists thus seem joined with the millions in Asia who have refused to accept the American economic empire, with the exploitative relationships implicit in the imperial design. As used by Braverman, the footage thus promotes a widening indictment of the failure of American liberalism. Without exposing a frame of his own film, Braverman succeeds in turning *The Sixties* into a powerful polemic. Few pictures more effectively demonstrate the potential of editorial control.

The films of Bruce Connor, one of the more noteworthy personalities in the American "underground" movement, represent another dimension of the compilation film. Though not so careful a craftsman as Braverman, he has a feel for the incongruous that compensates for what sometimes seems the total arbitrariness of his montage effects. His first effort, *A Movie* (1958), is an exercise in association constructed entirely from pirated studio footage. Cutting together shots from westerns, war films, travelogues, newsreels, and adventure stories, he concocts a kind of composite film experience, basically a parody of the Hollywood genres.

The tone is set in the first cut, which announces "End of Part 4" before a single image has appeared on the screen. Thereafter, runaway stagecoaches are bumped off the screen by careening race cars and stock cars, which in their turn give way to a limousine fatally plunging over a cliff. The strategy of arrangement is immediately clear. By setting "the chase" at the beginning of his film instead of at the end, Connor abstracts it from its normal context and invites us to look more closely at the visual conventions of chase scenes rather than at the participants.

Having begun at the end (complete with a "The End" title that follows the demise of the limousine), Connor completes the madhouse symmetry of *A Movie* by ending with a beginning. We watch a diver submerge and swim toward an undefined objective. Suspense mounts with intercuts to a school of fish accidentally stirred up by the diver's presence. Then as we return to the diver he disappears into a curious-looking underseas coffer which ought to hold either boundless treasure or a giant squid. But before we have the opportunity to follow the protagonist, the film abruptly ends, its development resolved only by the musical chords that suggest finality. As with the chase, here we have a "discovery sequence" handled without discoverer or discovery.

Insofar as these passages involve anything more than clowning, what we have is a technique that resembles the improvisations of jazz. The coherence comes from the rhythm and not the melody. Thus the chase scene has a peculiar kind of integrity, even though horses give way to motorcars and western landscapes are metamorphosed into racetracks. A set of movements is initiated, amplified, and then again curtailed, as we follow the cuts from horsemen on the hilltop, to cars racing helter-skelter, to the isolation of a single auto tumbling into a ravine. Given this bent of his imagination, the natural development of Connor's style is toward a purely musical form, which emerges in *Cosmic Ray* (1960). In this later picture Connor persists in his ironic treatment of American popular culture but conforms his visuals to the beat and lyrics of a Ray Charles song. While the tempo of the cuts (often of subliminal duration, like Braverman's) robs the individual images of their narrative import, they assume a collective meaning from the rhythmic tension and verbal content of Charles' performance. At this point the compilation film begins to resemble the purely lyrical exercises that constitute a further genre of the contemporary short film.

THE LYRICAL FILM

Transcendence of narrative form. Lyricism of the straight cut: Hilary Harris, Nine Variations on a Dance Theme. *Lyricism with more sophisticated opticals: Francis Thompson,* N.Y., N.Y.; *Ed Emshwiller,* Totem; *Norman McLaren,* Pas de Deux.

The compilation film hovers unsteadily between documentary and lyrical impulses. While Braverman and Connor seek satiric effects through the cuts they assemble, they are both keenly interested in the nature of the cut itself. This latter interest has led some contemporary filmmakers completely away from exposition toward the formulation of purely visual designs. Hence Hilary Harris, one of the most talented of American avant-garde editors: "The most exciting thing in film is movement. The rhythmic, pulsing, changing progression of images on the screen . . . can be endowed with all the power and magic and delicacy that one can imagine. . . . The action of shapes . . . can have a wonderful range and depth of communication, from the flick of a cat's tail to the majesty of the earth's rotation." [15] From these premises Harris concludes, "the abstract film is for me the most emotional and engrossing," since it is here, apparently, that the filmmaker has the greatest possible opportunity for "the movement and manipulation of images in time." And naturally, such manipulation is the particular province of the editor.

Harris' best-known film, *Nine Variations on a Dance Theme* (U.S.A., 1967), clearly illustrates this filmmaker's ability to generate movement by editorial means. "How do you create a life that is based on movement?" he asks, and then answers in the following terms: "The camera is a moving, interpreting eye, which in the editing process builds a form. It's a question of extracting kinetic elements from nature. Editing is the core of the art. The cut, although it seems to be an arbitrary thing, is a movement." Then, apropos *Nine Variations,* he adds: "The particular problem I dealt with in my film was to stretch, interpret and rearrange the dance, without destroying the original experience." The challenge is to respect the natural dynamism of the subject yet to accentuate and enlarge these movements through cutting. Remarkable for the simplicity of its approach, *Nine Variations* demonstrates the almost unlimited potential of mere shears and splicer.

Nine Variations is enacted by a single dancer in a single room without any special appointments or decor. It is shot on black-and-white stock with no conspicuous light accents, and nothing more elaborate than spiraling dolly shots for camera movement. There are no prisms, no mirrors, not even any zoom effects. The editing is similarly pruned of any sort of optical excess — no dissolves, superimpositions, inserts, etc., nothing but straight cuts. The dancer's movements are similarly uncomplicated. She rises from the floor and spins slowly around, embellishing this movement with a few hand gestures; then she gracefully returns herself to the floor. To respect the integrity of the dancer's performance, Harris opens the film by recording the dance without a single cut. Afterward, it is repeated eight times, altered in each repetition by more intricate cutting. Long before we get to the ninth variation, each of the dancer's movements has been broken down into split-second cuts and the gestures so enriched as to constitute an almost completely new experience.

---

[15] This and the following citations of Hilary Harris are from "Thoughts on Movement," reprinted in *The Movies as Medium,* pp. 90–91.

In the early sequences of *Nine Variations,* the cuts are infrequent and in no way startling: long shots alternate with close-ups; frontal shots are intercut with shots of the dancer's back; we look up, then down, then up again. The first complicated cut comes in variation five as the dancer rolls over in rising from a prone position. The movement of her torso is simple but Harris multiplies it by cutting quickly from three different camera mounts in clockwise rotation from one another. Each emphasizes a different contour of the woman's body, though the movements are virtually identical. This cut, which both complicates the gesture and extends it in time, is the key to the more intricate cuts that dominate the further sequences. Because of basic similarities of costume, lighting, and decor, the editor is able to match one thrust to another in a remarkably elaborate way. Flesh tones coordinate the matching of hand to foot, biceps to calf, calf to thigh: all appendages of the body thus participate in a continuous flow of energy. As close-ups become tighter and tighter, even distinctions between parts of the torso are obscured by the uniformity of dancer's costume and over-ridden by the dominant rhythm of movement. Such variety as Harris seeks is provided in subtle differences of lighting and decor: the hands are framed against streaming light from open windows; then the same movement is set against the textured brick of a relatively unlit wall; the hands then move against the uniform verticals of highly light-reflectant floorboards. The isolation and multiplication of these simple elements leads through the choreography of editing to a continuously renewed visual design.

While Harris works wonders with straight cuts from optically simple shots, other filmmakers have sought to integrate in their editing a richer body of plastic material. Francis Thompson's *N.Y., N.Y.* (U.S.A., 1957) attempts nothing less than the editorial animation of an entire cityscape. He works with footage shot through prisms, rotating concave and convex mirrors, and extreme wide-angle lenses that wildly distort perspective. Ordinarily, such material would be an editor's nightmare since none of the shots fit together in a conventional way. But through the use of dissolves and superimpositions as well as through the skillful timing of straight cuts, Thompson imposes a visually exciting design upon this apparently intractable footage. Steel and stone become mobile, fluid. Skyscrapers melt into one another, collapse, and reform like bits of glass in a kaleidoscope. Lines of compacted traffic stretch and snap back like rubber bands, crawl over and around each other like giant worms, while the integration of colors and thrusts supplies basic continuity. In speaking of his own work Thompson remarks upon how "I discovered the beauty of the fragment." Yet as is apparent from *N.Y., N.Y.,* what eventually emerges from the editing room is in no sense artistically fragmented.

Thompson's effort to plasticize inanimate objects links him to editors like Edward Emshwiller and Norman McLaren, whose background is basically in animation and cartooning. In their work of the 1960s, however, both McLaren and Emshwiller have experimented extensively in handling human subjects, engrafting further editorial movement upon the natural gestures of dance or mime. This usually involves the application of process-camera techniques even more elaborate than those of Braverman or Thompson. In films like *Totem* (Canada, 1963) and *Pas de Deux* (Canada, 1967), representative works of Emshwiller and McLaren, respectively, lighting, movement, and decor are controlled with the precision of an animation sequence. But the human figures, who are made to float, bilocate, vanish, and reappear, further enrich the visuals with the unique rhythm of a live performance.

In *Totem*, a film about the ritualistic roots of dance, the progression of images is toward increasing violence, as Emshwiller visually suggests the powerful instinctive drives that underlie the poised steps of a dancer. This development is handled through the optical imposition of increasingly starker color schemes, which saturate the later images in tones of blood and fire. But movement and perspective are also manipulated by the process camera. At one point a group of dancers successively leap toward the camera, a movement of no particularly remarkable significance. Once the footage has been developed, however, and then subjected to further elaboration in the animation studio, this gesture is strikingly transformed. The process camera creates a carefully timed zoom-in which exactly parallels the forward springing of the dancers. The result is that each figure makes what seems a preternaturally long leap at fantastic speed. The performers, while exhibiting their own muscularity and body tension, seem also propelled by the thrust of some unseen catapult. Through such techniques as this one, Emshwiller injects an element of primitive magic into the enactment of an otherwise ordinary ballet sequence. *Totem* thus achieves that balance between the natural and the ghostly which the editor evidently sought.

McLaren's *Pas de Deux* is another dance film, but one in which optical manipulation is used to suggest delicacy rather than power. Specifically, McLaren uses an animation technique called "displaced registration," which is made possible by a special kind of superimposition. In this process, the image from the original photograph is duplicated on a second strip of film, but duplicated in such a way as to slightly change its position in the frame (hence the term, "displaced"). This means that as the duplicate image is superimposed upon the original it occupies an area of the picture space either to the left or to the right of the

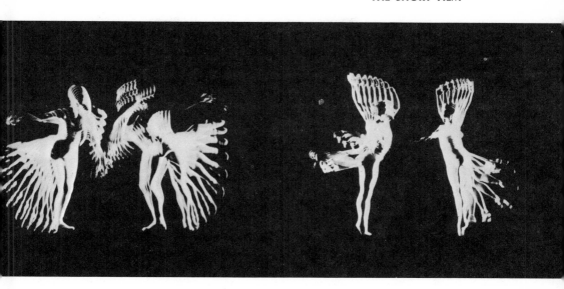

LYRICAL MONTAGE. Using an optical printer, one can superimpose images in such a way as to create the effect of secondary and tertiary figures unfolding out of the original shot. Here illustrated from Norman McLaren's *Pas de Deux*, this effect is radically different from either the cut or the dissolve yet remains part of the editor's repertoire. Courtesy of the National Film Board of Canada.

original. It may also, depending on exposure and printing techniques, be different in texture and tone from the original. Thus in *Pas de Deux*, the female dancer on screen as the film begins is soon joined by a partner, her ghostly double, who executes the same steps in absolute synchronization with her.

Since it is possible to create more than one duplicate image simply by displacing each of them a little further to the left or right, we need not be surprised at the introduction of several ghost dancers who seem to emanate from the live figure. Furthermore, once this ensemble has been called into being, the moves of each dancer can be choreographed separately, so that their steps no longer coincide either with each other or with those of the central performer. The other element of variety is provided by the differences of light tones that visually distinguish the emanations of the human figure. Utilizing an animationist's skill in the planning of movement, McLaren eventually introduces a second human figure with its own retinue of optical emanations, developing a miniature ballet with the two dancers and their celluloid partners. Rarely has the physical apparatus available to the contemporary editor been used to better purpose than in *Pas de Deux*.

List of Films Discussed

AMERICAN TIME CAPSULE   3 min.   PYR

BIRDS, THE   119 min.   SWA, UNI

COSMIC RAY   4 min.   AUD-BRA

EASY RIDER   95 min.   RBC, SWA

FANTASIA   not presently available

FOREIGN CORRESPONDENT   82 min.   FGE, TWY

GOOD EARTH, THE   138 min.   FNC

GUERNICA   not presently available

HIGH NOON   85 min.   CON

HIROSHIMA, MON AMOUR   88 min.   CON

LAST YEAR AT MARIENBAD   93 min.   AUD-BRA

M   90 min.   JAN

MOTHER   100 min.   AUD-BRA, MMA

MOVIE, A   12 min.   AUD-BRA, CAN

NIGHT AND FOG   31 min.   CON, PYR

NINE VARIATIONS ON A DANCE THEME   13 min.   RFI

NORTH BY NORTHWEST   136 min.   FNC

NOTORIOUS   101 min.   AUD-BRA

N.Y., N.Y.   14 min.   PYR

OCTOBER (TEN DAYS THAT SHOOK THE WORLD)   105 min.
   AUD-BRA, MMA

OLD AND NEW (GENERAL LINE)   76 min.   AUD-BRA

PAS DE DEUX   14 min.   PYR

PSYCHO   109 min.   CCC, UNI

SHADOW OF A DOUBT   108 min.   UNI

SIXTIES, THE   15 min.   PYR

STRIKE   90 min.   MMA, AUD-BRA

TOPKAPI   120 min.   UAS

TOTEM   16 min.   CAN

VITELLONI, I   104 min.   AUD-BRA

VIVA VILLA   114 min.   FNC

WAR AND PEACE   not presently available

WORLD OF '68, THE   4 min.   PYR

WRONG MAN, THE   105 min.   WAR

8
CONCLUSION

Integration of functions in filmmaking. Levels of collaborative achievement. Mechanical integration: "Mission Impossible." Failure of integration: The Misfits. *Technical and thematic integration:* The Searchers. *Some suggestions for the reorientation of film criticism.*

It is hoped that we have now looked closely enough at the diverse elements in the filmmaking process to notice that each has a separate history and poses unique artistic problems for the director and the specialists who assist him. As we see the individual demands of photography, of sound, of scripting or acting, and finally of editing, we get a fuller sense of the cinema's richness, its relationship to various other arts, and its own internal complexity. What we might lose in this analytical approach, unfortunately, is the integrity and multifaceted coherence which distinguishes every good film. For the several disciplines we have described ought to work harmoniously with one another to evoke a single theme, addressed simultaneously to the eye, the ear, and the mind.

Naturally there can be various artistic levels at which this harmony is achieved. These range all the way from the purely mechanical integrity of a good formula film to instances in which a personal moral vision is successfully mediated by the technical and professional disciplines essential to its articulation. In these latter cases, of course, the interaction among members of the production team is more delicate and the possibility of dysfunction is greater.

The collaborative tendency of filmmaking is suggested by the well-made formula film, or genre picture, which manages to transmit a unified impression without attempting to create a personal signature, the director's or anyone else's. In the 1930s, Hollywood formula films like the "Thin Man" series provided this type of entertainment, while today the genre picture is found both in the movie house and on television. The best of these, such as the "Star Trek" or "Mission Impossible" series from 1960s television, show how good production quality in shooting, acting, cutting, and orchestrating the sound track is entirely compatible with a mere made-to-market approach to the creative process. Presumably no one would think Bruce Geller of "Mission Impossible" a pantheon auteur, but his productions always exhibit imaginative staging, deft technical exposition, and meticulous internal balance. This gives them visual and theatrical excellences that derive not so much from personal vision as from the careful combining and proportioning of various solicited skills.

Even while we notice in "Mission Impossible" the relentless application of a formula ("Your mission, Jim, if you choose to accept it . . ."), we must commend each element in the production. The tape-recorded message that sketches the plot frees the hero to sort photographs, quickly introducing the protagonists without artificial dramatic exposition. The smoke from the self-destructing tape admirably motivates the dissolve that establishes a passage of time and provides for a working out of assignments. After the picture is underway, we sense how the distinct look of each principal actor eases identification, making possible concurrent development of several strains of plot and abrupt, dynamic cuts from one arena of action to another. Though the actors do not "perform," in the traditional theatrical sense, their cool, understated style is quite in keeping with the stiff-upper-lip courage they are supposed to exude. Nor are camera and sound track neglected. Talk is minimal, so that suspense can be sustained and the characters can remain mobile: drum taps mix with brass to vary the musical score while wild noise adds to the inventory of effects. At the same time, the deep-field effects of short-lens composition give the viewer insights that are often unavailable to the participants. We look down the barrel of the assassin's rifle as he draws a bead on his victim; we can see the escapee hidden in the suspended construction bucket while the military search party scrambles around the street far below. Although there is nothing in "Mission Impossible" to explicate thematically, there is much to admire at the level of interlocking crafts. It is hard to imagine a sonnet written by a committee turning out half so well.

The ironic thing about filmmaking is that this rather programmatic division of labor may be more successful than the single-minded effort to express a personal vision. There is the example of *The Misfits* (U.S.A., 1961) to remind us that in the cinema individual artistic aspirations are a rather ambiguous thing. The difficulty with this film, it seems to me, is that scenarist Arthur Miller gave director John Huston too well-wrapped a parcel. The script was passed into Huston's hands with a set of meanings already fully encoded into the dialogue. And because it was commendably well organized, apparently saying what Huston thought it should say, the director yielded to the temptation to leave it alone. He might much better have challenged his cameraman, his editor, and even his costume staff to think more inventively about their potential contribution to the finished product.

In assigning blame for the various misfittings of *The Misfits,* it would be too simple to say that the picture is "overscripted." That is perhaps true, but it doesn't go to the heart of the problem. The difficulty is that Huston, satisfied with Miller's treatment of the theme, did not work out roles for other members of the production staff. As a result, he laid himself open to the intrusion of clichés emanating from other departments of production. These are highly conspicuous in the look and performance of Marilyn Monroe as well as in the composition, lighting, and editing. Here, paradoxically, the close agreement of Huston and Miller as to the "meaning" of *The Misfits* led to fragmentation and imbalance in the practical execution.

Though Marilyn Monroe probably meant to play Roslyn according to Miller's conception, she brought to the performance quite a few of the calendar-girl clichés from her own earlier films. Miller's symbolic intentions are perhaps operative in the scene which introduces Monroe, as we find her secluding herself in an upstairs apartment, reluctant to get dressed and face the world. The fact that she is late for her divorce-court appointment and generally distraught in manner are the thematically relevant details. But these deglamorizing motifs which Miller has encoded into the script are largely effaced by the lighting technique and the bearing of the star herself. The familiar spot/flood plays affectionately upon her face as she sits in front of her mirror putting on makeup. She is wearing a highly ornamental slip carefully tailored to emphasize her bust. Upon rising, she strikes several decorative poses while pulling a dress down over her head, interrupting and delaying the process through her casual conversation with Isabel, friend and confidante. In one sense, of course, this behavior is perfectly in keeping with Miller's conception: it reinforces a thematic equation — undress equals mental and moral confusion. Yet at a more concrete level, it seems evident that the lighting, costuming, and theatrical execution conspire to carry us back to the commercially confected "Marilyn Monroe films" of the 1950s.

The photography of *The Misfits* is bedeviled by similar problems. Miller's script calls for a considerable use of scenic and architectural metaphor — an unfinished house, the glare of dancing lights, the vast emptiness of the desert itself. Whether for reasons of cost or taste, these details are not significantly incorporated into the film. Reno is not the madcap city-in-the-wilderness Miller had in mind; it is a sign on the back of a truck that we follow to Roslyn's apartment in the opening take. The composition is so tight, the image so closely cropped, that we could be in almost any American city: the symbolic potential of the scene is given no opportunity to emerge.

Ironically, the most memorable shot in the picture, far from extending the resonance of Miller's dialogue, has the effect of turning a meaningfully ambiguous remark into a sentimental cliché. At the close of the picture, Gay Langland is driving Roslyn back to Reno, and their conversation suggests the possibility of a permanent relationship, a new orientation. Miller, hovering close to mawkishness, puts into Gay's mouth a remark about using one of the neon stars of Reno to guide the couple "home." Here, if the scene were to be saved, the camera would have to either overlook the comment or treat it ironically. Instead, there is a disastrous cut to the star that Gay refers to, the one which presumably beckons the lovers to safety, security, and bliss. The conventional associations of the image, especially when so powerfully supported by the camera work and the editing, completely erase the ironies and uncertainties of the last scene. We have left the world that might have evolved from the material of *The Misfits* and returned to "happily ever after."

The case is otherwise, however, when all the elements of a film work in harmony. Take for instance *The Searchers* (1956), one of the best pictures ever directed by John Ford. Here the composition, the color, the cutting, even to a certain extent the sound track, speech, and theatrical performances cooperate to embody the theme of the film. *The Searchers* succeeds in conveying the values of Ford, mediating them through the work of the production team much more successfully than did Huston and Miller in *The Misfits*. Nowhere is this integration more evident than in the opening and closing scenes, where various talents are represented and each properly subordinated to the whole.

The Searchers deals with the approaching end of frontier days and the cultural obsolescence of those tough but unsocialized spirits who first ventured into the American wilderness. The scene is set in Texas during the late 1860s and the focus is upon Ethan Edwards (John Wayne), who, after several years of fighting and wandering, unexpectedly returns to his brother's home. His stay will be brief, since an Indian attack upon his brother's family soon sends him in pursuit of the Comanche tribesmen who have kidnapped two girls from the home. But in the opening sequence all our attention is concentrated upon the significance of Ethan's arrival. The scene provides the opportunity to contrast the qualities of settler and frontiersman, home and saddle, the wild and the tame. These several motifs, central to Ford's ideology of the West, are suggested in the contrast between indoors and outdoors, strongly marked in both the opening and closing scenes.

As is almost inevitable in a motion picture, the first hints we get about *The Searchers* are visual ones. The camera work is expertly supervised by Winton Hoch, who after impressing Ford with his Oscar-winning photography for *She Wore a Yellow Ribbon* (1949) handled much of this director's work in the 1950s, showing special skill with his composition in wide-screen formats, then first coming into vogue. In *The Searchers* the format is VistaVision, which is composed in an aspect ratio of approximately 1.75:1, considerably more weighted toward the horizontal than the prescope formats. Both lens and camera figure importantly in the initial framing of the image. The camera is situated inside the Edwards' house, with the exposure set for outdoors, barely visible through a door that is slowly beginning to open. At the outset the scope lens with its extension of the horizontal dimension emphasizes the darkness within the house, since the open door to the outside world admits light to only a small fraction of the picture space. It is to this tiny slit of light, however, that the eye immediately travels, for the door opens upon a picturesque landscape bathed in bright sunshine. At first there is no movement other than that of the door itself which, swinging outward, helps draw us toward the expanse of desert and buttes. Further emphasis comes from the low whine of the hinges and the silhouetted figure of a woman who, though inside, seems bent on scanning the far horizon. While the significance of the outdoor-indoor imagery is not yet defined, the contrast between the two worlds is already clearly established and their interdependence at least vaguely hinted at.

Once the door is fully open, the camera rouses itself and rolls slowly forward, as if drawn by the appeal of the outdoors and anxious to get beyond the protective but confining environment of the house. This relatively slight movement is highly significant, since the big VistaVision camera so rarely goes anywhere and since in a complementary episode at the close of *The Searchers* it will remain absolutely still. Very gradually (this gradualness is almost entirely lost in nonscope 16mm or video formats) light banishes darkness as the camera inches toward the door, following the lead of Mrs. Edwards who has moved out to the veranda, apparently looking at something in the distance. After the camera has rolled through the doorway, giving us our first unmasked view of the spaciousness and emptiness of the desert, we now perceive not only its beauty but something of its immense loneliness, and the threat to unprotected humanity that its vastness may hold. The subtlety of this camera gesture catches much of the ambiguity of the film as a whole.

At this point come the first cuts, introduced by Ford and editor Jack Murray to present the characters, quicken the tempo, and elaborate the relationship between desert and homestead. A dust trail tells us there is a rider approaching, but the first long-lens shot of the horseman is dominated not so much by this figure as by the butte behind him, richly red in the early sun and towering above the desert as a symbol of ruggedness and isolation. The association of the rider with this tower of strength (yet ironically an immobile and inflexible strength) is both inevitable and intentional. The next cut reverses the angle as the camera looks from the desert back toward the house, where Mrs. Edwards, leaning forward and putting her hand up to shade her eyes, seeks the identity of the visitor. The alternating shots of butte and veranda refine the contrast of indoors and outdoors: the porch is shaded while the desert appears parched and bleached by the sun. Mrs. Edwards' hand gesture further personalizes this contrast, since the harsh light of the sun obviously bothers her eyes. Finally, as the one-shot of Mrs. Edwards tells us, the homestead is the sphere of woman, while the desert, we would imagine, belongs to man.

The musical rhythm (Max Steiner's score is serviceable but not distinguished) now quickens, to some extent matching the faster pace of the cuts and the further introduction of characters. Mrs. Edwards is joined by her husband Aaron, then by her children, who appear first in one-shots, later as part of an assembled family. The domestic image is enhanced here not just by the gathering of the family but by certain elements in the decor: a son is carrying firewood and soon is joined by a pet dog. Significantly all these figures remain on the veranda, none venturing forth to greet the rider, though all register expressions of interest and excitement. After an appropriate interval the enthusiasm implicit in facial gesture is transferred to the sound track, as Aaron first wonders in a half-whisper, "Ethan?" and then the children begin to shout the name of their long-absent uncle. The dog's barking is the final choral effect.

Although dialogue plays only a small role in this scene, the actors have a crucial choreographic function. The homesteaders literally envelop the visitor, thus assimilating him into the family circle. Aaron's handshake establishes physical contact between the two worlds, after which Ethan walks slowly toward the house, flanked by the children and followed by Aaron. The lingering and affectionate look of Mrs. Edwards (this eye contact helps make Ethan the center of interest) suggests that she and Ethan were once perhaps something more than friends. If so, then in venturing into the wilderness he has given up more than just a roof over his head. In any event, as Ethan is escorted toward the house, the cuts become less frequent, relaxing the tension built up at the moment of the visitor's arrival. The camera now points unwaveringly toward the shaded veranda, focal point of the scene's symbolic decor; the desert is temporarily forgotten. The framing is wide, taking in all the figures on the set, thus implicitly offering an image of community in contrast to that of the isolated horseman. Though there is some hesitation and irony in the sparse dialogue (witness Aaron's almost grudging "Welcome home, Ethan"), it would seem that the traveler has been reincorporated into the sphere of home and family.

The further development of *The Searchers* reverses the expectations that the opening scene created. We soon see that Ethan's restless spirit can find no comfort in home and family, since after one night's sleep in his brother's cabin he volunteers to join a search party tracking hostile Comanches. Though his courage and fighting ability are always evident, we also notice that he is temperamentally unstable, quick to invent pretexts that justify his wanderlust. As a result of his insatiable thirst for adventure, he misses the raid on his brother's homestead in which Aaron and his wife are killed and their two daughters carried off by the Indians. The effort to find these missing girls and to avenge the death of their parents then becomes the sole purpose of Ethan's life. Here, ostensibly, he is performing a mission on behalf of the community — the effort to recover the lost children and secure the settlers against the Comanches. But as the unfolding of dialogue and image makes clear, this is really a private quest, a personal vendetta unconnected with any larger purpose. Unlike the young cowboy Martin Pawley who also undertakes the search, Ethan has nothing to return to when the trek in the wilderness is finally over. We see him at last disqualified for membership in the safe, civilized society his bravery and energy have helped to create.

The antinomies of home and saddle are kept in focus throughout *The Searchers,* then masterfully summarized at its close. The characterization turns upon the contrast between Martin and Ethan, reminding us often of the social instincts of the one and the almost complete alienation of the other. Martin, who will later successfully cross a homestead threshold, remains always in touch with his girl friend Laurie. He pays her a visit, writes her a letter, and gets back to civilization in time to prevent her marriage to Charlie McCorry. Ethan, on the other hand, seems to have more in common with the Comanches, his sworn enemies, than with the white settlers he has vowed to protect and avenge. In the course of his wanderings, Ethan speaks the language of the Indians, quotes Comanche theology (apparently as a believer), and when he finds the corpse of Chief Scar he scalps his enemy in the manner of an Indian brave. Like the missing daughter Debbie, whom Ethan finally finds dressed as a squaw and living in an Indian village, he has been so long absent from the world of the settler that he is completely estranged from its mores and routine. He seems utterly out of place each time he encounters organized society, whether at the army outpost or when he comes back to town where the stage is set for Laurie's wedding. These details foreshadow the last scene of *The Searchers*, where the door of the homestead is closed to Ethan and he wanders away into permanent exile.

The conclusion of *The Searchers* compares so closely with the film's beginning that almost every detail calls up a prior association, always with ironic implications. Again we look out through a doorway, this time from the home of the Jorgensens, Laurie's parents. This scene is also a homecoming, where Ethan turns Debbie over to the Jorgensen family and Martin Pawley claims Laurie as his bride-to-be. The same masking effect is operative, the same contrast between light and darkness is evident.

What has changed absolutely, however, is the response of the characters to Ethan. He stands only a few steps from the door as he puts Debbie in the hands of the Jorgensens. Yet their attention is exclusively devoted to Debbie as they escort her into the house, utterly ignoring Ethan. Then come Laurie and Martin, from several paces beyond Ethan, so that they must walk around him in order to cross the threshold. They do this, of course, while remaining so preoccupied with each other that they take no notice of Ethan. His physical presence is simply an obstacle in their path. Compared with the noticeable eye contact between Ethan and Mrs. Edwards in the opening scene, the fact that Ethan is now so completely neglected measures his diminished importance. He has ceased to have a place, even in the memory of the settled community. The capstone of this judgment upon Ethan is found in the behavior of the camera. In the opening scene it responded energetically to the magnetism of Ethan's personality, dollying forward to meet him. Now the camera remains motionless, studying the figures who come through the door, unmindful that they block our view of Ethan. When all but Ethan are safely inside the house, the door is slowly pulled shut, while Ethan ambles away into the desert. What he represents has become culturally irrelevant, and even the camera seems to have sensed this.

The Searchers illustrates paradigmatically how good films work. Every element interlocks with every other. The camera, the scenario, the actor, the editing process — all help to express the theme, none overruling or interfering with the contribution of the rest. At moments there is great virtuosity in the camera work, but when the gesture, posture, and speech of the actors become prominent then the lens plays a more passive role. Sometimes the cutting adds powerful symbolic effects (as when the editor matches the feet of Martin and Ethan plodding through the desert to the feet of the townsmen promenading at a square dance), but often the cuts serve simply to move the narrative forward as quietly and unspectacularly as possible. The sound track of *The Searchers* offers no particularly remarkable effects, though the combination of Evangelical hymns ("Shall We Gather at the River?") and western romantic music ("The Yellow Rose of Texas") emphasizes the taming of the frontier. Together these contrast with the "Ride Away" theme which suggests Ethan's relationship to the society that church, marriage, and romantic love have brought into being. Although it would be easy to imagine a more intricate sound collage, this could easily disturb the stylistic simplicity of the picture. Considering the potential of the cinema, sometimes it is essential to guard against a kind of artistic overload. Too many effects from too many quarters dissipate emphasis and risk fragmentation.

From this evidence it seems perfectly natural to conclude that filmmaking represents the mixing and merging of many talents. *The Searchers* is a coherent aesthetic experience; but it is also a moment in the history of wide-screen photography, a chapter in the respective careers of John Ford and John Wayne. Its script refers us to conventions of the anti-heroic Western which first touched Hollywood in the 1950s, while its editing style reflects the rather conservative conception of continuity which had prevailed in this genre since the beginning of sound. These facts about the picture reflect the various kinds of inspiration bearing upon its creation. Each has had a separate existence — the imagery, the plotting, the acting, the cutting — and each, after this moment of aesthetic convergence, will resume its independent status and follow its separate road. These are roads which the prospective film critic might profitably travel himself.

In the case of *The Searchers,* I have no trouble accepting the generally held belief that John Ford was substantially responsible for what happens on the screen. He was the man whose moral vision supplied the dramatic orientation and whose practical discipline organized the available skills, endorsed the decisive options. Even here, however, it would be instructive to know more about the director's relations with his various partners and their enmeshment in the traditions of their own crafts. It seems regrettable that we know so much more about John Ford than we do about Winton Hoch, Ward Bond, or even Max Steiner.

This brings me to a conclusion that is really an invitation. I am grateful for the impulse that has given us so many good books detailing the artistic aspirations of the film director, including the pioneering efforts of Andrew Sarris (*Interviews with Film Directors*) and Harry Geduld (*Film Makers on Film Making*) as well as the more recent interviews conducted by Joseph Gelmis (*The Film Director as Superstar*), Martin Rubin and Eric Sherman (*The Director's Event: Interviews with Five American Film-Makers*), and Irwin Blacker, Bernard Kanter, and Anne Kramer (*Directors at Work: Interviews with American Film-Makers*). But I would also like to see, for the sake of balance, more of the work represented in William Froug's *The Screenwriter Looks at Screenwriting*, Charles Higham's *Hollywood Cameramen: Sources of Light*, and Leonard Maltin's *Behind the Camera: The Cinematographer's Art*. In these interviews with subordinate members of the production team, we get considerable insight into the director's reliance upon the expertise of his associates. Unfortunately we have as yet no definitive effort to study the studio traditions that have shaped film acting and only the beginnings of a systematic inquiry into the evolution of film technology. Perhaps at this stage of cinematic study a thorough history of sound recording and transmission might be more valuable than further interviews with comparatively minor directors.

Some glimpse of the missing dimension in film criticism is provided by the various, rather uneven, books which describe the actual production of particular films. Lillian Ross' *Picture*, which treats the making of *The Red Badge of Courage* (U.S.A., 1952), is quite informative, although more gossipy than analytical. The same holds true of Deena Boyer's *Two Hundred Days of 8½* and Eileen Hughes' *On the Set of Fellini Satyricon: A Behind the Scenes Diary*. In spite of their analytical limitations, these works give us valuable profiles of the Fellini production team through impromptu interviews with composer Nino Rota, designer Danile Donati, or actor Alain Cuny. Seen in the context of their daily work, these figures become something more than mechanical extensions of the director's personality. More carefully scrutinized assumptions about the director's delegation of authority prevail in Howard Koch's *Casablanca: Script and Legend* and Pauline Kael's long introductory essay to *The Citizen Kane Book*. As Koch describes the scripting of *Casablanca*, we get the definite impression that it was first contrived as a vehicle for Bergman and Bogart, that it evolved into a political allegory under the aegis of Koch himself, and that only in its last stages was it shaped by director Michael Curtiz. As for *Kane*, Ms. Kael's special pleading for Herman Mankiewicz may run to excess, but the damage she does to the more inflated of auteurist assumptions seems to me quite severe. We need more data of this sort to temper the personality cult that has grown up around the film director.

In the last analysis, of course, the director remains a very important force in filmmaking. He sanctions the aesthetic choices and often controls the thematic input of a picture. It remains for his subordinates, however, to summon the photographic skills that generate a particular atmosphere, the writing skills that deepen characterization, the theatrical skills that make the hero credible or sympathetic. When the right relationship is achieved, the director's imagination is enhanced by those who put their talents at his disposal. Remembering this point, we should be less prone to overstate the role of the director and less inclined to use the word "collaboration" as a polite synonym for artistic sabotage.

List of Films Discussed

MISFITS, THE   124 min.   UAS
SEARCHERS, THE   119 min.   WAR

SUGGESTED FURTHER READING

Arnheim, Rudolph. *Art and Visual Perception*. Berkeley: California University Press, 1954.
   Though not explicitly oriented to cinema, the work deals exceptionally well with the significance of movement, design, and lighting — indeed with all subjects related to the figure in space.

Barsam, Richard M. *Nonfiction Film: A Critical History*. New York: E. P. Dutton & Co., Inc., 1973.
   The most recent and readable treatment of the underreported history of film documentary.

Bazin, André. *What Is Cinema?* 2 vols. Edited and translated by Hugh Gray. Berkeley: California University Press, 1971.
   Rich in historical information and critical speculation, Bazin's essays are among the best available. From the standpoint of subjects here under consideration, his two essays on "Film and Theater" are perhaps particularly valuable.

Belazs, Bela. *Theory of Film*. New York: Dover Publications, Inc., 1970.
   An older book, now republished as one of the classics of cinema criticism. His chapter "The Acoustic World" is especially recommended.

Clarke, Charles C. *Professional Cinematography*. Hollywood: American Society of Cinematographers, 1964.

A relatively nontechnical introduction to lenses, cameras, lighting, filtration, etc. Not oriented toward artistic questions, but solidly informational.

Color. Life Library of Photography. New York: Time-Life Books, 1971.

One of an important series of volumes that probably constitutes the best introduction to photography a layman could seek. Explains the theory, history, art, and special problems of color photography. Excellent illustrations.

Deren, Maya. "Cinematography: The Creative Use of Reality." *Daedalus*. Winter, 1960.

Fine treatment of the control achieved by perspective, selective focus, silhouette, movement, etc.

Donahue, Jay. "Focal Length and Creative Perspective," *American Cinematographer*. July, 1966.

Perceptive, relatively nontechnical treatment of the way lenses influence composition.

Duchartre, Pierre L. *The Italian Comedy*. Translated by Randolph T. Weaver. New York: Dover Publications, Inc., 1966.

Though much of the purely historical material has no relevance to the cinema, this book remains one of the best introductions to film acting, because of its attention to posture, gesture, costume, and facial inflection.

Evans, Mark. *Soundtrack: The World of Film Music*. New York: Hopkinson and Blake, 1974.

Covering such composers as Steiner, Prokofiev, Eisler, Britten, etc., this work fills a gap in film history and also offers insight into the medium.

Fielding, Raymond, ed. *A Technological History of Motion Pictures and Television*. Berkeley: University of California Press, 1967.

This anthology of essays from *The Journal of the Society of Motion Picture and Television Engineers* unearths an enormous amount of historical information on the technical bases of film art. Especially recommended are Charles Handley, "History of Motion Picture Studio Lighting"; Edward Kellog, "History of Sound Motion Pictures"; and Kenneth Mees, "History of Professional Black-and-White Motion Picture Film."

Gessner, Robert. *The Moving Image: A Guide to Cinematic Literacy*. New York: E. P. Dutton & Co., Inc., 1968.

One of the very few pieces of film criticism that attempts an analysis of the script. Repetitious and sometimes imperceptive, the book nevertheless commands interest because of the originality of its orientation.

Huntley, John, and Manvell, Roger. *The Technique of Film Music.* London: Focal Press, 1957.

Good analyses of sound scores supplemented by considerable historical information on various film composers.

Jeannides, Paul. "The Aesthetics of the Zoom Lens," *Sight and Sound.* Winter, 1970–1971.

A perceptive appraisal of the artistic significance of this new element in film technology.

Johnson, William. "Coming to Grips with Color." *Film Quarterly.* Spring, 1966.

Good historical material on the evolution of color cinematography augmented by interesting conjectures about color aesthetics.

Kirby, E. T., ed. *Total Theatre: A Critical Anthology.* New York: E. P. Dutton & Co., Inc., 1969.

Excellent background for anyone interested in the interdependency of film and theater. Especially recommended are Margaret Dietrich, "Music and Dance in the Productions of Max Reinhardt" and Nikolai A. Gorchakov, "Meyerhold's Theatre."

Kracauer, Siegfried. *Theory of Film.* Oxford: Oxford University Press, 1965.

Somewhat obsessed by the impulse to create categories, but perceptive within the framework of its assumptions. Good discussion of sound.

Lens, The. Life Library of Photography. New York: Time-Life Books, 1970.

Such matters as focal length, aperture, and depth of field are here dealt with both from a technical and artistic standpoint. Excellent illustrations.

Light and Film. Life Library of Photography. New York: Time-Life Books, 1970.

Another volume that maintains the high quality of the series. Good treatment of how light creates emphasis, atmosphere, etc. Excellent illustrations.

Lindgren, Ernest. *The Art of the Film.* New York: The Macmillan Company, 1948. 2d. ed.; London: George Allen and Unwin, Ltd., 1963.

Good topic-by-topic introduction to the cinema, which suffers somewhat from its not having been substantially revised since its original publication.

Magarshack, David. "Stanislavsky," *The Theory of the Modern Stage.* Edited by Eric Bentley. Harmondsworth, England: Penguin Books, 1968.

Analysis of both the theoretical assumptions and practical orientation implicit in the work of this stage director whose influence is pervasive in the training of today's actors.

Mascelli, Joseph V. *The Five C's of Cinematography.* Hollywood: Cine/Graphics, 1965.

Though artistically negligible, this analysis of composition, cutting, camera angles, etc., is practically well informed and helpfully illustrated.

Mast, Gerald. *A Short History of the Movies.* New York: The Bobbs-Merrill Company, Inc., 1971.

A readable historical survey distinguished by some highly original insights and no obvious limitations or omissions. Good bibliography and filmography.

Millar, Gavin, and Reisz, Karel. *The Technique of Film Editing.* London: Focal Press, 1968.

Illustrated descriptions of the mechanics of cutting, together with an informed history of various approaches to editing.

Nilsen, Vladimir. *The Cinema as a Graphic Art.* Translated by Stephen Gerry. New York: Hill and Wang, Inc., 1961.

Originally published in the 1930s, this Soviet cameraman's view of the cinema is one of the classic treatments of composition.

Nisbett, Alec. *The Technique of the Sound Studio.* London: Focal Press, 1962.

Not as inclusive as what one might hope for and unfortunately lacking an historical orientation. Nonetheless, a good introduction to a neglected aspect of cinema.

Ogle, Patrick. "Deep Focus Cinematography: A Technological/Aesthetic History." *Filmmakers Newsletter.* May, 1971.

A long, well-informed article that covers almost every aspect of this crucial topic.

Richardson, Robert. *Literature and Film.* Bloomington: Indiana University Press, 1969.

A rather conjectural, but highly intelligent, investigation of the similarities between film and literature as narrative media.

Roose-Evans, James. *Experimental Theatre: From Stanislavsky to Today.* New York: Avon Book Division, The Hearst Corporation, 1970.

Crucial to an understanding of stagecraft, choreography, lighting, etc., in their theatrical expression. Not explicitly oriented to cinema, but highly relevant as background to the motion-picture world.

Solomon, Stanley. "Modern Uses of the Moving Camera." *Film Heritage*. Winter 1965–1966.

Describes with highly relevant examples the aesthetic import of zooms, dolly shots, panning, etc.

Sontag, Susan. "Film and Theatre." *Tulane Drama Review*. Fall, 1966.

Very carefully argued discussion of the ways in which space, movement, etc., differ in theater and cinema.

Snow, William B. "Basic Principles of Stereophonic Sound." *Journal of the Society of Motion Picture and Television Engineers*. November 1953.

A purely technical exposition of how stereo sound operates, helped along by effective illustrations.

Spottiswoode, Raymond. *Film and Its Techniques*. Berkeley: University of California Press, 1966.

Probably the best layman's introduction to all aspects of the technical side of filmmaking. Slightly dated.

Walter, Ernest. *The Technique of the Film Cutting Room*. London: Focal Press, 1969.

Concerned with the how, rather than the why, of editing, the work is the most complete account of modern cutting-room practice. Covers sound as well as picture.

Wollen, Peter. *Signs and Meaning in the Cinema*. Bloomington: Indiana University Press, 1969.

An energetic, largely successful effort to create a fully viable film aesthetic from a combination of auteurist assumptions and a new, so-called semiotic approach to style.

Youngblood, Gene. *Expanded Cinema*. New York: E. P. Dutton & Co., Inc., 1970.

Investigation of the frontiers of cinematic technology with special attention to video tape and electronic editing as sources of special effects.

SUGGESTED FURTHER VIEWING*

ABEL GANCE: YESTERDAY AND TOMORROW   28 min. N-LEF
Homage to distinguished French director of the 1910s and 20s. Excerpts from his films with commentary.

ACTOR, THE   54 min. CCM
Studies the psychology of the actor, distinguishing among various modern schools of performance. Oriented to theater rather than cinema, though not without cinematic relevance.

ALL THE BOYS ARE CALLED PATRICK   21 min. PYR
Short film illustrative of the casual directorial technique of Jean-Luc Godard.

AMERICAN FILM, THE   37 min. N-LEF
A composite of excerpts exemplifying the styles of five American motion-picture directors. Material from *High Noon, North by Northwest, On the Waterfront, Friendly Persuasion,* and *Shane.*

ANIMATED CARTOONS: THE TOY THAT GREW UP   17 min. RFI
Study of the evolution of animation technique and stop-motion photography.

ART OF THE MOTION PICTURE, THE   20 min. N-LEF
Defines and illustrates the basic elements of filmmaking: composition, lighting, editing, movement, and sound. Oriented more toward art than technology.

ARTHUR PENN: *LITTLE BIG MAN*   30 min. TIME
Treatment of the career of this American director, mostly with reference to the making of *Little Big Man,* from which excerpts are taken.

AUTHORITY AND REBELLION: *THE CAINE MUTINY*   31 min. LCA
Excerpts from this feature-length film, suitable either for the study of script or the performing style of Humphrey Bogart. Commentary maintains dramatic continuity.

BASIC FILM TERMS: A VISUAL DICTIONARY   15 min. PYR
Excellent introduction to the vocabulary of the cinema with particular emphasis upon photography. Illustrates very clearly how lenses create different compositional effects, how the running speed of the camera may be altered, etc.

BIOGRAPHY OF THE MOTION PICTURE CAMERA   21 min. RFI
Traces the evolution of photographic apparatus, especially during the early days of cinema.

---

* List restricted to instructional films, excerpts illustrative of film history, and short films especially suited to classroom use.

CHARLOTTE ET SON JULES   15 min. MGH
    Short film illustrative of the style of Godard. Also interesting from
    the standpoint of the theatrical performance of Jean Paul Bel-
    mondo.

CIAO FEDERICO: THE MAKING OF *SATYRICON*   55 min. NLC
    Portrait of Fellini in the process of making one of his most extrav-
    agant spectacles. Useful insights into the director himself as well
    as into the relationship he enjoys with his production team.

CINEMATOGRAPHER, THE   17 min. N-LEF
    Examination of the role of the cameraman in filmmaking. Material
    usefully illustrative of contemporary (1970s) studio practice.

CLAY: ORIGIN OF THE SPECIES   8 min. CON
    Animation film by Eliot Noyes, Jr., which builds impressive effects
    into the mutation of clay forms. Interesting both from the stand-
    point of composition and of film editing.

CLOWN PRINCES   27 min. N-LEF
    Excerpts illustrative of the performance of silent comedy artists, in-
    cluding Chase, Lloyd, Turpin, etc.

CONSCIENCE IN CONFLICT: *A MAN FOR ALL SEASONS*   33 min. LCA
    Excerpts from this feature-length film, held together by summariz-
    ing commentary. Highly useful for the study of directorial tech-
    nique (Fred Zinnemann), scripting (Robert Bolt), and theatrical
    performance (Paul Scofield).

CRITIC AND FILM: *ODD MAN OUT*   35 min. MGH
    Commentary upon this feature film from the standpoint of struc-
    ture, lighting, mood, etc. Contains ample excerpts illustrative of
    each point made.

CRITIC AND FILM: *TWELVE ANGRY MEN*   25 min. MGH
    Another in this series of films made by the British Film Institute
    treating the aesthetics of motion pictures. Liberal excerpts with
    commentary.

DAVID LEAN: A SELF PORTRAIT   60 min. TWI, PYR
    Commentary upon the career of this well-known British director
    includes excerpts from his more recent films.

EDITOR, THE   15 min. N-LEF
    Treatment of the role of this member of the production team with
    emphasis upon his apparatus and studio activities as well as his
    contribution to the style and pace of a film.

ETERNAL TRAMP, THE   55 min. CCM
    Retrospective look at the career of Chaplin, especially in his role
    as silent clown, with excerpts of his vintage performances and
    routines.

EYE HEARS, THE EAR SEES, THE   59 min. TWY
Extended conversation with editor-filmmaker Norman McLaren, including valuable illustration of special effects achieved with an optical printer as well as other techniques distinctly characteristic of his style.

FATAL GLASS OF BEER, THE   20 min. TWY
Interesting blend of sight and sound gags makes this W. C. Fields performance highly useful for the analysis of comic technique.

FELLINI: A DIRECTOR'S NOTEBOOK   52 min. PYR
Search for insight into the creative instincts of this complex director is carried on with numerous impromptu and unsystematic references to his films.

FILM ABOUT FILMMAKING, A   18 min. IFB
Review of the process of filmmaking with attention to the various skills involved.

FILM EDITING: VALUES AND INTERPRETATIONS   30 min. N-LEF
Demonstration of how the same material might be handled in various editorial styles, each conferring a different emphasis and substance.

FILM MAKERS, THE: KING VIDOR   28 min. IU
Treatment of the career of this American film director with excerpts from his best known works, including *Our Daily Bread*.

FILM: THE ART OF THE IMPOSSIBLE   30 min. LCA
Rich sampling from various sorts of films, including *Birth of a Nation, The African Queen,* and *Lawrence of Arabia.* Commentary shows how the elements of a film are organized to elicit a certain audience response.

FLICKS, THE. I AND II   30 min. each IU
Running résumé of film history including highlights from various classic pictures of the silent era.

FRAME BY FRAME: THE ART OF ANIMATION   13 min. PYR
Introduction to both the technique and apparatus used in contemporary animation. Excellent background for study of experimental film of the 1960s and 70s.

FUN FACTORY   27 min. SEF
Extensive résumé of the career of Mack Sennett, including the classic chase and mayhem routines which he and his collaborators developed. Some useful material on the Sennett studio with its assorted contraptions and engines.

GOLDEN AGE OF COMEDY, THE   85 min. MGH
History of Hollywood comedy from the early 1900s, touching Sennett and Laurel and Hardy but also including excerpts from films of Jean Harlow and Carole Lombard.

GREAT DIRECTORS, THE   54 min. WOL
Treatment of the American film industry from the standpoint of its outstanding directors, including Alfred Hitchcock and Orson Welles. Excerpts illustrate the commentary.

HAPPY ANNIVERSARY   12 min. CON
Short subject starring Pierre Etaix, whose mimetic skills relate him to the tradition of silent comedy. The film also lends itself to analysis in terms of the broader aspects of composition and timing.

HOLLYWOOD DREAM FACTORY   50 min. RFI
Retrospective look at MGM studios, its stars and its stage props.

HOLLYWOOD: THE GOLDEN YEARS   60 min. SEF
History of the early studio era with emphasis upon the transformation of the industry with the coming of sound. Excerpts from the films of Valentino, Garbo, Mary Pickford, Douglas Fairbanks, etc.

HOLLYWOOD: THE SELZNICK YEARS   54 min. WOL
Extensive treatment of the big-budget superproductions of the 1930s and 1940s together with fairly extensive treatment of film conventions and techniques peculiar to this era. Many excerpts, including material from *Gone With the Wind.*

LAND WITHOUT BREAD   31 min. MGH
Excellent introduction to the astringent world view of film director Luis Buñuel. A bleak documentary on poverty in Spain.

LES MISTONS   18 min. PYR
Short subject directed by François Truffaut. Representative specimen of his approach to structure, performance, and composition as well as the themes of his feature films.

MAKING OF *BUTCH CASSIDY AND THE SUNDANCE KID,* THE
                                          45 or 52 min. TWY, EYR
Treatment of the staging and photography of this film, showing how technical problems are solved and difficult scenes enacted. Excerpts nicely illustrate how the finished product contrasts with the look of the preparatory efforts.

MAN AND WOMAN: *THE TAMING OF THE SHREW*   33 min. LCA
Excerpts from this film, bridged by summarizing commentary, nicely illustrates how theatrical partners (Richard Burton and Elizabeth Taylor) adapt their respective performances to one another.

MAN CALLED BOGART, THE   26 min. WOL
Emergence of the classic Bogart character in his work at Warner Brothers during the 1930s and 40s. Liberal excerpts allow the study of the distinctive Bogart style.

MIME OF MARCEL MARCEAU, THE   23 min. LCA
Not explicitly concerned with cinema, this conversation and commentary of the distinguished French mime throws much light on symbolic gesture and the movement of the body in space.

MOVIES LEARN TO TALK, THE   26 min. MGH
Examination of evolving sound technology illustrated with reference to representative films.

NEOREALISM   30 min. TEX
Analysis of the cinematic climate in post–World War II Italy which draws upon excerpts from Rossellini, De Sica, etc., to define the artistic aspirations of this period.

NEW FILM TECHNIQUES   60 min. CBS
Discussion and illustration of the new film technology unveiled to the world at the Montreal Exposition.

NEW SWEDISH CINEMA   40 min. SIS
Examination of the renaissance of Swedish cinema of the post–World War II period with attention to the general cultural climate and the directors associated with this renewal of an artistic tradition.

OCCURRENCE AT OWL CREEK BRIDGE, AN   25 min. CON
Adapted by Robert Enrico from an Ambrose Bierce short story, this picture is excellent for the illustration of composition, lighting, and sound score. It might also be profitably studied from the standpoint of cinematic structure.

ON LOCATION: *NIGHT OF THE IGUANA*   26 min. WOL
Another inquiry into the making of a specific motion picture, this one under the direction of John Huston.

PAUL NEWMAN: ACTOR IN A HURRY   26 min. WOL
Slightly gossipy but interesting glimpse of a major performer in American films of the 1960s and 70s. Some excerpts from his work.

PUDOVKIN   60 min. CCM
Detailed examination of the career of noted Soviet film director, conducted from the Soviet standpoint. Lengthy excerpts from the films.

SAD CLOWNS   26 min. N-LEF
Commentary and coverage of the films of Keaton, Langdon, and Chaplin.

SATYAJIT RAY   28 min. IU
Treatment of the career of the Indian director of the Apu trilogy, placing him in the setting of his native film industry. Excerpts included.

SERGEI EISENSTEIN   50 min. CCM
> Résumé of the career of this Soviet director which not only in-
> cludes excerpts from most of his best-known films (*Strike, Potem-
> kin,* etc.) but also offers glimpses of his sketches, cartoons, etc.
> Highly useful in spite of a sound track given over to political spe-
> cial pleading.

SOUNDMAN, THE   18 min. N-LEF
> Further film in a series devoted to the description of various cine-
> matic functions. This one describes and illustrates recording, mix-
> ing, and transmission.

STORY OF THE SERIALS, THE   27 min. SEF
> Many excerpts from this much neglected film genre, unfortunately
> balanced a bit too heavily toward the early (pre-1930) serials.

SWEDISH CINEMA CLASSICA   40 min. SIS
> Commentary with excerpts from the Swedish film of the 1920s, in-
> cluding the work of Stiller and Sjostrom.

THEATRE OF ETIENNE DECROUX   23 min. RFI
> Study of the technique and orientation of one of the most impor-
> tant schools of French mime. No direct reference to cinema,
> though useful for establishing the visual and physical dimension in
> acting.

TOKYO OLYMPIAD   32 or 39 min. TWY, PYR
> These excerpts from the feature-length documentary of the 1964
> Olympics are excellent for studying the photographic representa-
> tion of moving subjects. Also relevant to the treatment of editing.

UNSINKABLE BETTE DAVIS, THE   26 min. WOL
> Useful excerpts from Ms. Davis' most representative films, suitable
> for establishing her personal performing style as well as the studio
> look in lighting and decor from the 1930s.

FILM DISTRIBUTORS CODE

ADF
American Documentary Films
336 W. 84th Street
New York, N.Y. 10024

AUD-BRA
Audio-Brandon Films
34 MacQuesten Parkway
Mount Vernon, N.Y. 10550

AVCO
Avco Embassy Pictures
  Corporation
1301 Avenue of the Americas
New York, N.Y. 10019

CAN
Canyon Cinema, Inc.

Room 220 Industrial Center
Building
Sausalito, Calif. 94965

CBS
Columbia Broadcasting System
51 W. 52nd Street
New York, N.Y. 10019

CCC
Cine-Craft Company
709 SW. Ankeny
Portland, Ore. 97205

CCM
Crowell, Collier, and Macmillan,
Inc.
866 Third Ave.
New York, N.Y. 10022

COL
Columbia Cinematheque
711 Fifth Ave.
New York, N.Y. 10022

CON
Contemporary Films
McGraw-Hill Book Co.
Princeton Road
Hightstown, N.J. 08520

EYR
EYR Campus Programs
78 E. 56th Street
New York, N.Y. 10022

FCE
Film Classic Exchange
1926 S. Vermont Ave.
Los Angeles, Calif. 90007

FNC
Films Incorporated
4420 Oakton St.
Skokie, Ill. 60076

GRO
Grove Press Film Division
214 Mercer St.
New York, N.Y. 10012

IFB
International Film Bureau
332 S. Michigan Ave.
Chicago, Ill. 60604

IU
Indiana University
Audio Visual Center
Bloomington, Ind. 47405

JAN
Janus Films
745 Fifth Ave.
New York, N.Y. 10022

LCA
Learning Corporation of America
711 Fifth Avenue
New York, N.Y. 10022

LEA
Leacock-Pennebaker
56 W. 45th St.
New York, N.Y. 10036

MGH
McGraw-Hill Textfilms
1221 Ave. of the Americas
New York, N.Y. 10020

MMA
Museum of Modern Art
Department of Film
11 W. 53rd St.
New York, N.Y. 10019

NLC
New Line Cinema
121 University Place
New York, N.Y. 10003

N-LEF
University of Nebraska — Lincoln
Division of Educational Films
Media Center
Lincoln, Nebr.

PYR
Pyramid Films
Box 1048
Santa Monica, Calif. 90406

RBC
RBC Films
933 La Brea Ave.
Hollywood, Calif. 90038

RFI
Radim Films/Film Images
17 W. 60th St.
New York, N.Y. 10023

SEF
Sterling Educational Films
241 E. 34th St.
New York, N.Y. 10016

SIS
Swedish Information Service
825 Third Ave.
New York, N.Y. 10022

STA
Standard Film Service
14710 W. Warren Ave.
Dearborn, Mich. 48126

SWA
Swank Motion Pictures
201 S. Jefferson Ave.
St. Louis, Mo. 63166

TEX
Texture Films, Inc.
1600 Broadway
New York, N.Y. 10019

TIME
Time-Life Films
43 W. 16th St.
New York, N.Y. 10011

TWY
Twyman Films
329 Salem Ave.
Dayton, Ohio 45401

UAS
United Artists 16
729 Seventh Ave.
New York, N.Y. 10019

UNF
United Films
1425 S. Main St.
Tulsa, Okla. 74119

UNI
Universal 16
221 Park Ave. S.
New York, N.Y. 10003

WAR
Warner Brothers
Non Theatrical Division
4000 Warner Blvd.
Burbank, Calif. 91503

WOL
Wolper Productions
8489 W. 3rd St.
Los Angeles, Calif. 90048

WRS
Walter Reade 16
241 E. 34th St.
New York, N.Y. 10016

ZIP
Zipporah Films
54 Lewis Wharf
Boston, Mass. 02110

INDEX

Italic numbers denote pages on which illustrations appear.

Accident, 13
Acting, 14, 209–17
  body gesture, 217–39; physical comedy, 217–25, 239; *see also* Biomechanics, Constructivism, Expressionism
  nonprofessional, 8, 209–10, 254–56
  styles of, 239–59; formalist, 257–59; Hollywood studio, 240–47; improvisational, 254–57; Stanislavsky's, 247–54
  see also New York Actors Studio
Adalen 31, 57–58
Adrift, 69
Agee, James, 169
Agfacolor: *see* Film stock, color
Airport, 151
Alexander Nevsky, 30, 131–32, 136–39, 230
Alexandrov, Grigori, 137, 228
Alice's Restaurant, 266
Allen, Dede, 266
Allen, Woody, 239
Allures, 117
Alphaville, 202
Alton, John, 89–90
America, America, 97
American Time Capsule, 298–99
Anatomy of a Murder, 157–58
Andersson, Bibi, 13, 211–12, 215
Animation, 281, 298, 306–7
Anstey, Edgar, 148
Antonioni, Michelangelo, 13, 75, 213–15
  handling of color film, 115–16
  scripts for films of, 168–69, 190, 195–202
Archive footage, 8
Arrival of Train at Station, 25, 71
Artaud, Antonin, 254–55, 257

ASA (American Standards Association), 76
Astruc, Alexandre, 2
Auden, W. H., 148
August, Joseph, 5
Auric, Georges, 132–35
Auteur criticism, 2–9, 11
Avakian, Aram, 16–17
Avventura, L', 169, 196–201, 215, *196*

Bachelet, Jean, 56, 89
Bad Sister, 242
Band of Outsiders, 100, 202
Bank Dick, The, 56
Bartolini, Elio, 195, 198
Battle of Algiers, 58–60
Beast Must Die, The, 68–69
Beat the Devil, 14
Bergman, Ingmar, 11–15, 19, 211–14
  approach to scriptwriting, 19, 167–69, 179–83, 197, 202, 204
Bergman, Ingrid, 245, 288
Berkeley, Busby, 25, 136
Bicycle Thief, The, 75, 190–95, 199, *191*
Biomechanics, 217, 226, 228–31, 238–39
Birds, The, 263
Birth of a Nation, 10, 26, 79–80, *27*
Bitzer, Billy, 10, 79–81, 83
Bjornstrand, Gunnar, 13, 211–12
Blackboard Jungle, 215, *216*
Black Narcissus, 107
Black Orpheus, 110–11
Blind Husbands, 81
Blow-up, 75, 169, 197
Blue Angel, The, 91, 234–38, 240, *235*
Bogart, Humphrey, 5, 14, 240–43, 318
Bogdanovitch, Peter, 157
Bond, Ward, 318
Bondarchuk, Sergei, 251
Bonnie and Clyde, 30, 75

Boom, 13
booming, 32
Bourgoin, Jean, 110
Boyer, Deena, 318
Brando, Marlon, 6, 17–19, 210, 247–51
Braverman, Charles, 298–303, 306
Breathless, 100
Brecht, Bertolt, 202–4
Britten, Benjamin, 132, 148
Broadway Melody, 132
Broken Blossoms, 79–80
Brook, Peter, 255, 257, 259
Brooks, Richard, 215
Brownlow, Kevin, 16, 78
Brun, Joseph, 52
Buñuel, Luis, 32–33
Butch Cassidy and the Sundance Kid, 117
Butler, Lawrence, 143

Cabinet of Dr. Caligari, The, 84, 90
Cahiers du Cinéma, 2, 115–16
Camera, composing with, 24–31
    movement of, 22, 32–36; and sound
        mixing, 159–62; with zoom lens, 67–
        69
    shooting angle of, 36–37, 54
    types of, 7, 25, 99, 105, 146
    see also Lenses
Camera-stylo, 2
Camille, 75, 244
Camus, Marcel, 110
Canadian Film Board, 107
Capra, Frank, 241, 298
Carné, Marcel, 13, 89, 170
Carnival in Flanders, 173
Casablanca, 243
Casablanca: Script and Legend, 318
Chabrol, Claude, 68
Chaney, Lon, 126, 240
Chaplin, Charlie, 14, 29, 140, 239
    gestural style of, 209, 218–26, 248
Cherkasov, Nicolai, 230–31
Chinoise, La, 202–4
Choreography, 224–25, 232–33, 239
Chromatic aberration, 53
CinemaScope, 61–63, 65–66, 124, 147
Cinéma vérité, 99, 204
Cinerama, 61–62
Citizen Kane, 47–52, 142–45, *50*
Citizen Kane Book, The, 318
City Lights, 29, 221
Clair, René, 128, 132–36
Clockwork Orange, A, 29
Close-ups, 38, 40, 57, 213, 276
Cocteau, Jean, 13, 63, 133, 167, 169
Colem, The, 232
College, 223–24
Color photography: *see* Film stock, color

Color temperature, 76–77
Collinson, Peter, 163
Colpi, Henri, 16, 267, 293–94, 297
Compilation film, 298–303
Comstock, Daniel, 104
Confession, The, 60
Connor, Bruce, 298, 302–3
Conquest, 252
Constructivism, 226–28, 231, 239–40
Contempt, 112, 157
Conversation, The, 164–66
Cooper, Gary, 246, 264–65
Coppola, Francis, 17
Cops, 225
Cosmic Ray, 303
Costa-Gavras, 112
costume, 219–20, 224, 232–33, 235, 240,
    257
Cotten, Joseph, 245–46
Courtenay, Tom, 34
Coutard, Raoul, 10, 60, 99–102, 112
Crash effect, 67
Crime and Punishment, 43–46
Crime of Monsieur Lange, The, 171–73
Criminal Code, The, 131
Crystal-sync, 122
Cukor, George, 244
Cunningham, Lodge, 143
Cuny, Alain, 318
Curtiz, Michael, 14, 318
Cutting, 262, 265, 276
    see also Editing

Daniels, William, 78–79, 81–83, 127
Davis, Bette, 240, 246
Dean, James, 247–48
Decae, Henry, 10
Decor, 214–21, 225
    see also Constructivism, Expressionism
Demy, Jacques, 10, 99–102
Depth of field, 42ff
Deserter, 255–56
De Sica, Vittorio, 73–75, 190, 194, 196
Destiny, 232
Diary of a Mad Mousewife, 158–59
Dietrich, Marlene, 13, 91–92, 280
    acting style of, 239–40, 246, 251
    in *The Blue Angel,* 234–38
DIN (Deutsche Industrie Norm), 76
Displaced registration: *see* Superimposi-
    tion
Dissolves, 261–62, 265, 273, 280–81
Di Venanzo, Gianni, 11, 115
Divorce Italian Style, 155–56
Documentaries, 99, 210, 298
    sound techniques of, 120, 146, 148–54
Dolce Vita, La, 63–66, 195
Donati, Danile, 318

Don't Look Back, 150–52
Drew, Robert, 149–50
Drums along the Mohawk, 106
Duvivier, Julien, 170
Dylan, Bob, 150–52

Eastmancolor: *see* Film stock, color
Easy Rider, 263
Eclipse, The, 75, 116, 196–97, 214–15, *214*
Editing, 14–17
    basic principles of, 261–67
    of the short film, 297–307; compilation
        film, 298–303; lyrical film, 303–7
    see also Montage
8½, 11, 293, 296
Eisenstein, Sergei, 10, 19, 210, 255
    Meyerhold's influence on, 226–31
    montage, in films of, 14, 265–67, 269,
        272–79
    Prokofiev, collaboration with, 136–38
    use of wide-angle lenses, 43–44, 46–47
Elvira Madigan, 57–58, *59*
Emshwiller, Ed, 281, 306
Ensemble, actor's interaction with, 214–
    17, 220–21, 225, 239
    expressionistic concept of, 232–33
Establishing shots, 38, 40
Etaix, Pierre, 239
Expressionism, German, 29, 217, 231–40,
    259
    lighting techniques of, 83–84, 89–90

Fantasia, 281
Faulkner, William, 5
Fellini, Federico, 19, 155, 256, 318
    and camerawork, 10–11, 63–65
    editing, in films of, 13, 292–93, 296
    and neorealism, 10–11, 190, 195
Fesler, Bailey, 143
Feyder, Jacques, 173
Fields, W. C., 56
Film stock, 7, 12, 61–62, 64
    color, 75–77, 103–17, 263; Agfacolor,
        105, 107; Eastmancolor, 105, 107–8;
        112; Technicolor, 104–8; tripack,
        107–11
    orthochrome, 76–86
    panchrome, 76–78, 86–102, 239
    "pushing" of, 99, 112, 114
    sound negative, 122
    spectral response of, 53, 75–77
    speed of, 53, 75–76, 99; *see also* Light
        sensitivity
Filtration, photographic, 89, 112, 114–15
    see also Sound, magnetic
Fischer, Gunnar, 11
Flaherty, Robert, 83, 87, 148
Follow-focus composition, 54–55

Fonda, Henry, 106, 211, 240–41, 246–47
Foolish Wives, 81
Ford, Glenn, 215–16
Ford, John, 4–5, 54, 209, 241
    Nichols' scripts for, 168, 184–85
    and *The Searchers*, 312–14, 317
    Toland's collaboration with, 10, 47
Foreign Correspondent, 285–87
Forty-Second Street, 136
400 Blows, The, 296
Frames per second, 29–30
Framing, 38, 211–16
    see also Irising
Frankenheimer, John, 70
Freeze frames, 261
French Connection, The, 26
Frenzy, 282
Fresnay, Pierre, 176
Freund, Karl, 10, 32, 78
From Here to Eternity, 146
F/stops, 41, 99

Garbo, Greta, 240, 244–45, 252
Garmes, Lee, 10, 90–92
Gate of Hell, 108–9
Gaumont, Léon, 87
Geller, Bruce, 310
General, The, 224, *225*
General Line, The, 210
Germi, Pietro, 155–56
Gessner, Robert, 167
Gibbs, Anthony, 16
Gimme Shelter, 152, 257, 146
Glennon, Bert, 5, 55, 106, 280
Go-Between, The, 13
Godard, Jean-Luc, 115, 156–57, 209
    Coutard's photography for, 99–100, 112
    editing, in films of, 14, 16, 297
    and New Wave, 10, 267, 293
    as scenarist, 169, 202–7
Godfather, The, 17–19
Godowsky, Leopold, 107
Golden Coach, The, 109
Gold Rush, The, 209, 219
Gone with the Wind, 105
Good Earth, The, 279
Gospel According to St. Matthew, The,
    34–35
Graduate, The, 60, 112–14
Grand Illusion, 171, 173–78, 180, 197, 209,
    176–77
Grant, Cary, 288
Granton Trawler, 148
Grapes of Wrath, The, 47, 241
Great Dictator, The, 140–41, 239
Great Train Robbery, The, 26
Greed, 73, 79, 81–83, 127, *80*
Grierson, John, 148, 210

Griffith, D. W., 170
  Bitzer's photography for, 10, 80–81
  and editing process, 265, 268, 272, 279
Guernica, 293
Guerra, Tonino, 195, 198
Guillemot, Agnes, 16

Haller, Ernest, 10
Hand-held camera, 10, 35, 68, 99
Harris, Hilary, 303–5
Hawks, Howard, 4–5, 14, 242
Hecht, Ben, 5, 169
Hello Dolly, 136
Hemmings, David, 163
Henry V, 139
Hepburn, Katherine, 240, 246
High Noon, 264–65
High School, 153–54
Hiroshima Mon Amour, 293–97
Hitchcock, Alfred, 68, 112, 245, 263
  interest in editing, 14, 267, 282–91
Hoch, Winton, 313, 318
Hoffman, Dustin, 60
Hollywood functionalism, 240–47, 251, 255
Howe, James Wong, 10, 70
Hughes, Eileen, 318
Hunchback of Notre Dame, 126
Huston, John, 14, 242, 311
Hyperdevelopment: *see* Film stock, "pushing" of

Ibhaville, 297
Idle Class, The, 218
Il Grido, 169
Immigrant, The, 218
Informer, The, 185
In the Heat of the Night, 168, 251
Intolerance, 10, 25–26
Introduction to the Movies, An, 2
"Invasion from Mars," 141–42
Irising, 26–28
Iron Horse, The, 54–55
Itho, Kisaku, 108
Ivan the Terrible, 107, 132, 136, 230–31
I Vitelloni, 292–93

Jackson, Glenda, 254–55, 257–59
Jacobs, Lewis, 2
Jannings, Emil, 55, 234–38
Jaubert, Maurice, 132
Jazz Singer, The, 121, 131
Jesse James, 130
Jouvet, Louis, 210
Joyless Street, The, 28
Juliet of the Spirits, 293

Kadar, Jan, 69

Kael, Pauline, 318–19
Kalmus, Herbert, 104–5
Kalmus, Natalie, 105–6
Kammerspiel, 232–33
Kann, Stan, 125–26
Karloff, Boris, 240
Kazan, Elia, 13, 97, 248, 255
Keaton, Buster, 14, 29, 218, 223–25, 239
Key Largo, 14
King Murray, 117
Kinugasa, Teinosuke, 108
Knox, Alexander, 245
Koch, Howard, 141, 318
Krasker, Robert, 95–96, 102
Kubrick, Stanley, 115
Kuleshov, Lev, 265, 268–69, 272
Kurosawa, Akira, 3, 32, 57, 162

Lady from Shanghai, The, 143–45
Lady Vanishes, The, 283
Lang, Fritz, 157, 170, 232–33
Last Command, The, 55, *54*
Last Laugh, The, 32
Last Year at Marienbad, 263, 293, 295–97
Latham loop, 25
Lattudua, Alberto, 195
Leacock, Richard, 146, 149–50
Left-Handed Gun, The, 16
Lenses, 7, 10, 23, 37
  aperture (speed), 38, 41–42, 99; effect on texture, 38, 42–43, 47–48, 51–58; *see also* F/stops
  focal length, 38–43; normal, 38–40; perspective, effect on, 23, 42, 44, 56, 58, 60, 67–68; portrait (long), 38–40, 42, 52–60, 65, 116; telephoto, 7, 38–43, 53, 56–60, 66; wide-angle (short), 38, 40, 42–52, 62, 66, 116, 214, 276
  new optical systems for, 61–66
  special effects, 68–69; fisheye, 61, 70–71; zoom, 7, 28, 61, 66–69
Leone, Sergio, 211
Lessons with Eisenstein, 43
Levert, René, 156
Light-fogging, 112
Lighting, 73–117, 263
  with color film, 75–77, 103–17; contemporary innovations, 112–17
  with orthochrome film, 76–86; American naturalism, 79–83; German expressionism, 83–86, 232–34, 240
  with panchrome film, 76–78, 86–102; available-light photography, 10, 87, 94, 99–102; motif lighting, 94–99; studio look of 1930s and 1940s, 86–93
  studio lamps: arc, 77–79, 83–86, 88, 91, 104; tungsten, 86, 88, 104, 239

Light sensitivity, 41
Lindblom, Gunnel, 212
Little Foxes, The, 47
Lola, 100–102
Lola Montes, 63, 109
Loneliness of the Long Distance Runner, The, 34
Long Day's Dying, The, 162–63
Longest Day, The, 6, 121
Long Voyage Home, The, 47
Lorentz, Pare, 148
Losey, Joseph, 13–14
Love in the City, 196
Love in Vain, 146
Lower Depths, The, 32, 173
Lubitsch, Ernst, 75, 132, 136, 233, 244
Lumière, Louis, 25–26, 71
Lyrical film, 303–7

M, 282
McLaren, Norman, 281, 306–7
Magician, The, 11, 182
Mamoulian, Rouben, 244
Man and a Woman, A, 114
Mann, Anthony, 246
Mannes, Leopold, 107
Marat/Sade, 257–59, *258*
Marey, Jules, 25, 77
Marker, Chris, 16, 267, 296
Marnie, 75
Married Woman, A, 297
Martelli, Otello, 10, 64–65
Marx brothers, 14, 140, 239
Masina, Giulietta, 256
Matras, Christian, 63
Matting: *see* Superimposition
Maumont, Jacques, 156
Maxim Gorki's Return, 132
Mayer, Carl, 170
Maysles, Albert and David, 146, 152
Mechanical sound recording: *see* Sound, disc
Medium Cool, 68
Meerson, Lazare, 135
Méliès, Georges, 26
Merry Widow, The, 136
Method acting: *see* New York Actors Studio, Stanislavsky
Metropolis, 233, *234*
Meyerhold, Vsevolod, 226–32, 239, 247–48, 254, 257
Mickey One, 16–17
Miracle Worker, The, 16–17
Misfits, The, 311–12
"Mission Impossible" series, 310–11
Modern Times, 221–23, 225, *220*
Moana, 87
Mon Oncle, 110

Monroe, Marilyn, 311–12
Montage, in silent films, 267–78; continuity principle, 268–72; collision principle, 272–78
    in sound films, 278–97; new approaches, 291–97; studio specialization, 278–81; the suspense film, 281–91
    see also Editing
Monte Carlo, 136
Monterey Pop, 150
Mother, 269–72
Movie, A, 302–3
Muriel, 296
Murnau, F. W., 83–86, 170, 233
Murray, Jack, 314
Music, 124–27, 131–39, 264
Musical comedy, 132–33
Muybridge, Eadweard, 24–25, 77
My Darling Clementine, 4, 246

Naked Night, The, 12
Nanook of the North, 87
Naturalism, in acting, 254–55, 257
    photographic, 79–83
Neorealism, Italian, 10–11, 35, 291
    acting approach of, 254, 256
    scenarios in style of, 184, 189–96
New York Actors Studio, 13, 18, 247–48, 251–52
New Wave, 10, 267, 293
Nichols, Dudley, 168–69, 184–85, 187, 189
Nichols, Mike, 97, 112
Night and Fog, 296–98
Night Mail, 148
Nights of Cabiria, The, 256
Nine Variations on a Dance Theme, 304–5
North by Northwest, 283–85
Nosferatu, 29, 84–86, 90, *85*
Notorious, 287–88, *288–89*
Notte, La, 196–97
Nous, la Liberté, A, 133–36, *134*
Novotny, Vladimir, 69
Nykvist, Sven, 11–13
N.Y., N.Y., 305

October, 127–28, 273, 276–77
October Group, 171
Odd Man Out, 95–96, *96–97*
Odds against Tomorrow, 52
Oklahoma!, 62
Old and New, 273
Once upon a Time in the West, 211
One Day in the Life of Ivan Denisovitch, 164
One-Eyed Jacks, 6
On the Set of Fellini Satyricon: A Behind the Scenes Diary, 318

On the Waterfront, 248–51
Open City, 94, 190
Optical printer, 28, 307
Optical traveling, 67
Orthochrome: see Film stock, ortho-
    chrome

Pabst, G. W., 28
Painting with Light, 89–90
Paisan, 256
Palance, Jack, 157
Panchrome: see Film stock, panchrome
Panning, 22, 32, 67
Parade's Gone By, The, 78
Pas de Deux, 306–7, 307
Pasolini, Pier, 34
Passion of Anna, The, 212, 215, 213
Pawnbroker, The, 252, 253
Penn, Arthur, 16–17, 266
Pennebaker, Donn Allen, 146, 149–50,
    152, 154, 210
Périer, François, 256
Perinal, Georges, 135
Perkins, Tony, 246–47
Persona, 204, 212, 11
Persson, Jorgen, 58–59
Petrified Forest, The, 242
Phantom of the Opera, 126–27
Photographic sound recordings: see
    Sound, optical
Picture, 318
Pinter, Harold, 13–14, 168
Plough that Broke the Plains, The, 148
Poitier, Sidney, 215–16
Polgase, Van Nest, 280
Porter, Edwin, 26
Potemkin, 46–47, 136
    biomechanics and constructivism in,
        228, 231, 240, 229
    editing of, 273, 276–77
Prefogging, 112–13
Prévert, Jacques, 13, 168, 171–72, 179, 202
Primary, 149–50
Probyn, Brian, 163
Process camera, 298, 306
Projectors, 29–30
Prokofiev, Sergei, 131–32, 136–39
Psycho, 68, 263, 282, 287–90
Pudovkin, 137, 226–27, 255–56
    experimentation of, in editing, 14, 265,
        268–72, 276, 279, 291
Pumpkin Eater, The, 75

Queen Christina, 75
Que Viva Mexico, 10, 210
Quinn, Anthony, 155

Rabier, Jean, 68

Red Badge of Courage, The, 318
Red Desert, 115–16, 164, 214–15
Reed, Sir Carol, 95
Reinhardt, Max, 232–34, 240, 251, 254,
    259
Reisz, Karel, 16
Renoir, Jean, 13, 56, 89, 131
    scenarios for, 168–76, 204, 207, 209
Resnais, Alain, 10
    editing, in films of, 14, 16, 267, 293–
        94, 296, 298
Return of Dr. X, The, 242
Richardson, Robert, 167
Rink, The, 29
Ritual, The, 182
River, The, 148–49
Robe, The, 62–63
Rogers and Hammerstein, 132
Röhrig, Walter, 84
Roof, The, 190
Rope, 112
Rosher, Charles, 87
Ross, Lillian, 318
Rossellini, Roberto, 73, 256
Rossif, Frederic, 8–9
Rota, Nino, 318
Rotunno, Giuseppe, 10
Royal Journey, 107
Rules of the Game, 89, 171, 179, 204
Russell, Ken, 255, 259

Saboteur, 285
Sagiyama, Kohei, 108
Saint, Eva Marie, 247–48, 250–51
Sarris, Andrew, 5–6, 318
Satyricon, 75, 318
Scarface, 4–5
Scarlett Empress, The, 240, 251, 280
Schüfftan, Eugen, 89
Scope: see Lenses, new optical systems
Scriptwriting, 13–14, 167–69
    the anti-story, 169, 195–208; reconcep-
        tions of speech and action, 202–8;
        rejection of plot, 195–202
    picaresque structures of, 169, 184–94;
        action genres, 184–89; see also Neo-
        realism
    rhetorical structures of, 169–83; argu-
        mentative, 170–78; symbolic and as-
        sociative, 179–83
Searchers, The, 312–17
Seconds, 70, 71
Sennett, Mack, 14, 29
Sellers, Peter, 252
Sequences from a Cinematic Life, 190
Servant, The, 13
Set design: see Decor
Seven Samurai, The, 35–36, 57, 3

Seventh Seal, The, 180–82, *181*
Shadow of a Doubt, 245–46, 286
Shamroy, Leon, 63
Shanghai Express, 91–92, 102, *93*
She Wore a Yellow Ribbon, 313
Shoeshine, 94, 190
Shoot the Piano Player, 102, 112
Short films, 297–307
Shostakovitch, Dimitri, 131–32
Shoulder Arms, 219
Shutter, synchronized, 25
Signs and Meaning in the Cinema, 4–5
Silence, The, 12, 212
Silent cinema, 217–25, 239
  montage in, 267–78
  and sound, 124–29
Silliphant, Sterling, 168
Sixties, The, 299–302, *301*
Ski the Outer Limits, 30, *31*
Slow motion, 7, 29–30
Sound, basic technology of, 119–66, 288
  disc recording system, 121
  magnetic recording system, 121–22, 124, 145–66; electronic, 163–65; filtered, 162–63; mixing, 120–21, 123, 159, 162, 267; off-speed, 159, 162; and voice-over commentary, 158–59, 162–63; wild-sound, 120, 146–55
  optical recording system, 121–22, 129–45; music, 131–39; voice-music-effects mix, 140–45
  stereophonic, 124, 146
  see also Music, Silent cinema, and sound
Sound effects, 123, 163–65
Spaak, Charles, 168, 178–79, 202
  script for *Grand Ilusion,* 171, 173, 175–76, 209
Special effects, 7–8, 89, 262–63, 267
  see also Sound effects
Spectral response: *see* Film stock, spectral response of
Spellbound, 245
Split-screen printing, 267
Sprocket wheel, 25
Stagecoach, 4, 185–91, 197, *187*
Staging: *see* Constructivism, Decor, Expressionism
Stanislavsky, Constantin, 227, 241, 247–56
Steiger, Rod, 247–54
Steiner, Max, 314, 318
Sternberg, Josef von, 13, 55, 75, 90–91, 233, 280
  and *The Blue Angel,* 235, 238–39
Stewart, James, 143
Stopped-down apertures, 41–43, 47–48
Strada, La, 155
Strange Cargo, 132

Stranger, The, 144
Strasberg, Lee, 248, 255
Streetcar Named Desire, A, 248–49
Strike, 46, 128, 136, 240
  and constructivism, 228, 231, editing of, 272–76, *274–75*
Superimposition, 261–63, 265, 273, 306–7
Surtees, Robert, 112–14

Targets, 157–58
Tati, Jacques, 14, 239
Technicolor: *see* Film stock, color
Technology, film, 6–8, 24, 71, 149
  lens, 23, 37, 47, 53, 56, 61–67
Temptation of Dr. Antonio, The, 293
Terra Trema, La, 291
39 Steps, The, 283
This Is Cinerama, 146
This Sporting Life, 75
Thompson, Francis, 305–6
Three Musketeers, The, 162
Throne of Blood, 159, 162, *160–61*
Through a Glass Darkly, 11–13, 182
Thulin, Ingrid, 13, 210–12
Tilting, 22, 32
Tin Star, The, 246–47
Tisse, Edouard, 78
  collaboration with Eisenstein, 10, 43, 46–47, 210, 278
Todd-A-O, 61–62
To Die in Madrid, 8–9
To Have and Have Not, 5
Toland, Gregg, 5, 10, 47, 49, 51–52, 56
Tomassini, George, 283
Tom Jones, 29
Topkapi, 264
Tora! Tora! Tora!, 121
Totem, 306
Tracking, 22, 32
Tracy, Spencer, 240–41
Tramp, The, 219
Treasure of the Sierra Madre, 14, 243, 280, *243*
Tripack, integral: *see* Film stock, color
Truffaut, François, 28–29, 282, 296
  collaboration with Coutard, 99, 102, 112
  and New Wave 10, 267, 293
Two Hundred Days of 8 1/2, 318
200 Motels, 7–8
Two of Us, The, 73
Two or Three Things I Know about Her, 157
2001: A Space Odyssey, 114–15, 257
Two Timid People, 128–29

Ugetsu, 33, *32*
Ullmann, Liv, 13, 212

Umberto D, 35, 190, 292
Undercranking, 26–27, 29–30

Varda, Agnes, 16
Veidt, Conrad, 233
Vertigo, 285
Video tape, 7–8
Vierny, Sacha, 10
Vigo, Jean, 132
Virgin Spring, The, 11-12
Viridiana, 32–33
Visconti, Luchino, 10, 190
Vitaphone system, 120–21
Vitti, Monica, 213–14
Viva Villa, 279–80
Vivre sa vie, 100, *101*
Vogel, H. W., 77
Voice, 140–45, 152–53, 238–39
Voice-over commentary: *see* Sound, mag-
    netic
Von Harbou, Thea, 170
Von Stroheim, Erich, 79, 81–83, 176, 209
Von Sydow, Max, 13–15, 57, 211–13, 215
Vorkapitch, Slavko, 279–80

Wada, Sanzo, 108
Wagner, Fritz, 10, 84–86
Waller, Fred, 62
War and Peace, 264
Warm, Hermann, 84
Waterloo, 251
Watt, Harry, 148
Wayne, John, 3, 209, 312, 317, 246
Weekend, 204–7, *205*
Wegener, Paul, 83–84, 232–33

Welles, Orsen, 210, 246
    use of sound, 19, 131, 141–44
    Toland's photography for, 10, 47–51
Westerner, The, 47
Westerns, 26, 211
Wexler, Haskell, 67–68, 97, 102
Who's Afraid of Virgina Woolf?, 67, 96–99
Widerberg, Bo, 57
Wide-screen formats, 61–66, 313
Wiene, Robert, 83, 170, 233
Wild Child, The, 28–29
Wild Strawberries, 11, 182–83, 204
Winter Light, 12, 212
Wipes, 261, 265–66
Wise, Robert, 52
Wiseman, Frederick, 153–54
Wizard of Oz, The, 105
Wollen, Peter, 4–5
Women in Love, 259
Woodstock, 114, 257
Woolfe, H. Bruce, 298
World of Apu, The, 34
World of '68, The, 299
Wright, Basil, 148
Wrong Man, The, 286–87
Wyler, William, 10, 47

Yamasaki, Kazuo, 32

Z, 26
Zabriskie Point, 169, 215
Zappa, Frank, 7
Zavattini, Cesare, 168, 190, 194–96, 291
Zero for Conduct, 131
Zone focusing, 57